D0859793

everybody eats there

everybody eats there

william stadiem
& mara gibbs

ARTISAN

Copyright © 2007 by William Stadiem and Mara Gibbs

All rights reserved. No portion of this book may be reproduced—
mechanically, electronically, or by any other means, including
photocopying—without written permission of the publisher.

Published by Artisan
A Division of Workman Publishing Company, Inc.
225 Varick Street
New York, NY 10014-4381
www.artisanbooks.com

Library of Congress Cataloging-in-Publication Data

Stadiem, William.
  Everybody eats there / William Stadiem and Mara
Gibbs.
    p. cm.
  ISBN-13: 978-1-57965-322-4
    1. Restaurants—Guidebooks. 2. Cookery,
International. I. Gibbs, Mara. II. Title.
  TX907.S7155 2007
    647.95—dc22   2006047824

Design by Nicholas Caruso

Printed in the United States of America
First printing, February 2007

10 9 8 7 6 5 4 3 2 1

PHOTO CREDITS

New York: courtesy of Rao's. **London:** Savoy Grill, courtesy
of Gordon Ramsay Holdings. **Paris:** courtesy of Restaurant
de La Tour d'Argent. **The Continent:** Harry's Bar, Venice,
courtesy of Cipriani. **The Far East:** courtesy of Tenichi, Tokyo.
The Americas: courtesy of Hominy Grill, Charleston. **Los
Angeles:** Fountain Coffee Shop, courtesy of the Beverly
Hills Hotel.

R0410356423

THE CHICAGO PUBLIC LIBRARY

Contents

OAKLAND PUBLIC LIBRARY

Introduction

My baptism of starfire into the world of celebrity restaurants occurred in the late 1970s, with my first lunch at Ma Maison in Los Angeles. At first I thought I had arrived at the wrong address, that of a Rolls-Royce dealership, with countless classic cars out front. And because the restaurant had an unlisted number, I couldn't call from a pay phone to get proper coordinates. But when I saw Swifty Lazar get out of his white Aston Martin, I knew I was at the right place.

Ma Maison had a little cottage in the back, but nobody ate there. Instead, everyone was seated out behind the hedges in the California sun in what looked like a garden supply store, all lawn chairs and AstroTurf. The first famous person I noticed was Orson Welles, enormously Falstaffian, draped in a kind of black muumuu, eating copiously all by himself. I had loved *The Man Who Would Be King,* and was thus doubly wowed when I saw its stars, Sean Connery and Michael Caine, eating together. At another table was my screen hero Steve McQueen. And at still another was Jack Nicholson with his then inamorata Anjelica Huston, and her Olympian father, John. Jacqueline Bisset was lunching that day, looking more like a movie star than I could have imagined. There were a lot of other impossibly beautiful women and more table-hopping and cheek kissing than at any wedding that I had ever attended.

Believe it or not, I even remember what I ate that day: duckling "two ways," separate courses of the fowl, one *confit,* one *grillé,* exactly like I had savored at the then-two-star Chez Michel in Paris, where magical things appeared from the kitchen near the seedy Gare du Nord. But I had never seen a star at Chez Michel, and I had never seen stars kiss a cook before, either, as they were all doing with the young Austrian in *toque blanche* who kept popping out into the garden to take his bows. His name was Wolfgang Puck.

And what was *I,* a mere mortal, doing in that garden of Hollywood Eden? I was there to interview Madame Claude, the legendary Paris matchmaker, who was fleeing the long arm of the French law on charges not of pandering (the French were *so* sophisticated in those matters) but of tax evasion. Hollywood seemed pretty sophisticated as well, for nearly every man in the house came by our table to kiss her hand: Swifty, George Peppard, Gene Kelly, the mogul Ray Stark, the studio head David Begelman, who may have been disgraced in the press but was treated as a god here. Madame Claude was the dear friend of Claude Terrail, the *boulevardier* owner of La Tour d'Argent and the uncle of Patrick Terrail, who owned Ma Maison and who played the French card to the hilt, Madame Claude being the ultimate ace.

Later that same week, back in New York, I saw Michael Caine again, this time at Elaine's, which had its own stars but nothing like the every-day-is-Oscar-night concentration at Ma Maison. And then, a week or so later, there Caine was again, in London, at the restaurant he then owned, Langan's Brasserie. We couldn't go on meeting this way, I joked to him. He got it.

I thus got hooked on celebrity restaurants as the perfect fusion of two of my all-consuming passions—a great meal and a great party. And I turned this avocation into a paid vacation by writing columns for *Interview* and *Tatler* about this intersection of food and fame, and then becoming a restaurant critic for *Buzz* and then *Los Angeles.* Because I had never cooked a meal in my life, I have been highly dependent on restaurants, a pure consumer. And a very fussy one. But I was always as interested in society as gastronomy, and my writings on the restaurant scene around the world have always been as Winchellian in spirit as they have been Larousseian.

Where did you eat? Because of my enviable sideline, that's the first question people ask me whenever I come back from a trip. Not what wonders did I see, not what dramas did I witness, not what hotels did I stay in, but what restaurants did I go to? For so many people, restaurants have become a shorthand about the culture, the history, the ambience of a particular place. Food is now the window into the society. Where, how, and what people eat is the quickest, and tastiest, way to get a snapshot of how they live, and why we might want to emulate those lives, if only for a brief while, or in our wildest dreams.

If restaurants are one kind of shorthand, celebrities are another. If a star (of screen, playing field, corridors of power, wherever boldface reigns) goes somewhere, or does something, then it must be worthy of curiosity, if not emulation, or so the thinking goes. Where food is concerned, the current instinct, in our celebrity-driven world, is to eat where the stars do. There is a certain logic to it all: people with all the money, all the connections, all the information, ought to know the best places. The stars, for their part, tend to eat where other stars eat, hence the celebrity restaurant, epitomized by the longed-for Ma Maison, a fabulous gathering place of the rich, the famous, the powerful, the best and the brightest, the flashiest and the luckiest, eating memorable cuisine in an unforgettable atmosphere.

Of course there are numerous star places that are considered egregiously awful exceptions to this definition of the celebrity restaurant, where the food really does bite. However, even in the most scorned rookeries, there are invariably delicious things to consume. You just have to know what to order, sometimes off the menu. No star goes out of his or her way to eat badly. They may be foolish, but they're not stupid.

Think about your own priorities, your own mythology. What will you remember more, talk about more, brag about more: a Lucullan lobe of foie gras, a melting pork belly, the *dernier cri* in *crème brûlée,* or seeing Bill Clinton tablehopping to flirt with Sharon Stone, Tom Cruise meeting Woody Allen, Madonna devouring vegan pizza, Sumner Redstone squaring off against Rupert Murdoch some enchanted evening across a crowded room? The stars tend to stay in your mind long after the food has left your stomach. But that's the whole point here, to have your stars and your foie gras, too, all under the same roof, the way I did with that Puck duck in the shadow of Connery and Caine.

In 1970, I met a young California dreamer in London who I thought had come up with the coolest idea in the world, serving fabulous charcoaled California burgers to burger-deprived Londoners. He was Peter Morton, and he had this little restaurant on the Fulham Road called the Great American Disaster, which led to the Hard Rock Cafe, which led to empire. Later, I met Morton's sister Mara Gibbs, who was not only the pickiest eater I had ever met, but, for her tender age, the most knowledgeable person about restaurants around the world, and their inside machinations, I had ever come across. She had eaten everywhere—and I mean *everywhere*—and always with the chefs and owners. Mara was the last word (actually, the first) on what was new and happening on the restaurant scene in New York, London, Paris, Aspen, the Caribbean, wherever famous people were hungry. She was known as "the concierge." Not only did her brother rely on her for where to eat while surveying his Hard Rocks around the world, but so did half of Hollywood—the producers, directors, stars, agents, et al. with whom she worked in the film business. Mara was the Delphic oracle of restaurants. She and I traded hot tips for years, and then we came up with the idea of sharing the wealth with the public.

Hence this book. The bottom line here is that the celebrity restaurant is an unforgettable three-ring circus of food, fame, and fun. Assuming, that is, that you can get in, and that if you do, you don't feel left out. That is why this book has been written, to explore and demystify the fascinating yet forbidding world of these restaurants. These are the restaurants you want to go to, but you hate feeling like an alien. Yet because *our* knowledge is *your* power, you won't have to. The purpose here is to enable outsiders to feel like insiders at the most exclusive dining places in the world. The world of celebrity restaurants is a rather tiny global club, albeit one that can't really keep you out. You may not be able to live in the Malibu Colony, or afford to sleep at the Hotel du Cap, but for the price of a meal, you can see exactly how the rich and famous really live. It's the cheapest price of admission imaginable to the greatest show on earth. If you're addicted to the idea of seeing stars, up close and personal, the restaurants herein are your surest bet to do so. This book will be your membership card to the celebrity food club.

A number of the restaurants in this book have been around for centuries, and most of them for decades. It takes longevity to create a classic, and this is a book about classics, classics that have retained both their vitality and their primacy in the hunger pangs of the world elite. But a lot of the legends that are still around have become culinary Madame Tussauds; they don't make this book's cut. Nor, conversely, do the supertrendy *tables du moment*. One of the book's criteria for inclusion is the authors' sense of the restaurant's being in existence, and being in favor, five years from the date of publication. Many of the owners of today's superhot places don't even *want*, much less expect, their sizzlers to be around in five years. They are playing the game of trend, and that game depends on accelerated depreciation. When you're hot, you're hot, and when you're not . . . , well, thanks a lot, but *ciao*, baby.

Just as the trendoids have been 86-ed in this volume, very few of the current temples of gastronomy make this book's honor roll, either. Yes, Robuchon is in (but only in Tokyo), as are Passard and Puck. But Ducasse, Keller, Vongerichten are not, and not because their food isn't wonderful. It's that it may be *too* wonderful, too complicated, too confusing, outshining the stars themselves and taking way too long to consume. Celebrities, as you will see, tend to prefer the simpler pleasures. And that simplicity is the over-riding hallmark of most of the classics in these pages. A lot of the greatest of the greats are founded on one simply amazing dish: the suckling pig at Casa Botín, the roast chicken at Ami Louis, the bratwurst at Kronenhalle, the stone crabs at Joe's, the carpaccio at Harry's Bar, all uncomplicated classics that avoided becoming clichés and, with a near Pavlovian response formation, have ravished the palates of generations of supernovas.

While a number of these restaurants are top secrets of the gourmandis-ing elite, others have been written about in articles and guidebooks, but usually in a brief paragraph, never all in one volume and never in depth. Although this book will serve up the great dishes, make you very hungry, and explain pre-cisely what to order, and how to get a perfect, emblematic meal in each place, this volume is much more than a food book. All of these restaurants have a vivid history, with owners and chefs often as colorful and outsize in personality as their famous patrons. How they got, and keep, these patrons is a key part of the story, as are the power politics of the restaurant world in each city in the book. And while there is a "food pack" of stars and moguls who are habitués of *all* of these dining shrines, each city and each restaurant has its own unique set of celebrity patrons who illuminate where you are and provide indelible insights into the place and its culture. Even if you never get to the place, this book will make you an armchair insider, the toast of cocktail parties. Plus it will give you lots to dream about.

In compiling this volume, our approach was the ultimate foodie fantasy—around the world in eighty meals. We had been to most of these places in our travels, knew them and loved them. Our only problem was one of exclusion. So many meals, so little time, so few pages. Great cities and great restaurants have, of practical necessity, been forced to wait until another volume. We left out Las Vegas, St. Bart's, Shanghai, New Orleans. . . . But we'll be back. The book thus does not pretend to be all-inclusive, though there is nothing anywhere better than what lies within. What follows is a global strategy for gourmet and gourmand travelers who want to see stars and *be* stars. And it can work. For although these restaurants need their celebrities, they need *you* more. A smart customer is always king, even in these caravansary of fame.

everybody
eats
there

York

La Grenouille
The Frog Pond

There are several perennial nominees for the quintessential New York meal: a hot dog in Coney Island, a prime steak in Brooklyn, spaghetti and meatballs in Little Italy, curry in the East Village, Chinese takeout in a high-rise. Those are all vintage New York, to be sure. But the meal that captures the power and the glory of the Big Apple—the meal that established the bona fides of restaurantdom here, that allowed New York to become the restaurant capital of the world—was the haute snob, haute cuisine, power-seating blowout at a French temple of gastronomy in Midtown. Like the Jewish delis, these French temples are falling fast. Most of the big names—Lutèce, La Caravelle, La Côte Basque—have given up the ghost in recent years. But La Grenouille, arguably the most elegant temple of them all, is still proudly standing. And its congregation may be the richest, most connected, most powerful worshippers in the old-time religion that is food.

Located in a quaint Tudor cottage off Fifth Avenue that used to be the stable of the city's top abortionist, La Grenouille is incongruous amid the anonymous towering skyscrapers of Fifth and Madison that have turned Midtown Manhattan into almost another Dallas or Houston. Almost. Because Dallas and Houston don't have anything like La Grenouille, not even close. Inside, the restaurant has a unique rosy glow, aided in part by the five-foot-tall floral masterpieces, the deep red banquettes, the red silk wallpaper, and the electric bulbs that are painted pink. Until recently you could never look in: the big window into the bar was draped by curtains. But now the curtains have been pulled back, and from the street you can get a glimpse of the spectacular room, with its rows of banquettes around the perimeter, filled with the high and mighty sitting side by side, chic to chic. If you're not in one of those banquettes, you probably don't belong. At La Grenouille, it's On the Wall, or Not at All.

Who are those high and mighty? The Rockefellers. The Astors and Vanderbilts, or what's left of them. The tycoons, like Henry Kravis and Ron Perelman. The designers, like Calvin Klein and Oscar de la Renta. The heirs and rulers of "appearance" fortunes, like Ronald Winston (son of Harry) and Ronald Lauder (son of Estée). The press lords, like Si Newhouse and Conrad Black before he was indicted (Black threw a surprise party here for his wife that cost $42,000—chump change that makes shareholders feel chumpish). Rich Texans like the Bass brothers. In fact, rich Americans from all over who can get this formal thrill only in New York, and barely anymore. Foreign royalty and plutocracy—Rothschilds, Agnellis, Hohenlohes, Hapsburgs, whoever's in town. The Donald, because he can. The mix of La Grenouille is the mix of Manhattan, old-money WASP, *Our Crowd* grandee Jews, techno-dollar Wall Streeters, Euroclass, brash Trumpish arrivistes, megawatt media presences.

The only group in short supply at La Grenouille are movie and rock stars, who always chafed at the dress code, which has now been opened up, like the curtains. You'd see Michael Eisner, but not Brad Pitt; Clive Davis, but not Tina Turner. But you'll see more than enough. If you can handle the ego battering of being the stranger at a party, where the men are on the front page of *The New York Times,* and the women, if a little too old for *Vogue* and not in the *Times* themselves, are right there in *Town & Country.* La Grenouille is probably the last place in New York, outside the charity-ball circuit, where women can wear their jewelry and their couture dresses out in public. It's a very private public, but public nonetheless.

And you can, too. La Grenouille may not give you a banquette at the entrance, the Babe Paley seat, but it will greet you with open arms. It dropped its required necktie policy, opened its curtains, and offers a bargain prix fixe panini menu at the bar. These are all signs of changed times, casual times, funky times, the end of elegance. At one point, not long ago, over 40 percent of La Grenouille's reservations were no-shows. "We were irritating our customers," concedes owner Charles Masson, whose parents opened La Grenouille in the go-go year of 1962, when coming in black tie was not unusual. Now it's "irritating." See? They *need* you. So you sit in the middle of the room, even the back room. The flowers are the same, and so is the food. Think positive. Think pink.

As for the cuisine, it's nowhere as haute as you might expect: no pressed duck à la Tour d'Argent, no *lièvre à la royale* out of Escoffier, no Alain Ducasse razzle-dazzle or Alain Passard vegetable fantasia. La Grenouille's menu is very straightforward, old-school French, but not a school you couldn't get into. The menu is pretty much club food, fancy Paris club food: smoked salmon, grilled Dover sole, steak *au poivre*. The most complicated you can get is veal kidneys flamed with cognac, but nobody orders that, except maybe Pinault or Arnault when they're in town doing a takeover. The most famous appetizer is the baked little neck clams, which are like the clams *oreganata* you get in Little Italy, but made with butter and not olive oil, a little drier than you'd get downtown. There are frogs' legs on the menu, *bien sur*, sautéed Provençale, but they can't compare to the just killed croakers you find in Chinatown. In the old days Truman Capote's society "swans" would usually start with lobster-tarragon ravioli, which passed for fusion in those simpler times, then move on to French-as-you-get *quenelles de brochet*, and finish up with *oeufs à la neige*. The "Capote option" is still on the menu. It worked then, it works now.

Even if the food isn't three-star complicated, the wines rise to the presence of the superrich. Expect to drink wonderfully and pay accordingly. The service is old-school perfect, and not at all scary, other than the waiters' suits being more expensive than yours. The room is as blissfully quiet as it is elegant. Silence is golden, and a rarity in buzzy Manhattan. To go with their big sticks, the rich speak softly.

The first Charles Masson, founder of this noble house, goes back to the very beginning of the French revolution in sophisticated cooking in America.

The year was 1939. The place was the World's Fair, held in Flushing Meadow, Queens, where the Mets now play. Masson *père* was a waiter at the restaurant of the French Pavilion, the hot food ticket of the festival, under the *aigle* eye of big boss Henri Soulé. Soulé had been maître d' at the famed Café de Paris on l'Avenue de l'Opera, a three-star extravaganza that gave Maxim's and La Tour d'Argent a run for their francs in the prewar period.

Soulé was a bourgeois, squat, rotund, unprepossessing young man from near Bayonne, in the French southwest; he was precisely the sort of person he himself would relegate to Siberia. An unabashed snob, he was deeply influenced by the arrogance and caste systems of Maxim's, where he was never able to land a job. The excludee thus became the excluder. When the war broke out, Soulé and his crew were stranded in New York. Making the best of an awful situation, Soulé found some investors, and in 1941 opened his own restaurant. It was called Le Pavilion, trading heavily on his association with the Fair and France without getting a license from either, on Fifty-fifth Street and Fifth Avenue, across from the St. Regis Hotel. Charles Masson, another middle-class boy, from Belfort, near the Swiss border, became Soulé's maître d'.

Playing his new game by the Maxim's rulebook, Soulé helped New Yorkers, a highly psychoanalyzed group to begin with, even then, to embrace the icy joys of insecurity and inferiority complexes. Remember the Avis "We Try Harder!" ads, one of Madison Avenue's most brilliant campaigns? Well, Henri Soulé made New Yorkers try harder—a lot harder, especially those *near* the top but yet so, so far away. As Soulé's right-hand man, Charles Masson was a junior Torquemada, flagellating the egos of Manhattan. As if World War II wasn't painful enough. With the postwar boom, the ego thing got a lot worse, so bad in fact that Charles Masson could no longer stand his role as Soulé's whip hand. He quit Le Pavilion eventually and went to sea, albeit to a floating island of more snobbery, the S.S. *Constitution,* where he became headwaiter.

Masson's wife, Gisele, stayed behind in Manhattan raising two sons, Charles and Philippe. She was part of the expatriate French community that often visited the Fifty-second Street art studio of Bernard Lamotte, a spark plug of New York's French set who gave swell parties for the likes of Garbo, Chaplin, and Dalí. Lamotte painted the vividly elegant murals of Paris for Le Pavilion as well as those of Saint Jean de Luz for Soulé's new offshoot, La Côte Basque, where Capote trashed all his swans in a famous *Esquire* article that burned all the tiny terror's bridges to the Soulé-fed high-society Capote craved. One of Lamotte's most famous wartime guests was the aviator and author Antoine de Saint-Exupéry, who wrote *The Little Prince* while staying at the studio. Charles Masson was an amateur painter and was also a visitor of Lamotte, and of the little French restaurant La Vie Parisienne on the ground floor.

By 1962 the Soulé juggernaut had taken the life out of La Vie, and Lamotte had moved out as well. Strolling down Fifth Avenue one day, Gisele Masson, who had gone to work for Christian Dior and wanted her sailor to come home from the sea for his two boys, saw a for-lease sign in the window. Then she did something she thought her husband would kill her for: she signed a long-term lease for all of $4,000 a month, and presented it to Charles as a fait accompli. Charles did not kill his wife; he accepted his fate to own a Manhattan restaurant. He named it for Gisele; his nickname for her was "ma petite grenouille" (my little frog). La Grenouille opened in December 1962. No little frogs came through the doors, only big ones, very big ones, the ones who had been fattened up by Henri Soulé but couldn't get fat, or French, enough.

In a city that couldn't get enough flagellation, La Grenouille was an instant smash, so much so that within two years Charles Masson bought the whole building for $385,000, one of the great real estate moves in New York history. Taking a break from being grandmaster of the seating follies, Masson would go upstairs and paint. Eventually, though, the upstairs space was converted into one of the most charming country-French private dining rooms in the city.

What initially made La Grenouille was its embrace by John Fairchild, whose family owned *Women's Wear Daily*, the bible of the rag trade. Fairchild, a master of the Manhattan exclusion game, loved to publish lists—what's hot, what's not, what's in, who's thin, that sort of thing. La Grenouille was on the top of every list. It soon became the darling of the rag set, both sellers and buyers. When it became the darling of Jackie O, who was then Jackie K, the Massons were made.

Henri Soulé died in 1966, at sixty-three, of a sudden heart attack in the kitchen of La Côte Basque. Charles Masson died in 1975, of malignant melanoma acquired from too many escape trips to Florida to lie in the sun without a seating chart. His wife and sons took over and kept La Grenouille the same as it ever was, as long as they could. Eventually Gisele, in her eighties, retired to Brittany, and the brothers split, leaving Charles junior, in his fifties, in control of the restaurant, if not of the revolt against formality and the assault of the celebrity chefs. At La Grenouille, the celebrities are in the banquettes and the cooks stay in the kitchen. The twain do not meet.

Charles left his art studies at Carnegie Mellon to join the restaurant after his father died. He has loosened the place up, dropping the ties, even dropping the waiters' tuxedos, all to try to attract a new generation of Babe Paleys and Halstons and Henry Kissingers. Whether Nicole Richie and Tom Ford and Karl Rove can step up to the Limoges plate here remains to be seen. "We have tried to become more user-friendly, less huffy-puffy," Charles says. But when it all gets to be too much, Charles Masson goes upstairs to relax in a little six-by-eight garret under the roof, as French a space as exists in New York today. What does he do up there? He doesn't read the *Social Register*, as Henri Soulé used to do, or *WWD*, to see what's hot, or "Page Six," to see who's cool. La Grenouille is way beyond that. Who comes, comes. Charles Masson may drop the ties, but he doesn't hustle business. When he comes up to his French garret, he sketches, just like his father, just like Bernard Lamotte. Art, even more than food, runs in this house. ★ ★ ★ ★ ★ ★ ★

Da Silvano
Village of the Damned

GREENWICH VILLAGE

Da Silvano isn't a restaurant; it's a buzz machine. The unassuming little store-front trattoria in Greenwich Village, on the Avenue of the Americas near Houston Street, creates more press than any restaurant in New York. Small wonder. Those twin towers of Condé Nast, Graydon Carter of *Vanity Fair* and Anna Wintour of *Vogue,* are Village neighbors and treat the trattoria as their neighborhood kitchen. Richard Johnson of "Page Six" is a fixture. Not only are the employees of the "beautiful people" press on the meal plan here, but so are the owners: Newhouse and Murdoch, to name two. Not to mention all the beautiful people themselves. Da Silvano is a restaurant that other restaurants die for, even restaurants like La Grenouille, who covet Da Silvano's youth demographic and envy its captivation of the Old Guard on the "casual" nights when they're trying to be neither old nor guardish.

Why, oh why, is this trattoria different from the countless other trattorie that make all New York one giant, sprawling, olive-oil-splattered Little Italy? Because, to quote Confederate general Nathan Bedford Forrest, Da Silvano got there "firstest with the mostest." It might be said that for all its Italians, New York went for almost a century without a "real" Italian restaurant, beginning with the first waves of immigration after our Civil War. It was 1860 when the warrior-patriot Garibaldi liberated the lower half of "the boot," known as the Kingdom of the Two Sicilies, from French rule. But the promised reforms never materialized, and millions fled from everywhere between Naples and Palermo to come to the cities of America's East Coast in search of opportunity, any opportunity. Wanting to forget the past and change the future, these immigrants quickly assimilated, and they created a new Americanized cuisine, which could be called "New York Italian," a hearty red-sauced fried-meat-rolled-in-cheese, pasta-on-the-side fare whose apotheosis was veal Parmesan and whose apostle to the heartland was Chef Boyardee, not Mario Batali.

That was what Silvano Marchetto arrived to from Florence in 1968, when he was in his own roaring twenties. The Florentine had wanted to become an engineer, but he couldn't get into engineering school. Little did Marchetto suspect that he would ultimately become a social engineer. Instead he drifted into cooking school in Florence, then drifted around restaurants in Switzerland and France before landing on these shores, where he took a waiter job at the Derby Steak House on MacDougal Street in Greenwich Village, the home of many so-called Italian places that did less than zero to make Marchetto homesick. The Derby, learning of Marchetto's training, invited him to work in the kitchen. He refused. He simply couldn't bring himself to make the bastardized Italian food in what he saw as this gastronomic Village of the damned. Instead, he began looking for a place where he could pursue his credo, "to thine own self be true." He knew he couldn't fail. He had no competition.

Actually, Marchetto had one competitor: Alfredo Viazzi, a Genovese (the port, not the crime family) who had worked his way around town and had been the true love of Elaine Kaufman, whose own American-Italian restaurant uptown opened in 1963. Elaine's was gaining favor with the literary set, mainly because Elaine let a lot of starving writers run tabs, and many of them hit it big and were forever loyal. But Alfredo Viazzi refused to serve veal Parmesan, or manicotti, or spaghetti with meatballs. He opened a little place on Hudson Street, near the White Horse Tavern (where Dylan Thomas drank himself to death), and called it Trattoria da Alfredo. He made three different pastas a day and three different main courses, just like you would get in a little *tavola calda* in Rome. The pastas were al dente, the fish were lightly grilled, there were vegetables no one had heard of.

At the time, New Yorkers' idea of a great Italian meal was Mama Leone's in the Theater District, or drinking wine out of a centurion's helmet in the way-over-the-top Forum of the Twelve Caesars at Rockefeller Center, only slightly less of a spectacle than the Rockettes. So Alfredo was as much terra incognita as Hispaniola was to Columbus. And because it was in the Village, where eccentricity was not just tolerated but almost required, New York beat a path to Alfredo's door. Even the great Paul Bocuse had come and raved about it; all New York's top French chefs followed him, on their nights off.

Silvano Marchetto saw himself differently. Alfredo Viazzi may have been from Genoa, but he had become a New Yorker. Alfredo's was in the Village, but not of it. He was uptown, as was his crowd. The food was Italian, all right, but from every region, from Torino to Milazzo, not true to his regional roots. Viazzi, a Renaissance man, had written a best-selling novel and was trying to produce off-Broadway shows. He was married to Jane White, a superconnected actress whose father, Walter, was the head of the NAACP. The restaurant was Viazzi's way station on the road to media stardom. Whatever it was, it was a success, and its long lines proved to Marchetto that there was room for another. Marchetto saw himself as *pure*. He was a Florentine, and he would cook only the food of his Tuscany. In 1975, with his eight years of savings from the Derby, he found a tiny brick-walled storefront on Sixth Avenue for $500 a month, and started his own, very personal trattoria. He was going to do it "his way," not the way of Sinatra, which was the way of Hoboken, the way Marchetto found inedible, an insult to Italian culture, a culture based on perfect, simple food.

At the beginning, Marchetto did it all himself—cooking, waiting, dishwashing. It quickly paid off. He was discovered by the downtown Warhol art crowd, who had been going for years to a little trattoria around the corner on Houston Street named Ballato's. But Mr. Ballato, who fed all the great midcentury artists—Rauschenberg, Johns, Lichtenstein—as well as all the big dealers, like Leo Castelli, was very old and ailing. The closest port in this storm was Da Silvano. For Marchetto, it turned out to be the perfect storm, in which the artists brought their dealers who brought their rich clients, who happened to be famous. Rave reviews from the local food press followed. Gael Greene and Mimi Sheraton were wowed by the authenticity. Marchetto had a hit his first time at bat.

Da Silvano's success was quickly noted, and a wave of attempted knockoffs began. The biggest challenge came from one of the first busboys Marchetto was able to hire, in 1980, a struggling actor named Pino Luongo. Luongo rose to become Marchetto's manager, then defected in 1983 to start the Silvanoesque Il Cantinori nearby. Luongo was backed by two Greeks, who seem to own not only all the coffee shops in Manhattan (the Belushi cheeseburger routine from *Saturday Night Live*), but also seem to have a hand in *every* restaurant, regardless of ethnicity. Marchetto cried Judas; Luongo cried "goal"; and the trattoria wars began and are still raging, with new combatants seemingly every day for the last two decades.

Luongo went on to open Le Madri, Sapore di Mare in the Hamptons, a chain of Coco Pazzos, Centolire, and restaurants in the Barneys stores. But Silvano Marchetto stayed on the block, holding the fort and making it bigger, more secure. He bought the two spaces on either side of his original cubbyhole, but never tore down the walls, which might as well be the walls of Troy. The original cubbyhole remains the sanctum sanctorum, while the new rooms might as well be somewhere far away up the Hudson, Sing Sing perhaps. Marchetto also opened a cheaper version of himself, Bar Pitti, a few doors away. When Luongo left in 1983, he took most of Marchetto's Italian kitchen staff with him. Marchetto responded by replacing them with Ecuadoreans. Despite Marchetto's exacting supervison, word of the "South Americanization" of once pure Tuscany got out. Da Silvano wasn't what it used to be, people carped. The critics agreed, and the raves morphed into "over" pans. His ex-wife but still bookkeeper was terribly burned in a freak fire on a ski holiday in New Mexico. Marchetto himself had a stroke.

But Marchetto was a survivor, in the best only-in-New-York sense. The critics, the foodies, the trendies, all may have moved on to the next of-the-moment hot spot. But the stars stayed true. Oddly enough, celebrities have their own honor code. Once they embrace a place, they are loath to move on. Perhaps it's out of self-interest, a fear that a new place may not worship them the way the old one did. Perhaps it's that they really couldn't care less about the food. Perhaps they just loved that forty-seat cubbyhole, their own private Tuscany. Perhaps they liked the outdoor terrace, on one of the deepest sidewalks in the city, where you could see the Village in all its glory without being Rollerbladed. It's as close to a piazza as New York gets. But perhaps, and most likely, they just loved Silvano Marchetto.

Near sixty but perpetually turning twenty, Marchetto is still right here. He's always here. Even if the kitchen can be inconsistent, he never is. A little man with terrific Italian gray hair, barbershop quality, Marchetto is a renowned fashion plate. There's a bit of the Portofino beach-stud/gigolo look, as Marchetto drips in gold chains and bracelets and flaunts sixty expensive watches (though not at once), as well as tortoiseshell sunglasses, night and day. There's some Palm Beach preppie, too, pink and lime Lilly Pulitzer trousers, Brooks Brothers button-downs. And there's some ghetto fabulous—the Rome ghetto, that is: bright red Alfa Romeo coveralls, red Ferrari sneakers by Fila. To go with the gear, he is always collecting cars, Italian cars, which he often proudly double-parks outside to show off, and he somehow never gets a ticket. But how could he? He is Il Duce of this block.

Obviously, do not expect to sit in the cubbyhole, or the alfresco cigar bar that the terrace has become, unless you come with a king or kingmaker. You go to the side rooms, where the brick walls and travel posters are the same, but the exclusiveness is not. Do not expect to get the love treatment from Marchetto, unless you're a looker, and then you will see that, for the aesthetically gifted, America is truly a land of opportunity. He's a dreadful flirt, and only his immense charm and uniquely unintelligible English syntax save him from sexual harassment charges. Do not expect to get out of here for anything under a hundred dollars a person, before wine. This is the big league, and you have to pay to play. And, even at these stratospheric prices, do not expect to eat as well as you might in the mamaland, the long and seductively appetizing menu notwithstanding. The Ecuadoreans still run this kitchen, and sometimes they get Tuscany down, but sometimes they leave it in the Andes. You have to know what to get, and you have to put yourself into Marchetto's hands, if you can somehow entice him into noticing you. One good way is to seek his advice on a vintage wine. He's a passionate oenophile, and this will win *respect*, which is a key concept in the Italian lexicon.

You can't go wrong by starting with cured meats. Marchetto has a prime source, maybe even a friend at customs, for some of the best hams and salamis you will taste on these shores. The flavor is that of an ancient smokehouse in Volterra, not the Boar's Head plant in New Jersey. There is a difference, a huge one. The bread here can be peasant heaven or cafeteria hell, depending on demand and time of day. Da Silvano likes to fry, and fry well. The fritto misto, served on butcher paper, does credit to tender calamari and company. And when soft-shell crabs are in season, even though they belong to the Chesapeake Bay and not the Ligurian Sea, Da Silvano does them as well as anyone in Manhattan. Ditto the humble bluefish, another New York sea fave. Pastas can be oversauced and overcooked, so speak your mind, and try to order the peasant delight of orecchiette with rapini and crumbled fennel sausage. There are the usual grilled fish and lamb and Tuscan steak, all fine if you insist you want them undercooked, which translates to normal. If Marchetto has taken a shine to you, he may insist you partake of his *panna cotta* with truffles. Most people finish, hours and bottles later, with the homemade blood orange sorbet, best in the city.

Speaking of which: beware of truffles here, if price is any object. Truffles are investment banker food, food that separates the Masters of the Universe from the day traders. For all the stars here, Silvano Marchetto loves investment bankers. And he loves truffles, for their taste, for their *respect*. Some years ago, Warren Beatty ordered a special of tagliatelle with white truffles. When he complained about the niggardly portion of the fungus, Marchetto came over and shaved some more. Still not enough, Beatty caviled. Eight shavings later, Beatty was happy. The tariff for the dish was $500. And that was some years back. Beatty wasn't price sensitive. You may be. So let the eater beware.

Although everybody in New York does eat at Da Silvano, a nasty 2004 incident at the restaurant endangered its standing among a demographic coveted and courted by every restaurateur in the Big Apple: the high-rolling, truffle-eating African-American elite, from street rappers to Time Warnerers. On the night in question, a group of black bankers, lawyers, and broadcasters were celebrating at a table next to that of Princess Michael of Kent, who felt they were celebrating too much. "Go back to the colonies," she told them as she left one A table for another, more removed from the fray. Colonies? What colonies? The black celebrants assumed somewhere in Africa, like Rhodesia or Sudan. They were not amused, especially upon learning that the princess's father, the Baron Von Reibnitz, had been an "honorary" member of the Nazi Party, whatever *honorary* meant.

Nonsense, replied "Princess Pushy," or "Pushy Galore," as the British press had dubbed the aristocrat for her imperial, imperious manner. She claimed to the gossip press that the colonial reference was to the olden days when people had manners. The princess's many Manhattan friends, like society costume jeweler Kenneth Jay Lane and society decorator Mario Buatta, all Da Silvano habitués, stood up for her nonracist honor. Her Park Avenue hostess claimed that what the princess really said was, in changing tables, "Let's go to the colonies," aristo-speak for Siberia. Whatever she said, neither P. Diddy nor Halle Berry nor Vernon Jordan, Silvanoites all, has been reported in the cubbyhole since. But all true Silvano-ites, including the Terminator, tend to be trattoria recidivists. Odds are, they'll be back. ★ ★ ★ ★ ★ ★ ★ ★ ★ ★ ★

Starman

If every film critic since Pauline Kael has had to write under her long shadow, the food critics after Craig Claiborne have had an even tougher act to follow. As the first restaurant critic of *The New York Times,* the Francophile from Sunflower, Mississippi, basically invented the profession, borrowing the star system from Michelin and gracing it with some of the most authoritative, Hemingwayesque gastro-prose ever written. Gael Greene may have her hats, and Mimi Sheraton her wigs, but Craig Claiborne's gimmick was no gimmick, just unalloyed, totally self-confident good taste.

Claiborne's personal life, which he shockingly laid out in his 1982 autobiography *A Feast Made for Laughter,* was by contrast all about insecurity. Molested by his father, smothered by his mother, whose boardinghouse gave him his passion for southern hospitality, Claiborne fled Dixie, first to study journalism at the University of Missouri, then the navy, then to a halfhearted PR career in Chicago and New York. Uninspired, in 1949 he chucked Madison Avenue to follow his muse, moving to France, learning to eat, and to live. He came back to serve his country once more in Korea, then followed his discharge by enrolling in the best Swiss hotel school in Lausanne, after which, facing reality, he returned to New York to begin a food-writing career at *Gourmet,* hired by James Beard (they grew to hate each other). His first position was receptionist, though he kept at it until he was on the masthead.

Through a Mississippi good-ole-boy connection, in 1957 Claiborne got hired at the *Times* for the "ladies'" job as food editor. He quickly made it his own and began doing star ratings, which rank-obsessed New Yorkers literally ate up. Claiborne himself was not impressed, actually depressed, by the state of restaurants in the city. For all its melting-pot global population, New York, compared with Paris, didn't compare at all. It was more like melting-pot London, home of gray roast beef and grayer Wimp burgers. Lutèce, when it opened, was given by Claiborne the same one-star rating as the hot dog and coffee chain Chock full o'Nuts. And Lutèce was damned grateful for it.

The only restaurant up to Claiborne's standards was Henri Soulé's Le Pavilion, which got four stars and thus began the *Times*'s long romance with Gallic temples of gastronomy. Hotel school alum Claiborne was undoubtedly impressed by Soulé's by-the-Escoffier-book pomp and ceremony, something even a great Neapolitan place like Grotta Azzurra in Little Italy could never match. Claiborne rarely gave an Italian restaurant more than two stars. But Claiborne was like New York's drill sergeant: on his watch, all the city's restaurants began to shape up and aspire to more than three-martini lunches and five-scotch dinners. Like London in the 1990s, New York in the 1960s came of age as a world-class food town. In time Soulé spin-offs such as La Caravelle, Café Chambord, and La Côte Basque, as well as Soulé rivals like Quo Vadis and Lutèce, which tried harder and harder, were admitted to Claiborne's four-star inner sanctum.

Claiborne was indeed an awful food snob, but he was always open-minded, and had a flawless, ecumenical palate. He ignited the Szechuan food craze by giving four stars to Shun Lee Dynasty, and played Pancho Villa to the heretofore nonexistent Mexican revolution when he gave three stars to the funky El Parador Café. He also put his fellow southerner "K-Paul" Prudhomme and his ragin' Cajun blackened cookery on the national map. Because New Yorkers respect their paper of record more than any other urbanites, Claiborne's perch at the *Times* was pretty much papal, and he never abused his enormous power.

Well, actually, only once, and it nearly destroyed his enormous credibility. One night in 1975 Claiborne was watching a fund-raising auction on the New York PBS station. On a whim, he bid $300 for a dinner for two anywhere in the world, sponsored by American Express. And he won.

Right away, never-more-excited Claiborne flew off to France with his best-selling cookbook collaborator Pierre Franey, a Burgundian who had been executive chef at Le Pavilion before becoming a vastly better paid vice president of Howard Johnson. Franey compensated for the shame factor by writing high-toned tomes with Claiborne, who was actually not that great a cook himself and thus needed Franey's expertise. After trying a lot of fancy candidates, the two superfoodies chose the then most expensive restaurant in Paris, the tiny Chez Denis, in the 17th. Because Claiborne *was* the food press, the world press paid *beaucoup* attention to the planning of what became billed as "the meal of the century." Claiborne and Franey planned a *grand bouffe* of thirty-one courses (shades of the French Laundry to come) that included ortolans, cocks' combs, truffles galore, foie gras, beluga, rare fish and game, plus wines like a 1918 Chateau Latour and, for dessert, a Madeira from 1835.

The actual meal, when Claiborne and Franey rejetted to Paris to devour it, cost $4,000, an astronomical sum. Plus Claiborne, ever the critic, found plenty wrong with it: the presentation of the cold dishes, like the quail mousse tart, he deemed "mundane." A lobster dish was chewy, and the oysters not warm enough. This imperfect perfect meal, which made the front page of the *Times,* created a perfect storm of dreadful press. Over a thousand letters to the editor were received, the great majority of them from appalled readers. Not since Marie Antoinette apocryphally said "Let them eat cake" did a food commentary produce such outrage. Even the Vatican weighed in against the food pope, denouncing the escapade as "scandalous." Externally at least, Claiborne took the entire contretemps with his usual sangfroid. The thing that really amazed him, he said, was that he left the table without feeling "that stuffed."

Claiborne retired from the *Times* in 1986, with a send-off at the Four Seasons catered by twelve of America's celebrity chefs, including Prudhomme, Wolfgang Puck, Daniel Boulud, Andre Soltner of Lutèce, and Barry Wine of the Quilted Giraffe. For all the controversy of the Chez Denis affair, Claiborne never tired of a long meal and eventually all those courses, combined with all that alcohol, took their toll: Claiborne developed hypertension and all sorts of wages-of-sin health problems that forced him into dreaded low-fat cookery before shuffling off, in 2000, to the celestial Chez Denis at the ripe old age (for a food critic) of seventy-nine.

Rao's and Gino
Gun-shy

Tuscan shmuscan, a lot of New Yorkers might say. Veal Parmesan. You gotta problem with that? Don't knock New York's old school (sometimes reform school) Italian food. This *Soprano* fare is what America grew up on, and nowhere is it better or more atmospherically presented than at Rao's, in what used to be Italian Harlem, 114th Street and the surely misnamed gangland redoubt of Pleasant Avenue. Perennially festooned with Christmas lights, the woody, boothy, Godfatherly Rao's is without question New York's hardest-to-get-into restaurant, both because of its century-old Mafia mystique and because of the huge demand for its eight or so tables. It is perhaps the only restaurant where you can find Tony Bennett both on the jukebox and in a booth next to the jukebox. To see John Gotti across from Woody Allen, Fat Tony Salerno across from Norman Mailer, Paul Castellano across from Beverly Sills, any mobster across from Bill Clinton—this is the New York melting pot on acid, and it's a thrill. And to hear names of waiters and regulars—like Johnny Roast Beef (he owned a deli), whom Martin Scorsese cast in *GoodFellas,* and Angelo Cheesecake (bakery) and Charlie Ding Ding (candy store) and Rao busboy Tommy Salami—is music to the ears of any armchair capo. Americans love their Mafia, and Rao's is as vicarious a thrill as you can get. Plus the food is great. People are thus dying to eat here.

It's surprising that there haven't been more murders at Rao's. Officially, there's been only one, at least on premises, but it was a good one. Twas the night or two before Christmas 2003. The current owner of Rao's, Frank Pellegrino (otherwise known as Frankie No, because that's what he says to reservations seekers) was leading a sing-along at the packed bar. Frankie No had a recurrent role on *The Sopranos* as, ironically, the FBI bureau chief, and has moonlighted as a singer for years under the name Frank Anthony; he is a big patron of musicians (though he once said no to Madonna at the door). Accordingly, after singing a few tunes himself, Frankie No insisted on a song from a visiting Broadway soprano named Rena Strober, who belted out her version of "Don't Rain on My Parade." A tippling, thirty-something midlevel hood in the Lucchese crime family named Albert Circelli decided to rain on it, and gave an unsolicited invective-intensive review that would have made Frank Rich blush. Another smaller-time Lucchese hood, the sixty-something Louis Barone, had liked the number. Besides, this was no way to treat a lady.

She deserved respect. Accordingly, Barone pulled out his Smith & Wesson and shot Circelli in the back as he was exiting into the cold Harlem night. Justice was served, frontier justice, as Rao's is truly a New York version of a Wild West saloon. Barone pleaded guilty to the murder, but the lady got her respect, and Frankie No picked up everyone's bill. Miss Strober turned the disaster into a success, mounting a one-woman nice-Jewish-girl-walks-into-gangland-bar show called "Spaghetti and Matzo Balls" at the cabaret Don't Tell Mama. Only in New York.

Getting into Rao's is harder than getting into Harvard. The tables are like time-shares. Somebody important "owns" each one for a certain time every night of the week (it's closed weekends). So the trick is to find Frankie No a sing-ing gig. Then you might get fed. Small wonder Rao's is populated with Broadway and Hollywood quid pro quo types. But if you're resourceful and persistent and patient and able to plan many months in advance, you can get in.

Once you're in, getting uptown is a seminal New York adventure. Take a cab or a Town Car, and watch Manhattan morph from Fred Astaire to Malcolm X as you cross the Maginot Line of Ninety-sixth Street and head east. It may seem hard to believe that a century ago, Italians fled the tenements of Mulberry Street to Pleasant Avenue, with its East River views and East

River breezes, which they saw as their promised land, as idyllic as Greenwich or Larchmont. The surrounding blocks are now burned-out, Dresden-like, in dire need of urban renewal, if not full-out gentrification.

There are only a few Italian vestiges left: Patsy's famed pizzeria, Our Lady of Monte Carmela church, a barber, a baker, a social club, more black Cadillacs than you'd expect. Parts of *The Godfather* were shot (pardon the expression) here. There was a famous butcher shop, supposedly a front for Godfatherly activities, that the locals joked hadn't sold a pork chop for forty years. And there's Rao's, which, except for the chauffeured Rollses and stretch limos out front, looks like a little neighborhood bar.

The little bar has been here, fairly unchanged, since 1896, when the immigrant Charles Rao bought the small saloon belonging to an adjacent brewery. Charles's son Louis Rao ran the place as a speakeasy during Prohibition. Louis was a George Raft character, Chesterfield coats, spats, haircuts at the Waldorf, the kind who was supposed to die in a hail of bullets. Instead Louis went gently, replaced at Rao's by brother Vincent, who traded the mobster look for the cowboy one. Vincent loved to cook, and to do so in his ten-gallon hats and Texas boots. Vincent's wife, Anna, an elegant "broad" who inspired Woody Allen to create the Mia Farrow character in *Broadway Danny Rose*, was an even better cook than her husband. Her recipes were what caused the "outing" of Rao's in a three-star review in *The New York Times* in 1977. When the pugilistic Norman Mailer met the critic Mimi Sheraton, he turned on her for ruining his favorite place. Since the author had once stabbed a wife for less, Sheraton had cause for concern. But she lived to write the foreword to the hugely successful Rao's cookbook, bought by everyone who couldn't get a table.

Anna Rao's nephew is Frankie No, who now runs the place. He has a son, Frank Jr., who might well be called Frankie Yes, for he has a Broadway restaurant called Baldoria (which means "blow-out") with lots of tables, serving Rao's recipes. But there's nothing like the real thing, as the kitchen at Rao's cooks every dish, New York classics all, to order.

But first the ritual: You have a strong drink at the eight-seat bar, poured by Nicky the Vest (he owns lots), and play some Bennett or Sinatra, or the Temptations, if you must (you probably won't get shot, since it's on the jukebox), and get high on the heavenly scent of sizzling garlic and olive oil. An hour later, you take your seats, and Frankie No tells you what to eat. No one looks at a menu. No one dares.

There are things you *have* to eat, beginning with the seafood salad: a lukewarm medley of the freshest, lightly steamed shrimp, squid, scungilli (so beloved by Little Italians), lobster, and more, in a delicate bath of lemon and olive oil. This is an Atkins delight, a meal in itself, but it's only the beginning. You'll be sharing it, whether you want to or not. Rao's is family style; in a room full of egotists, no egotistical food fetishes are tolerated. It's their way or the East Side Highway, or maybe the East River. The other must dish at Rao's also owes a lot to citrus: the legendary lemon chicken, the best chicken dish in the city, maybe the best this side of Paris's Ami Louis. A recently slaughtered bird (Rao's has got good butcher connections) is first half-grilled, then finished off in a sauté pan with olive oil and lots of lemon juice. It comes out charred, crisp, juicy, pungent, everything you want in a bird. In fact, Rao's should call the dish "the jailbird." But they don't get cute here.

Between the fish and the fowl, you'll have a pasta, the best of which is the simplest spaghetti *aglio-olio,* but the *vongole* is fine as well. For greens, the sautéed escarole is dreamy, another garlic fest, as is the cold broccoli with oil and lemon, which seems to be the Rao's elixir. And what about the veal Parmesan? Probably the best in town, but you won't have room for it. Save it for your next visit, five years from now when your name comes up again on the waiting list. Whenever, you'll still have years of bragging rights for getting in at all.

Still hankering for veal Parmesan? With a side of history? Then there's no better place than Gino, which opened in 1945 across from Bloomingdale's. Aside from the prices, Gino is identical to what it always was, and always will be. Gino is the most constant, consistent restaurant in the city, and the most quintessentially "New York," in that it draws a cross section of the most interesting, glamorous, motivated people on the planet and gives them a great meal and a great time in a quintessentially urban-sophisticate environment.

The Truman-Eisenhower era after World War II was the last halcyon period in New York history, the boom years of Madison Avenue, the elegant skyscraperization of Park Avenue, the arrival of the postwar best and brightest, the building of the United Nations, the emergence of the city as the undisputed capital of the world. Afterward, race and war and drugs and crime turned the city into a dirty word for decades before its current comeback. Gino captures New York's 1950s moment of power, glory, and hope in a simple, delicious, yet deeply urbane way. The people who eat at Gino may be the most worldly people you'll ever see under one roof. They've been everywhere, know everyone, seen it all. And Gino is where they come. So it must have something.

What it definitely has are zebras, the trademark-hallmark of the cozy, thirty-table rectangular room. The walls are covered with red wallpaper depicting parallel rows of zebras gracefully running from a hail of arrows. If you look closely, one zebra in every large-small pairing is missing a stripe near its tail. The wallpaper, which looks ancient, has actually been replaced many times, but always with the unintended flaw in the tail. The owner, Gino Circiello, had wanted to get the zebras right the first time, but the wallpaper was already up by the time he caught the missing stripe. Not wanting to inconvenience his customers, Gino let it hang. Later, not wanting to give his customers even the slightest shock of the new, he replicated the stripeless ass with every redo. That's the way this place is. Even well into the age of the cell phone, there is still a forties wooden phone booth with a folding door in the front of the room. The regulars didn't want to see it go.

Among the regulars have been Marilyn Monroe, who would eat here alone and with Joe DiMaggio and Arthur Miller (but not à trois); Frank Sinatra, who came here with his beloved Dolly every Mother's Day; and Ed Sullivan, who planned his "really big shew" here every afternoon. This is Gay Talese's favorite restaurant, and that of a lot of the La Grenouille and Da Silvano people who like to stay in the neighborhood, Bloomingdale Country, the gateway to the Upper East Side. There are models, and designers, and diplomats, and stars, and trophy wives, everyone who loves to shop across the street or over on Madison, plus so many of the owners and workers of the glam shops themselves. That's a lot of beautiful people, usually dressed to kill or thrill.

What all these people have in common is that they will have to wait in line for a table. They will have a manhattan, or a martini, or a whiskey sour at the bar by the phone booth, which can be more sardined than the Lex IRT at rush hour, and they will cool their Prada heels. While the Noo Yawk Italian fare may be similar, Rao's and Gino couldn't be more different. Rao's is a club that basically no one can get into. Gino is a democracy where no one can get an upper hand, not even the black hand, as the Mafia used to be known. The one Gotham constituency that is not represented at Gino is the goodfellas. If they want to go uptown, they do it All the Way, to Rao's.

Aside from the veal *parmigiana* (they spell it the right way here), which comes delightfully and old-fashionedly carbo-loaded with a wonderful potato croquette *and* a side of spaghetti marinara (beg for al dente, and the old-timey clip-on-bow-tied waiters might oblige), the things to get at Gino are the baked stuffed clams, or the grilled bluefish with sautéed escarole, or Ed Sullivan's chicken Gino, which in Little Italy would be called *scarpariello*, or shoemaker style, in a Rao-esque garlic-oil sauce that you scarf up with the heels of Gino's fine, crusty bread, which used to come from the great Zito bakery in the Village until it closed in 2004. Salads, which may please the models and the pretty perfume girls from Bloomingdale's, are as dull as they were back in the 1940s and haven't evolved here into anything vaguely Californian. Vegetables are invariably overcooked, just as they were in 1945, but somehow that works fine to sop up more of Gino's gutsy, oily white and red sauces. Go atavistic for dessert and order the rum cake, an alcoholic blast from the past.

The voyage of the founding father here is a paradigm of Italian restaurant creation in New York. Gino Circiello, born in Buenos Aires in 1912, was a fashion plate himself, again of the George Raft school, but with Rudolph Valentino's slicked-back hair. His Italian-born father was an itinerant chef who had gotten the family back to Capri just as World War I erupted. Already multilingual from growing up in the Argentine, Gino went to work as a junior waiter in the grand hotels of Venice, but wanted to come to New York. He arrived the month of the stock market crash of 1929. Bouncing all over East Coast hotels, from Atlantic City to Palm Beach, he wound up at the Waldorf-Astoria as a bartender. Gino loved cruising up and down Lexington

Avenue, behind the Waldorf, and noted that there wasn't one Italian restaurant anywhere near Bloomingdale's. He found two similarly ambitious Italian friends, and they found a spot in a brownstone that they could rent for $400 a month (it's well over $25,000 today). They bought a used mahogany bar on the Bowery and some wooden tables that are still there, and opened shop. The zebras came from Gino Circiello's dream to be a big-game hunter. By the time he retired in 1985, he had managed to get to Africa and shoot a real one of his own, with stripes on the behind. The trophy skin was his home's conversation piece. Gino Circiello died in 2001 at age eighty-nine, having sold Gino to his three most loyal waiters. He came in until the end, making sure that nothing had changed. He can rest easy. ★ ★ ★ ★ ★ ★ ★ ★ ★ ★ ★ ★ ★ ★

Peter Luger
Last Exit to Brooklyn

BROOKLYN

As with Rao's, the very process of going to Peter Luger is a key part of the mystique. Anyone can go to the Palm or Morton's or Ruth's Chris Steak House for a prime steak, and they wouldn't even have to go to New York to do so. But to cross the rickety Williamsburg Bridge, with its stunning views of the East River and the glittering skyline, and to arrive in, until its recent hipsterfication, what was very much a bombed-out, abandon-all-hope infernal urban wasteland, made a statement—both about you, for having the courage and the cab fare to cross the bridge, and about Peter Luger, for having survived as

Gotham's King of Meat for well over a century in what was always, even in the best of times, an Outer Borough.

Peter Luger is New York's oldest great restaurant, New York's finest old restaurant, a charter member of that club of world-class one-dish, mostly male, temples of testosterone: Lawry's in Los Angeles (prime rib), Joe's Stone Crab in Miami (fried chicken—fooled you!), Ami Louis in Paris (roast chicken), Casa Botín in Madrid (suckling pig), Kronenhalle in Zurich (bratwurst). But Lawry's, which in America comes closest to Peter Luger in concept, is a low-priced mass feedery. Stars come, but so does everyone else, particularly countless tour buses of Japanese gastronomes who never saw beef this good that was so cheap. There's nothing exclusive about Lawry's, and it's as easy to get to as it is difficult to get to Luger. No, you have to work to get to Luger, and you have to pay, Wall Street leveraged-buyout money, to step up here. Plus they don't even take credit cards, except their own. So Luger is a true in-your-face, money-talks, bullshit-walks New York challenge: no pay, no play.

If you have the dough, Luger makes you feel good, real good, about yourself. That's what a great steak can do, and Luger has the best in all Meatland. Luger, which sells ten tons of beef a week, is the pinnacle of a long tradition of great steakhouses in New York City. Many of them, like the original Palm and Pietro's, and the late, lamented Christ Cella, Danny's Hideaway, and Pen and Pencil, were clustered together in the East Forties, near the abbatoirs that went down in 1947 when the United Nations went up; East Forty-fifth Street used to be called Steak Row. Now there are so many pretenders to the Luger throne that every street seems like steak row. But there is only one Peter Luger and only one Brooklyn, so you have to go.

Don't expect Luger to be a celebrity restaurant the way that Mr Chow* or Nobu or Da Silvano is. Even at the height of now faded Atkinsmania, no celebrity, except for sports stars, not even the aging action heroes, wanted to admit that he (and especially she) was a big-time beefeater. It's like saying you're pro-capital-punishment, or pro-fur. But that's exactly what Peter Luger says about you, that you're a big-tipping, big-tippling, carbo-mainlining,

---

* Part of this restaurant's "high style" is to drop the prosaic period in abbreviating Mister.

bloody carnivore. Not a pretty picture, eh? Too cavemanish?

Good stuff for "Page Six." But the reason the gossip columnists are not over here in Williamsburg outing the gluttons is that they're here gluttonning it up themselves, as are so many of the stars and bigwigs (male and female) whose favor they wish to curry, not microwave. So don't be shocked when you see the Thin People here: Uma Thurman or Gisele Bundchen tucking in across from Rudy Giuliani or Jeff Katzenberg or George Clooney or Quentin Tarantino or John Cusack or Benicio Del Toro. Or The Donald and bride Melania. On any given night, especially Sunday night, the famous French chefs like Eric Ripert of Le Bernardin fill the house. They're all thin, so eat up. Maybe if you pay enough for a steak dinner, as you will here, you won't gain any weight from it.

The drill here is simple, once you're in (weekends take enormous months-in-advance planning, unless Howard Rubenstein handles your **PR**). Getting out of your limo and ducking into Luger under the canopy is nowhere as terrifying as it once was. You can even take time for a stroll around New York's new Bohemia without risking life and wallet. Save the wallet for Luger. Once you go in, you're back in 1887, the year Peter Luger started this joint. Have a Dortmunder Union in a big frosted mug to soak in the German beer hall atmosphere. New York used to be full of these *hofbrauhauses*, and Germans used to run the town back in Peter Luger's days, before they got muscled out by the immigrant Irish, Italians, and Jews, all of whom peacefully, if boister-ously, coexist here. Luger is a study in oak: oak bar, oak tables, oak chairs, oak paneling, dark and light. There are coat hooks on the wall, sawdust on the floor, and the only real decoration is provided by giant ceramic steins. The noise is as deafening as a rumbling subway train. *Danke Gott* no one can smoke anymore, as the place was such a miasma you could barely taste anything.

When you get to your oak table, you will be waited on by a burly someone named Adolph or Dieter or Helmut, Fatherland old-pro types who will never show you their head shots. They might, however, slip you a prospectus for their own restaurant; Luger knockoffs owned by former servers, like the new (but old-looking) Wolfgang's, are all the vogue in

Manhattan now. Luger is spawning steakhouses the same way Le Pavilion spawned French temples. These waiters, among the best paid in America, *give* orders rather than *take* them: "You vill haff ziss!" And so you will.

Everyone starts with a shrimp cocktail, although the protein is highly superfluous, because that is the American Way in steakhouses, and it is as good as all-American frozen jumbo shrimp can be. Next is the Luger salad. There's nothing salad-y about it, just alternating huge slices of almost taste-less white Bermuda onion, and not-that-red "beefsteak" tomatoes, which must grow in a hothouse as large as the old Ebbets Field. What makes the salad is the Luger "special sauce," a ketchupy-Worcestershiry-Heinz-57-y amalgam that brings back every memory of your childhood nongastronomy in Akron or Pascagoula. The onions and tomatoes are perfect vehicles for the sauce, as are the fine German breads and salt rolls.

But stop dipping. The Hindenburg is about to land, in the gargantuan form of the "Luger steak for two," a crusty blood-rare porterhouse charred to perfection on the grill from hell, sliced into huge pieces. It is set before you on a slant, the steak platter propped up by a little dish, so that the combo of meat juices and butter atop the steak creates a deep dipping pool to spoon over the steak. Also over the excellent, giant, hand-cut, fried-in-don't-ask-what potatoes that spawned the frozen horror known as "steak fries" that are ubiquitous in bad restaurants near and far.

The steak more than lives up to expectations: salty, beefy, aged, hot, succulent. But what seems to make this steak different from all others is its greater thickness, which allows more of a yin-yang effect between the slab's carbon crust and bloody center. Toothsome may be a word for it. Of course Luger has *the* inside track for the prime-est of the prime from the wholesale purveyors at Hunt's Point Market, so quality as well as cooking comes into play here. As you're sopping the meat in the buttery *jus* and gnawing on that T-bone, you might console your formerly slim self that Peter Luger's owner Sol Forman ate *two* of these monsters every day and lived to be ninety-eight.

Forman died in 2001, but he passed the restaurant on to his daughter, who with her daughter goes to the all-male meat market almost every day to claim their steaks. Sol Forman had made his fortune owning a metalware factory across from Luger, and he did all his business lunches and dinners at the steakhouse. When the original and imperious "the customer is always wrong" Peter Luger (who would taste every complained-about steak and usually refuse to redo it) died in 1941, the restaurant hit the skids. The neighborhood was declining, filling up with Hasidic Jews, whose kosher rules forbade the eating of Luger's hindquarters (not to mention its *über alles* German-ness). Luger's son closed it in 1950.

Forman had been eating at Luger for twenty-five years, and he needed a place to take his clients. He was the only bidder when the restaurant was auctioned off. A rave from über-critic Craig Claiborne in *The New York Times* was proof that Forman had kept the Luger faith. And because Gothamites respect the *Times* as gospel (at least before Jayson Blair and Judith Miller), the four-star review generated a new legion of the faithful; there are over eighty thousand Peter Luger charge-card holders today. Sol Forman opened only one Peter Luger branch, near his home in Great Neck. Always one to mind the store, he didn't believe that the franchise system could ensure consistent quality. The result of Forman's passion and focus is on your plate.

Extras? Aside from the potatoes, there is a very rich creamed spinach here, which doesn't set a standard, but will have to do if you want something green. Yes, Luger recently added a Caesar salad, just as they have added a grilled salmon. But if it hasn't been on the bill of fare for at least a hundred years here, it fails the test of time. So skip it. If you're dying to experience the cardiology advances at Columbia Presbyterian Hospital on this trip to the Apple, finish yourself off with a huge wedge of cream cheese cheesecake from S&S, the great Bronx purveyor to steakhouses, and proof that Brooklyn isn't chauvinistic where quality is concerned. They have to go to Hunt's Point, also in the Bronx, to get the meat, so why not throw in some cheesecake, too. So take the cake, already, lay out the cash, pop three Lipitor, and ask Adolph to carry you to the limo. ★ ★ ★ ★ ★ ★ ★ ★ ★ ★ ★ ★ ★ ★ ★

East Side Story

Oh, WASP, where is thy sting? At Swifty's, the successor to Mortimer's, the Upper East Side playhouse of the *New York Social Register.* Until the 1970s, when they were muscled aside by the multiethnic Big Swinging Dicks of Wall Street, the WASPs ruled New York, or at least its class-driven aspirations, usually achieved by imitative outsiders through Ivy League educations, white-shoe jobs, and the charity circuit. The term was an acronym for White Anglo Saxon Protestant, and the idea was that this was America's English-style aristocracy. However, the roots of New York's WASPs were anything but aristocratic: Dutch farmers, who became Roosevelts, and *Mayflower* refugees, who became the guys you can still see playing backgammon and squash at the Racquet Club on Park Avenue. In the post–Civil War era, when "society" was really created, the big names were the Astors, who got their start as fur trappers, and the Vanderbilts, whose patriarch went from stevedore to commodore. Money thus always talked, though perhaps not as loud as now.

There are plenty of Muffies and Lindsays still on the Upper East Side, even if some of them began their lives as Miriams and Lindas. Even today, a lot of the strivers in the most upwardly mobile of cities are preppie-clubby wannabes. Just look at Ralph Lauren (Bronx né Lifschitz) and the empire he spawned. When it comes to food, the real WASPs seem to have developed a genetic predilection for the chicken à la king-y glop they were served at their boarding schools and later at their clubs, and on the rubber-chicken charity circuit. Enter Glenn Bernbaum, a preppie, WASPy wannabe, who founded Mortimer's on Lexington Avenue in 1976. It was the first and only restaurant for Bernbaum, who had been an executive at the Custom Shops shirtmaker and who so risked losing his own shirt that he stayed on at his day job for Mortimer's first four years.

Chronicled by Tom Wolfe and Dominick Dunne, Mortimer's became a club of its own for the Brooke Astors themselves, as well as for WASPy banking-rich Jews like fashion-plate social X-ray prototype Nan Kempner; fashion-plate creator, the very WASPy Bill Blass; and the ultimately WASPy Jackie O. Most Americans confused the Irish Catholic Kennedys' muscular Harvardness with WASPiness, which became shorthand for upper class. Enter all the Jewish, Irish, Muslim, whatever, Harvard Business School–minted investment bankers and their Pine Manor and Wellesley wives who came of age and of Croesusean wealth at this time and who had caught Ralph Laurenitis along the way. Mortimer's became *their* place, too.

Hence there was an entire Manhattan zip code bereft when Glenn Bernbaum died in 1998 and his will declared that Mortimer's be shuttered forever. *"Après moi, rien"* was Bernbaum's posthumous message to his flock. The WASPs thus went into a long gastronomic Babylonian captivity at La Goulue, the Madison Avenue temple of Eurotrash. But the decor at La Goulue was too beautiful, the food too complicatedly French (even though it could be tasteless enough for the WASP palate). Plus all those Euros trying to be preppy was really annoying to the Old Guard. No, La Goulue was *trying* too hard, and the key to WASPdom is indifferent effortlessness. Muffie needed a place of her own.

Finally, in 1999, the dream came true in the form of Swifty's, just a few blocks down Lexington from the Bernbaum locus. Bankrolled by a group that included Kempner and Blass, and decorated by the "prince of chintz" Mario Buatta and his partner Anne Eisenhower, Swifty's managing partners came from Mortimer's: manager Robert Caravaggi, Mortimer's maître d', whose own father had owned the old society shrine Quo Vadis; and chef Stephen Attoe, who was from England and knew all about clubby WASPs. Sadly, Nan and Bill and Jackie are all now eating twinburgers (dainty four-ounce bunless patties beloved of the lunch bunch) and Miss Porter's–style creamed spinach with Glenn at the Mortimer's in the sky. But for those still in the heaven that is both Louis Auchincloss's and Woody Allen's Manhattan, Swifty's is there doing a good doppelgänger act.

The restaurant is named not for Hollywood superagent Swifty Lazar, but for Bernbaum's pug (the only living creature he ever loved, according to all), who resembled the shaved-headed, diminutive Lazar. Lazar himself would have hated Swifty's. He would have seen it as too much of a waxworks, no stars, no producers, no action. The Brooklyn-born Lazar was totally self-created and true to his own egomaniacal self. He didn't need a Ralph Lauren template. The only preppies he had any use for were Andoverites Humphrey Bogart and Jack Lemmon.

The trick about Swifty's is knowing where to sit. Not that as an outsider you'll have that much choice. There's a submarine-narrow, Mortimerian brown bar room with tables scrunched along a wall, then a slightly more comfortable square chintzy room in back with dog paintings and Nantuckety scenes. Everybody looks the same in both rooms, men in navy blazers and pink pants, women in anything *tasteful,* from Jil Sander to Lilly Pulitzer. In one room you might see Carolina Herrera, and in the other Caroline Kennedy Schlossberg.

One *must* be the Siberia, but no one seems to know, including the charming, lean and hungry Caravaggi, who is far sweeter on his own than he was allowed to be under the cantankerous Bernbaum, who, if he didn't fancy the cut of your jib, would leave you stranded at his bar for hours and never call you to table, good or bad. Caravaggi is an artist like Caravaggio in his seating strategies, keeping old lovers a room apart, playing Cupid with new ones, helping society feuds simmer and burn out. But he also welcomes outsiders, if you seem decorous and potentially East Sidey. A broker today, a hedge fund tomorrow, so it never hurts to be nice to all.

The food at Swifty's is not only a lot better than Mortimer's, much of it is also quite good. It's as if Bernbaum felt it was WASPier to serve bad food, that gourmet fare was for ethnic peasants, and thus ordered Attoe to look up but cook down. Now Attoe is on his own, and defininitely cooking up. Yes, the twinburgers, and the cardboardy paillards and the creamed spinach are all right there, and the curried chicken salad with banana and avocado and mango chutney is exactly what you might get in the ne plus ultra of women's clubs, the Colony over on Park. The crab cakes are still there, too, but they're fresher than ever, as is all the fish. Swifty's must have a good society fish man in Palm Beach, or maybe Hobe Sound, as the red snapper and pompano or any Gulf fish is as good as you can hope for in Gotham. Swifty's chopped Cobb is better, gutsier, than Michael's, a Hollywood dish worthy of the human Swifty rather than the canine one. And the French fries are fresh and crisp, if not quite Balthazar's.

The ladies who lunch tend to save their best for last, and the desserts are as sweet and rich as the women are. There are girly, and girly-man, over-the-top sugary indulgences such as a baked apple with butterscotch sauce, banana Foster, baked Alaska, pumpkin pie with nutmeg ice cream, and a pine-apple upside-down cake. These are all country club desserts, but A-list clubs like Round Hill or Piping Rock. No matter how much they pack away at the end, you *never* see a fat person at Swifty's, as if all the women were perpetually paying their respects to Nan Kempner by miraculously being richer and thinner than mortal women in the isle of Manhattan's less exalted quadrants. So make yourself your clubbable best and join the party, which is as easy to get into these meritocratic, money-talks times as New York Society is ever likely to be.

The thing about Swifty's is that its lions and lionesses tend to be fifty-plus. To see the beautiful cubs of the chintzy social jungle, the best game park on the Upper East Side is Via Quadronno, just off Madison in the Seventies and steps from such neighborhood bulwarks as the Whitney, Sotheby's, and the Carlyle. Via Quadronno is the coolest sandwich-and-ice-cream shop in New York, and nowhere except perhaps Cipriani Downtown has a more drop-dead attractive clientele. Via Q, inspired by a Milan sandwicherie called Bar Quadronno (name of the street), is as Euro as can be, a few outdoor tables, a long espresso and gelato bar, a sunken tiny eating area with hard monastic seating, and some Italianate art on the walls. This is not a place to linger, but everyone does, because if you stay long enough you'll inevitably run into someone you know, or want to know, from Martha Stewart to native East Sider Gwyneth Paltrow to Ralph Lauren himself to all the Gothamophile Euros who love the WASP look and outprep the master at his own game.

What makes Via Q so hot is not merely its prime location and its throw-away charm. The homemade, totally Italian, many-flavored, many-splendored ice creams and sorbets are arguably the best in town, ditto the cappuccino. And the sandwiches are up there, rivaled only by 'ino (short for panino) in the West Village. The key is great Italian bread and great imported meats like *speck, bresaola,* pro-sciutto, mortadella, *soppressata,* and cheeses like mozzarella, fontina, Camembert, taleggio, sliced thin and toasted perfectly. The most popular panino is the *tentazione:* prosciutto, smoked mozzarella, arugula, shrimp, and a creamy pink mayonnaise. These delicate, petite gourmet creations are light-years from Manganaro's meatball heroes in Hell's Kitchen, which for decades was the state-of-the-art Italian sandwich in New York. Now it might as well be Martha Stewart's kitchen.

Although Via Q looks like a short-order snack bar, you can eat full meals here. There is a soothing pureed vegetable soup sworn to by neighbors with colds, as well as a few daily pastas and risottos, like a dreamy lasagna, cooked to Milanese perfection by the largely Chinese-mainland staff (don't forget where Marco Polo got it). Plus Cipriani-level carpaccios, and model-pleasing salads with beautiful baby greens. It's staggering what the tiny kitchen can do, especially under the constant pressure, as the place is packed from breakfast to dinner.

Still, it's the sandwiches that are the main draw, for New York is a sandwich town that until the recent panini renaissance was losing its Jewish delis and hence its carbo mojo (see page 51). So it had to be the Italians, the *real* Italians, flying in on Alitalia to the rescue. The sandwich savior behind Via Quadronno is a former music executive named Paola Della Puppa, who had made a career shift to New York to be maître d' at Sant Ambroeus, a few blocks down Madison. Sant A, which opened in 1983, was part of a small Milan chain of deluxe espresso-gelato bars and the first of its kind to open in Manhattan. Sant A quickly became the darling of the Uptown art world, holding its own with such nearby casual rivals as Eli Zabar's EAT and the Three Guys Coffee Shop, which surely has the toniest clientele of any Greek diner in this city, or even of tony Mykonos. But Sant A was slightly formal, with a padded and swagged pink dining room that served full, delicious Italian meals. It was too grand to want to be a panini stand.

It was somehow too grand to last forever, and its lease was sold to Paris's Fauchon in 2001. But in 2006 Fauchon sold it back to the Sant A family, sort of like a colony in the Triple Entente days of yore. The Sant A people were doubtless cognizant of the unexpected smash down the block of the uprooted but resilient Della Puppa, who has gone on to open Via Q branches in Hong Kong, Tokyo, and Coral Gables, with many more planned. Panini are proof that man, preppy man for sure, can indeed live by bread alone. ★ ★ ★ ★ ★ ★ ★ ★ ★ ★ ★

Elaine's and Primola
Walking the Line

Presenting yourself to Elaine Kaufman is like going for a full-body scan. You worry that there's something wrong with you. You may have cancer from the nitrites in those Papaya King hot dogs you love, clogged arteries from Peter Luger, God knows what. You may be just fine, too. But you wouldn't bet on it. So it is with Elaine, the city's most ruthlessly eagle-eyed restaurant-gatekeeper since the late Henri Soulé. Elaine is to New York what Regine used to be to Paris: the supreme arbiter of Who Belongs and Who's Out.

Say you've written your first best-seller. Hollywood is nibbling. Where else to celebrate but Elaine's, the only restaurant in America that is so devoted to writers, of all people. You want to sit in "the Line," that Murderers' Row of ten tables on the right wall as you enter this old saloon on Second Avenue and Eighty-eighth Street. This is where America's greatest writers sit, or have sat: Norman Mailer, Gay Talese, William Styron, Philip Roth, Irwin Shaw, James Baldwin, and, of course, Woody Allen, who has eaten more meals here than any other famous person in any famous restaurant on earth.

You've booked, of course. But you don't dare ask for "the Line." It's like asking someone if you can kiss them. It's up to Elaine. First you have to find the place, in the upper stretch of Second Avenue. There's a hideous yellow awning out front. So this is the place? Don't ask. You come in, with the most attractive companion you can conjure up. The Big Boss, closing in on eighty, greets you coolly, checks you out, gets your name, sends you to the bar. You wait maybe fifteen, twenty, thirty minutes as Elaine greets, not so coolly, some of her regulars—David Halberstam, Nora Ephron, Pete Hamill, Mike Nichols and Diane Sawyer, David and Helen Gurley Brown, Martha Stewart, Joan Rivers, George Steinbrenner—with hugs and kisses and a walk down the Line. Those are long, long minutes.

Finally Elaine comes to get you. She walks the Line, or, more accurately, waddles it. You follow, heart aflutter. But then she takes a hard left, into the adjacent row, and keeps walking to the back. She seats you, only one row away from the Woody table, but the gap might as well be the Pacific Ocean, or the Mindanao Trench. You thought you were in, but you're still on the waiting list. You're filled with doubt, fears that Elaine knows something you don't, that Hollywood will dump you, that you'll never hit the list again. Your only consolation is that it could be worse. You could have been taken two, or even three, rows over. Or the horror of it if Elaine had taken a right and not a left, and had taken you into the walled-off side room, where you can't even *see* the famous people. That would have been a death sentence. At least there's hope for another night, another table, another chance to make the Line.

With the death in 2005 of George Plimpton, who everyone thought would live forever, the mortality of Elaine's has become an issue. Everyone thinks Elaine will live forever, too, but Plimpton's exit has shaken the confidence of the city's literati. The crowd of world-beaters who made Elaine's, or who Elaine made, in the 1960s and 1970s, is getting old, really old, if not clocking out. So many of the great clients have gone recently: Bobby Short, Alan King, Anne Bancroft, Marlon Brando, William Styron, Ahmet Ertegun, not to mention such less lately lamented every-nighters as Jerzy Kosinski and Mario Puzo and Peter Maas and Rudolf Nureyev. Among the living, these people have been legends for forty years or more. But it takes time to become a legend, and . . . well, you do the math. Some once young but now, alas, middle-aged writers like Jay McInerney and Winston Groom are fixtures here, but they're in the minority. Elaine's is the Lion Country Safari of American letters, all giants, no midlisters.

Furthermore, the young Brooklyn lit set—Lethem, Safran Foer, et al.—is not following their elders to Elaine's. Maybe it's not ironic enough for them. Maybe they're afraid of not making the Line. The point is that there isn't a new generation of Elaineians waiting in the wings. But if Elaine's days are numbered, so are your own. The point is to get there now, while it's still in its glory, because if you want to see New York's finest (as well as a few top cops), this remains the place.

On the subject of cops, one of the most colorful, telling incidents here took place in 1998, when Elaine was brought down to the precinct house on charges that she assaulted a D-list customer who wasn't spending enough at the bar. The man from Memphis was with his date, from Little Rock, at the bar after midnight. The date, who was driving, was not drinking, and that somehow piqued Elaine, proof that she doesn't spend all her time cosseting Gay and Norman. The Memphian claimed that Elaine chided the couple for cheapness, called them "white trash," and taunted them that there were plenty of other southerners in house that night, even some on the Line, who could afford to spring for dinner.

The southern man stood up for his lady's honor by impugning Elaine's. He called the queen of the literary night "a pig." Elaine responded, he said, by clawing his face and drawing blood. Not bad for an old dame. Elaine didn't dispute her annoyance at the couple taking up her prime bar space with only one drink between them, but the lit queen denied using the "white trash" expression. "I'm a New Yorker, and that's not a New York expression," she told the press, conceding, "I might have said other things." As for the assault, she claimed self-defense, for the southerner was "in my face. He could have had a knife or something. I've seen it before." All her waiters backed up the proprietor's account of the event, and the charges in this case of southern hospitality manqué were ultimately dropped.

The incident is silly, but telling, because it illuminates Elaine's character, her toughness, her extremism in defense of her institution. Elaine Kaufman was born in 1929 in Manhattan and high-schooled in the Bronx, a true Depression baby. Her downwardly mobile father was a prosperous merchant with a dry-goods store who ended up peddling socks in the street. Elaine started out skinny, really skinny, though at one point she was up to over 350 pounds. Along the way, she worked as a fabric cutter, sold stamps and lipstick, then decided to go bohemian, dyed her hair green, and moved to the Village "to be around beatniks" in the 1950s.

Elaine always loved restaurants. One Village night at an Italian joint, the Portofino, she was swept away by a dashing fellow waitperson, the aforementioned Alfredo Viazzi (see the Da Silvano section, page 8), just off the boat, where he had been a steward, from Genoa. She was so swept that, after an endless lunch the next day, they moved in together two weeks later. For the sake of togetherness, Elaine took a waitress job at Portofino, where Alfredo, who would in a decade give New York an education in *la vera cucina italiana*, gave an early one to his inamorata, plus a primer on how to run a restaurant. Eventually, the restaurant owner decided to sell, and the lovebirds bought it, on time—a long, long time. Although Elaine loved running Portofino, Alfredo knew he was destined for greater things. He wanted to be Fellini, Pirandello, not a chowhound. Accordingly, he created a tiny theater in the back of the restaurant to stage his own plays. Elaine thought Alfredo's concept stank. Their fights rivaled those of Patterson and Johansson. He called her a *porchetta grassa*, a fat pig, fighting words in any language. Eventually they split up, viciously, with Elaine going Greek (taverna-style, that is) on her mate, smashing every dish in the joint.

Still, Elaine was bitten and smitten by the restaurant bug. She wanted another, but she had no money, plus she was a woman, and no one in the early 1960s would believe that a woman could run a restaurant all by herself. She thus found a male partner, a Village bar owner with expansion fantasies. They each put up five grand, Elaine's borrowed from her sister. Ten thousand went nowhere in 1963; any place in a decent neighborhood started at fifty thousand. So Elaine found a divey place in an indecent neighborhood called Yorkville, a tenement-filled German-Hungarian ghetto populated by Park Avenue doormen, handymen, and nannies, before they wrote diaries. The place was an old Hungarian bar with an Italian name, Gambrino's. Elaine knew Italian food from Alfredo, so she found a seventy-five-year-old retired

Italian cook who dried his own pasta on a clothesline on the kitchen ceiling. There were eight tables to start, all of them empty. There was no foot traffic in this netherland, no Park Avenue types wandering east out of curiosity, no loyal Portofinians coming uptown to lend support, nothing. Nothing, that is, except some starving authors.

The first was the penurious patrician Nelson Aldrich, who lived around the block and was teaching in nearby Harlem. Aldrich had just come back from Paris, where he had toiled on the *Paris Review* with fellow penurious patrician George Plimpton, whom Aldrich brought in. A chain began, and writers begat producers, who begat actors, who begat press. Many of the original "Elaine's Boys" had little money, and Elaine would let them run tabs, sometimes for years. Gambrino's pre-Elaine had been something of a betting parlor, and Elaine somehow inherited an ability to pick the right horses. Many of her Boys—Plimpton, Talese, Halberstam, Tom Wolfe, Bruce Jay Friedman, Terry Southern, Dan Jenkins, Arthur Kopit, Pete Hamill, to name a few—Hit It Big. And they stayed loyal, Remembering When.

A few years into Elaine's success, she and her bartender-partner got into an Elaine's fight when he wouldn't let Truman Capote in. "We don't serve fags" was his excuse. Elaine turned around and bought him out, and soon such luminaries as Leonard Bernstein, Tennessee Williams, and Andy Warhol were joining Capote in what was more a salon, a party, than a conventional restaurant. Soon Woody Allen would join the club, and Michael Caine, and Liza with a *Z*, and Jackie with an *O*. Even Frank with an *S* came in, on nights off from his beloved Jilly's on Eighth Avenue. Roman Polanski became a regular and ended up winning a libel suit against *Vanity Fair* for saying he groped and romanced a Scandinavian model at Elaine's just after his wife, Sharon Tate, was murdered in 1969 by Charles Manson. Mia Farrow testified that she ate at Elaine's around the same time and that the famed playboy was beside himself with grief and on good behavior, despite the distaff temptations always around at the restaurant, temptations many a lesser playboy has been unable to resist, regardless of circumstances.

Today, you don't see that many models at Elaine's, not the young ones in any case. What you see are legends, model legends like Christie Brinkley and Cheryl Tiegs, actress legends like Lauren Bacall and Mary Tyler Moore, sports legends like Reggie Jackson and Walt Frazier, and, of course, literary legends like Mailer and Talese. They all come late, after the theater, after the charity benefits, after the parties. They come to prolong the night and relive the glory days. Nobody has a bad time in Elaine's, not even in Siberia. But Plimpton is gone, and you can feel the tick of the clock, if not see the grim reaper.

Oh, and the food: the food at Elaine's is probably the most maligned in Manhattan. It's a bum rap. If you got this fare in Cleveland or even foodie Seattle, you'd think you had died and gone to Parma. Elaine's customers may have started out starving, but they ain't starving now. They wouldn't put up with bad food. There is also a surprisingly noble wine list, assembled by Elaine in large part to satisfy oenophile Woody Allen. Woody has moved on; the wines remain.

The menu, which no one has ever seen, is classic New York Italian, similar to Gino, though everyone tends to order the same few dishes: crunchy well-fried zucchini, al dente spaghetti Bolognese, the best grilled veal chop in the city, pink and thick and juicy. Drinks are what you might expect, generous and expertly mixed. Elaine's is actually more a bar with food than a restaurant with drinks. The fancy Woody vintages notwithstanding, this dark-walled, dark-ceilinged hideaway is still the saloon it always was. Take away the endless book jackets of major best-sellers lining the walls, and, atmospherically, you could be at any old-time East Side watering hole. But actually not. That's only if you take away Elaine, who almost never strays from this, her home. Elaine, whom so proudly we hail, is what makes Elaine's. She is every celebrity's best friend, and good luck on her becoming yours.

Actually, to pan Elaine for her food is to do her a double disservice. Not only is her food perfectly fine, but she also spawned, albeit inadvertently, an entire school of superdelicious (yes, better than the original) East Side Italian restaurants run by her former employees. Because Elaine likes to fight, and because these barmen and waiters, being around the rich and famous, couldn't help but catch the unique Manhattan virus of ambition, it was inevitable that Elaine's employees would move on and move up, though geographically, most of them seem to be the prisoners of Second Avenue, which is New York's Appian Way of trattorias.

Top of the lot, which includes Elio's, Nicola's, Parma, and more, is Primola, which is where Woody Allen defected to, and not because of any dustup with Elaine's but because Primola may have the very best Italian food in the city. Talk about purity. Virtually everyone at Primola, from chef to busboys, is not only from Italy, rare for any Italian restaurant in America, but also from one city, Bari, that cradle of wonderfully rustic fare on the Adriatic. What they make is not the entrails and odd sea creatures the poor Baresi eat, but the best possible versions of the prime-est steaks and finest fish, Italian style, that rich New Yorkers eat. Movie stars and sports heroes and billionaire Wall Streeters tend not to be so adventurous foodwise, so Primola makes it real easy for them.

Primola looks like an updated Elaine's: a rectangular room, a juke-box, knowing Italian waiters in shirtsleeves. Plus a Line of its own, lined up with Woody and Soon-Yi; Brad and Angelina; Wasserstein and Perella, when they were partners; Perelman and Barkin, when *they* were partners; play-boy-banker (a uniquely New York–London species) Teddy Forstmann and Elizabeth Hurley or whoever is the reigning beauty of the moment; George Steinbrenner; Derek Jeter; Jason Giambi; Neil Simon; Ralph Lauren; Rudy Giuliani; the big architects, like Charles Gwathmey and Richard Meier, who are the new superstars in this city.

Unlike at Elaine's, they're all here to eat, not so much greet. They start with a complimentary plate of magnificent hams and salamis and Parmigiano-Reggiano, hacked off a straight-from-Parma giant wheel. This could be a meal in itself, but it's only the start. Next, the Players actually lighten up with a pasta course, most often the gossamer, best-ever spaghetti primavera, a sym-phony of finely diced market vegetables in an olive oil sauce with hints of garlic and tomato. This is the dish that made Sirio Maccioni. But at Le Cirque,

Maccioni Frenchified it with tons of cream and cheese, turning springtime into winter. Butter and cream are alien to the Barese kitchen. The Primola primavera may well be Manhattan's most delicious health dish, a must for the Masters here who have reason to want to live forever. All the tomato sauces are cooked separately, not doctored from a single vat, and they sparkle. When soft-shell crabs are in season, have them here; the kitchen is masterly at lightly sautéeing seafood. And, yes, they make a mean grilled veal chop, but nobody here gets it, since that's what they eat at Elaine's. Remember that a lot of these "A" people go to both, but far more often to Primola, which is their neighborhood canteen, while Elaine's is much more ceremonial. Dessert is house grappa, which is all you'll have room for, though gluttonous epicures swear by the tiramisù.

Because restaurants on this level do not compete on good food alone, what makes Primola shine? Yes, Giuliano Zuliani, an old Elaine's hand, is a charming, convivial host, bearish and gusto-ish, the kind of man athletes and cops would love. He has two other East Side restaurants, Girasole and Canaletto, held to Primola's standard and always a fallback if the Line is full. Yes, the waiters know their regulars and cosset them, as well as being sweet as pie to you, which is different from Elaine's, where you *are* where you *sit*, and are pitied accordingly. Yes, the tables are spacious, and you can breathe, if not converse, very well. But what really seems to make Primola, to set it apart from the almost-as-good, more *Social Register*-y Sette Mezzo on Lexington, is its jukebox. You can hear Little Peggy March, and Lesley Gore, and especially every great doo-wop group, with the emphasis here on "wop," and all pride, no prejudice: the Del Vikings, the Five Satins, plus all the Italo-American folk heroes like Dion, Fabian, Frankie Valli. This is the best 1950s–1960s East Coast American (not English, not Motown) jukebox in the world, the greatest hits of your (depending on your age, but to the boomers here) youth, when your ears were pressed to the radio in Raleigh or Wilkes-Barre or nearby Massapequa listening to Cousin Brucie on WABC, and you were dreaming of how you would take Manhattan someday. And now you have. So have another grappa, and stay right here, cause these are the good old days. ★ ★ ★ ★ ★ ★ ★ ★

The Four Seasons
and Michael's
Power of the Press

What does it say about New York's most famous restaurant that its most famous dish for its most famous patrons is a baked potato? Not a baked potato with caviar or truffles, although that can be had here for around $150 a spud. No, it's a regular Idaho with nothing but some fine olive oil and a grind of black pepper, a cross between the Mediterranean diet and the Boise diet, that currently goes for around $20, off the menu, of course, as famous dishes for the famous go, the most expensive baked potato anywhere. What the tuber says is that the restaurant, the Four Seasons, is about power and control, and a little perversity, more than about cooking, even though the kitchen here is capable of turning out some of the finest, most inventive dishes in the city. But those dishes are for foodies and regular people who don't have the world to run. The baked potato is for those who, as in the Hebrew National ads, "have to answer to a higher calling." These earthmovers don't have time for the frivolities of gastronomy.

For an out-of-towner, or an outside in-towner, having lunch at the Four Seasons's moderne-clubby Grill Room (as opposed to its splashy, bar-mitzvah-royal Pool Room) is like getting tickets to the *Late Show with David Letterman*. You will see a lot of famous people, but you're definitely in the audience, not center stage. Who will you see? Big men in dark suits eating baked potatoes: Tom Brokaw, Dan Rather, Vernon Jordan, Henry Kissinger, Si Newhouse, Barry Diller, Reverend Al Sharpton, mega-banker Felix Rohatyn, mega-agent Mort Janklow, mega-Canadian Edgar Bronfman Jr., who owns the place. And it's not all guys: Barbara Walters, Martha Stewart, Anna Wintour, and Katie Couric all call this home for lunch. And you *will* get in. You may not sit in certain power banquettes reserved for these regulars, but there are usually free seats. Like the chief cheerleader everyone was too scared to ask out, so she sat home alone on Saturday nights, the Four Seasons is so grand and intimidating that most people don't think they're *worthy* of being here, and never even try. Besides, for all its power and glory, the Four Seasons, since it opened in 1959, has been a roller coaster of success and failure. The place knows about hard times. It *wants* your business, *needs* your business, believe it or not.

No restaurant could have higher overhead. Designed by Mies van der 43 Rohe and Philip Johnson as part of the landmark Seagram Building on Park Avenue, the Four Seasons has a fortune in art by Picasso, Miró, Pollock, Lichtenstein, Rauschenberg. Rothko was to be added to the list, but when the populist artist found out the place was to be for the capitalists, not the labor (he envisioned a workers' cafeteria), he bailed out. There are huge ficus trees in the Pool Room, a fortune in silver and china and crystal and trolleys and fancy uniforms for the army of servers, the best ingredients flown in from across the globe. In this top-dollar piece of real estate, the tables are so widely placed you think you're in the Great Plains. It's so quiet you can almost hear the wind sweeping down these plains, although not the world takeover plans being hammered out at the next table, seemingly miles away. For the power elite, this is a day place, the canteen that Rothko would have liked to bomb. All the action takes place in the soaring two-level Grill Room, where many of the oldest clients sit on tall perches, like Roman emperors watching the gladiators below fight it out.

Because this is lunch theater, as opposed to the dinner theater at Elaine's, you'll want some food to nibble on while you watch the spectacle. It'll take a lot more than the baked potato to fill you up. The spa-cuisine-style menu, which obviously changes with the seasons here, may seem superfluous to the emperors, but it will turn you on. You've never seen so many enticingly healthy choices, a veritable Canyon Ranch in the canyons of Manhattan. But it's not all spa. Although there are bad goodies like Caesar salad, lobster bisque, Maryland crab cakes, a buttery Dover sole, and shad roe with bacon, the things that grab your attention are a bison carpaccio with rocket (Brit-speak for arugula, maybe to please Anna Wintour and Tina Brown and the countless Anglophiles in the media elite); a "toss" of baby vegetables in a ramp vinaigrette; tortelloni with morels, sage, and more of those ramps, a leeky veg that has taken Manhattan like Graydon Carter; an ahi tuna burger; a roasted black bass with barley risotto.

While prime of stock and provenance, the food is slightly timid of taste, as if the chefs were worried that the emperors and empresses might actually pass on the potato and *try* something else. But the chefs didn't want to pump it up too much for fear of getting a thumbs-down and being thrown to the lions, or to Mario Batali. Desserts, which the royalty will never order, have no such restraint: the chocolate velvet cake; the pineapple strudel, a nod to the kitchen's Swiss roots; the "forbidden rice pudding," a jab at the power-eaters' severe diets. Despite a cellar full of great vintages, the imperial drink in the Grill Room, next to the bar, ironically, is Diet Coke. The wine is for the weddings and other festivities in the Pool Room.

The current coowners (with Mr. Bronfman) of the restaurant are Alex von Bidder, a military-precision proper Swiss and Cornell Hotel Administration School grad who had worked for the "Queen of Mean" Leona Helmsley at her Park Lane Hotel, and Julian Niccolini, a Tuscan and also a Helmsleyite, who is an expert on wine, women, and, to a lesser degree, song. They came to the Four Seasons at the restaurant's and the city's lowest ebb (*Daily News* headline: "[President] Ford to City: Drop Dead") in the mid 1970s and courted power, starting with publishers like Simon & Schuster's editor-author Michael Korda, who memorialized the Grill Room in his book *Power!*, and Mort Janklow, a lawyer who became the king of book agents by repping Nixon's henchmen Haldeman and

Ehrlichman, plus Judith Krantz. Today, the austere, Von Clausewitz–like von Bidder runs the operation, and the ebullient, Bacchus-like Niccolini runs the show. The latter adores attractive women, and rolls out the red carpet accordingly to those endowed by nature if not by their family. Any woman who tries hard enough thus has a shot at royal treatment here.

Von Bidder and Niccolini are the end of a distinguished line of restaurateurs who have stepped up to the challenge of a restaurant that at first glance would seem like a slam dunk. But the odyssey of the Four Seasons is evidence of just how hard the luxury restaurant business is. The creator of the Four Seasons was Joseph Baum, a Cornell-trained hospitality executive from a hotel family who went on to head Restaurant Associates, a concept-dining empire whose first hat trick was creating a successful gourmet restaurant in the highly unlikely venue of Newark Airport. From Newark, Baum took RA into Manhattan, with the over-the-top Forum of the Twelve Caesars, which would have made Brutus blush, and La Fonda del Sol, which would have done the same to Pancho Villa. Baum's tour de force, his class act, was the Four Seasons. But despite its concept as being a gourmet "American" restaurant (James Beard was an early consultant), Baum could never contain his passion for flambéing things.

By the early 1960s, all the restaurants were hits, so Baum created more and more. Among dozens, he acquired Mama Leone's, New York's ultimate Italian tourist attraction (some might have said trap); he rebuilt Tavern on the Green in Central Park; and he created Zum Zum, a highly sophisticated fast-wurst chain. But Baum had gone too far, too fast, and by 1970 RA stock had sunk from a high of $47 to $2. And the Four Seasons's American angle was more stigma than lure. It simply couldn't compete with Le Pavilion and its continental ilk. France ruled New York in those days.

RA ultimately merged with the Waldorf cafeteria chain and dumped most of its high-end ambitions, along with Baum, who never would give up. He bounced back in 1976, opening Windows on the World in the World Trade Center, which aped the elegance of the Four Seasons but was too big to match its cachet. Windows was a huge hit, however, as was Baum's revival of the Rainbow Room atop Rockefeller Center. Baum, a numbers man turned showman, died at seventy-eight in 1998.

Meanwhile, back at the Seagram Building, a succession of Hungarians tried to breathe life into what was looking like an elegant albatross. First was George Lang, who went on to become the impresario of the Upper West Side's Café des Artistes, with its risqué murals, and to rebuild Gundel, which might be described as the Four Seasons of his native Budapest. The very worldly former violinist Lang tried to Frenchify the Four Seasons, to no avail. He even hired a trio to jazz up the morbid Grill Room, also without any luck.

Then came two more Hungarians from inside the bleeding Restaurant Associates, Paul Kovi and Tom Margittai, who had worked together at the Waldorf-Astoria, which for decades was a training ground for New York restaurants similar to what the Savoy was in London: Everybody Worked There. Their hotel background may explain the Four Seasons's history of cutting-edge restraint and essential conservatism. Then again, Si Newhouse and Felix Rohatyn and all the other dark-suit moguls are not exactly radicals. They're grand-hotel types themselves, hence the fit. At a fire sale in 1973, RA unloaded (taking a down payment of a mere $15,000) both the Four Seasons and Forum of the Twelve Caesars on the Hungarians, the latter of which they themselves quickly closed, bringing its two Swiss chefs over to the Seagram Building to rescue what was becoming a very foreign "American" restaurant.

Kovi and Margittai had a long, long run, from 1973 to 1995. Their Euro-American rejiggering of the Four Seasons jelled perfectly with the rise of California cuisine and the foodie movement in general, plus New York itself came back from the brink. What better place to symbolize New York's survival than this stunning Gotham temple of Americana, Hungarian style. In 1995, Kovi and Margittai sold the restaurant to the Seagram company, with the Bronfman family installing long-term loyalists von Bidder and Niccolini as their partners. In the years since, New York has just gotten better and better, and so has the Four Seasons, which has proven that it can rise, with aplomb, to any occasion. For instance, when an antifur activist crashed into the Grill

Room and threw a dead raccoon on the table of the fur-loving Anna Wintour, Julian Niccolini was said to have suavely picked up the carcass, turned to the protester, and asked her if she'd like him to put it in the fridge for her. Of course, Joseph Baum might have gone Niccolini one better. He would have flambéed the darn thing.

When it comes to American food and the power lunch, the Four Seasons has only one chief rival, and that is Michael's, off Fifth Avenue right behind the Museum of Modern Art. "21" used to get this crowd decades ago when it was family owned, but it has changed hands so many times (now Orient Express owns it) that the personal touch has been lost to institutional ossification; without the original hosts Jack and Charlie, "21" is 86. The Big Boys want that glad hand, and no hand is gladder than that of Michael McCarty, the Michael of Michael's. There is no restaurateur in the city more all-American than he. His success in the heart of heartless Manhattan is remarkable in that Michael's symbolizes the thing that Manhattanites are supposed to hate and scorn more than any other: Los Angeles. (Remember the Woody Allen joke in *Annie Hall* that LA's only cultural advantage was turning right on a red light.)

Michael's is a branch of the original Michael's in Santa Monica, which ranks with Chez Panisse in Berkeley as one of the chief progenitors of California cuisine. California cuisine might well be defined as Provençal cooking on a surfboard: great local ingredients, great French technique. Michael's made its name with lots of wonderful salads from area farms, and good fish and meats from area purveyors, simply grilled with even more Golden State veggies. The food was good enough to begin turning *California* in New York eyes from a new-age space-cadet dirty word to a mouthwatering Pavlovian hunger trigger, a trigger that Michael McCarty knew exactly when to pull.

When Michael's in Manhattan opened in 1989, it was something of a homecoming for McCarty, who grew up in Briarcliff Manor and prepped at the Hill School in Pottstown, Pennsylvania. McCarty, a hale fellow well met with a bone-crushing handshake who dresses in Palm Beach pinks and limes, would have made a fine Wall Streeter, or an even finer host of one of those Upper East Side preppy bars, in the John Lindsay era when preppies ruled New York. Instead, he got the food bug. It started when he attended an Exeter-Andover year-abroad program in Rennes, France. He liked France so much that after Hill, he went straight to Paris and to cooking school, hotel school, *and* wine school, collecting diplomas from the Cordon Bleu, the École Hôtelière de Paris, *et* l'Academie du Vin. But he also needed a real American degree, and to that end he headed west to Boulder, where he graduated from the University of Colorado, then America's reigning party school, where his French skills made him big party man on campus.

Perched on the Continental Divide, McCarty succumbed to the lure of surf and sand, as well as that of opportunity, since LA in 1979—the year he opened Michael's—was, notwithstanding the recent wild success of Ma Maison, still a restaurant desert, though about to bloom. There was a lot of Ma Maison in the twenty-five-year-old McCarty's new venture: the outdoor garden seating, the unlikely location in then seedy Santa Monica, the simple, clean nouvelle cuisine. But Michael's was a far, far lovelier *endroit* than Ma Maison, whose garden was a reverse-chic AstroTurf-ed toolshed; Michael's garden was Versailles by comparison. And Michael had modern art on his walls, art by California artists who would soon be discovered, art that would later be worth a fortune. Plus there was Michael himself. Unlike Ma's intimi-datingly grand French supersnob Patrick Terrail, McCarty was a good ole American party boy. No unlisted numbers here, no power seating, just good food and drink. Stars, at least the laid-back Santa Monica stars like Jane Fonda in those days, would come to Michael's. But it was much more for artists and writers—and foodies, Chez Panisse South, as there seemed to be something of a shuttle between the two French-inspired California kitchens.

Michael's was such a hit, and such a media sensation, that by the end of the go-go 1980s, McCarty had not only Michael's in New York but also places called the Rattlesnake Club in Washington, D.C., Denver, and Detroit. His biggest project was creating his own luxury hotel on what was known as Santa Monica's Gold Coast, a strip of palazzos by the sea where Cary Grant kept house with Randolph Scott, and where the Kennedys gamboled with the Lawfords and the Rat Pack. The gold had become tarnished, supplanted by the Malibu Colony. But McCarty had found a defunct club, the Sand and Sea, and was planning to turn it into an international "must" destination.

Talk about hubris. Soon after unveiling his plans, McCarty was beset with a series of plagues. First was the liberalism of Santa Monica—the People's Republic of Santa Monica, as it is known. His plan was decried as elitist by the elitists here (takes one to know one), and a referendum squashed it completely, forcing the high-flying McCarty into Chapter 11. Next came an area recession, then the Malibu fires, which burned down McCarty's home, then the Northridge earthquake, which destroyed most of his vintage California wine collection. He sold the D.C., Denver, and Detroit restaurants, while in LA Michael's seemed to fall off the radar of happeningness. Also, the stigma of having failed at the hotel venture hurt McCarty in a town where "losers" have a rare form of celebrity cooties.

No man being a prophet in his own country, McCarty concentrated on New York, where he had the mystique of the new kid in town, the cool surfer dude with all the greens (not greenbacks). And Michael's on Fifty-fifth Street just got hotter and hotter, as New York's many secret California Dreamers all came out of the closet here. The space, which used to belong to the dowdy Italian Pavilion, has been California-ized, all blond woods and modern art (Hockneys, Grahams), widely spaced big tables filled with big Cobb salads, views of the garden in back and the street in front through capacious bay windows.

On a sunny day you could almost be in Santa Monica, except for all the dark suits. Just about every big publisher, book agent, broadcaster, and media presence can be found here at least one lunch a week, and maybe more—not to mention the power breakfasts, which rival those at the Regency Hotel. You'll also see The Donald, The Clinton, Ralph Lauren, pleased as punch that the waiters are dressed, as they are out west, in Polo prep. And most of the time you'll see Michael, tan, bouncy, slick-haired, ever preppy, working the room, breaking fingers, bruising ribs with his trademark greeting. Even though it's much less formal here than at the Four Seasons, it's also much harder to get in at lunch, because it's so much of a media clubhouse.

If you do get a lunch table, odds are it'll be overlooking the garden, which is all very California but not very New York. The moguls here like seeing the street. The service is obliging, the famous grilled chicken and matchstick fries are the same, and Michael will surely give you a warm hello if not a trip to the hand specialist, but it's still not the same. Nor are you the same as The Donald, so try to be grateful.

But you can't, and you can't help it. New Yorkers, in particular, seem to thrive on rejection, from the early grades at St. Bernard's to the later ones at Collegiate, on to Harvard, and then Columbia Law or Med. And yet they still go on to make a billion dollars. So who is left to reject them but Michael McCarty, who gladly rises to the task and exiles the superstrivers to the garden. Big deal? To them, yes. But to a normal foodie, from a normal city, rejection may not be the same masochistic delight. If you're not in media res, as it were, you might ask, why bother? You can eat as well or better at so many close-by places without feeling so inadequate.

Still, the salads are delicious here, a fine niçoise with sushi-grade rare tuna; a tasty mix of baby lettuces with charcoaled chicken, jalapeños, sweet peppers, onions, and goat cheese, that cornerstone of California cookery. But it is the Cobb, from the Brown Derby, that is Michael's go-to greenery. Be warned: Just because it's green doesn't mean it's not fattening. The Cobb is loaded with chopped eggs, bacon, blue cheese, avocado, all of which the power lunchers pick out and shove aside. Again, you may ask, what's the point? *They're* the point. The salad is merely a green backdrop. ★ ★ ★ ★ ★ ★

Dinosaur Deli

In the midcentury heyday of the New York delicatessen, there were far more celebrities at Lindy's, Reuben's, or the Stage than there were at Le Pavilion. The latter was a society haunt; but if you were front-page famous, you preferred to stuff your face with a sandwich like Reuben's that was as famous as you were. And you did it for public consumption: the great columnists Walter Winchell and Ed Sullivan spent almost as much time at Reuben's as they did at the Stork Club, and both had sandwiches named after them. Lindy's on Broadway was the hangout of Damon Runyon, who wrote about it as "Mindy's" and immortalized it in *Guys and Dolls*. The World Series fixer and legendary gangster Arnold Rothstein had his last supper at Lindy's before being shot to death. Babe Ruth loved Lindy's; so did J. Edgar Hoover. It was most famous for its cheesecake, which became the definitive New York dessert.

Reuben's, which was across from the Plaza and closed in 1966, had a paneled ambience as refined as the Racquet Club. Its namesake sandwich was a corned beef, Swiss cheese, coleslaw, and Russian dressing combo on toasted and buttered rye, as unkosher as you could get. You certainly didn't have to be Jewish to love Reuben's. Frank Sinatra (cream cheese, Bar-le-Duc, tongue, sweet pickle on whole wheat), Dean Martin, Judy Garland, and Barbara Stanwyck all had concoctions in their names.

The Stage, on Seventh Avenue, was another matter, a raffish, fluorescent neighborhood deli mobbed with all the luminaries of Broadway. The owner, Max Asnas, known as "the corned beef Confucius," was more recognizable in New York than Henri Soulé. The Stage not only named all its sandwiches after stars, it also pioneered the practice of festooning its walls and windows with autographed head shots, a practice that spread from delis to laundries and throughout this starstruck city. Again, you didn't have to be Jewish: Marilyn Monroe as well as Lunt and Fontanne loved the Stage, as did Joltin' Joe and Wilt the Stilt and other sports legends, perhaps the only people who had metabolisms high enough to finish the sandwiches.

A block away on Seventh was (and is) the Stage's chief rival, the Carnegie, which offered even huger sandwiches. Instead of being named after stars, the Carnegie's sandwiches were christened in clever *jeux de mots* after Broadway or movie hits: Hamalot; Nosh, Nosh, Nanette; Bacon Whoopee; Nova on Sunday. The Carnegie was even the star of the film *Broadway Danny Rose,* which got Woody Allen the exclusive honor of having his monicker on Carnegie's biggest monster sandwich—corned beef *and* pastrami, which really should have been named after Linda Lovelace or her opus *Deep Throat.*

But just as *Broadway Danny Rose* was about the vanishing Damon Runyon world of showbiz, the deli became a vanishing world itself. The great cholesterol scare of the 1980s turned New York's *fressers* into Italophiles and Mediterranean dieters. Not only did Lindy's and Reuben's close, but Max Asnas passed on as well. Leo Steiner, the impresario behind the Carnegie, died young in the 1980s. Without a Broadway-size personality, the delis were forced to survive on legend alone, and the Pritikin-led assault on the food turned a habit into a guilt trip. As people moved out of the boroughs, the great delis of the Bronx, for instance, did not travel with them, and did not survive. Meanwhile, the new colonization of Brooklyn did nothing to revive the deli. The young hipsters were interested in gastropubs and pork belly, not delis and pastrami.

The last great deli in Manhattan, the strictly kosher (as the uptowners were not) Second Avenue Deli, survived the street murder of its owner-impresario Abe Lebewohl, but not the gentrification of the Lower East Side. Metastasizing rents forced Lebewohl's brother Jack to close the place in 2005. All that remains is Katz's on Houston Street, famous for its motto "Send a Salami to Your Boy in the Army" if not its star-studded clientele. Actually, since the Lower East Side became "in," more celebs come to Katz's now than ever before. Nothing is better than a fatty corned beef sandwich to soak up the excesses of a trendy binge. The Stage and Carnegie still have their stars, if only for their location, if not their food, which has sadly declined. Also, eating a "Fran Drescher" or a "Richard Simmons" or even a "Jay Leno" or a "Mayor Bloomberger" somehow isn't the same as an "Ethel Merman" or a "Milton Berle." Still, the most telling death knell for the deli was the fact that Seinfeld and company, those urban icons of their modern time, did not hang out at one. Broadway Danny, R.I.P. ★ ★ ★

Balthazar
Virtual Paris

SOHO

The power lunch is all well and good, but what about the City That Never

Sleeps? What about Downtown, where all the action is now? What about the

stars and other cool people who *don't* wear suits? If these are your questions, your answer is Balthazar, which is the most authentic-*seeming* French brasserie anywhere outside France, maybe even inside France. Balthazar looks so Parisian that you automatically assume that looks can kill, and that the food has to be inversely proportional to the decor, that this has got to be a Gallic theme park where you have a Pastis and bolt. But you're wrong. Inspired by a triumvirate of smoky Parisian brasseries—Balzar, Bofinger, and Lipp—Balthazar has far better food than any of them, plus more movie stars, French ones, too. It's one of the best huge restaurants on earth, and one of the most beautiful. The only problem is the hypoglycemia that will knock you out as you wait, and wait, for the table you've booked weeks in advance. You can always buy a loaf of its bread, among the best in New York, to hold you and sop up the booze, which you need to deaden the noise. In any event, Balthazar is well worth the migraine you'll get waiting for it.

Located in what was once a leather warehouse in what was once a foreboding industrial wasteland, Balthazar and its neighborhood of SoHo are now as Establishment as the Four Seasons, or the Knickerbocker Club, for that matter. SoHo is like a cast-iron stage set, a playground of the rich. The power is there, the funk is gone. And Balthazar is the best stage set in the area. Step off the corner of Spring and Crosby right into fin de siècle (nineteenth-century) Paris, though the reality is quintessential fin de siècle (twentieth-century) New York. Despite the smoky mirrors, the high, high ceilings, the red leather banquettes, the long, long zinc bar, the distressed, smoke-eroded walls, and the enticing bakery and kitchen aromas that transport you instantly to France, the chic, hip (and hop) crowd is pure high-energy only-in-Manhattan, partying like it's 1999. The only difference today is the no-smoking law. If ever there were a restaurant for smokers, Balthazar is it. But, as they say in Paris, *tant pis.*

If you come to Balthazar to see stars, look in the left-front quadrant banquettes as you enter the fray. Anyone and everyone can be there, but you're most likely to see Manhattan-chauvinist thesp types like Uma Thurman, Chloë Sevigny, the *Sex and the City* girls (where else); Hollywood visitors staying at the nearby Mercer Hotel (Keanu Reeves, Russell Crowe, brandishing a cell phone); New York rock-and-rollers like Billy Joel and Mariah Carey; and lots of youngish hip art dealers and Wall Street wheeler-dealers. But, hey, you ask, why aren't *they* waiting? Because there's a special "fast track" private number possessed by the elite public relations firms, where, with any reasonable level of plugged-in-ness, you, too, can leapfrog the "bridge and tunnel people," as the late Steve Rubell of Studio 54 so ungraciously labeled the people from the Outer Boroughs whose frustrations at the velvet rope created Studio's legend. Private number, eh? But didn't owner Keith McNally say, very publicly and over and over, that he couldn't care less about stars, that Balthazar was a brasserie for the people, and not just *the* people? Sure, Keith.

You do, however, have to hand one thing to McNally, who is known for his stellar scenes, and stellar clientele, but not necessarily for his stellar fare: this time he went flat out for the food, hiring two of four-star Daniel Boulud's most talented sous chefs to make brasserie food at the highest level, without becoming the pretentious travesty that can be haute. So forget the stars. They're only five or ten of the two hundred seats that turn over at least three times any night. And forget the girls, even though Balthazar always has a few Kate

Mosses lounging around, getting thinner. If you want models, you can walk a few blocks over to West Broadway to Cipriani Downtown, where Giuseppe Cipriani (son of Arrigo, and lord of the Manhattan Harry's Bar empire) serves his family's Bellinis, carpaccio, and risotto pimavera to the elite of Elite (the agency) as the world's most famous dirty old men (Harvey Weinstein, Mick Jagger, Jack Nicholson, photographer Peter Beard) and some famous younger ones (P. Diddy, L. DiCaprio) watch the show. Or *are* the show.

But Cipriani Downtown isn't virtual Venice; it's absolute New York. And, notwithstanding its Harry's pedigree, food isn't the thing there, beauty is. Balthazar, on the other hand, is a beautiful food experience. Its New York hordes are here to be in Paris and eat in Paris, and that the kitchen can serve so many so well is remarkable. And the service, by nonactors in white aprons and black ties, may look brasserie-ish, but it's very kind and smart and not surly Parisian at all.

The hardest thing is choosing. Most people start with a platter of *fruits de mer*, which, to be fair, are the one weak link at Balthazar, for the raw seafood in New York can rarely match the best that Paris can ship in from nearby Brittany. So save the sixty to a hundred dollars, and have the best onion soup in town, which is just as good as the old stuff in Les Halles, plus the totally authentic *brandade de morue* and the *rillettes*, which you spread on Balthazar's addictive bread.

Then everyone has the steak *frites*, not for the steak, which can be stringy and chewy (as most Paris brasserie steaks are), but for the *frites*, Balthazar's pride and joy, the best in New York—and in Paris, where a fresh-cut fry is getting as hard to find as a classic Deux Cheveaux. Cohead chef Riad Nasr once told an interviewer that his "secret ingredient" was peanut oil. He uses Idaho potatoes, cuts them in five-inch-long slices, a quarter inch thick (the typical restaurant matchsticks get too cold too fast and all you taste is grease), soaks them overnight, then dries and double-fries them. It's a level of care that few places even try, and never a huge place like this. The result is an addiction—crisp, hot, mealy, sea-salty—that keeps people coming back. But don't waste them on a steak, when the roast chicken is far better. Because of Balthazar's volume, the chickens turn over constantly. They don't dry out from neglect and are crisp skinned and succulent. The duck confit is just right, too, and a good vehicle for the fries, as are the mussels and rare burgers.

Come to think of it, you could probably have the fries with a tart green salad as a meal in itself, then finish off with a cinnamon bun from the top-notch French bakery here, and be blissful. And no one would scold you for not ordering enough, or not eating a balanced diet. That's what brasseries are all about—cravings and impulses at all hours. If you like eggs and croissants, Balthazar does a great breakfast, which may be the best time of all to come here, because all the power breakfasters are in Midtown, and the cool people are still sleeping off Bungalow 8.

The one star you are unlikely to see at Balthazar is the lodestar of the downtown restaurant scene, proprietor Keith McNally, who also owns the red-hot Paris simulacrum Pastis, and the red-hot Old New York simulacrum Schiller's Liquor Bar, and new ventures that are always in the works. Keith began his conquest of Downtown in 1980 with Odeon, created with his brother Brian, who went on to establish Indochine; 44, at the Royalton; Canal Bar; and Café Lebowitz. This brother act has only one parallel in all hip restaurantdom, the Costes in Paris. But the brothers Costes work hand in hand, while the brothers McNally can go for years without speaking to each other. Whatever, they've both got the Midas, or rather Nobu, touch, in that they rarely lose, an unlikely instinct for two lower-class sons of a stevedore-turned-cabbie from London's downscale Bethnal Green.

Keith McNally likes to brag that he never ate at a proper restaurant before he was seventeen, even though he started working in the hospitality trade as a bellboy at the London Hilton on Park Lane when he was sixteen. Keith was a pretty-boy teen, though; he was discovered at the Hilton and had a desultory acting career in a couple West End plays, one with John Gielgud, and in a never-seen film with Michael Redgrave. Still, Keith was bitten by the movie bug, and he came to New York in 1975 at age twenty-four. Arriving as an illegal alien, he wanted a career in "arty" films (otherwise he would have gone to Hollywood). Instead he learned the art of dessert, ending up a busboy at the Serendipity ice cream parlor a block from Bloomingdale's. He soon moved up to Downtown at One Fifth Avenue, which was designed to approximate a deco ocean liner. He started as an oyster shucker, then became a waiter, and finally manager. He also fell in love with a One Fifth waitress, Lynn Wagenknecht, whom he would marry.

By 1979, Keith was emboldened to go out on his own and found a 1938 cafeteria in the then wasteland now known as Tribeca that needed very little work to become Odeon, the restaurant that "made" the neighborhood. Stars have always been a key element in McNally's success. At Odeon the pivotal stars were the producer Lorne Michaels and the cast of the new and seemingly unlikely-to-succeed show *Saturday Night Live*, who had taken a shine to McNally at One Fifth and followed him to Odeon. John Belushi would come into the kitchen to make his own cheeseburgers, a little more sedately than in his famous Greek-diner skit on the show. Odeon was as big a hit, in its own way, as *SNL*.

The married McNallys (Brian went off on his own) followed Odeon with Café Luxembourg near Lincoln Center, and then Nell's, whose namesake Australian hostess had costarred in *The Rocky Horror Picture Show*. Proof that the McNallys were not just about scene was Nell's serious chef, Rose Gray, who went on to cofound the River Cafe in London. Keith started Lucky Strike in 1989 just as SoHo was really taking off, then he took off himself, to his great love, Paris, and to his other great love, film. With his newfound wealth, he had made an art movie in New York called *End of the Night*, which no one saw. His two-year pursuit of his dream in the land of *Cahiers du Cinema* cost him his marriage and his three restaurants, which he gave to Lynn. But it seeded the idea for Balthazar and Pastis, Paris on the Hudson. McNally, the angry young man, has never once looked back in anger. ★ ★ ★ ★ ★ ★ ★ ★

London

The Savoy Grill
Savoy Truffle

English aristocrats used to be as suspicious of fancy chefs as they were of dentists. A preoccupation with food, fine food, was perceived as somehow "foreign," effeminate, unseemly, un-English. Real men didn't eat quiche, or foie gras, or even a Napoleon, except at Waterloo. Why waste time at table when you could be off colonizing India, or at least foxhunting?

Thus it was that in the late 1960s, the chef at Mirabelle on Curzon Street in Mayfair, London's most exclusive restaurant, was Polish, and never came out of the kitchen. Craig Claiborne of *The New York Times* admired the place, especially for its deep list of important wines and for its British classics like smoked Scottish salmon and grouse, Colchester oysters, Dover sole. The menu listings were inexplicably in French, which may have explained why Mirabelle's clientele was heavily foreign: Aristotle Onassis, J. Paul Getty, the Aga Khan, the Maharanee of Baroda, Darryl F. Zanuck of Twentieth Century–Fox. The real English aristos preferred Claiborne's other London favorite, the roast beef palace Simpson's in the Strand, which was the only British restaurant to win one of the nine *Michelin* stars the guide handed out in London in its first offshore edition in 1972. Not surprisingly, 7 of these restaurants were French. By comparison, Paris had 103 starred restaurants in the French *Michelin* of that same year. There wasn't much competition, but there wasn't much interest, either. Albion clearly wasn't into food.

Today London has over three dozen *Michelin* stars. It's still not Paris, but it's a lot closer. Moreover, its non-French foreign restaurants, which *Michelin* is generally clueless about, are up there with New York's. The rotten boroughs of bangers and mash and Scotch eggs have become a world of epicurean delights. The transformation is all about money, owing largely to the "Big Bang" of 1986, in which the xenophobic restrictions of the London Stock Exchange were dramatically relaxed. The result was the Eurotrashing of the City, London's financial center, as merchant bankers and other moneymen from all over the Continent (and other continents, too) poured in to make their fortunes. With fast money came a desire to spend it, and restaurants catering to these Eurodollar divas sprung up overnight. The opening of the Chunnel in 1994 further accelerated London's rising food sophistication. No longer was England an island of Wimpy bars unto itself.

As the old Virginia Slims ads used to say, "You've come a long way, baby." The evolution of London from gastronomic wasteland into foodie paradise in the last two decades has been way beyond remarkable. No other city could possibly go so quickly from being so indifferent to food to being so obsessed. "London Dining: It's Not as Bad as People Say," trumpeted the headline of a 1972 *New York Times* piece by food critic Raymond Sokolov that singled out the Connaught Grill as the best of a sorry lot, describing its cuisine as "high mundane." Today no one would dare an act of such lèse-majesté. Critics grovel and gush over Gordon Ramsay, London's three-star Escoffier, lest he toss them out of his eponymous temple, as he did the feared London *Times* food writer A.A. Gill. Ramsay's wunderkind predecessor, the three-star Marco Pierre White, himself set the tone by heaving guidebook titan Tim Zagat out of Mirabelle after White bought the place. Don't tread on me.

But the celebrities of London, the ones who went to Mirabelle in the 1960s, are still going to Mirabelle today. They still go to the Ivy and Le Caprice, just as they have been for decades. They go to the storied dining rooms of the storied hotels, the Connaught, Claridge's, the Savoy, just as they ever did. That the latter three are controlled by Ramsay, and Mirabelle by White, has something to do with it, but it's more likely the other way around. Tradition dies hard, even in a London that's on the cutting edge of trend.

It's also a class thing, like everything else of this Sceptered Isle. Ramsay and White, poor country boys in awe of the Establishment, just had to have a piece of the rock, the same way upwardly mobile diners had to sit in the same room with their betters to feel that they had truly arrived.

When you say "everybody eats there" in London, that "everybody" is somewhat different from the "everybody" in Los Angeles or even New York. A waiter at the Savoy Grill in the 1960s prepared a seating chart of "everybody's" favorite tables. Here are some of the categories and the names: statespeople Winston Churchill, Eleanor Roosevelt, Prince Rainier and Princess Grace, ex-King Umberto II of Italy, the Prince of Siam, Edward Heath; tycoons J. Paul Getty, Nubar Gulbenkian, the Seifs, who owned Marks & Spencer; Greeks Aristotle Onassis, Stavros Niarchos, Livanos, Goulandris; publishers Lord Beaverbrook, Lord Shawcross, George Weidenfeld, Victor Gollancz; auto racers Graham Hill, Stirling Moss, Donald Campbell; boxer Primo Carnera; golfers Gary Player, Arnold Palmer; high culturists Margot Fonteyn, Maria Callas, Artur Rubinstein, Georg Solti; English stage legends Noël Coward, Laurence Olivier, Vivien Leigh, Michael Redgrave, John Mills, Charles Laughton; directors Alfred Hitchcock, Carol Reed, Vittorio De Sica; stars Errol Flynn, Orson Welles, Douglas Fairbanks Jr., Charlie Chaplin, John Wayne, Danny Kaye, Judy Garland, Ava Gardner, Gina Lollobrigida, Doris Day (que sera, sera). Elizabeth Taylor and Richard Burton had the prime table at the entrance. Bing Crosby and the Marx Brothers sat up in the balcony, out of the fray. There was a special table for maharajas, and another one for "Prince" Mike Romanoff, who often came over to get ideas of "class" for his Beverly Hills restaurant. Here at the Savoy Grill was the clientele to end all clienteles. No wonder Gordon Ramsay had to have it.

Soon after this chart was prepared, along came the Beatles. And the Stones. And Mary Quant. And Biba. And the King's Road. And the Chelsea Drugstore. And the entire youthquake whose epicenter was Swinging London, a London that the great people at the Savoy Grill were so insulated from that it might as well have been Uganda. The Beatles even wrote their own homage to the luxuries of the Grill, "The Savoy Truffle," but they had no intentions of storming the maître d'. (Mick Jagger, who had social aspirations, probably felt otherwise.)

Today Gordon Ramsay has the Savoy Grill totally in his big soccer hands. The first thing to think about at the Savoy Grill is not so much the food as the pedigree, for the Savoy has the greatest show-business lineage of any hotel anywhere. Its theatrical roots go back to its founder, the impresario Richard D'Oyly Carte, the producer of Gilbert and Sullivan. To showcase their operettas, Carte built the Savoy Theatre in 1881, the first of its kind to have electric lights. In 1889, he opened the Savoy Hotel, so out-of-town theatergoers would have a place to sleep after seeing the Savoyards. That all the rooms had electricity, and that most of them had private bathrooms, made the Savoy, with its unique electric elevators, the most futuristic hotel of its day.

But the Savoy's reputation as the pinnacle of innkeeping was sealed when Carte hired Caesar Ritz to come over from Paris to manage the Savoy. Ritz brought his chef, Escoffier, to run the kitchen, and suddenly the two greatest names in hospitality were holding court in the Strand. And what a court it was. Escoffier created dishes for Sarah Bernhardt, Lillie Langtry, Nellie Melba (peaches and toast), and the Prince of Wales, later King Edward VII. It was a revolutionary fusion of royalty and celebrity. The Savoy Grill opened in 1904, in the expansion that would give the hotel its inimitable nouveau-deco look. The Grill was originally called the Café Parisien, an Escoffier attempt to lure in society ladies, which was quickly dropped. The Grill has been a man's world ever since. The ultimate party, the equivalent of Truman Capote's Black and White Ball at the Plaza, was the "Gondola Dinner," hosted in the summer of 1905 by Wall Street tycoon George Kessler, for which the then-new legendary entrance court of the hotel, with its golden statue of Count Peter of Savoy, was transformed into Venice. Enrico Caruso entertained. He was paid £450, a fortune at the time. That court, the only street in the British Isles where cars drive on the right, rather than the left, was immortalized in *The Long Good Friday* as the spot where Bob Hoskins, playing a gangster-tycoon, is hijacked in his Jaguar by the IRA.

Given the preponderance of flashy dressers on a recent visit, the "new" Savoy seems to be heavier on the gangsters than the tycoons these days, though one shouldn't judge Versace wearers so harshly. The Savoy is now part of a chain, the Fairmont Group (as in the grande dame Fairmont of San Francisco's Nob Hill), owned by the Saudi billionaire Sheikh al Walid Bin Talal, who is expanding Fairmont luxury resorts all over the Persian Gulf. As part of the transformation, Gordon Ramsay took over the Grill. Much of the venerable clientele, especially the old, pre–Rupert Murdoch Fleet Street press lords who had made it their local, felt a major sacrilege had occurred, especially after Ramsay hired Los Angeles decorator Barbara Barry to spiff up the Grill and accomplish what Escoffier could not—make it more alluring to the ladies who lunch. The Beverly Hills influence is apparent; the fusty deco masterpiece, which used to feel like a dining room on the *Titanic*, now feels like it's going down with the ship. The Hollywood makeover has a strong whiff of the Polo Lounge crossed with Houston's.

Running the kitchen is Ramsay's chief protégé, another French-trained wunderkind named Marcus Wareing, who won his own *Michelin* star at Pétrus in Saint James's. Anyone looking for the Grill's famous "school food" (as in Eton and Harrow), roasts and plain fish and steak and kidney pie and such, is likely to be disappointed. The new Grill kept some of its old dishes, like the Welsh rarebit and the omelette Arnold Bennett, with smoked finnan haddie, named after the essayist and chief propagandist for Britain during World War I.

Now you can start with a lobster and quail egg gratin in a mushroom "puff," a nomenclature that surely has the old boys in paroxysms of bad puns. Wareing's attempt at school food is something called a mushroom "mushy" with a pea coulis and carrots. It will delight vegans and the ladies who lunch, but probably not the beefeaters of yore. Yes, there is a filet mignon, albeit in a foie gras and artichoke sauce, and there is the classic turbot, fancied up in a sage *jus*. Wareing won't leave well enough alone. The riffs on the originally plain classics are what separate the chef from the cook. The problem is, the schoolboys don't want chefs. They want cooks, surly Eton and Harrow Cockney cooks, who knew how to inflict the culinary pain so essential to building a proper young Englishman's character. Sort of like caning, it's a Brit thing. For all its complications and embellishments, Wareing's food is tasty and fine, but it's unlikely you'll remember a single dish (too many ingredients are tough on the memory) the way you would the old Grill's giant, golden brown grilled Dover sole, truly London's king of the sea.

If you insist on going "schoolish" with smoked Scotch salmon or grilled Channel plaice, you might be better off just next door at Simpson's in the Strand, owned by the Savoy but not Ramsayfied, where true Brit is the order of the night. The Grill wants to be challenged. It wants its patrons to eat its foie gras parfait, its asparagus velouté. Food for girls or girlie-men? A lot of tough-looking rich guys are wolfing it down, and their gorgeous molls are lapping it up. What Winston Churchill might think of his favorite London haunt is anyone's guess. ★ ★ ★ ★ ★ ★ ★ ★ ★ ★ ★ ★ ★ ★ ★

La Famiglia
All in the Royal Family

FULHAM

The 1960s swingers of London, young and old, had no interest in grouse, whether it was labeled "Scottish" or "D'Ecosse." The pretenses of neither the English stately home nor the French temple of gastronomy spoke to them. What did was pasta, and all things Italian, which became the lingua franca, or rather Latina, of an entirely different group of "everybodies."

The war of these two worlds may best be summed up in an anecdote told by Alvaro Maccioni, proprietor of La Famiglia at the World's End end of the King's Road, which has the most glittering show-business clientele of any restaurant in London. One night in 1967 at Alvaro's original trattoria, called Alvaro's, on the King's Road, Keith Richards complained to Alvaro about the weird old man who wouldn't stop staring at him. That weird old man, Alvaro told the rough Stone, was King Umberto II, the deposed ruler of Italy, who had slipped away from his table at the Savoy Grill to see what the rest of the world was so excited about. "See how important you are? You have to be flattered," Alvaro said. Alvaro's "everybody" kept getting bigger and bigger. His proudest moment was seeing General Moshe Dayan and Jordan's King Hussein, who had recently fought each other in the Six Day War, across the dance floor from each other at Alvaro's disco Arethusa. The King's Road was more than living up to its name.

Today the "royalty" at La Famiglia tends to the likes of Tom Cruise and Tony Bennett, although the "trat" was Lady Diana's second favorite restaurant after her beloved San Lorenzo. Like his Tuscan cousin, Sirio Maccioni of New York's Le Cirque, Alvaro Maccioni has spent a lifetime catering to the rich and famous. A graduate of Lausanne's famed École Hôtelière (alma mater of Craig Claiborne), and trained in the best Swiss hotels, Alvaro came to London in the 1950s to the best job any aspiring restaurateur could have, as a waiter at Mirabelle. He was convinced that the Polish chef was a spy. Alvaro waited on royalty but was most impressed by the entertainment celebrities— Olivier, Alec Guinness, the impresario Sir Lew Grade. In 1959, also impressed by the stars, two of Alvaro's fellow Mirabelle waiters, Mario Cassandro and Franco Lagatolla, mortgaged their homes to start up London's first authentic trattoria, La Terrazza, on Romilly Street in the heart of Soho.

There were a lot of quasi-Italian restaurants in the raffish, theater-land-adjacent neighborhood, places like Quo Vadis and Bella Napoli, but they were Italian in name only. "They served French hotel food," Alvaro remembers, without nostalgia. "They put *cream* in the *carbonara*, cream in the *marinara*, cream in everything. Sacrilege! And there were no ingredients, no French beans, only lima beans." With no real competition, La Terrazza took off. A year later, in 1960, Mario and Franco were able to persuade Alvaro to leave the security and prestige of Mirabelle for their brave new *mondo*. His first task was to lure customers down to La Terrazza's cellar, which was decorated like the Grotta Azzurra in Capri. It was beyond Siberia, no one wanted to descend to that dark pit. First, Alvaro changed the decor to all-white minimalist. Then, running the front desk, he told each reservation requester the big lie that downstairs was fully booked. Soon "everybody" wanted to sit downstairs, to which he gave a name, the Positano Room. "They want exclusivity," he says with a shrug and a smile.

His next challenge was the food. It started when Frank Sinatra was planning to pay his first visit. Word was out that the Chairman wanted baby octopus salad. Baby octopus salad? In London? No way! But Alvaro found a way. He went out to London's East End and found a fishmonger at Billingsgate Market who could supply the Big O for Mister S. "Yeah, baby." A new dish, Sinatra Salad, was born, and everybody ordered it. The same monger, who specialized in cockles and mussels, which was the fare London's poor people ate, also became a source for *vongole veraci*, and La Terrazza became known for its spaghetti with clam sauce, heretofore unknown in this land of kidney pie.

The movie world poured in, Olivier and Guinness from Mirabelle, and new faces like Julie Christie after winning the Oscar for *Darling*, and her costar Laurence Harvey. By 1963, the Italians were doing so well that they decided to challenge Mirabelle itself by starting the lavish *alta cucina* Tiberio just across Curzon Street in Mayfair. The clientele included deluxe call girls Christine Keeler and Mandy Rice-Davies, who rocked English politics in the Profumo scandal the same way Mario and Franco rocked English dining. Soon there were eight restaurants and a listing on the London Stock Exchange.

"The 1960s didn't really begin until 1965," Alvaro observes, and by then he was ready to strike out on his own. Raising money from a La Terrazza client who was in the aerosol spray business, Alvaro started Alvaro's right next to Mary Quant's emporium on the King's Road. He had wanted to call it Michelangelo, but that other Michelangelo, the director of the ultimate Swinging London film *Blow-Up*, talked Alvaro into going eponymous. There was no dress code, revolutionary in a formal men-in-bowlers city where even

La Terrazza required a coat and tie. And, more revolutionary, an unlisted phone number. The matchbooks gave no address, either, just a picture of Alvaro with his fingers to his lips and the inscription, "If you know where I am, don't say where I am." But the Beatles and the Stones knew, and in Swinging London, that was all there was to know.

The hits kept on coming. First there was the equally unlisted disco Arethusa, then a chain of London's first authentic thin-crust pizza restaurants, for which Alvaro made headlines by delivering a pie to Sinatra while the Chairman was reveling at Annabel's, the ultrasnooty private club in Berkeley Square. During the Charles Manson reign of terror in Los Angeles, the first place the police came looking for Roman Polanski was at Alvaro's. The royals started coming. Princess Margaret danced at Arethusa with Sammy Davis Jr.

But then in 1975 the world changed, following the first oil embargo. The newly rich Arabs, from all over the gulf, descended on London, buying up Mayfair and Belgravia, and making the city their own secular Mecca. London almost overnight went from being one of the world's cheapest cities to one of its dearest. A dinner at Mirabelle that had cost $25 was now well over $100. Part of the allure of London was the Beatles, but the Beatles were gone; another part of the allure was the bargain, and now that was gone. The party of Swinging London ground to a sad halt.

In 1978, Mario and Franco sold their holdings to a dog food company. Alvaro Maccioni, too, sold his holdings at the top of the market. But after a few years of being and nothingness, he got back into the game by opening the white-walled, plant-filled, star-photo festooned La Famiglia in the late 1970s. All his old customers came back, as did most of London, and the result is a long-running hit. The classic Italian fare is as simple and good as ever (the *penne arrabbiata* is London's gold standard, and the Florentine steaks have that authentic banks-of-the-Arno sizzle), so much so that local swells flock to Alvaro's summer cooking school outside of Florence. And you can still get a Sinatra Salad, off the menu, of course, but that's what exclusivity's all about. ★ ★ ★ ★ ★ ★ ★ ★ ★ ★

Roux the Day

The antifancy English mind-set has created a profound ambivalence on the part of the British elite toward the country's two wunderkind three-star chefs, Marco Pierre White and Gordon Ramsay. On one hand, there's nothing effete or effeminate about them. White is a poor boy, a big bad boy, from Leeds, as angry a young man as anyone John Osborne ever conjured up. Ramsay is a bad boy from Glasgow, a former soccer player, also angry as hell, to wit his hit TV series *Hell's Kitchen*. They both have empires and are self-made macho millionaires. Yet their empires are built on elegant French technique, and therein lies the rub for the old-school English, as well as most stars, who simply can't deal with all the French pomp and pretense and want a steak or a sole or, if they're feeling global, maybe a bowl of pasta. They want to retreat to the familiar, to the Savoy Grill, to the Connaught Grill, to Claridge's, whose restaurant might as well have been called a grill, or to that other Mayfair fair lady, Mirabelle, tried and true blue. But White and Ramsay have the last laugh, as they cry, "Gotcha!" If the aristos and celebs wouldn't come to the chefs' temples, the chefs would take over *their* temples. And so they did.

What the two working-class heroes have in common is that both learned their craft from the Roux brothers, Albert *et* Michel, whose Le Gavroche was the first British restaurant to win three *Michelin* stars, in 1982. Formal, fussy, too slow and too grand and too rich and creamy for lean and hungry T-shirted Hollywood types, Le Gavroche (Albert Roux) has only two stars today and feels a bit old-fashioned. The prices are not, easily $500 for two, with appropriate wines. Le Gavroche's sister restaurant, the Waterside Inn (Michel Roux) in Bray, near the Fat Duck, still gets three stars. Talk about pilgrimage destinations. Les Roux still reign as the fount of British foodiedom. The brothers, now in their sixties, come from Charolles, in the bread basket of central France, growing up around the glories of the Gallic larder. They initially came to England to work as private chefs to the superrich, including both Astors and Rothschilds, before opening their first place in Chelsea. It led to star after star and an empire that stretched as far as a Waterside Inn in Santa Barbara (now closed) and an alumni roster that reads like a *Burke's Peerage* of British chefs.

The Roux empire was a major inspiration to both White and Ramsay, who also trained under White, six years his senior. Both had their three stars when they were thirty-three. The idea became not only to get six stars, just as the Roux had done in their prime, but to get even more stars, and get them faster. White, who was so arrogant about his skills that he cooked French haute cuisine without ever having visited France (the big, tough guy was also terrified of flying), first came up with the idea of redoing the classics in the mid 1990s.

Before buying Mirabelle, backed by media conglomerate Granada, White bought the Café Royal, London's first "celebrity" restaurant, where Oscar Wilde got into lots of trouble. The Royal was founded in 1865 by a Parisian wine merchant, and London's bohemians embraced it as a continental oasis in the foggy wet desert of Victorian repression. George Bernard Shaw dined here with Wilde, trying in vain to persuade him not to sue the Marquess of Queensberry for libeling him as a homosexual. (Truth proved to be a defense.) Before White took it on, the Royal had become a touristy roast beef parlor, a bad imitation of Simpson's in the Strand.

"I want all the great dining rooms in London," White declared with the subtlety of Napoleon. Yet White was as good as his boast. There was Quo Vadis in Soho (with art by Damien Hirst), the Criterion in Piccadilly, the Belvedere in Holland Park, Drones in Belgravia, Mirabelle . . . great landmarks, fourteen in all, and counting up. If there were a National Trust of restaurants, it seemed as if White would own them all. White liked empire building so much that he stopped cooking altogether at the turn of the new century and handed back his *Michelin* stars. There was nothing more to prove in the kitchen. It was on to the boardroom.

The only way the ultracompetitive Ramsay (he is a footballer, after all) could compete with his mentor's capitalistic orgy of acquisition was to become a televison star, both in England and America, and to snare the restaurants of London's, and probably the world's, most legendary hotels. Otherwise, all the two bad boys could do was try to out-outrageous the other, throwing customers out, abusing the help, turning the kitchens into sadistic boot camps. "I never treated anybody as bad as a kid named Marco Pierre was treated in Leeds," White once said, trying to defend himself. But he had a special poor boy's detestation for the spoiled City bankers who were making him a rich boy. Once he threw out an entire bachelor party of fifty-four. "It was ten months before I threw out my first customer. But I was like a serial killer. Once I got a taste for it, I couldn't stop," White says. On another occasion, a City toff demanded French fries, which weren't on the menu. So White went back in the kitchen, cut the spuds, boiled them, blanched them, fried them in beef suet, served those perfect *pommes frites* on a silver platter, and then presented the fellow a bill for twenty-five pounds for the dish. The banker blanched and raged, but White stood firm. That's what the banker got for not asking the price. "An hour of my time. Twenty-five pounds." White revels in the anecdote about the most expensive chips ever made.

Although White is no longer interested in stars, Mirabelle, alone of all his famed locales, still gets one, as does each of Ramsay's three hotel dining rooms, each staffed with one of his disciples. White's food at Mirabelle isn't all that different from Ramsay's at the hotels. One can split hares, or *lièvres,* in *haut*-speak, that White's food is pure French and Ramsay's is modern British cooking using French techniques. But in the end, it's all pretty much fabulous French food similar to what you'd get at similarly *haut* places across the Chunnel.

At the Connaught, Ramsay has renamed the restaurant Menu, but he hasn't tampered too much with its elegant clubby wood paneling. Yes, there is some new checkered carpeting and some unobtrusive modern art, and vaguely feminine pistachio-colored curtains, maybe to make the ladies feel more at home. But in contrast to the Savoy Grill, there's no massive Polo Lounge-fication going on. The Connaught still feels like a country house, the most expensive country house you'll ever visit.

In his effort to court the female vote, Ramsay has installed Britain's most acclaimed young woman chef, Angela Hartnett, who, being half Italian, has created a menu at Menu in her own image. Notwithstanding the pastas, risottos, and lots of rosemary and thyme, Menu still feels far closer to Le Gavroche than to La Famiglia. It's beautifully executed fare, but it's extremely mannered and polite, as is the crowd, heavy on country club Yanks on Bond Street shopping sprees.

Then there is Claridge's, where Ramsay himself is in command of the kitchen. He divides his time between here and his tiny, fourteen-table, three-star flagship on Royal Hospital Road. The soccer chef has bragged that he can run the two miles between restaurants, shower at Claridge's, and be in his chef's whites in a matter of minutes, but it all sounds redolent of Clark Kent. Unlike the unexciting Chelsea venue (it's all on the plate, they say), the high-ceilinged Claridge's space is a deco knockout, a trip back to the Noël Coward heyday of London in the 1930s.

The designer here, Thierry Despont, knew how to leave well enough alone. There is a leather-walled "fumoir," or cigar bar, at the entrance filled with smoky fat cats. Inside are lots of fashionistas, and lots of ordinary foodies and architecture buffs, albeit none of them look like the people who actually *stay* at Claridge's—dowdy old-money types or wannabe aristos. All the froufrou on the menu would send most of them in retreat to their rooms, where they would call for room service and pray Ramsay won't splash their club sandwich with truffle oil.

Here's what you might eat: Start with one of Ramsay's acclaimed soups, like a cream of pumpkin with Parmesan and truffle shavings, or the rare something actually light, like a Charentais melon soup, spiked with basil and white crabmeat. Ramsay makes great salads aimed at the lunch ladies: a Scottish lobster salad with baby asparagus; marinated loin of tuna with pickled white radishes and frisée. But sometimes he overdoes it, as in a tiger prawn ravioli atop a bed of sautéed lettuce, lemongrass, and a caviar vinaigrette. Can't imagine Margaret Thatcher, or even Sienna Miller, eating that, can you? Main courses are very Frenchified: A *dorade* filet in a vanilla sauce. Roasted brill in a cucumber-chervil velouté. "Black-leg" (a local rara avis) chicken breast poached on a bed of heavily truffled pureed potatoes (don't call them "mashed" or Gordon might toss you). Desserts are luscious, like passion fruit "three ways"—tarte, parfait, and *glace;* a frangipane tart with mascarpone; a caramelized banana financière. You need to be a financier to pay for it; the bills always run to nearly two hundred dollars a person.

Despite Ramsay's track-star protestations, London food critics have all noted that most of the cooking is done by the talented Mark Sargeant. With his growing empire and his television demands, it would be naive to expect the captain of this team to be around all that much. But Ramsay is a true celebrity himself, so when his craggy countenance does emerge, it's a major sighting, as big a kick as, say, Liam Neeson or Bono or Sir Paul. British food's other rock star, Marco Pierre White, has pretty much gone Garbo. You're highly unlikely to see him walking the floors at Mirabelle. Which leaves you with his braised pig's trotter with morels, as haute bourgeois French a plate as the new Anglo haute cuisine can offer. Even with Madonna and Guy Ritchie at the next table, the foodie challenge may be too much. ★ ★ ★ ★ ★ ★ ★ ★ ★ ★ ★ ★ ★ ★ ★ ★ ★ ★ ★

Cipriani
Tit for Trat

So loyal are the stars to La Famiglia that today only two of London's now countless "trats," one old, one new, can give it a run for its clientele. The new rival is the new arrival, Cipriani, a branch of Harry's Bar in Venice. There is also a London Harry's Bar, a very private dining club a few blocks away in the dead center of Mayfair, close to Claridge's and the Connaught. The Venetian Ciprianis *detest* the London Harry's Bar for taking its name in vain (see page 80) and founded this outpost to show England the real thing. Mayfair is truly dead in the evening. Except, that is, for the lines of Bentleys and hordes of paparazzi camped outside Cipriani. The moment you arrive, a wave of insecurity washes over you. You recall the Stones' song "Beast of Burden." "Am I rich enough?" You'll never be rich enough for Cipriani. But Sir Mick himself may be sitting in the front room, bringing it all back home. Inadequate though you feel, you cannot resist the siren call of masochism, to crash this club that may *have* you but will never *need* you.

It's the same "A" but slightly louche Donald Trumpian mogul crowd as Cipriani Downtown in New York, lured by the spectacular Amazon (and not dot-com) goddesses draped all over the tiny tables. If they remind you of Veruschka in *Blow-Up,* you ain't wrong. (Veruschka had the classic line of the film, emblematic of London's coming of age. When the David Hemmings photographer runs into her at a Mayfair pot party and says, "I thought you were in Paris," Veruschka takes a deep hit of her joint and replies, "I *am* in Paris.") Most of the Cipriani girls are, like Veruschka, six-foot-tall Russian and Ukrainian models (Chernobyl seems to have caused a growth mutation), who have arrived in London in the wake of the billionaire Moscow oligarchs who have taken to England in the new millennium the same way the Arab-petrodollar set did in the 1970s. After all, as Samuel Johnson said, "When a man is tired of London, he is tired of Life."

Aside from the distaff floor show, the most amusing thing about Cipriani, which has the intimately low tables and flattering lighting of the Venice original, is its witty "living porthole," an animated yacht window at the entrance showing a blind loop of rolling blue sea. It's almost hypnotic, if you can take your eyes off the *ballet Russe,* with tycoons and rock stars hopping from table to table kissing one another, and flirting with the girls. The porthole is the design of David Tang, the Cipriani of Hong Kong, who has partnered with the real Ciprianis in London. He also has the red-hot—both as in the East Is Red and as in packed with "everybody"—China Tang in the Dorchester (see page 87).

The Venetian menu is irresistible, the actual food perhaps less so. There's so much scene going on that the kitchen can be distracted. No one cares. Safest bets are the Venetian Harry's Bar classics, the Bellinis, the carpaccio, the risotto primavera. As for the latter, instruct your handsome, smooth but possibly indifferent waiter firmly to tell the kitchen to keep stirring and to take their time. If the risotto comes out in less than twenty minutes, it ain't Venetian. If you have to, drop the name of big boss Arrigo Cipriani. Drop anything you can. Cipriani has one of the most alluring, eat-me menus there is, but concept and execution are two different things. ★ ★ ★ ★ ★ ★ ★ ★ ★ ★ ★ ★ ★ ★ ★ ★ ★ ★ ★

San Lorenzo
To Di For

KNIGHTSBRIDGE

The food has likewise never been the selling point at the other Italian contender to London's celebrity throne, San Lorenzo in Knightsbridge, the fave not only of Lady Di, but also of all Sloane Rangers, that special breed of well-born, well-bred stylish English girl, the epicenter of whose world of power shopping and ambitious, eye-on-the-prize dating is Chelsea's Sloane Square. These Sloanies loved the idea of rubbing shoulders with the likes of Jagger, Clapton, and Bryan Ferry, or eyeing legends like Omar Sharif and Peter O'Toole reuniting after *Lawrence of Arabia,* all the while eating simple Italian pastas and salads that would allow them to keep the Twiggyesque or Jean Shrimptonian figures that would attract Lord (never settle for Mister) Right.

While Alvaro Maccioni took the high road through Swiss schools and Mirabelle to become a celebrity sustenancer, Lorenzo Berni took a far less auspicious path. A native of Forte dei Marmi, the Tuscan beach resort that fueled the Los Angeles food revolution, Berni was a merchant seaman who jumped ship for a short visit to London, only to get stranded when his ship sank. Eventually he opened La Taverna Spaghetti Garden in pretrendy Westbourne Grove. He met his wife, Mara, an Alitalia air hostess. And in 1963, admiring the success of La Terrazza in Soho, they found a location on

Beauchamp Place behind Harrods and set up San Lorenzo. Meals cost one pound, and people brought their own wine. There was no real decor, just a garden effect with a lot of potted palms.

Things muddled along until one day Sophia Loren poked her head in. She was making *A Countess from Hong Kong* with Charlie Chaplin and Marlon Brando out at Pinewood Studios, which was also where Peter Sellers, in ardent pursuit of Sophia, was shooting *After the Fox*. She was homesick and asked if San Lorenzo could make her a lunch basket for the set. They agreed, and their Greek baker began putting *SL* on the loaves they put in the basket. She thought it was the most wonderful personal touch, narcissistically never noticing that it was the restaurant's initials as well.

Sellers was jealous of the good food Sophia was eating. But not wanting her secret source revealed and ruined, Sophia refused to tell him. (She withheld sex from the ravenous Sellers as well.) But somehow Sellers found out, and one night he showed up at simple little San Lorenzo with fiancée Britt Ekland and Princess Margaret and Lord Snowdon. The royalty-mad tabloids picked up the rendezvous, and a new restaurant star was born. Soon the rockers were coming in—Jimi Hendrix, Marianne Faithfull—and the mods like Twiggy and Lulu, and then came the rest of Hollywood, from Gloria Swanson to Lauren Bacall to Barbra Streisand to Jack Nicholson, to all the James Bonds, Connery to Brosnan. All the tennis stars came during Wimbledon. Boris Becker ate the exact same dinner of *tagliata di manzo,* sliced filet with arugula and mashed potatoes, for seven years following his first championship in 1985.

San Lorenzo's Beauchamp Place is far less glittering than it was when it opened. Then it was antique row, and every store had some special cachet. Now it's turned slightly downmarket, but San Lorenzo is as upmarket as ever. It hasn't changed its swinging 1960s fern-bar, motel-art, faux-Mykonos decor. But that's part of its throwaway charm, wherein you pay Claridge's prices for ambience evoking that of London's most picturesquely named 1960s hotel chain, the Go-Gotels.

San Lorenzo has a warren of smallish rooms on different levels. It's hard to know what is heaven and what is hell, because Siberia seems to vary daily. But all the celebs do tend to sit together in whatever the designated "A" room is. You probably won't be in it, because stars tend to be xenophobic, and Lorenzo and Mara are very protective of them. They also feed them the same exact simple Italian recipes that won Sophia's heart and stomach forty years ago: al dente pastas, al dente fish, al dente meats, no complicated sauces, no confusing frills. Familiarity here breeds loyalty, not contempt. But even though you may eat the same dishes that a star eats here, you probably won't sit like one, and you might just feel like a second-class citizen, depending on your ego. Odds are, you're not going to get kissed by Mara, which in London restaurant circles is akin to being knighted. If that makes you feel insecure, San Lorenzo isn't for you.

One other reason the stars love San Lorenzo is that all the foliage and blind corners give them something to hide behind. Also, the policy of no credit cards tends to separate the serious money from the expense-account crowd. San Lorenzo's prices were, and remain, not for the faint of heart. Outside of Annabel's, it's still the most exclusive club in town, without actually being one. Having turned down countless franchise offers, Lorenzo and Mara still hold court every day. The old stars keep coming in, and the new ones like Gwyneth, Madonna, Colin, and Orlando follow in their big footsteps. San Lorenzo is a major tradition in a land where tradition is the coin of the realm. ★ ★ ★ ★ ★ ★ ★ ★ ★ ★

Hurley Birley

A big step up in exclusivity from Nobu and the Ivy is a restaurant that no concierge, not even the redoubtable Martin of Claridge's, can get you into. That's because Harry's Bar, a few blocks from Claridge's on South Audley Street in Mayfair, is a private club. It is also that rarity of rarities, a private club with great food, Italian food of all things. Just try ordering *spaghetti alle vongole veraci* at Boodle's or White's in St. James's, the imperial men's clubs, and see the looks you'll get. Not that you'll get into Boodle's or White's, either, but those are clubs of a different stripe. Harry's Bar is part of a chain of four Mayfair social-dining clubs that are unique in all the world in that they welcome women and are as much about sex as they are about power. Only New York has tried to emulate them, with Doubles, and more recently Soho House. But the four London clubs—Harry's, Annabel's, Mark's, and George's—are the original vision of perhaps the world's greatest commercial host, Mark Birley, a man who can barely be imitated, much less duplicated.

The secret of the clubby success of the towering, six foot six, and supremely Savile Row–dapper Mark Birley, an old Etonian now seventy-five years old and ailing, is that he is probably the best connected man on earth. Mark himself was married to Lady Annabel, the daughter of the Marquess of Londonderry, who left him for tycoon Sir James Goldsmith but remained best friends. Her daughter Jemima married Pakistani cricket star Imran Khan and is at this writing the consort of Hugh Grant. Mark's sister Maxime, like Gloria Swanson, married French nobility, a de la Falaise. Her daughter, and Mark's ravishing niece, Loulou, was the right hand of Yves St. Laurent, while Loulou's daughter Lucie is married to the son of Keith Richards. Mark's son Robin's girlfriend Lucy Helmore is the ex-wife of Bryan Ferry. You need a flow chart for all the connections. It didn't hurt that Mark Birley started with a flying leap. His *branché* father, the famed artist Sir Oswald Birley, painted portraits of Queen Elizabeth, Churchill, Mountbatten, Eisenhower, and Gandhi, and entertained them all, with his stunning bohemian Irish wife Lady Rhoda, at their Sussex estate Charleston Manor.

Mark Birley began his post-Eton career inauspiciously as a face-in-the-crowd adman at J. Walter Thompson. His first advertisement for himself was opening the first Hermès shop in London in the Burlington Arcade in the late 1950s. But retail wasn't his forte, and in 1963 he conceived of Annabel's, a luxury, members-only private restaurant-disco that fused Boodle's with the Savoy Grill: aristos, thesps, foreign Croesuses, and the Aga Khan with gorgeous women were the key to it all.

Annabel's, located in the basement of a chic Berkeley Square private casino, took right off, and even the Beatles donned neckties to get in. Ironically, Mark Birley was hoist on his own petard when, one night at the club, its namesake Lady Annabel was swept off her feet and into divorce and remarriage by member tycoon Jimmy Goldsmith. Still, Birley took it with aplomb, as did Annabel, when she found that Goldsmith had another wife and family across the Channel in France.

Annabel's is like a British Arabian Nights, none of which created a bigger stir than when Lady Di and Fergie crashed Prince Andrew's bachelor bash disguised as raiding policewomen. For all its high jinks, Annabel's looks country-house sedate: low lights, velvet sofas, endless paintings of Jack Russells, whippets, corgis. It's the formula Birley followed for Mark's and George's, the latter named for a bartender and designed as a more casual "Junior Annabel's" for the (designer) jeans-wearing progeny of the blue-blooded 1960s swingers. The food tends to be Ivy-ish, if not nursery-ish. But the drinks are strong.

Harry's Bar is completely different. Birley got the name, and the financing for it, from James Sherwood, the American founder of Orient Express. Sherwood had bought the Hotel Cipriani in Venice, and the rights to the Harry's name, from Arrigo Cipriani, who still held on to the original Harry's Bar, and used that as the basis for his own empire (called Cipriani). Arrigo's London Cipriani is an in-your-face to both Sherwood and Birley. (Flow charts, again?) Cipriani had previously attacked Sherwood's redo of the hotel as something from Adnan Khashoggi's yacht. He wrote in his memoir about the endless mirrors, where "New Jersey druggists could . . . admire the reflection of their heavy gold necklaces and medals."

You won't find many "New Jersey druggists" at Harry's Bar in London, unless their name happens to be Merck. The L-shaped Victorian room is hung with red and cream Fortuny wallpaper covered with 1930s travel posters of Deauville and St. Moritz as well as black-and-white *New Yorker* cartoons by Peter Arno. One has a waitress being pinched by a naughty customer. "Sorry, sir, this isn't *my* table," reads the caption. Only the low chairs will remind you of Venice. The food, served by waitresses in nanny uniforms, can be even better than what you find in Venice (or at the London Cipriani): amazing razor-thin fried zucchini, tagliatelle with pheasant Bolognese, a silver trolley with a delectable roast breast of veal. For dessert the nannies pass out yummy imported Italian chocolate bars. All this can cost more than $250 to $300 a person, the biggest bill in Albion. You probably won't have to worry about it, since you probably won't be going. But take heart. Mark Birley and his clan may be out as well, unless a currently very bitter roiling dispute with Sherwood can be resolved. If not, the Birleys may well start a new Italian food club, and this time, maybe you can get on the list. ★ ★ ★ ★ ★ ★ ★ ★ ★ ★ ★ ★ ★

The River Cafe
High Tide

The River Cafe is less a restaurant than a living cookbook. Many regard it as the best Italian restaurant outside of Italy; it is certainly the best Italian restaurant anywhere run entirely by non-Italians. The River Cafe is owned by two women: Ruth Rogers, an American from Woodstock, New York, a Bennington dropout who never cooked before professionally; and Rose Gray, an aristocratic Englishwoman who ran the kitchen of Nell's nightclub in New York, not a confidence-inspiring résumé item. Yet they run a splendid ship, right on the Thames in Hammersmith. And some of the many other non-Italians in the kitchen have done quite well for themselves since the RC opened in 1987, most stupendously Jamie Oliver of "Naked Chef" fame, not to mention April Bloomfield, whose gastropub the Spotted Pig in New York won one of *Michelin*'s first American stars.

Yet there is a strong Italian sensibility at work here. Ruth Rogers is married to Sir Richard Rogers, one of the world's great architects, who designed the Pompidou Centre in Paris, as well as Lloyd's of London's new headquarters and the highly controversial Millennium Dome. Sir Richard was born in Florence; his family name is Ruggiero. He is as Italian as his colleague Renzo Piano, and he worships great simple food. The impetus to founding the café, which sits on the striking premises of the Rogers design studio, was that Sir

Richard knew it was the only way he was going to get a decent lunch in Hammersmith. Rogers's mother, who spent most of her life in Trieste, coached her daughter-in-law on the Italian virtues of freshness and simplicity.

Elizabeth Taylor once made a movie in London called *Hammersmith Is Out*. Now Hammersmith Is In, thanks to the RC, a pilgrimage shrine for foodies, as well as for stars, who have the chauffeurs to drive them there. It can be an hourlong trip from central London, each way, which can cost a fortune in a black cab. Its location is thus the RC's version of San Lorenzo's no-credit-cards policy, a winnowing device. The result is a Spago-like array of limos and fancy cars parked outside.

Unless you knew Sir Richard was involved, you'd be hard-pressed to guess there was anything architectural about the place. Inside, the RC looks less like a shrine than a warehouse, or an unfinished rest stop on one of the motorways. There's a long open kitchen with a wood-burning oven, and a big plain rectangular room, with windows opening out to the Thames, which can be great in springtime, but more like springtime for Hitler in the drear of winter, when it's dark by four. The Thames here is actually quite pretty and winding, but it's no Arno. The view across the water is not of some Palladian villa but of the old Harrods furniture warehouse.

Still, the crowd looks very worthy of the transport outside, casually rich. Aside from being the unofficial canteen for Tony Blair and his circle, the RC's notable habitués tend to be brainy, talkative media types like Barbara Walters, Harvey Weinstein, the star of *The Weakest Link*, big London publishers, BBC execs, and Film4 producers. There are so many vacationing New York foodies here that if you close your eyes the din sounds like Zabar's on any given Sunday. But there are no bad tables, and none of San Lorenzo's or Cipriani's gut-wrenching insecurity here. All the tables have river views; the beautiful people are scattered equally among the normal ones. The River Cafe is about wonderful food, not power seating. Despite all the Bentleys outside, nobody drives this far and through such hellish traffic to want any further torture over status anxieties. Getting there is masochism enough.

Lack of decor and acoustics notwithstanding, the food is more than worth the trouble. From the fresh pomegranate-Prosecco Bellinis to the grilled squid with chili, the al dente wild mushroom risotto (the equal of anything in Milan), the crab tagliatelle, the oven-roasted turbot, the lemon tart, every dish sings of the marketplace. You forget that the preparers are from Scotland, Poland, New Zealand. In the kitchen, they might as well all be Bolognese. Notwithstanding Alvaro Maccioni's warning, "When *Michelin* gives a star to an Italian restaurant, run in the opposite direction," that caveat doesn't apply here. "We're not an Italian restaurant," Ruth Rogers insists. "We just make Italian food." Do they ever, but not in any kind of precious way that would scare away the antichef gourmet-phobic aristocrats of yore. It's not like going out to the three-star, avant-garde Fat Duck in Bray. That's for the slick Eurobankers in the City. Real men don't eat foam, but they do eat risotto. Bring it on. ★

The Ivy and Le Caprice
Ivy League

PICCADILLY CIRCUS

If you want to eat British-British, keep it simple, and see stars, there is no better choice than the Ivy, in the heart of theaterland. The problem is that it's so good and obvious a choice that you can't get in unless you're a star yourself or you book months in advance, which seems sort of, well, French, given such a seemingly unpretentious restaurant. The Ivy reputedly gets over a thousand calls a day, to four receptionists, for reservations. Why? The restaurant has been around since 1911, but it hasn't been fully booked all those years. In fact, it had many cycles of hard times. It was by no means a Savoy Grill, but rather an unassuming theater café that got a lot of big stage names by virtue of its location. Its name supposedly came from a prophecy Sarah Bernhardt pronounced to the original owner: "The acting profession will cling to you like ivy." But when two aspiring restaurateurs, Chris Corbin and Jeremy King, took it over in 1989, the tired old Ivy was clinging for dear life.

Corbin and King gutted the place and created a stained-glass and wood-paneled, art-filled, Connaughtian ambience that everyone mistakenly thinks is pure 1930s glamour but is actually contempo artifice. Many people also mistakenly assume that the LA Ivy and the London Ivy are related, which is a good thing for both places. They are both showbiz colossi, they do serve the same constituency, and they both offer enticingly wide arrays of chauvinistic comfort food. While the LA Ivy's menu leans south by southwest, London's Ivy goes back to nursery school. Favorites here on West Street are the salmon fish cake, the shepherd's pie, fish and chips, the sticky toffee pudding, and a special creamy dessert called "Eton Mess." It's hardly *Michelin* fare, but the fact that it's not putting you through any gourmet gauntlet is the essence of its appeal. Look around the room, at everyone from Sir Harold Pinter and Lady Antonia Fraser to David and Victoria Beckham, from Andrew Lloyd Webber to Elton John, from Kevin Spacey to Johnny Knoxville, and you'll get the idea, if not a table. If you don't, you're in good company. Jennifer Lopez was barred here, declared out at the plate after three strikes of being a no-show.

Corbin and King, known as the Batman and Robin of the London dining scene, have accomplished three miraculous resurrections: first of Le Caprice, behind the Ritz Hotel in Piccadilly; then the Ivy; and then J. Sheekey, an ancient down-at-the-heels fish house with an A-plus West End location. The two men understand stars. Corbin had been the manager of the Michael Caine–owned Langan's Brasserie, the hottest celeb restaurant of the 1980s, while King had run the door at the actor-packed Joe Allen's in Covent Garden. The smallish Le Caprice, which opened right after World War II, was in those dark days one of the few places one could eat in splendor in London. The gourmet of gourmets, oil billionaire Nubar Gulbenkian, lived upstairs in Arlington House and was key in putting Le Caprice on the world food map. In the swinging 1960s, Le Caprice, with its liberal dress policies, became the favorite crossover restaurant for the Carnaby Street miniskirt–Sergeant Pepper set, who wanted something other than pasta for a change.

Once life turned capricious on Caprice in the Arab-dominated 1970s, Corbin and King swooped in and bought it for a song, hanging the creamy walls with giant David Bailey blowups of Deneuve and Shrimpton to inspire remembrances of 1960s past. A lot of 1960s legends love it here, and not just for the narcissism of seeing themselves up on the wall. The crowd here tends more to publishing, journalism, and style (Anna Wintour, preindictment Conrad Black, postprison Jeffrey Archer) than the thesp-filled Ivy and J. Sheekey's. The menu, very close to the Ivy's, harks back to school, not to Gulbenkian, fish cake and the like. The eggs Benedict are thought to be definitive, though there is a central-commissary feel to most other preparations, something corporate about it all.

That corporate thing is not just an illusion. Corbin and King actually sold out their restaurants in 1999. The buyer was Luke Johnson, who had made his fortune in the Pizza Express chain. But Corbin and King had created such a seamless operation that nobody felt it had changed hands, and the reservation waits got even longer. In 2005, Johnson himself sold out to Richard Caring, a clothing tycoon (supplying third-world-made garments to Topshop, etc.) wanting to make a splash going from rags to dishes. Caring liked to make grand gestures. He once paid over $300,000 at a charity auction to have dinner with Elton John, and on another occasion hired the Winter Palace in Saint Petersburg for another charity blowout. But the Ivy and company seem to be owner-proof. Dependent upon neither celebrity owners nor celebrity chefs, they are dependent only on the celebrities themselves, who for some inexplicable reason in their fickle world have remained completely loyal. Corbin and King meanwhile have embarked on a new venture, an all-day brasserie with an Ivyish comfort menu called the Wolseley in a converted Piccadilly showroom for that now extinct automotive brand. It's packed with stars, too. Celebrity hunger, it seems, is infinitely elastic. ★

China Tang, Hakkasan, and Yauatcha
Enter the Dragons

MAYFAIR and SOHO

With the grande dame classics being declassicized and Frenchified and the theaterland favorites being corporatized and standardized, a power vacuum has arisen in the world of London celebrity restaurants. Into this breach have sprung several wise men from the East bearing their own exotic culinary versions of frankincense and myrrh. These Asian dining entrepreneurs got hip to the fact that in the newly foodified London, neither man nor superstar man can live by fish cakes alone. That's probably why Nobu on Park Lane is by total consensus the hottest restaurant in fish cake land. Wherever it is, Nobu seems to be the hottest restaurant. Maybe it's because Nobu's miso cod, or his soft-shell crab hand roll, or his *tiradito,* is the Hollywood fish cake. And the entire world, being Hollywood-mad, wants to eat what the stars do.

Nobu on Park Lane is so successful that, as in New York, it had to clone itself next door to handle the overflow. The names range from Hollywood A, like Tom Cruise and George Clooney, to London B, like golden oldies Cliff Richard and Cilla Black. Hordes of garmentos follow Naomi Campbell here, while hordes of heirs and heiresses follow Jade Jagger. But hordes there are, night and day, putting the Armani-clad waitstaff to the task. Part of Nobu's London notoriety stems from a close encounter of the third kind that tennis ace Boris Becker enjoyed in a Nobu pantry with an eastern Euromodel. This dangerous liaison engendered a baby, a paternity suit, and a painful divorce, making it the most expensive sushi meal of all time. And Becker didn't even order *fugu*, the big-bucks blowfish.

The best way to crash the all-star party that is Nobu (or the Ivy or Cipriani) is to stay at one of the grand hotels and have the grand concierge book you a table. Knowing Martin at Claridge's, the reigning Jeeves of the profession, is almost as good as being a FOB (friend of Bob, as in De Niro, the star capital behind the wasabi). The second best thing is to find the *next* Nobu. Currently leading the pack is Knightsbridge's Zuma, which translates as "second wife" in Japanese and sounds like the LA beach, which is a good sound in sun-and-star-mad London.

Zuma has a German chef and Indian financing, which doesn't seem to bode well for its raw fish. But then again, neither does red-hot Koi in LA, where the sushi men are from Bangladesh. Nipping on Zuma's heels is Sumosan in Mayfair, another unorthodox combo of a Japanese restaurant owned by a Russian woman with North Korean sushi chefs from Moscow. In Moscow, which has gone sushi mad, there are very few Japanese but countless North Koreans, from the old Communist days of the USSR, who pretend to be knife men from the land of the rising sun. Sumosan is superhot because of its bait, or jailbait, of gorgeous Russian MAWs (model-actress-whatevers) who call the place their canteen. It caters the parties of Roman Abramovich, a transplanted oligarch who owns the Chelsea football team and is currently London's highest roller.

If all this Japanese table-hopping is too inscrutable and too un-London for you, you might try as an alternative the superhip Chinese restaurants, a trend originated in the 1960s by Michael Chow that has been given a second life by two Eastern contemporary visionaries, David Tang and Alan Yau. Because of England's long ties to Hong Kong, the Anglo-Chinese connection seems somehow deeper and far more organically "British" than the nearly nonexistent Anglo-Japanese one. But first, Mr Chow, which is still in its original space in Knightsbridge but now part of the Conran group (Bibendum, Quaglino's, Almeida, and many more). Somehow the Conran restaurants, for all their style and panache, are simply too big, too mass-market, and thus fly over the Hollywood radar. Intimate Mr Chow is the exception, and nostalgic stars still drop in, hoping to see a miniskirt ascend the flagpole staircase. But somehow P. Diddy and the hiphop crowd, who make the LA and NYC Chows their home, haven't embraced the London Chow. Hence it remains more an artifact than a nerve center. But Michael Chow has had his own resurrections, and he knows that trends can turn on a dime, or a euro, and that any moment, especially once he is showcased next to Nobu at the Vegas Hard Rock Hotel, Chow London could get hot again.

Before Michael Chow, there was no such thing as a sophisticated Chinese restaurant in London, notwithstanding that Britain owned Hong Kong at the time. Only in England, whose ruling class was obsessed with good taste but equally dismissive of anything that tasted good, could the magnificent cuisines of an entire empire be ignored. Michael Chow brought Chinese food into the limelight, but only through the vehicle of chic. Not only was he from a leading Beijing theatrical family, with a sister who was a Chinese film star, but he also married Grace Coddington, a top model turned trendsetting British *Vogue* editor. Chow himself dabbled in acting, with small parts in gangster films. He also ran a cool *Shampoo*-ish hair salon. He thus had the connections, the éclat, the location, the new concept, the right time. Mr Chow was an instant smash, filled with everyone from the Stones to the Beatles, the Rothschilds to the Hanovers.

If anyone has the right stuff to step into Michael Chow's footsteps, that man is David Tang. "You live in Hangzhou, you marry in Suzhou, you die in Luizhou, but you eat in Guangzhou," says Tang, citing an old Chinese proverb. Hangzhou is the prettiest place in China, Suzhou had the most beautiful women, Luizhou has the best wood for coffins, but Guangzhou, formerly Canton, has the best, simplest, purest, healthiest food. And that's precisely what David Tang is committed to serving in his own burgeoning empire in this country of empires.

Tang, in his early fifties and very Anglo old school, is to the empire born. Like Chow, he came from a distinguished family, but unlike Chow, also

89

a very rich one. His great-grandfather had a bank in Hong Kong, his grandfather a private transport line of double-decked London buses. His father, who was knighted, was a horse breeder. David Tang was sent to school in England at thirteen. He read physics at the University of London, then philosophy, before he got practical and became a solicitor, at the distinguished firm of Macfarlanes, which happened to represent some of the key figures of the 1960s transformation of London, such as Mark Birley of Annabel's and Mary Quant. In the 1980s Tang went back to China and taught Western philosophy at Peking University. Next he became an oil wildcatter, off the coast of China. He couldn't find a drop. So once again he tried something completely different: retail. In 1994 he opened Shanghai Tang, in Hong Kong, a totally stylish East-West contemporary men's and women's clothing store that also sells a huge array of home furnishings and gifts. The success here led to branches in New York and Singapore, and then to something again completely different, the China Club restaurants, in Hong Kong, Beijing, and Singapore, which quickly became the most glamorous dining venues in all Asia.

"I started the restaurants as my own way to correct annoyances," Tang says, then enumerates some of the things he hates about dining out: waiters interrupting conversations; messy, empty tables after the main course has been cleared ("the best time to judge a restaurant is 10 P.M., not 7"); lukewarm food (Tang breaks Chinese all-dishes-at-once tradition by serving course by course). He detests fusion, he scorns Szechuan fare as loaded with lard, and he bans MSG in everything. The result is the delicate, delicious Cantonicities served at his newest venture, China Tang. The restaurant is in the space recently vacated by the Dorchester Club, owned by Harrods' Mohammed al-Fayed (father of Dodi), in the cellar of the Dorchester Hotel, now owned, like the Beverly Hills Hotel and the Plaza Athenée in Paris, by the Sultan of Brunei. Grand hotels seem to be the collectibles of the Muslim elite.

Can Tang succeed where someone so illustrious as al-Fayed could not? He's not worried. As at his coventure Cipriani, Tang has filled the Dorchester space with witticisms. There's a big screen with a live offshore feed of the Shanghai Bund, with the junks sailing by the deco skyscrapers. There is a large admonitory painting of the pope right outside the bar. And the bathrooms are the coolest on earth, with an Alistair Cooke-ian voice intoning the complete Edward Lear's "The Owl and the Pussycat": "O lovely pussy! O Pussy my love, what a beautiful Pussy you are!" One trip to the loo, and you won't *need* MSG.

The food, from the fresh mango and lychee juices to the perfect hot-and-sour soup, the fried tofu, the prime pepper beef, and the very warm Peking duck and steamed fish, is as upscale as you can take Chinese, served in a palatial, Forbidden City–like maze of rooms with ancient chests and price-less silks. If only the boisterous crowd were more imperial. Instead, similar to the Savoy Grill, China Tang seems like a reunion of the Krays, the storied East End mobsters. The women are very cinematic, albeit out of Fellini rather than Antonioni. But maybe these are London foodies. Maybe you have to be big and thuggish to make enough loot to come here. There are Indian maharani types in saris and impassive Russian hit men in black leather and Nigerian princes in tribal robes, and it all seems like central casting. "I want drama, the *wow* factor," Tang says. He's got it. The Mick Jaggers, David Frosts, Joan Collinses, Phil Collinses, Saatchi and Saatchis, they are all pals of David Tang. They come, too. But they tend to sit in the private rooms.

Alan Yau, forty-four, is an entirely different kettle of steamed turbot. Yau grew up poor, very poor, in a small village near Hong Kong. His father, from the Hakka group, the "wandering Jews" of Southeast China, wandered to London when Yau was twelve. Yau *père* eventually opened a chop suey joint in the town of King's Lynn. Alan Yau tried to break away. He came up to London and read politics and philosophy at City Polytechnic. But after a series of dead-end jobs, he ended up back working with father, who now had a take-out place in Peterborough. Dreading the prospect of becoming his father's cook, in 1992 Yau tried to break away again, this time by starting, on the very cheap, a futuristic noodle shop in Bloomsbury called Wagamama. The concept was a healthy Asian McDonald's, and it was sheer genius. Forty branches later, in 1997 Yau sold out for a fortune, which he used to open Hakkasan in 2002, in a menacing alley off Tottenham Court Road, and Yauatcha in 2004, in a hooker-intensive Soho market street. The concept here is to serve the pinnacular gourmet Chinese cooking of Singapore (the "fat city," which is to Asian food what Bologna is to Italian, or Lyon to French) in the atmosphere of a futuristic Shanghai brothel. Again, the concept was genius, and the two restaurants transformed their environs into chic destinations; both now have *Michelin* stars.

The food at Yau's glittering Vegas-y temples is superb, the best dim sum in Europe, served night and day, all flavors, all colors, all textures. You'll never want to go to Chinatown again. It's the best pre- or posttheater food fix in London, and it's full of stars who want to get in and out fast, Broderick and Lane, Spacey, Judi Dench, Kristin Scott Thomas. But it's not a place that empties out at showtime. Showtime is all around the clock. The fish, meat, and vegetarian dishes are all unique, incorporating Thai, Malay, Javanese, and Indian influences, as well as every region of China. Yet nothing feels gimmicky, overdone, or contrived. It's Chinatown, Jake, but Chinatown via Singapore. Again, it can be hell getting in, and a greater hell, noise-wise, once you're in. But who ever said Shanghai brothels were supposed to be quiet? ★ ★ ★ ★ ★ ★

Sweetings
City Slickers

THE CITY

What if all this is too, too much? If the Savoy Grill isn't what it used to be, and the Ivy isn't what you think it is, and Nobu is Hollywood and Hakkasan is a hemisphere away and Cipriani is . . . Isn't there a place where famous people go to eat real English food in a real English atmosphere? You bet! David Tang loves it, and Michael Chow, and half the starred chefs in London would go there if only it weren't open Monday through Friday for lunch only. The place is Sweetings, the best fish house in the City, and the city, a Victorian gem (on Queen Victoria Street to boot) unchanged since 1890—except for the electric lighting. Wiltons on Jermyn Street is of a similar ilk, but in its move from its truly venerable digs to its *faux*-venerable current ones, something has been lost in translation. At Sweetings, all is as it has ever been.

You want celebs? Here you get London's true celebs, its pinstriped moneymen. You stand in line—and it can be a long line, no favorites—with Hambros, Rothschilds, Goldsmiths, Hansens, Whites. And you sit with them at long wooden counters (there are only two tables). The place is owned by fishmongers, and you feel like you're right in the market, even though the nearby Lower Thames Street Fish Market was demolished a few decades ago. You eat succulent smoked salmon with buttered brown bread, grilled Dover sole on the bone, or deep-fried plaice, with old-fashioned homemade chips. Forget green vegetables; real Englishmen don't touch 'em. You wash it all down with a tankard of Black Velvet (Guinness and champagne). And then you have a true Welsh rarebit with a glass of port. Then you light up a Havana and walk back to the office and make a huge deal that will pay for an eternity of your wife's luncheons at Gordon Ramsay. But, as Fred and Ginger sang, ho, ho, ho, who's got the last laugh now. ★ ★ ★ ★ ★ ★ ★ ★ ★ ★ ★ ★ ★ ★

93

Paris

La Tour d'Argent
Tour de Force

5TH ARRONDISSEMENT

Nobody walks to the world's oldest, most famous, and most spectacular restaurant, La Tour d'Argent. Such gastronomes are driven, and not merely vehicularly. But not to walk to "the Tour" is to deprive yourself of the utter fabulousness of the foreplay to the experience. You start out on the Right Bank and head across the Seine, down the ancient streets of the Île Saint Louis, past the flying buttresses of Notre-Dame. Every literary and cinematic image of Gallic grandeur and elegance and romance, from Quasimodo to Belmondo, from Emma Bovary to Audrey Hepburn, is in that walk.

You cross one more bridge over to La Rive Gauche and onto the Quai de la Tournelle, and there it is, the five-story "Tower of Silver," to be literal, or "Tower of Money," to be correct. You're greeted by a doorman in enough Napoleonic livery to keep him warm in a Moscow winter, and then led through a *petit trianon* of salons by a footman in full dress. Just about every movie star who ever shone is right there, in photos on the walls, alongside de Gaulle, Eisenhower, Kennedy, Nixon, Picasso, Chagall, Dalí, you name them. Yet any gallery where Toscanini hangs with Bowie, where Queen Elizabeth hangs with Tina Turner, where Einstein hangs with Schwarzenegger, is far more than any mere sentimental journey.

You proceed into a plush paneled elevator, the one that the late claustrophobic superproducer Aaron Spelling, who also refused to fly, mistook for the entrance to the wine cellar, and whose response necessitated the SOS dispatch of a sizable rescue squad. Another attendant, this one suave in a tuxedo, rides you up six flights, then—*wow!* It's the most drop-dead view in the entire world, Notre-Dame in all its glory, plus every spire, every gargoyle, every garret, that combine to make Paris the most beautiful, most cinematic, of all cities.

Until very recently you would next be received by the most cinematic of all restaurant hosts. Claude Terrail, who died at eighty-eight in 2006, had until the last few months of his long and incredibly soigné life played polo every week, went shooting in season, cruised the Bois de Boulogne in his Ferrari. Regally tall, he had all his hair, was resplendent in his Lanvin suit, Charvet shirt, Hermès tie, plus his trademark boutonniere—a walking Rue St.-Honoré. For decades he had been one of the reigning playboys of the Western world, as his photos with his pals Porfirio Rubirosa and Gianni Agnelli and girlfriends like Marilyn Monroe, Rita Hayworth, and Ava Gardner readily attest. Up to the end, when Terrail was ailing and having great difficulty seeing the hands of the stars and grandes dames he had kissed for the last seventy years, he was aided on his walks through the dining room by assistants. All the more reason to visit now, as *plus ça change* here will never be *la même chose.*

Terrail had always ridiculed the notion of "A" tables and "Siberias," notions that made his nephew Patrick Terrail's Ma Maison in Los Angeles *the* template for scary, starry restaurants. "Here we have no bad tables," Terrail said, waving at the endless views of the Paris skyline, from the luxuriously spaced, blissfully quiet tables. "Patrick's effort"—note Claude's carefully contemptuous choice of words—"was an exercise in masochism." Dismissing the entire concept as a failure of hospitality, he quoted his dear friend Barbara Hutton: "The best table is where *I* sit." Sort of like, *"L'état, c'est moi."* Or *"Après moi, le deluge."* Echos of monarchy, grandeur, power. We are in France, after all.

Terrail or no Terrail, the Tour is still the best "date" restaurant on earth. Everyone dresses up in their often recently purchased Avenue Montaigne chic-ery, stuff you could rarely wear back in increasingly casual America.

The Tour is also a place where women wear fine jewelry when they're putting on the dog. There's no way you can possibly overdress. Once attired, you must order a fine wine from the Tour's 500,000-bottle cellar, the one Terrail put up a false wall around to trick the occupying Nazis. And you might as well splurge on luxe ingredients: Belon oysters, foie gras, the ultimate smoked salmon, truffles galore. Even though the Tour has in the past few years lost two of its heretofore taken-for-granted three *Michelin* stars, nobody is better at doing simple dishes to perfection: sole meunière, grilled Charolais beef.

But if it's your first time, have the duck. *Caneton* à la Tour d'Argent, or pressed duck, is the restaurant's signature classic, the most famous duck there is, except for maybe Donald. (Walt Disney was a loyal patron.) The Tour has been numbering the ducks served here since 1890. In the ring-a-ding 1950s, Sinatra and his pals, who were turned on to the Tour by Grace Kelly, by then of Monaco, dubbed the restaurant "The Duck Joint," and the name stuck. Nearly a million ducks have been served (imagine, to some future horror, a regal Gallic version of the golden arches, with a digital tally board). Each customer gets a special certificate, with a number, suitable for framing. Don't sneer. Both Theodore and Franklin Roosevelt had the duck. So did Emperor Hirohito, before World War II. So did the Duke of Windsor, in a kind of last supper, shortly before he abdicated.

The duck has quite a pedigree. It comes from the same farms, in the Atlantic marshland near Nantes, that have been raising ducks since 1650. The canals there are protected by law from industrial development, so it's as pure as fowl can be. Above all, it tastes as good as its lineage. The roasted duck is flattened in the famous silver duck press, which looks like a torture device from the Spanish Inquisition. The pressed breast is served in a heart-stopping Madeira and cognac sauce made from the duck's blood, with constantly replenished sides of *pommes soufflés*, the labor-intensive, wonderfully hot potato balloons first served in the court of Louis XIV. (Think about the modern world outside of frozen French fries; we've come a long way, baby—downhill.) The second duck round is something you might find in Napa, a simple fire-grilled leg with a light mesclun salad.

While you're catching your breath for dessert, you might reflect on the history in which you're basking, history being a scarce commodity in contemporary restaurants. An eating spot of some sort has stood on this hallowed ground since 1562, although restaurants, as we know them, didn't really come into their own until after the French Revolution. Then the court chefs, at least the ones who weren't guillotined, opened public places of their own, to "let them eat cake"—for a price. By the late nineteenth century, La Tour d'Argent, operating out of the ground floor of its current premises, was already one of the top restaurants in Paris, its place secured by its 1870 Christmas "game" dinner during France's war with Prussia, when the chef served elephant soup, antelope terrine, roasted camel hump, and kangaroo stew.

Claude Terrail came from a venerable family of hoteliers, who owned, among other glamorous properties, the George V and the San Regis. In 1947, when Terrail took the reins of the Tour from his father, the restaurant was a true island of luxury in a sea of postwar rationing and deprivation. For Americans, though, such luxury was relatively cheap, certainly when compared to that of Henri Soulé's Manhattan gastronomic temples, Le Pavilion, La Côte Basque, and Chambord. Now that the war was over, Americans could have the Real Thing in Paris at a fraction of the cost of the New York facsimile.

To page through the Tour's *livre d'or* of the late 1940s is a walk through the stars. Terrail had three from *Michelin* when *Michelin* really was the bible of gastronomy, and hundreds from Hollywood: Garbo, Dietrich, Swanson, Chaplin, Gable, Cooper, Bogart, Flynn, Chevalier. Of course, Chevalier. They had faces then. And names, too. In 1950, invited by Orson Welles, Terrail first visited America, was embraced by the Darryl Zanuck polo set in Palm Springs, dated Marilyn Monroe, and capped things off by marrying Hollywood royalty, in the person of Jack Warner's daughter, Barbara. The marriage, for which Barbara moved to Paris, lasted three years, although Terrail's romance with Hollywood continued. He had a grand affair with Ava Gardner, who showed up, famished, one night at the Tour after the kitchen had closed. Terrail, no cook at all, tried to make her something. Gardner pronounced it the worst meal of her life but fell in love with him anyhow.

Before the dawn of the age of the celebrity chef, Terrail became the first celebrity *patron*. He was the first to spin off the Tour into a lower-cost bistro version, La Rotisserie du Beaujolais (down the quai); the first to take the show on the road, to Tokyo, where the Tour still thrives; and the first to have a presence in Hollywood, albeit the unauthorized one of his nephew. The big names still come to the Tour: Paul McCartney with his vegetarian designer daughter Stella (the Tour caters to every whim); Prince Sihanouk of Cambodia; Bill Clinton, who loves to eat more than any other ruler; and Woody Allen, who's been in love with Paris and the Tour ever since *What's New Pussycat,* among whose many stars was Romy Schneider, again one of Claude Terrail's celebrated girlfriends.

So, over dessert of wild strawberries that would be the envy of Ingmar Bergman and pistachio ice cream that would shame Häagen-Dazs, raise a crystal goblet of your Chateau d'Yquem to Claude Terrail. And to his dashing (what else?) twentyish son, André, by Claude's last wife, a stunning (what else?) Finnish model, who now will try to fill Claude's custom shoes at the Tour. But Terrail assumed that he had at least a decade left to get the boy in shape. Ah, hubris. Ah, sweet bird of youth. Let us hope that Terrail *fils* can somehow replicate his father's magic and enable the Tour to carry on for still another century. ★ ★ ★

Madame Publicité

If you want to eat like the stars eat in France, you cannot rely on your concierge alone, nor upon your own wit, charm, and savoir faire. France, cradle of the imperious maître d', can be a tough ticket indeed—forbidding, impenetrable, nasty. But great food and great fun lie past the Maginot Line at the door. It can be so hard that even the stars aren't always confident they'll be able to eat like stars. While *People* readers may see a star, the maître d' at Ducasse or Gagnaire might see a Dallas cowboy, a Topeka hayseed, a Reno rube. But there is a solution: Yanou Collart, the Belgian-born, Paris-based queen of restaurant publicity, the woman who took Paul Bocuse and Michel Guérard out of the kitchen and onto magazine covers and television screens. A lot of Hollywood's biggest names have been retaining Collart for decades to make their stays in France something out of *Funny Face* or *Gigi* rather than *The Out of Towners.*

Tom Cruise and Nicole Kidman did it. Sherry Lansing and William Friedkin do it. Nicholson, Stallone, and Schwarzenegger are all Collart's *chers amis.* But isn't this like paying for free love, you wonder. Well, *mon cher,* nothing in Paris is *free.* The big players retain Yanou Collart to get them the best dining experiences for the same reason that another generation of big players retained Madame Claude, the sexual den mother to the global elite, to introduce them to the world's most beautiful women. Like James Bond, nobody does it better.

Collart is a sixty-something, still gorgeous former film publicist who used to be driven from Lasserre to Lucas Carton in her trademark vintage Rolls-Royce. Collart understood the grand gesture, and that such gestures got grand press. She put the now Governator on the map when he was an unknown muscleman in *Pumping Iron* by posing him with a posse of showgirls from the Crazy Horse Saloon, not topless as usual but clad in demure designer frocks. Collart understood the powerful nexus between food and sex; she made chefs seem like sexy beasts, rather than spattered stove slaves. The food and sex writer Gael Greene, whom Collart included on many a foie gras and champagne junket though *Michelin*-land, marveled in her memoirs at Collart's ravishing good looks, her couture suits, her genuine diamonds, her perfect, braless cleavage, her naughty jokes. Collart's own immense sex appeal rubbed off on the chefs. If *she* liked them, they had to be hot.

On a more serious note, it was Collart who announced to the world that Rock Hudson had AIDS. She has been tireless in countless charities, pulling in all the biggest names in food to support worthy causes. Nothing seems to loosen a checkbook like a three-star meal. Collart's grand home office is right off the Champs-Élysées, between the George V and the Plaza Athenée, where she can get you in if you cannot. Recently, she's been focusing more on culture than on food, helping Jerry Lewis with his Legion d'Honneur. But in a country where culture *is* food, Collart is never that far removed from the restaurant scene. So if Ami Louis hasn't been that amicable or Le Stresa claims Tom Ford has booked the whole place for a private party or you want to take the TGV to Troisgros but can't handle the logistics, call Collart, who can always manage to pull a *lapin* out of the old *chapeau.* ★ ★ ★ ★ ★ ★ ★ ★ ★ ★ ★ ★ ★

Davé and Chez Omar
Reverse Chic

If you were rich enough to eat at La Tour d'Argent and its liveried, truffled ilk every night that you were in Paris, how could you not? In the not-so-old days, that's what rich people did, following, if not waddling, in the Diamond Jim Bradyish footsteps of the legendary global gourmands—Farouk, Gulbenkian, the Aga Khan, Onassis, Getty. Today, eating creamy *Michelin vaut le voyage* feasts every day seems like sheer torture, like the force-feeding of geese whose livers are being fattened up for the kill. For stars, of screen and elsewhere, it's more than a matter of a surfeit of cream, calories, and cholesterol. Stars have enough pomp and ceremony in their daily lives; they don't *need* any more at dinner. Furthermore, at a place like the Tour, the restaurant is the real star, not the stars who eat there. And stars, their "just folks" protestations notwithstanding, don't like to surrender a whit of their centrality of attention.

Enter Davé ("Dav-ay" to you), perhaps the hippest restaurant in Paris. And as far as Chinese restaurants are concerned, on the global scale of trend, maybe even hipper in Paris than Mr Chow is in New York and Beverly Hills. In terms of decor and presentation, there is none; Davé is the anti-Tour. But in terms of a guiding restaurant persona, Dave Cheung ranks right up there with the Tour's Claude Terrail, and is infinitely less intimidating, albeit even more of an arbiter of status. Dave may be the most ebullient, gossipiest, most vivacious restaurateur anywhere. Imagine Jackie Chan crossed with Liz Smith. Full of aphorisms and bons mots, Dave is a human fortune cookie. Once you've registered on Dave's radar, which isn't easy, he never forgets a thing about you, and he flatters you to death. When you come back, Dave provides the world's warmest welcome in the world's coolest city.

Davé is located behind a bright red lacquer door (shades of *Raise the Red Lantern)* in a backpackers' lodging called the Hotel Montpensier, on the gloomy Rue Richelieu near the Comédie-Française and the Palais-Royale. There is a sign in Davé's window that always reads COMPLET, or full. Because you've booked, you venture in. Once your eyes adjust to the red velvet bordello darkness of the place, illuminated only by a fluorescent fish tank, you wonder where the stars, or anyone else, is. "Brazil" is playing on the house Muzak. Cheap paper flowers decorate the tables. At nine o'clock, prime dinnertime in Paris, the joint is dead. But then out comes Dave, the anti-Claude, in his Marc Jacobs sweatshirt, his Comme des Garcons vest, his red scarf. Fifty-something, with wild salt-and-pepper hair, he looks like a hip Caltech professor. Because Dave, who is multilingual, either liked the sound of your voice if you were brave enough to book yourself, or he knows the concierge at your chic hotel, he makes you feel like you're the greatest American to hit Paris since Gene Kelly. Like you've scored the hardest reservation in town, even as he leads you to the empty back room, Siberia to the cognoscenti, or Kashgar, to keep the analogy Chinese. Somehow Dave gives you the impression that, as with that other great host at the Café Americain in Casablanca, this could be the beginning of a beautiful friendship.

As you nibble cold shrimp crackers and peruse the tattered, grease-stained sparerib, spring roll, moo-shu-standard-issue Cantonese menu, you can't help but look at the countless snapshots on the walls, all taken by, and often with, Dave. There's no one to ogle at the tables, but *everyone* is in those snaps: Mick, Keith, Leo, Gisele, Roman, Keanu, Cher, Sting, Naomi, Warhol, Lichtenstein, Rauschenberg. Plus all the supergarmentos: Yves St. Laurent, Tom Ford, Calvin Klein, John Galliano, Karl Lagerfeld, Donatella Versace, Donna Karan, Anna Wintour, who throws her big parties at Davé. But where are they, you despair, wondering if it's not too late to slip out and make it into the Balzar for some *poulet roti* and other brasserie comforts. Forget this nutty idea about eating Chinese food in Paris, of all places, just to see stars.

Somehow, not expecting much, you hang in there. You order some not-bad rosé and some food, which turns out to be quite tasty. A special of "Thai" shrimp, spiked with lemongrass and cilantro: the shrimp are fresh, which you'd never find in America; the sauce sprightly. The broccolini is perfect, as is the tofu. It should be, because this is what all the top models, for whom Davé is their canteen, invariably order. There is fine crispy roast duck, and greaseless fried noodles, and classic lemon chicken, which everyone except the models invariably orders. It's not razzle-dazzle Chinese, like Uncle Tai's and David K's in New York in the roaring eighties, the heyday of spicy Szechuan cooking: no General Tso's chicken, or Colonel Wang's beef (all those incendiary dishes had martial names). But the generals are gone, and Davé's still standing. For all the catcalls, Davé's food is fresh and simple and doesn't get in the way of good times. In fact, it's every bit as good as, and similar to, Mr Chow's, minus the glitzy packaging and the fancy noodle-making displays. No wonder the stars like it.

But where *are* they? you despair. Just as you round the turn to home, and are finishing up your delicious canned lychees, just like the ones at Mr Chow, *they* start to arrive, after ten-thirty, Spanish style. First to enter is "BHL," Bernard-Henri Levy, the celebrated intellectual-as-rock-star, with his gorgeous actress wife, Arielle Dombasle. They have a love-in with Dave, and are seated up front, by the fish. Then comes David Schwimmer, with a beautiful date. Another love-in, plus one with the BHLs, with whom the *Friends* star would seemingly have little in common. There must be a community of celebrity that unites all boldfaced names. Schwimmer also eats with the fishes. As does actress Kristin Scott Thomas and her French husband. Director Wim Wenders. Photographer Nan Goldin. Gaggles of models come in, platters of tofu come out. Is that Charlotte Rampling? Or are preternaturally high cheekbones simply the price of admission here? In seeming seconds, the place has gone from *vide* to *complet*. So many beautiful people are sitting in the back room that forlorn Kashgar could pass for Shanghai's Bund.

Dave is table-hopping like a whirling dervish, kissing, charming, snapping his camera, popping champagne. He complains to everyone how put out he is that his pal Tom Hanks didn't stop in once while filming *The Da Vinci Code,* but that his pal Sofia Coppola *lived* here while filming *Marie Antoinette.* In a way, Davé is the house that Coppola built. Born in Hong Kong, Dave came to Paris in his teens and worked in his family's small restaurant until he started his own in 1982 on the nearby Rue St. Roch. One of his first customers was the actress Aurore Clément, who was married to Dean Tavoularis, Francis Coppola's production designer. The Tavoularises brought in Coppola, who brought in everyone in Hollywood. At the same time, the restaurant was discovered by that other ultimate tastemaker, photographer Helmut Newton, who stumbled into Davé after a fashion shoot in the Tuileries across the street. Newton and his wife, June, brought in the models, who brought in the garmentos, and then the world.

Dave moved to his new location a few years ago, but he prides himself on always minding the store, never leaving town. "They want me. They need me." *"Le restaurant, c'est moi. N'est-ce pas?"* He notes, without gloating, how tough a restaurant town Paris is, so tough that even Nobu had to close his operation here. "You can't make money in France," he says. "You can have a name (like mine), but no money." Then he giggles madly. "Most of the time, it's no name *and* no money. If I were in London, after twenty-five years, I'd own my own building. Here I still rent." But Dave is not complaining. All he needs is love, and he's got it, from tough customers from I. M. Pei to Oliver Stone, people who have eaten the finest Chinese food on earth but still call Davé home, sweet home. It's living proof that flattery will get you everywhere.

Paris's other temple of reverse chic is Chez Omar, which, in simplistic terms, is a Moroccan Davé. Actually, the eponymous *patron* here is Algerian, as are most of the city's countless *couscouseries,* but for some reason perhaps fathomed by repeat viewings of *The Battle of Algiers*, the shorthand for North African dining is "Moroccan." Here's looking at you, kid. The laconic, ironic Omar is more like Bogart's Rick than Davé's Dave, but he presides over an equally starry court. He's cocky and preppy, in a Ralph-Lauren-goes-Casbah kind of way. His restaurant is far grander than Davé, a high-ceilinged, smoky, fin de siècle tavern near the Marais that hasn't been rebuffed since the Dreyfus Affair. It's got charm. It's got good food. And, most unusual for a celebrity restaurant, it's got value. The vegetarian couscous, the nonfat *plat* that lures in the models, who in turn lure in the stars, is Omar's "money dish." Yet at twelve euros, it barely costs any money at all. It's Paris's ultimate gastronomic loss leader, a testament to Omar's business genius. Throw in some cheap, lusty Algerian red wine, finish off with home-brewed mint tea, and, with all the eye candy for dessert, you don't need anything from the tempting platters of baklava and supersweet North African pastries.

In his definitive 1969 *Paris Dining Guide*, the great food critic Waverly Root lists six North African restaurants, but even he is hard-pressed to differentiate one from another. Things haven't changed. Whether Omar makes the best couscous in Paris is beside the point. Whatever, it's a fine couscous, whether the delicate steamed semolina grains are topped with fresh vegetables alone or with *mechoui* (barbecued lamb), or grilled lamb or chicken kebabs, which are all fine. The animal protein is "guy food," though local folklore is that any model who crosses this gender-protein line is sending out signals of carnality, as opposed to anorexia. Omar is also considered to serve the best steak *au poivre* in the city, and the accompanying fresh peanut-oil *pommes frites* are state-of-a-vanishing-art. The steak *frites should be* tops here, as Omar got his start in 1962 as the steak *frites* chef at La Coupole, the landmark 1927 art deco brasserie in Montmartre, which, like most of Paris's landmark brasseries, has gone corporate—swallowed, like the Balzar, Julien, Vaudeville, Boeuf sur le Toit, by the leviathan catering chain Flo Prestige. The bodies remain, but the souls have been snatched.

Omar left La Coupole in the early 1970s to try his luck at his own place on the King's Road in London, but he just missed the magic of the

Swinging 1960s. He returned to Paris to open his Chez in 1979. His timing now was perfect; the Marais was beginning to take off. To Omar's loyal core constituency of artists, like Cesar and Arman, who remembered his grill work at La Coupole, was added the fashion people, who are to Paris what film people are to Los Angeles: the arbiters of chic. Romeo Gigli was the first. Then Naomi Campbell brought Linda Evangelista and Christy Turlington, the girls who wouldn't get out of bed for less than $1,000 an hour, to eat three-dollar couscous. Then came Gene Pressman, the Barneys heir, with Kenzo, Yohji Yamamoto, Agnes B. Catherine D (as in Deneuve) soon followed, with culture czar Jack Lang. When Roman Polanski brought in Lee Radziwill, Omar was a made man. The Beautiful People were his, and they have never left. Like the exclusive nightclubs Castel and Les Bains Douches, which have never lost favor, Chez Omar has managed to stick, to become a classic, a touchstone of stability in the shifting sands of trend. ★ ★ ★ ★ ★ ★ ★

Chez l'Ami Louis
The Bird Is the Word

3RD ARRONDISSEMENT

If La Tour d'Argent is "The Duck Joint," Ami Louis is "the chicken coop." But while there are endless temptations on the Tour's bill of fare, it is almost impossible to resist, time and again, the elemental siren call of Louis's seventy-euro *poulet*, which is *sans rival* as the biggest, juiciest, most succulent, not to mention most expensive roast chicken to ever grace a restaurant table. The stenciled lettering, dating from the 1920s, on the windows facing the run-down Rue du

Vert-Bois, near the old garment district in the 3rd arrondissement, proclaims *foie gras de Landes*, rather than the chicken. And the foie gras is great indeed, and great big. But if you have it, there's no room for the bird, and the bird is what everybody comes here for. And everybody means *everybody*, from Arletty to Oprah, from Sartre to Jagger, from Brigitte Bardot (when she ate meat) to Angelina Jolie, even if she usually doesn't. The less-than-no-frills Ami Louis has a coal stove for heat, bare lightbulbs, and a treacherously steep passage down to the very exposed ancient toilets that has sent more than one reveler to the hospital. There are fewer than fifty hardwood seats in this moldy, crumbling time warp, and they're the fifty hardest seats to get in this capital of cuisine.

From its founding in 1920, Ami Louis (Chez l'Ami Louis is its official name), which still is the quintessence of a vintage Brassaï photograph, has always been a theatrical hangout. The Louis who opened the place sold it in 1931 to the chef Antoine Magnin, who catered to the *Enfants du Paradis–Grand Illusion* crowd. Magnin specialized not so much in chicken as in "seasonal" food: the first baby peas, white asparagus, suckling lamb for Easter, venison and woodcock during the hunting season, and, above all, that foie gras *du landes*. He served it fresh, and he served it dear, and for decades ordinary diners were intimidated by Ami Louis's celebrities, and by its celebrity prices, however much they yearned for its unique big-bucks rusticity and its country-in-the-city fare. Magnin died in 1987, allegedly in his nineties, never having missed a day in the tiny, hot kitchen. His longevity was a testament to the "French paradox" regarding Gallic survival in spite of massive cholesterol and saturated-fat intake.

Was it the red wine? Or was it the roast chicken, which the Goldwyn, Mayer, Warner moguls of Hollywood, nostalgic for their Old World grandmothers, embraced as *their* dish in Paris? They dispatched their stars on pilgrimages to share this "must taste" experience. The Paris-based columnist Art Buchwald memorialized the "celebrity chicken" in syndication throughout the 1950s, and the world, or at least the *beau monde*, got hooked. In 1986, just before Magnin's ascent to the kitchen in the sky, a French "baby mogul" named Thierry de la Brosse, then a hotshot at Cointreau who had eaten at Ami

Louis with his parents since his gilded childhood, teamed up with the longtime Breton headwaiter Louis Gadby to buy the place and preserve it forever.

Gadby, a squat, white-coated, full-brown-haired human postcard of provincial France, is himself a French paradox: he simply doesn't age. His glittering American clientele call him "the Great Gadby," and he beams at the adulation. Maybe it *is* the chicken, which is more like a Great Auk—a giant, parchment-skinned airship of a fowl, served in its own pan juices and a side of watercress. It takes a good hour to eat, hands on, using the baguettes to sop up all those delicious, unsalty juices. Gadby loves to come by and watch your progress, a "we do chicken right" smile illuminating his otherwise stolid countenance. Or maybe it's the *pommes Béarnaise* (from the province of Bearn), one of the greatest potato dishes anywhere, the platonic ideal of hash browns, a thick, crispy, golden buttery cake topped with lots of garlic and parsley. There are other potatoes, too. Ami Louis is famous for its *pommes allumettes,* or matchstick fries, but they're good only for a minute, and get too cold too fast. Habitués ask for the thicker classic *pommes frites,* but unless you don't trust the French paradox to work for you against the butter, the *Béarnaise* is the ticket. Salads, for some reason, are awful, no better than any commercial bistro's. But the bracingly tart lemon sorbet is just what you need, and all you can handle, by the end of this *grande bouffe.*

The de la Brosse–Gadby partnership seems to have lost sight of Magnin's seasonality. There are specials each day, but nobody who comes here once a year or once in a lifetime, depending on if a table is ever free, can seem to resist the call of the barnyard. And having done so fabulously here, the Ami Louis boys have partnered with Alain Ducasse in restoring the classic bistros Aux Lyonnais and Benoit to their former luster. But there the food has been somewhat Ducasse-d: so many choices, so many complications. At Ami Louis, the old bird still rules the roost, and always will. It's a one-dish wonder, but what a *merveille* it is. ★

Arpège
Promise Her Anything

7TH ARRONDISSEMENT

Michelin stars and Hollywood stars are generally incompatible. The latter's laid-back life in sweats, not to mention their obligations on the stuffy rubber-chicken ballroom circuit, make them hate to dress up. Furthermore, the attention demands of haute cuisine run up against their attention deficits, at least for any matter other than themselves. Fancy restaurants evoke the classrooms that most of the stars dropped out of; fancy waiters, the authority figures whom they rebelled against. That's why they go to Davé and Omar. But there is one siren call that stars do heed, and that is the call of health and longevity. Who wants to die when you've got everything? Hence that is why, of all Paris's three-star temples of gastronomy, the one where you're most likely to spot stars is Arpège, which the chef Alain Passard has transformed into a temple of vegetables.

Arpège is not exactly vegetarian. While red meat has been banned, Passard can do splendid things with fish and fowl. But if he has his way, and the stars have theirs, it will be a night of magnificent vegetables, taken to an outer limit that only one of France's acknowledged superstars can go to. Besides, Arpège, despite its tony location in the haughty *septième,* right near the Hôtel des Invalides, has no dress code. So if Hollywood wants a big food night out, without the risk of gaining weight, this is their place. Not to scare the dudes away, but Arpège is kind of a "chick restaurant," and not in the avian sense of Ami Louis, but in the Nicole Kidman–Liz Hurley–Posh Spice sense. Beautiful women, who can never be too rich or too thin, see vegetables as talismanic, and flock here accordingly. But Jack Nicholson likes it, too, maybe for the girls, maybe for the veggies, maybe for both.

Despite its august neighborhood, there is nothing very temple-ish about Arpège, except its prices, which are terrifying: The vegetable prix fixe is 240 euros, or nearly $300. A respectable wine here will run another $300. These are movie-star prices—not for animal protein, perhaps, in these expensive times, but for vegetables, it's a lot to swallow. Granted, this is star food. But it's not a star room. It's a simple, moderne blond wood space of far-apart tables with leather and metal armchairs, filled with mostly rich Brits and Yanks, and fewer French people, with some Cesar (or is it Arman) sculptures of cellos and violins, as well as tied cords of dried asparagus stalks, an homage to the greenery that awaits you. There is also a downstairs room that accommodates the overflow, but avoid it if you can. Locals call it "the dungeon."

The coed service staff is very young and multiculti, people you might find in a seminar at the Sorbonne. The slightly older, smiling maîtres d's wear plain dark suits, and aren't at all intimidating. Alain Passard is nowhere to be seen. You ask if he's cooking tonight, and the entire staff assures you he's hard at the stoves. You're also assured by the centrality of the bread station: there are huge dark peasant loaves that Passard bakes, like the famed Poilane bread, but bigger and better. Immediately on being seated, huge slices of this crusty, yeasty, chewy bread are placed before you, with a thick-as-cheese wedge of salted butter from St. Malo to slather on it. This may be the best bread and butter you'll ever eat. You sip your $200 Burgundy and you're relieved that, in spite of the vegetables-only to come, you know you won't leave hungry.

As an *amuse-bouche* you get a hollowed eggshell with the softest scrambled yolk flavored with intense maple syrup. It's not very vegetarian, but it's an early-Passard ambrosial signature. Perhaps it's an answer to the chicken-or-the-egg conundrum. Since you're not getting the chicken, the egg comes first. You worry again how abstruse this meal is going to be. And then the greenery starts coming. Many of the vegetables, the captain informs you, had been picked that morning in the garden of Passard's château in Le Mans, a three-hour TGV train ride away. This is vegetable aristocracy. Wait a minute! A chef with a château? At these prices, why not? Where do you think Wolfgang Puck lives? A Hollywood condo? Please.

The first course is an onion ravioli in a cabbage consommé, which tastes much more interesting than it sounds. You're glad you have that bread at hand to "clear your palate," when in truth you're scarfing it down to sate your hunger. Next comes a single cold white beet in a sweet-and-sour sauce made with honey from Passard's château beehive. Again, that bread sure comes in handy to lap up the sauce. You tell yourself that this is the only sane way to do fancy food in France, the light way, the right way, then you wish you had preceded this evening with a big chicken at Ami Louis.

The third dish is a crusty gratin of sweet baby onions with intensely green mustard greens on top, sort of an onion *rosti*. It's *almost* filling, but not quite. Oh, for some of Louis's *pommes Béarnaise*. You're paying, and paying through your teeth, *not to eat*, you think. And then you console yourself on how thin and Kidmanesque you'll look after this repast and still have bragging rights of having been to the temple.

Then comes a gossamer risotto with the best Parmigiano-Reggiano, topped with baby endives. Imagine Italian food that didn't stick to your ribs. Next, three carrots, one white, one yellow, and one blood orange, in an intense Venezuelan chocolate mole sauce. There's an almost cocaine-ish rush to the sauce, Bugs Bunny meets Pablo Escobar, and you pretend you're getting high. Or maybe you're just light-headed from hunger. Your mouth waters as you see a chicken go by. It's a dish from Passard's Breton grandmother, chicken steamed in hay. How you gonna keep it down on the farm, after it's seen Paris? You want that chicken badly, but as this is an exercise in virtue, you bite your tongue and stay pure.

Finally, your main course, a *couscous aux legumes:* giant chickpeas, tiny cauliflower and broccoli, carrots, turnips, beets that make the baby vegetables of California's Chino Ranch seem clunky and graceless. But it's a tiny main course, ephemeral, gone in a few bites. You wish you were at Chez Omar, with a side of fries for good measure. But you're in a temple. Kill those heresies. Maybe dessert will fill you up. You pray for something rich and chocolatey and creamy and decadent, the stuff that explains why vegetarians are often so much more ample than you'd think they'd be. Some puff pastry, let-them-eat-cake-obnoxious confection, Sun King food, not gardener fare.

You get a tomato. Tomato? Tomahto? Let's call the whole thing off. All right, so it's the most famous tomato in the world, Alain Passard's brainy, witty exposition that the big red globe is a fruit, after all. It's a tomato that rated a long piece in *The New Yorker*. How many tomatoes get written up in *The New Yorker*? This is a star tomato. It's very caramelly, stuffed with twelve ingredients: cloves, pistachios, orange zest, ginger, star anise, whatever. It takes hours and hours to cook. It takes seconds to eat. It's delicious, all right, but no more delicious than a perfect ripe garden tomato, with some salt, pepper, and balsamic vinegar. Then again, is Nicole Kidman any more beautiful than so many of the women you see on Bondi Beach in Sydney? But she's a star. And this tomato is a star. And there you have it.

When you're paying the bill and figuring out how to mortgage your house to pay for this trip, the real star, Monsieur Passard, emeges from the kitchen. He's vegan-thin and at fifty still looks like a choirboy, curly blond hair, fair blue eyes, dimples, jeans, and polka-dotted Converse sneakers. He seems chummy with most of the diners. Fellow château owners? But he greets each table and is as modest as a choirboy in accepting the effusive encomia. Come to London, come to New York, come to Dallas, they all beseech him. But, to Passard's credit, he's no franchiser, no Vegas guy. Opening a small vegetable boutique at the food hall of the Galleries Lafayette department store is as entrepreneurial as he gets. And you have to love any chef who can come up with Passard's great line about why he turned off meat and on to vegetables. "I couldn't keep having a creative relationship with a corpse." No wonder Woody Allen eats here. ★ ★ ★ ★ ★ ★ ★ ★

Voltaire
Voltaire Died Here

If you're ready for some *real* French food, arguably the best—and indisputably the best-peopled—bistro in Paris is in a historic building directly across the Seine from the Louvre. Not only did Voltaire die in the apartment above the restaurant in 1778, but during World War II, the restaurant's cellar was a center and hotbed of resistance activity. So this is one bistro with two important historical plaques above its door. The place is so modest that it has a door that's almost impossible to see. All you do see is an unprepossessing little bar-café, a place for a quick Pastis or a ham sandwich with the shopkeepers of the neighborhood. Little would you suspect that behind the bar is a beautiful, elegant, tiny wood-and-leather dining room, a French take on an English club. A bust of the philosopher stands in a place of honor. There are barely fifteen tables; it's as tiny as Ami Louis, but far quieter, more discreet. If you're not famous, it's the perfect place to have an affair. But because you're not famous, you're probably not going to get in, not on an impulse.

Voltaire, romantic and cozy, is a couple's place. Liz and Dick, Sartre and Simone, the Duke and Duchess of W, Dodi and Di. And not just dead couples. It's also a neighborhood spot, with neighbors like Mick Jagger and Ambassador Pamela Harriman, who adored popping in for dinner. The École des Beaux Arts is around the corner, and so the Voltaire is a great favorite of the big art dealers. Leo Castelli took most of his meals in Paris here. Tom Hanks was on the Voltaire meal plan while filming *The Da Vinci Code* across the way. Jack Nicholson is a regular. So is mogul Sherry Lansing, and her husband William *(Exorcist)* Friedkin, who was married to French national treasure Jeanne Moreau, who had come here with her boyfriend Pierre Cardin. And on and on, six degrees of Kevin Bacon, who, strangely, is *not* a regular.

A key to the Voltaire's appeal is its fabulous, hand-stenciled menu. It changes every day, but it's a compendium of France's greatest hits. A recitation of the day's specials could make lovers of us all: *terrine de chevreuil, omelette au fromage, 6 Belons, 12 escargots, turbot poche hollandaise, coquilles St. Jacques poêlées aux échalotes, filet de boeuf Béarnaise, boudin noir grille, cerises fraiches pochees pétales de roses.* . . . If Voltaire had had his last supper here, it would have been to die for. However, for all the enticing classics on the menu, most of the regulars seem to have the same meal: *potage aux legumes,* a lusty vegetable puree; *poussin roti à l'estragon,* tarragon chicken, with a side of what most agree are the best *pommes frites* in the city of fries; and *framboises, glace vanille,* raspberries with vanilla ice cream. There are seductive wines and champagnes, ports and cognacs, perfect for the affair you can never have, so love the one you're with.

One of the reasons the celebs are so loyal to the Voltaire is that there is no one more accommodating and discreet than the Picot family, from Berry, near Tours in châteaux country, who have owned the place for the last seventy years. After all, they were resistance heroes, so they know discretion like Alain Passard knows vegetables. The current patriarch, Jacques Picot, in his seventies but with the energy of a crack-of-dawn farmer, is as unpretentious as his patrons are grand. He wears a blue apron, washes the dishes himself, and spryly pops up and down to the famed wine cellar, where all the bravery took place in the dark days of the German occupation. His son Antoine, as elegant and refined as dad is robust and lusty, is a product of the best hotel schools in France and the Monaco kitchens of Alain Ducasse. But there's no froufrou at Voltaire, just the Picots and three old-school waiters, a great kitchen and a room of legends. What else is there? ★ ★ ★ ★ ★ ★ ★ ★ ★ ★ ★ ★ ★ ★

Le Relais Plaza
Grand Hotel

8TH ARRONDISSEMENT

Paris is one of the few cities (London and Bangkok, too) where you can eat as well in hotels as you can outside of them. No grand hotels are grander, or have more illustrious histories, than the Ritz, the Crillon, the George V, the Bristol, the Meurice; and few hotel restaurants anywhere are as lavish or luxurious. The *grandpère*, however, of the over-the-top luxe caravansary is the Plaza Athenée, on the Avenue Montaigne, which Christian Dior put on the fashion map in the 1950s and which now vies with the Rue St.-Honoré as Paris's most elegant thoroughfare of conspicuous consumption. Lately, however, that consumption is becoming a little too conspicuous. Ferraris with Qatar plates and Humvees with PLO stickers jam the porte cocheres. Rich Arab playboys smoking the best Havana cigars stink up the Aubusson tapestries in the lobby, while towering blond Ukrainian call girls take up all the antique couches. The hotels seem so overdone, so luxe, with enough winter flowers to give you vernal catarrh, that they seem like Dubai-based imitations of the real thing, the thing that they are, or used to be. Of course, there's a reason for the Persian Gulf breezes blowing through these hallowed halls where Roosevelt and Churchill used to tread. The Ritz is owned, famously, by Egypt's Mohammed al-Fayed, the George V by Arabia's Sheikh al Walid bin Talal, who has huge WELCOME signs in Arabic engraved into the hotel pediment, just so you don't forget who's hosting here. And both the Meurice and the Plaza Athenée are owned by the Sultan of Brunei. If you've got it, flaunt it, seems to be the territorial imperative, as the Muslim presence in France is being felt at both the bottom and the top of the social pyramid.

For all the flash and cash, the art nouveau masterpiece Plaza Athenée, which opened in 1911, is flat-out the most fun, the most self-mocking, of this otherwise somber, pompous, money-talks lot. Take the Bar Montaigne. Of course, it can't compare historically with Hemingway's beloved Rue Cambon bar at the Ritz, but it's not a waxworks, either. Designed by Patrick Jouin, a disciple of Philippe Starck, the Bar Montaigne looks like a giant igloo, with a huge bar seemingly sculpted out of a cake of ice. When you put your glass down the bar lights up. There's a vast wall safe of rare cognacs, and an equally vast choice of stogies. Heating the igloo up are lots of those towering Ukrainian "models" who here actually turn out to be Tunisians with great plastic surgery. It's more louche than anything in Las Vegas, and a lot more fun. This was Mata Hari's hotel, and the intrigues are thicker than ever.

But what about the food? You half expect to find a branch of Chez Omar, but what you get is a stop-at-nothing three-star Alain Ducasse extravaganza. About a third of the diners are women in burnooses eating in gaggles. Gigolo alert! Much more fun can be had at the hotel's "casual" Relais Plaza, a landmark deco room that opened in 1936. With the rise of Dior and the New Look, the Relais became the canteen of the designer set. It has never since lost its cachet. That Yves St. Laurent dines here, often alone, every Sunday night speaks volumes as to the Relais's position in the Paris firmament. The Plaza Athenée was the location for that final *Sex and the City* episode wherein Big proposes to Carrie. It's that kind of place, one for grand gestures and big moments, and the Relais is the best part of the hotel. It's a total classic, the haute Paris of Cole Porter songs and Fred Astaire films, the Paris of rich, sophisticated Americans abroad, like the Fitzgeralds and their friends the Murphys. If living well is the best revenge, you can still come to the Relais, just like in the good old days, and get yours.

The blast from the past begins the minute you enter the room, which feels exactly like a 1930s ocean liner, all sleek woods and soaring columns and engravings of elongated nymphs and zodiac symbols. "You're the Top" is being tinkled on the ivories by a refugee from "Shall We Dance?" The manager, the Bavarian Werner Küchler, is straight out of central casting, the smoothest, slickest restaurant man in Paris, a one-man exploder of the myth that Germans have no charm. If you enter the Relais through the hotel, there's a "walk of fame" with black-and-whites of the dashing blond Küchler (a ringer for Marlon Brando as the tragic Nazi in *The Young Lions*) embracing virtually every great person on earth over the last three decades while he's ruled this roost. And, oh, the women—Kennedy, Kelly, Callas, Gardner, Bacall, Dunaway, Dietrich, Adjani, Ardant, Deneuve, Loren, Seberg, Sagan. This is murderers' row, the Mount Olympus of pulchritude, talent, and style.

But what can the Relais do for an encore? The clientele here is totally chic, Neuilly BCBG *(bon chic, bon genre)* types, Bev Hills trophy wives, Greenwich preppies, Park Avenue and Park Lane Masters of the Universe, French tycoons like Arnault and Pinault (ten points to anyone who can tell them apart), Gstaad skiers in for shopping, elegant Lebanese who'd pass for St. Tropez except for the worry beads. Every table has a story. There's an aging Chinese dragon lady with a dead ringer for Leonardo DiCaprio caressing her endless red fingernails. There's an ancient Gloria Swanson type cuddling chic to chic with a Gwyneth Paltrow lookalike dripping in diamonds from Harry Winston next door. There are lots of stunning, *GQ*-meets-*Vogue* perfect couples that you know will finish this enchanted evening on the floor at Castel.

The service is by model-level waitresses sans attitude, resplendent in designer farm-girl white uniforms, amazingly efficient for being so radiantly pretty. Mr. Everywhere, Herr Küchler, runs the tightest of ships. The Relais kitchen, helmed by a protégé of Ducasse down the hall, is most famous for its *escalope viennoise* (Wiener schnitzel to Küchler) and its *oeufs benedictine* (eggs Benedict to us Yanks), evocative of a Manhattan Upper East Side haunt, like Mortimer's of yore: simple clubby food, but the execution here is French at its best. Lobster salad, spit-roasted veal, truffle risotto, sole meunière, the menu is a Trans-Europe Express of continental delicacies, all state-of-the-art. The kitchen is particularly skilled at dessert, having won the sugar

Olympics for best pastry in the world, something called an "Oreade," which is *not* an Oreo for billionaires but a magnificent chocolate mousse–raspberry concoction wrapped in edible gold leaf. If French women don't get fat, one way they do is by eating at the Relais. A Küchler kookbook (which he's too discreet to write, of course) would be the ultimate regime of the rich and famous. ★

Costes
Haute Snobisme

1ST ARRONDISSEMENT

What good is a visit to Paris unless you're made to feel inadequate? To be ridiculed for your best Wellesley French, trashed as a fashion victim by a snotty store clerk, intimidated by people far more glamorous than you ever dreamed of being, or exiled to Siberia by some haughty captain who can't stop reminding you that you're not in Kansas anymore, but that you *should be*. That's the good old Paris, but it's not the Paris of today. Now the boutiques are desperate for your business, the Arabs who have taken over the grand hotels are wonderful hosts who have an almost southern sense of hospitality, and the Siberia thing was really an invention of the supersnob French restaurants of Manhattan, which felt they had to overcompensate in hauteur what they lacked in ingredients and technique.

Still, if you somehow *need* insecurity to keep you on your toes, hie yourself to the Hotel Costes on the Rue St.-Honoré, next to the Place Vendôme, which is the red-hot center of Paris cool. The Costes is the local of the top models, the top photographers, the top designers, and, most important, the top publicists, who create the South Sea Bubble that is Fashion, the grand illusion that makes us long for what we cannot have and what we can never be, and spend, spend, spend, trying to achieve this Impossible Dream. The Costes is named for its owners, three brothers and one sister from the very provincial province of Auvergne, country kids who have taken Paris by storm and become its ultimate arbiters of status and style, at least where hospitality is concerned.

The Costes used to be the down-at-the heels Hôtel de France et Choiseul, a favorite of baby-boom Ivy League and Seven Sisters types who in the 1960s and 1970s liked the idea of sleeping across from the Ritz for under ten dollars a night. Enter the Costes in 1996 and their newly anointed designer Jacques Garcia, whose simply red, lush, antique- and Buddha-statue-filled interiors are as maximal as the Costes's original discovery, Philippe Starck, were minimal. They call Garcia's decor Napoleon III, but it's more like Napoleon on acid, or Napoleon goes to a New Orleans–style bordello in Tokyo with Madonna. But just as with Starck in the 1980s, *tout* Paris loved it, followed, inevitably, by *tout le monde*. If the Costes build it, they will come, and indeed they did.

The intimidation, however, is part of the Costes charm. If you can call fear and loathing charming. It begins on the hotel's Web site, which basically provides riddles rather than informs. Want to sleep here? Better know somebody. Want to eat here? Better be gorgeous. Entering the hotel, whose dining rooms and lounges take up the entire first floor, surrounding a central courtyard, which is a *plein air* delight in clement weather, you are intercepted by a phalanx of six-foot Amazons in black who gloweringly tell you the empty rooms are "fully booked." If you have been lucky enough to be able to make a reservation, they let you stand around for about half an hour waiting for your table, as they break into huge smiles and whisk in "the chosen," who often arrive with big dogs that are virtual fashion accessories. You will never see taller, thinner, younger, chic-er people on the planet, and your own self-esteem will never be lower.

If they ever deign to seat you, you may end up in your own cozy little four-table warren. It may have the cool Jacques Garcia look, all right, but you may be segregated with other uncool outsiders like yourself, sort of like the fraternity rush party in the opening scene in *Animal House,* in which the blind, the lame, the halt, the fat, and the Pakistanis were all led to the losers' corner "to meet some great guys you'll really like." To the Costes's credit, they don't have two kitchens, one microwaving Birds Eye for the rubes from Omaha, the other steaming live fish for the Perfect Ones. No, there's one kitchen, one menu, and the kind of simple "model food" that could make us all a size zero.

The Costes fare, which involves lots of vegetables, is not intellectualized Arpège haute cuisine, but more health-store-counter fare: carrot juice, endive salad, steamed vegetables, string beans in olive oil, vegetable soup *"pour francois girbaud,"* as the menu for this fashion café says. But you can also get a great club sandwich, a chicken curry, sweet-and-sour shrimp, a langoustine risotto, a perfect egg-white omelette *fines herbes*—sort of like the Relais Plaza, but with less fanfare, and far surlier service. And for kids and those postbulimic runway stars who actually need to *gain* weight, Costes wittily offers a fattening option, its "menu *'lou': 'pas pour les grands'"* of a hamburger, French fries with ketchup *and* mashed potatoes, followed by a huge slice of "gâteau au chocolat." Like Burger King, Costes lets you have it your way, if they only let you in.

The king of the Costes empire is Gilbert Costes, who, if he didn't own the joint, the model-gatekeepers might not even let in. In his fifties, rumpled, Gap-clad, with the look of a weary prizefighter, Gilbert looks anything but chic. He doesn't have to try. He and his older brother came to Paris in the early 1970s to work as waiters at Lasserre, the then darling of the Hollywood set, with its great gimmick roof that opened with every fleeting ray of sun and closed with every frequent downpour. Costes barely remembers the stars he served; the biggest impression was made by the local politicians, artists, writers—Pompidou, Dalí, Malraux. The two brothers left Lasserre and bought their first café, the Tabac D'Orléans in Montparnasse, in 1975. By 1984, two more siblings had arrived from the outland, and they made their big breakthrough, the stark, Starck-designed Café Costes off the Rue St. Denis in the *sentier,* the largely Jewish garment district.

Café Costes was in the right place at the right time. The neighborhood, next to the demolished Les Halles markets and adjacent to what had been the biggest streetwalker area in Paris when Shirley MacLaine starred in *Irma la Douce,* was gentrifying. The Pompidou Centre had just gone up, and the artists were flocking in. Café Costes became their local, and, as in New York's SoHo and Tribeca, where artists trod, trend would follow. In 1986, the brothers opened another Starck place, the Café Beaubourg, right across from the museum, to accommodate the overflow. "We became the new Flore and Deux Magots," Costes says proudly, referring to the adjacent Left Bank literary cafés that reigned for decades as the center of intellectual life in a city where *intellectual* is not a dirty word but the quintessence of cool. "We just want people to be comfortable, and we're open to new ideas, new fashions" is all Costes will say about his innkeeping philosophy. What about the snobbery, the elitism, the looksism? Costes laughs it all off. "We don't seek publicity. It seeks us."

The Costes went on to get the vaunted commission to open the first restaurant in the Louvre, the always jammed Café Marly. And then they built this hotel, which has become the hipsters' Ritz. Gilbert knows how influential he is on such trendsetters as Ian Schrager, André Balazs, even Alain Ducasse, whose chain of Spoons was inspired by the Costes. The new Miami Beach seems like an homage to the Costes style, but Gilbert has resisted endless offers to put his own mark there. "Too seasonal," he says, dismissing Florida. "Too expensive," London. "Too far," New York. Gilbert Costes is a country boy in the big city, *his* city now, and he doesn't like being too far from the roost he clearly rules. ★ ★ ★ ★ ★ ★

How the Mighty Have Fallen: Maxim's

For most of the twentieth century, Maxim's and La Tour d'Argent reigned as the two most famous restaurants in the world. They both had three *Michelin* stars, when that meant the world in gastronomy. (Only two other Parisian restaurants had three stars in the early 1950s, when the Americans came back to France: Laperouse and Café de Paris. The former still exists, in oft changed hands, the latter long gone.) The Tour had its duck, but Maxim's had its Billi-Bi (cream of mussel soup) and sole Albert (more cream, lots of vermouth). The Tour may have had the best view, but as a sheer institution Maxim's was even grander. After all, it is the only restaurant to have a classic operetta written about it, Franz Lehár's cancan-flaunting *The Merry Widow*. It was the more beautiful, and its art nouveau decor—curved mahogany doors, stained-glass ceiling, pre-Raphaelite murals of gamboling naked nymphs (which inspired New York's Café des Artistes, among many others)—was a national landmark. Maxim's was more expensive. And it was far, far more intimidating, having invented the concept of power seating. As Roger Viard, Maxim's grandest of maître d's, sneered to *The New York Times* in 1979, "It's normal that if we don't know you, you don't get a good table." This king of restaurants was the restaurant of kings, of Farouk, of Umberto, of Rainier, of the Aga Khan, of the Shah. It was the restaurant of Getty, Onassis, the Windsors, royalty, aristocracy, plutocracy. Even Hollywood stars got a little nervous coming here. After all, they were merely employees of the studios. Maxim's was more for their bosses, but even the Goldwyns and the Mayers watched their step across the nouveau threshold. For all its beauty, history, and cuisine, the Fear Factor was Maxim's most powerful weapon.

But now Maxim's has no stars. It's not even in *Michelin*. Or Frommer's or Fodor's, for that matter. Everybody went there; nobody goes there. Nobody except fearless Russian billionaire types who don't read guidebooks or newspapers or anything, the types who are buying all the grand villas on the Riviera, the big yachts on Sardinia, the Gulfstreams. They want the best that money can buy, the big names, and Maxim's has, or at least had, the biggest name in restaurant-dom. What could have possibly happened?

The answer is Pierre Cardin. In the late 1970s Cardin was the most power-ful designer in the world. He was selling over a billion dollars' worth of franchised goods a year, in nearly a hundred countries. Cardin—not Chevalier, not de Gaulle, not Peugeot, not Chanel—was the most famous name in France. The only name Cardin himself worshipped more than his own was Maxim's, which he saw as the great emblem of France, at least *la Belle France.* Maxim's was up for grabs, and the octopus Cardin wanted to grab it.

One of the reasons Cardin may have identified so strongly with Maxim's is that, for all their Frenchness, they both had Italian roots. Born in Venice in 1922, the son of a wine seller, Cardin soon moved with his family to Avignon. He had dreams of being an actor, of kicking up his heels at posttheater midnight suppers at Maxim's. But the hand that life dealt him made Cardin a tailor's apprentice in Vichy during World War II. He also learned accounting during the war, working in the business office of the Red Cross. The fusion of sewing and business skills resulted in an empire, as Cardin became known as the Napoleon of licensors.

Maxim's was founded in 1893 as an ice cream parlor right off the Place de la Concorde, the dramatic scene of revolutionary beheadings, by a now forgotten Italian immigrant, who sold it to a Frenchman named Maxime Gaillard. He turned it into a bistro, and following the Anglophilia of England's then imperial heyday, Gaillard dropped the *e* from his first name and added the English apostrophe, to make the enterprise seem that much chummier. He redecorated his bistro in 1899, for the upcoming 1900 World's Fair, the one for which the Eiffel Tower was built. Neither the tower nor Maxim's has been altered since.

Until around 1930, Maxim's was as much an elegant brothel as a great res-taurant. It was known as the place to take or find a mistress, but never a wife. This was the age of the courtesan, the *grande horizontale,* and Maxim's was the place to find her. Maxime died, and in 1932 the new owner, the Vaudable family, gave the place what was called by one sniffy aristocrat "a moral face-lift," and hired the most arrogant waiter in Paris dining history to keep the joint in order and make it safe for wives. This was Albert (as in "sole"), and he became the first "star" restaurant personage. During World War II, the Germans ousted the Vaudables and Albert, and installed their man Otto Horcher in what would become the Nazis' favorite Paris haunt. Horcher, who let Vaudable steal thousands of bottles of his own wine, ended up in Madrid after the war, and founded Horcher's, still the grandest Maxim's-style restaurant in that city of paella and suckling pig.

With Liberation, the Vaudables got their restaurant back, and Maxim's had a new golden age, an age of jet-set Croesus-rich sybarites, led by Onassis with first Callas and then Jackie. Onassis sat in the same red plush left-corner banquette in the main room every night he was in Paris, which of course became *the* place to sit (and the right side of the room became Siberia). At lunch, however, the A-tables were in the narrow entrance hall known as "the Omnibus," because of its resemblance to a motorized streetcar. The new captain, Viard, became the preeminent social arbiter in the city; where you sat was who you were, and international society cowed to his whims. "You must preserve a certain elegance," Viard insisted. To wit, he established black-tie Friday evenings, with an orchestra and strolling violinists and cheek-to-cheek dancing, which were the hottest ticket in all Paris. Few Americans were welcome. "Americans wear practically anything," Viard once complained. "It's shocking."

Like Cardin, the Vaudables began taking their show on the road. Tokyo, which loves a famous name like nowhere else, was a smash. Chicago, a disaster. Mexico City, a toss-up. Maxim's got the catering franchise at Orly Airport, and later established a beachhead at the new Charles de Gaulle, as well as at the airports in Lyon and Marseilles. But by 1977, Louis Vaudable was seventy-seven, and getting tired. Enter Cardin. First he became partners with the Vaudables. But after four years he spent a reported $20 million and bought them out, or swallowed them up, depending on how you look at it. Napoleon did not have partners. To celebrate, Cardin sponsored a gala exhibition "La Belle Epoque" *("La Belle Epoque, c'est Maxim's,"* Cardin said) and opening ball at New York's Metropolitan Museum, welcoming a guest list of eight hundred, many of them jet-set aspirants of Fifth and Park whom captain Viard had heretofore exiled to Siberia.

Cardin envisaged a global chain of Maxim's—New York, London, Brussels, Beijing, Rio, just for starters. He wanted Maxim's hotels, with a prototype planned for Palm Springs and another in New York, at the old Gotham (now Peninsula). He wanted Maxim's tableware, chocolates, peanuts, perfumes, flowers, a chain of elegant fast-food places called Minim's. Everything was a disaster. Haute cuisine did not travel well, and the restaurants were panned everywhere. Furthermore, a Californianization of dining was sweeping the world—down with cream sauces, down with ties, black and blue, down with stuffiness—and Maxim's got caught in the backlash against formality. All the restaurants failed and closed, as did the hotels. Cardin overestimated the power of the brand. The world knew *his* name, which had trickled down to supermarkets in Bogotá and Manila, but only a tiny elite knew Maxim's—enough to be snobbish with, but not to make a fortune on. Even the French turned on their icon, the cruelest indignity being *Michelin*'s stripping Maxim's of its stars. Now the emperor truly had no clothes.

For both Cardin and Maxim's, there has been a long slide down, although Cardin, now in his mideighties, is still a billionaire. And Maxim's is still patronized by billionaires, albeit of a different, less social ilk than Getty and Gulbenkian. There's no bar at Maxim's wherein to go and have a drink, but you can schedule a tour on Saturday afternoons. It's not black-tie Fridays, but they don't exist anymore. *Sic transit omnibus.* ★ ★ ★ ★ ★

Le Stresa
and Le Cherche Midi
Romanesque

8TH and 6TH ARRONDISSEMENTS

When it really comes down to it, it often seems as if the French prefer eating Italian to eating French. At least the famous ones. No restaurant in Paris, or perhaps anywhere else, has a higher celebrity-to-table ratio, not even the tiny Voltaire or Ami Louis, than Le Stresa, right behind the Plaza Athénée. Although it's named for a town in northern Italy on Lago di Maggiore, there is nothing even vaguely Piemontese about the place, which originally opened in 1951 but in 1975 was sold to the five Faiola brothers from Sperlonga, on the coast between Rome and Naples. What they run is a perfect small-town trattoria, totally unpretentious, with delicious homemade grandma food, that has caught the fancy of the most demanding clientele.

It took the Faiolas ten years of hard labor before Stresa became famous, but since 1986, in the world of big-time food, the Faiola boys are made men. Even Italians love the place, bold-face Italians like Agnelli, Mastroianni, Zeffirelli, Bertolucci, and American goodfellas like De Niro, DiCaprio, Scorsese, Tarantino. The big designers, Italian and other, all love it: Armani, Valentino, Versace, Ferre, Dolce and Gabbana, not to mention Givenchy, Lagerfeld, Klein, Ford, McQueen, de la Renta, and the big models like Naomi, Cindy, Gisele, Elle, Kate. And the big artists: Schnabel, Bleckner, Koons. All the stars, from Rock Hudson to Hugh Grant, from Audrey Hepburn to

Angelina Jolie. The rockers Bono, Elton, Mick. The politicians Berlusconi, Chirac. The moguls Rothschild, Redstone, Trump, Arnault, Pinault. The highest compliment of all is the patronage of star chefs: Robuchon, Bocuse, Ducasse, Verge, Gagnaire, Senderens. They all eat here. There are no bad tables, and the only sad part of it is that the place is so small that there may be no room for you.

The room is a classic wood-paneled rectangle, with red leather banquettes and tiny wooden chairs (no fatties here). The abstract art on the walls was donated by those great French foodie-artists Cesar and Arman, and the big-scale model Ferrari was a gift of a grand prix racer friend of the brothers, who are as warm and down-home as if they'd never left little Sperlonga and never saw a star. The atmosphere is very evocative of the great 1950s gangster film *Le Cercle Rouge,* which was a grand tour of 1950s Paris by night, although you never see gangsters here.

Like most exclusive Paris restaurants, Stresa is closed on weekends, when its clientele is ostensibly away at their châteaux. Lunch is even more of a power play than dinner, so the evening may be the best time to worm your way in. Whenever you go, the Faiolas will treat you royally. What to eat? Anything you'd order in Rome. They import the best prosciutto, the ripest melons. The lasagne is hot, meaty, cheesy, and crusty; grandmother would be proud. If you want a name pasta, the Delon is simply a *checca* variant: raw ripe tomatoes, olive oil, mozzarella cubes. Belmondo is spicier: tomato sauce, olives, peperoncini. Better than all is the risotto primavera, an all-veggie rice dish that Alain Passard would admire and that is even better than the classic of the genre at Harry's Bar in Venice. The most-ordered dish on the menu is the low-cal grilled scampi, and there's a huge dessert business in sorbets and wild strawberries. Wines are grand but nonessential. The most-ordered drink here is Coke Lite (the Euro euphemism for Diet).

With all the legends here, it's surprising that there have been no reports of catfights over tables, thrown plates between rivals, drunken high jinks. The brothers are blessed peacemakers who've done their homework and know exactly who's who, and who to separate. There's a quiet back room, which some of the biggest stars, from Cary Grant in days gone by to Tom Cruise to Karl Lagerfeld, when he's feeling fat, actually prefer. Whatever seat they give you, seize it with gratitude, as you take the break from haute cuisine that for most of Stresa's clientele has become a permanent vacation.

To call Le Cherche Midi the poor man's Le Stresa would be selling it very short. A more accurate description would be the "casual" Stresa. Not that Stresa is formal, but it is a power spot, in a power neighborhood. Cherche Midi is *the* neighborhood trattoria for the Left Bank. It has a wildly misleading French name, after its street, one of the great boutique streets of Paris, particularly for shoe fetishists. Its owner, Nello di Meo, is an Italian who grew up in France but never lost his Roman epicurean roots. He's one of the most elegant of restaurateurs, mainly because his restaurant is his hobby. Di Meo's day job is his highly prestigious modern art gallery on the Rue Jacob, across from the École des Beaux Arts. Le Cherche Midi, which di Meo, a lapsed lawyer, started in 1978, is the gallerist's labor of love, and it shows. The food is possibly even better than Stresa's, and the crowd a little less intense, perhaps, but equally decorative. Plus Cherche Midi is open all weekend, for those who stay away from their châteaux, and even those stragglers who happen to be château-less, at least for the moment.

Cherche Midi is tiny—ten tables inside, three outside under the awning for the diehard sidewalk crowd, in denial over the Paris weather. There is a joke of a smoking/no-smoking division, which amounts to a two-foot corridor dividing the room. The French all smoke, and most others do as well. There seems to be a direct correlation here between glamour and nicotine. The room has green banquettes, yellow walls, ceiling fans. The waiters, all Italians, are in jeans. There's a tiny bar, with an alluring marinated vegetable antipasto, just like in Italy, and a giant mortadella, also just like home. Take the mortadella. It's sublime, as delicate as foie gras, and eat it with the country bread from Poujauran, the best bakery in the city. Di Meo is a stickler for provenance: he gets the best bread, best hams and sausages, best cheeses, best sorbets and ice creams from Berthillon on the Île St. Louis. You could make a stellar meal on the outsourcing alone. But the kitchen is fine, too, turning out three different pastas and three different main courses every day. There's a gutsy, down-on-the-farm cheese ravioli with a heady tomato sauce, and a definitive veal Milanese, perfectly fried and topped with baby arugula and Passardian tomatoes. The fish, which Di Meo buys at the fish market every day (part of his labor of love), is the freshest, simply grilled and lightly cooked.

Cherche Midi is the platonic ideal of a little trattoria in Parioli, where the rich people live in Rome. And because it's in Paris, you have the best of both worlds. It's also very Upper East Side, like Sette Mezzo, with a lot of the same faces, although here the food is literally and figuratively far closer to home. The restaurant is understandably a great favorite of Americans, one of whom is that great trendsetter John Fairchild, of *Women's Wear Daily*, and that other demographic of trend barometry, the heads of all the big modeling agencies. Hence the models are here, and all else will thus follow. From the glory days of Maxim's in the Belle Epoque, beautiful women have been the flypaper that made a restaurant hot, and nothing has changed ever since. Even when they're with their chic, blond, streaked, sleek aristocrat wives, and their spaniels and Great Danes, the dashing BCBG French prepsters in their Lacostes and their Tod's can't keep their eyes from roaming the perpetual *défilé* that is the Cherche Midi. *Cherchez la femme! L'amour toujours.* This is Paris when it sizzles, so put feminism aside and enjoy the show. ★ ★ ★ ★ ★ ★

The Co

ntinent

Kronenhalle
Clockwork

It's Michael Chow's favorite restaurant. And David Tang's. And Mark Birley's. In fact, if you ask most restaurant titans where they'd like to have their last supper, you would think they would nominate somewhere preheavenly, like La Tour d'Argent, or somewhere otherworldly, like El Bulli. But no. Most hospitality pros, the ones who have been to the Mountain and have seen the Other Side, these arbiters would sigh and say Zurich's Kronenhalle, a temple of simplicity that may well be the most classic, most gratifying, most perfectly run restaurant in the world. Kronenhalle is pure clockwork, but, then again, isn't that what Switzerland is all about?

You may not think of Zurich as a food town, but it is. It's a money town, and money talks. All those gnomes want quality, and they get it, big time. Rodeo Drive, Bond Street, Via Monte Napoleone, none are grander shopping venues than Zurich's Banhofstrasse. A trilingual city, Zurich has first-rate French, Italian, and German restaurants. It has perhaps Europe's most sublime, Old World hotel, the Baur au Lac, which has been in the same family for centuries. And it has the Kronenhalle. Many savvy travelers check in to the Baur and take all their meals at the Kronenhalle, just a ten-minute walk down the edge of the lake, with the snow-peaked Alps shimmering in the distance. Talk about heaven.

As you walk uphill from the lake, you might miss the restaurant entirely, as there is no sign outside, only some ancient lanterns hanging from the mouths of gargoyles, topped with golden crowns. There are three possible entrances, one to the bar, another leading upstairs, and, the least obvious, the door nearest to the lake; this third door leads to the soaring two-story main dining room. You feel as if you've stumbled into a private banquet at a castle in another century. There is a rush of warmth, of fabulous smells, of food, of perfume, of money, of color, of elegance. Everyone you see is beautiful, splendidly dressed and coiffed, rich, rich, rich. Giant roasts are being carved, champagne corks popped. There are coats of arms around the pediment of the room, which turn out to be the insignia not of the regal families on the floor, but of the guilds of Zurich: butchers, bakers, candlestick makers, quite literally. And there is art, great art: Picassos, Mirós, Bonnards, Kandinskys, Chagalls. Art like you've never seen in a restaurant before.

A black-suited captain greets you and takes your coat, and, Zurich being Zurich, where the only bad thing is the weather, your umbrella. He puts them in a giant coatrack in the center of the room, festooned with guilt-less minks from the fearless clientele (no thieves in Zurich). You think you're going to be invited to join this swell party, but you're wrong. The captain will most likely send you upstairs, or to a lower-ceilinged anteroom. Wherever you go, the atmosphere will be similarly baronial, clubby, dark paneling, creamy red leather seats, museum art, and beautiful people. But the main hall of the Kronenhalle is for the *crème* of Zurich society, and unless you go back to Charlemagne, try not to feel too left out. Recently, George Bush (the original one) and the Aga Khan sat in the anteroom, gorging on bratwurst and drinking beer, and having the time of their life. You will, too.

The menu is tiny, unadorned, unpoetic: salmon, herring, caviar (if you must) to start, a few veal dishes, steaks, rabbit, game, two or three fish. There's no hype, no food lust engendered by the *carte*. So ignore it, have a draft Löwenbräu or a Pilsner Urquell or some house Burgundy (the house has a long history with Burgundy, so the house wine is great), and watch what everybody else is having. The food lust will quickly set in. Giant steaks, T-bones, that look even better than Peter Luger's, come out with copper pans full of vegetables you won't see in Brooklyn. A waiter with a trolley is carving a carcass of something divine, something alien. What is it? you ask. Goat. But it's not on the menu, you sputter. Don't ask. Nothing's on the menu, but everything is right here. There's the biggest veal Milanese you've ever seen, enough for two plates. But the most beautiful dish of all, the Kronenhalle signature, is the bratwurst, the biggest and best bratwurst in all sausagedom. Why this brat is different from all other brats is that it comes from the house's master *metzger* (butcher) in St. Gall, which is to bratwurst what Strasbourg is to foie gras; and that, unlike other brats, which are a blend of pork and veal, this one is all veal. It's white and smooth on the inside, grilled brown and snappy on the outside, served with an onion marmalade and *rosti,* the golden buttery Swiss potato cake that, like the brat, is crisp without, melting within, the Matterhorn of potato dishes. That's what's great about the Kronenhalle. Whatever it serves is the best that dish can ever be.

Inspired, you dive in. You start with the raw herring, which the Kronenhalle imports from Holland in barrels, then cures in olive oil to get rid of any brininess. You're a little trepidatious, like with sushi the first time, but one taste of the fish and you're hooked. It's as pure as a fine oyster, spiced up with finely chopped apple and onion; perfect appetizer that it is, it only makes you hungrier for what's to come. You see someone having a cucumber salad, and you go for that, and it takes cucumbers to a new dimension. There's only a hint of dill in the vinaigrette, a note that elsewhere is invariably overplayed; here it's a symphony. Then the bratwurst arrives and exceeds all the hype, as does the chocolate mousse in the capital of chocolate, lighter than air, sweet, but not too sweet, addictive. You want more and more, and all you can do is make a reservation to come back the next day, which is very common among first-timers here.

Before you leave you are greeted by a Shelley Winters look-alike, a stylishly dressed-up one, who has been working the various rooms and somehow keeping the supposedly dour burgher-tycoons in stitches. This is the *patronne,* Vreni Gerhartz, the granddaughter of the family that has owned the

Kronenhalle since 1925, and she is the embodiment of gemütlichkeit. She won't let you go, and besides, who wants to leave the Kronenhalle, ever. She gives you a tour of the art, Picasso's self-portrait, talks about getting Chagall drunk over his protective wife's objections, self-deprecates about being a model for her pal Botero, who actually has a skinny wife.

Vreni jokes about everything. Her name comes from the Egyptian word meaning "one who consoles you." "It's the most common name in Switzerland," she says. "Every milk cow is called Vreni." She points out a few framed photos: Thomas Mann, James Joyce, who was the only patron the restaurant ever comp'ed. "Otherwise he would have starved. Poor man didn't have a penny." She recounts Bill Gates's recent visit, looking like a poor student in a ratty pullover, albeit one who devoured a whole saddle of veal. Einstein used to conduct after-class seminars here, and Albert Schweitzer was a regular. But Lenin, who drank across the street at the Odeon Bar, never crossed the threshold.

Vreni reads you some of the mottos of the guilds, like this from the bakers: "Bad times are for a man when he suffers from hunger, but he is a peaceful man if he has his daily bread." She holds up the *buerli,* or peasant roll, that you have eaten far too many of, and tells you of the centuries-old bakery that has been supplying them. The Kronenhalle is all about tradition, yet Vreni realizes that she may be the end of a great line. When her grandparents, the Zumstegs, took over the "K" in 1925, it was on hard times. It had originally been founded in 1797, as the restaurant of the Hotel Golden Crowne, and after a century of prosperity, it was running out of steam. But her grandmother Hilda—whose floor-to-ceiling portrait by Verlin dominates a wall and evokes a John Singer Sargent—and her uncle Gustave were sticklers for tradition, and they wouldn't let go. For Gustave, the place was a hobby. He lived mostly in Paris, where he had made a fortune in the silk trade and was a major art collector. "He paid for every one of these paintings," Vreni says, exploding the myth that the starving artists traded their canvases for bratwurst. She introduces you to the chef, a Paul Bunyan type who harks back to a golden age when giants ruled the stoves. "He was in the pope's guard at the Vatican," Vreni confides, but he preferred to cook.

Vreni wanted to go to medical school, but her grandmother insisted she join the restaurant. "She thought there were enough doctors. Now instead of making people healthy, I'm making them ill." She sweeps her arm out with a roar, gesturing at the Herculean cholesterol consumption all around her, urging you to have more chocolate mousse, or maybe a crème brûlée, also perfect. She also confides that she nearly died recently of a brain aneurysm, takes "thirty pills a day," and despairs that neither of her two daughters may go into the business. You get the sinking feeling that the Kronenhalle, which seems timeless and endless, like Tennyson's "The Song of the Brook" ("Men may come and men may go, But I go on forever"), might have a finite future.

So you go back to the Baur, which you feel will never be Starwooded, and exult in the marble baths and the linen sheets. You sleep the sleep of angels. And then you come back to the Kronenhalle the next day for a Last Supper, of white asparagus from Cavaillon, and roast baby chicken with rosemary and garlic that could give Ami Louis a crisis of confidence (à la recherche du Frank Perdue), and more *rosti*, plus an order of vinaigrette *kartoffelsalat* (because you can never get such a delicacy in mayonnaise-crazy America) and more chocolate mousse. If you want meat and potatoes, this is as good as it gets. Because you want to come back, over and over, you say a little prayer for Vreni, with her cute cow name, and hope she will be *la vache qui rit* forever. ★ ★ ★ ★ ★

Harry's Bar
The Granddaddy

VENICE

Kronenhalle may be a perfect restaurant, *the* perfect restaurant, but its influence is limited by its location. For all its culture, wealth, scenery, and charm, Zurich is still on the periphery of the grand tour. It has never captured the world's imagination. Venice, on the other hand, is everyone's City of Dreams. And Harry's Bar is the preeminent place to drink, dine, hang out, whatever in this dreamily impossible city on the sea, so it is the most influential of all restaurants. Harry's fuses Italian food, global celebrities, the ultimate in romantic locations, and an American pedigree to create a surefire formula for success. While it can't compare to the colossus Nobu, it has an even more glamorous, more exclusive, more celebrated clientele. Wherever Harry's goes—whether Fifth Avenue, West Broadway, Davies Street—the Fabulous People will follow. It's not so much Venice that everybody wants to recapture; it's Harry's. Still, Harry's is a symbiosis that could have happened only in Venice.

It didn't start with Hemingway, who was an amazing writer but anything but a food critic. He was a Chicago-born reporter from Kansas City who happened to put Europe on the map for Americans, and for that everyone, Europe and America, is eternally grateful. But he was no A. J. Liebling, no Joseph Wechsberg, no Waverly Root, no Craig Claiborne. Hemingway was a sportsman, a bon vivant, but no effete intellectual epicure. He was a real guy who loved a great place, and that's what Harry's Bar is: a great place, with great food, but nothing fancy, nothing pretentious. And that seemingly effortless simplicity, in essence, is what makes any place a "celebrity" restaurant—assuming, of course, the celebrities discover it. Call it "the Hemingway test." If Mr. H would love it, so would the world.

But before Hemingway, there was Harry: Harry Pickering, a young American doing a "travels with his aunt" grand tour/flight from the Depression at home. Young Harry was anything but a culture vulture. In fact, he was an early alcoholic, which is why his family dispatched him abroad, to grow up and dry out. Bad call. Harry couldn't have cared less about the Duomo, the Doge's Palace, Canaletto, or Bellini. Actually, Bellini, yes—the cocktail, not the artist. But it didn't exist yet. Instead of the churches and the museums, Harry spent most of his time hanging out at the bar of the German-owned Europa Hotel, where his new best friend was the bartender, a kindly gentleman originally from Verona named Giuseppe Cipriani.

One day Harry came to Giuseppe distraught. His aunt had disappeared with her new gigolo (those were the days), leaving poor Harry with a little dog, a big hotel bill, and no money. Since Giuseppe was his only acquaintance in Venice, and he wasn't quite sure how to break the news by wire to the folks, he asked the bartender for a loan of ten thousand lire, a princely sum for a wage earner who had begun his hospitality career in a Veronese pastry shop at three lire per hour and then worked in a number of grand hotels, from France to Sicily, before settling in Venice. Giuseppe was a soft touch, and, to his family's consternation, lent Pickering the money he barely had. Then Pickering disappeared, to even greater family consternation.

A year later, Pickering returned, with no explanation, but with the ten thousand lire to return. Plus forty thousand more in interest. Pickering also now had a sense of mission in life. He wanted to do something, and he wanted Giuseppe to do it with him. The mission? Open a bar. Giuseppe had come to believe that there was a place for a freestanding little casual bar in Venice, outside the grand hotels like the Europa, the Danieli, the Bauer, the Gritti, away from the snooping eyes of the hall porters and pompous staff. Despite the

Depression, Americans were coming to Europe to escape Prohibition, to drink, to have fun. Giuseppe wanted to give them their own place in Venice, and now he had a backer. With those forty thousand lire, Harry's Bar was born.

Harry's opened on May 13, 1931, at the end of a dead-end street that was near the Piazza San Marco but, because there was no bridge, had to be reached by gondola. Harry's was thus born hard to get into. There was never a sign outside, just the name Harry's Bar etched on the windows. Again, born low-profile. This being nautical Venice, the place was designed to look like a ship's bar, and because the space was small, everything, from the chairs to the tableware, was scaled down, miniaturized to look in proportion. Nothing ever got bigger. The famous low three-legged tables were a matter of form following function. The floor was highly uneven, so the tables were designed simply, so as not to wobble. Such is the genesis of classics.

The bar took off right away, so much so that Giuseppe hired an old hotel mate to whip up some dishes designed to appeal to rich Americans, weaned on bland club food at home and fancy French food on the road. The initial results were some grilled ham-and-cheese sandwiches and some chicken-à-la-king-glop-ized, Frenchified Italian food; noodles with lots of ham and cheese (Americans love that old ham and cheese) plus cream, shrimp with cream and brandy, veal with lots of cream. Giuseppe had been awed by the Diamond Jim Brady fanfare cuisine of the grand French hotels where he had toiled. This is what you give fine people, he concluded, not spaghetti with tomato sauce. This stylized comfort food, while greatly expanded upon, remains the core of the classic menu today.

But the initial draw of Harry's were Giuseppe's great cocktails, particularly his martinis—American gin martinis, not the plain vermouth of the same name, served in those miniaturized glasses that kept people ordering more. The best customer of Harry's Bar was its namesake owner, Harry Pickering, who never left. He was, however, more interested in imbibing than in business, and after a few years he sold out to Giuseppe. He never looked back in anger at Harry's Bar's success; like all Americans, Harry was loyal to Harry's, going there every day whenever he returned to Venice.

During World War II, the Americans left, and Harry's Bar, because of its American associations, came under the heavy jackboot of the Fascists. The name was Italicized to "Bar Arrigo," and Giuseppe Cipriani was ordered to put up a sign, JEWS NOT WELCOME, as if the local Jewry were martini-ing it up in those dark days. Eventually, Harry's was taken over by the officers of Mussolini's navy, who turned it into their canteen.

After Liberation in 1945, it was tit for tat, as both the Americans and English claimed Harry's as *their* canteen. Hemingway arrived in 1949, and instantly decided to divide his time between Harry's in Venice and the Locanda Cipriani on the lagoon island of Torcello, which Giuseppe had created as a restaurant and six-room inn overlooking the island's two ninth-century Byzantine churches. Hemingway set *Across the River and into the Trees* at Harry's and then won the Nobel Prize for literature, and then *tutto il mondo* discovered the world of Cipriani, which expanded once more in 1958 with the creation of the Hotel Cipriani. The hotel was replete with an orgiastic swimming pool, across the Grand Canal from Harry's on the island of Giudecca, which quickly became one of Europe's premier resorts, as did the Villa Cipriani in the cool hills of nearby Asolo, which joined the empire in 1962.

In addition to the prose of Hemingway, one drink and one dish created in the postwar boom also cemented Harry's Bar's global renown. The drink was the Bellini, inspired by a seasonal surfeit of fresh white peaches and Giuseppe's affection for a pink-hued masterpiece by the fifteenth-century Venetian artist. He squeezed the peaches, added some local Prosecco, and a star was born. The dish was carpaccio, again named for a Venetian painter celebrated for his intense reds and whites, who was having a major exposition in 1950. At the same time, Harry's had a regular, the Contessa Mocenigo (Italian aristos loved Harry's as much as the American tycoons, perhaps *because* of the New Worlders, who the Italians found amusing and refreshing), who had gone on a raw-meat diet, a high-protein precursor of Atkins. The ever accommodating Giuseppe, inspired by the art exposition all over the city, sliced some raw filet mignon paper thin and did a Jackson Pollack–like slashing of a made-up mustard-mayo mixture all over the beef. *Voilà!* Carpaccio!

He pretended to the contessa that this was an ancient and recherché Venetian specialty, which of course it wasn't, but contessas tended to go for lineage. Whatever, the dish stuck, and still sticks.

The Big Names came, and kept on coming, as the jet set colonized postwar Europe and Venice was one of their prime haunts. Barbara Hutton, Doris Duke, Gianni Agnelli, the Aga Khan, Capote and his "swans" from Park Avenue society, Liz and Dick and Frank and Ava and Katharine Hepburn and David Lean making *Summertime* in 1954 and Zanuck and Spiegel and their countless mistresses and all the rest of Hollywood. Even Queen Elizabeth and Prince Philip got into the sideshow in 1960, dining at the Locanda Cipriani, the first restaurant ever visited by the queen in a private capacity. At the Locanda, very few star portraits adorn the walls, only those of the queen and Prince Philip, and another of Lady Di and Prince Charles. The exiled king of Italy gets one, and there are three of Hemingway. But pride of place goes to Kim Novak, who gets ten, which may say something about Who Matters in Cipriani-land.

Giuseppe Cipriani died in the early 1970s, and his dashing karate-black-belt son Arrigo (Harry to you) became the new Bellini-ator. In the 1980s Harry was joined by his own dashing rising son, Giuseppe, who helped his father spearhead the invasion of Manhattan, which, now with numerous out-posts, could not have been more successful. A darker spot was the loss of both the Cipriani Hotel and the Villa Cipriani in Asolo, sold in the aftermath of the passing of the Guinness beer baron Lord Iveagh, who was Giuseppe's financial partner in that expansion. A particular thorn in the Cipriani side is the ownership of their namesake hotel on Giudecca by American container kingpin James Sherwood (of Orient Express train and hotel fame), who, Arrigo Cipriani is fond of noting, ate only hamburgers at Harry's Bar. In a complex legal tangle, Sherwood, not Cipriani, licensed the Harry's Bar name to Mark Birley in London, who now is having his own battle with Sherwood over control of London's most exclusive private restaurant. Meanwhile, young Giuseppe C has opened what has quickly become London's most exclusive public restaurant, Cipriani. What's in a name? Everything.

Meanwhile back at the ranch, the beat goes on. And on. Harry's Bar, flaunting its American roots, now has stars-and-stripes awnings. It is still the most exclusive table in Italy, especially in the tiny downstairs bar area, where the only Americans you will see are those you have seen on the cover of *People, Time,* or *Fortune.* Upstairs is far more luxurious, with stunning views over the Grand Canal to the grand white church of Santa Maria della Salute. But nobody in the know *wants* to sit there; the only views that matter are those of the stars, or the even more starlike aristos, each making a grand entrance through Harry's unchanging wooden vestibule. As the bartender of the Gritti Palace tells his charges, "Harry's isn't a restaurant. It's a theater."

Wherever you sit, no orchestra ducats ever cost as much. That Bellini will set you back fourteen euros. And they disappear fast. The vegetable risotto, a diet favorite of the rich and slender, is forty-five euros. The famed retro shrimp Thermidor is sixty-five euros. A Tuscan steak is sixty-seven. That's pretty dear humble pie if you're sitting upstairs. Of course you can economize, and stargaze, by having drinks only at the tiny bar. Be warned, however, that you will never feel more marginalized, if even extant. The barflies inhabit a parallel universe at Harry's. The people sitting down, the beautiful people, the chosen, do not know these others exist. They look straight through them, the way rich Indians look through the outcaste beggars on their way into a temple. It's more than a little disconcerting.

Once you sit down, high or low, you'll get the smoothest, most professional service anywhere, from the blue-suited captains and the white-coated waiters. No one will give you a head shot or ask if you're having a nice day. Familiarity breeds contempt, and there's none of that at Harry's, not at these prices. Often Arrigo himself is around, making the rounds, and making every woman feel even more beautiful than she is, which is no mean feat with this distaff lot. This consummate host is a true ladies' man, and it shows. For men and women, kings and queens and drag queens, too (Venice is *très gai* and loves costumes, not merely at Carnivale), Arrigo remembers birthdays, anniversaries, and dietary quirks, and always has the last flattering word.

The food is equally pro, starting with the buttery, briochelike dinner rolls, and the hot, slightly burned white toast, the smell there just to slake your hunger. The food is, as always, comfort fare of a high order. But questions have arisen about consistency, and whether the comfort of the fare can transcend the discomfort of the check. The white *tagliolini* baked with ham is as it always has been, as is the scampi Carlina, named after Arrigo's sister, who used to run a branch of Harry's over on the Lido (even Harry's can fail, here, as well as in Buenos Aires, where the currency crisis proved too much even for the Ciprianis). The Carlina is a sauce of tomatoes, capers, Worcestershire sauce, and pickles that is evocative of a Bloody Mary—good bar food, albeit maybe not at sixty-five euros.

A recent risotto primavera evoked Knorr's onion soup mix, and a fritto misto evoked the fried clams at Howard Johnson, both classic American comfort food for the infinitely elastic nostalgic spender. But even billionaires draw the line. One Croesus hit the roof when he saw that the fries with his big-bucks Tuscan steak were frozen. The captains were as abashed as kids caught with their hands in the cookie jar. Back to the kitchen they went, and out of the kitchen they emerged, with perfect hand-cut spuds, fried in olive oil, a real treat. So you just have to be tough and speak up. Harry's can rise to any challenge; you simply have to challenge them. For dessert there's as much cream as most main courses, in the decadent chocolate cake, even in the ostensibly light lemon meringue pie. But, hey, this is fat-cat food, so live it up today and diet tomorrow.

It's enormous fun to go with a Harry's regular and get the downstairs royal treatment while watching the floor show, getting the skinny on each fat cat making his or her grand entrance through the vestibule. Bolivian tin kings, Macao gaming lords, Saudi arms merchants, crypto-Nazis, ex–Madame Claude call girls, not to mention Woody Allen, J Lo, Beyoncé. Between the Biennale, the Regatta, the Venice Film Festival, Carnivale, whatever, there's always somebody superfamous in town, and they're invariably at Harry's. And even if you strike out, it's top sport just to watch all the gorgeous people who *look* like they belong downstairs, like they own the place, get the bum's rush to the second floor, where, adding insult to insult, the waiters try to sell them cookbooks and Bellini mix.

Of course, if all these status games get too much, you can always have a kinder, gentler version of the Harry's experience by taking a two-hour slow boat to Torcello and Locanda Cipriani. The food is the same, if not better, and less than half the price. It's a little dowdy, in an English *Separate Tables* kind of way, but that's why Queen Elizabeth and Lady Di came here. And that's why Hemingway came to stay. The views of the Byzantine churches are breathtaking, the birds sing, and for once you can see why they call Venice "La Serenissima." Before you leave, you must visit the larger church, Santa Fosca, and see the famous whole-wall mosaic *The Last Judgment*. It's supposed to be the battle between heaven and hell, but it also may remind you of the equally desperate struggle on the ground floor of Harry's Bar a millennium later. ★ ★ ★

Al Moro
The Gold Standard

ROME

If most people's favorite food is Italian, and most people's favorite restaurant is Harry's Bar, wouldn't that make Harry's most people's favorite Italian restaurant? Not by any means. Harry's Bar shouldn't really be classified as an "Italian" restaurant. Harry's has very much its own cuisine, which draws from New York men's clubs and grand fin de siècle French hotels as much as from the Veneto. Harry's is sui generis. Harry's is Harry's.

And Al Moro is Al Moro. For those who get around a bit, this tiny 1929 trattoria, hidden in a private, empty winding lane that feels like a serene time warp behind the tourist nightmare that the Trevi Fountain (as in "Three Coins in . . .") has become, is *the* perfect Italian restaurant. The menu is state-of-the-art *cucina della nonna*, or "grandma food," the Italian home cooking of the best ingredients, simply and perfectly prepared, that is so wonderful because you can eat it every day and keep wanting it tomorrow. Many foodies, in the interest of that divine simplicity, take all their Roman meals at Al Moro. It's easy to see why.

Not that Al Moro is a friendly, happy-go-lucky *dolce far niente* kind of place. It's dead serious, totally uptight. It only *looks* like fun. There's a rumor that Tom Cruise was asked to leave when one of the owners spotted him squeezing a lemon on his grilled sole. Not putting Parmigiano on his *spaghetti vongole*, but squeezing a lemon on some fish, for St. Pete's (we are in Rome) sake. And Tom Cruise, whose mere presence would put any restaurant on the global star map. Of course, no one will confirm or deny the rumor. But no one who knows Al Moro would dismiss it as preposterous, either. Stars are ephemeral, food eternal, and in the Eternal City food trumps stars any day. At Al Moro, tampering with the *correct* way to serve fish is akin to defacing the Pantheon. *Keep* your Pantheon, you might say, but only if you hadn't eaten at Al Moro. Once you have, you gladly do exactly what they say.

The crowd of men in dark suits on the Vicolo delle Bollette at five of one gives you the impression that Al Moro is about to be raided by the authorities. At precisely one, they storm the doors. They *are* the authorities, it turns out, Italian senators and ministers and other bigwigs from the nearby SPQR offices, but they're only here to eat. You wait your turn in line, and once you reach the threshold you're met, not particularly greeted, by the elegantly towering, senatorially balding Franco Romagnoli, the proprietor and son of the founder, in a shirt and tie you'd die for. That's from Battistoni, you want to ask, so you can get the same for yourself. But you're terrified to be so familiar with such a glowering presence, who could instill fear in the most arrogant captain of Maxim's in its nasty heyday. Roberto Benigni he is not. You stammer your name, mentioning that you booked months ago. Signor Romagnoli (don't call him Franco) looks at you with a how-could-I-let-this-in-*here* puzzlement and hands you off to an English-speaking waiter in a tan coat who leads you into the *sala americana*, as the back-room Siberia is known.

Before you get there, you can't help but be transfixed by the bounty dominating the entire center of the entrance room, Valhalla. There are no humans in this high-ceilinged chamber filled with modern art. The seats are all empty. But the food is there. It's a still life of the best of Italy, *funghi porcini*, the first asparagus of the season, a pot of just shelled baby peas, *puntarelle*, that uniquely bitter Roman green, eggplant simmering in fragrant tomato sauce (double, double toil and trouble, fire burn and eggplant bubble), giant prosciuttos and mortadellas and wheels of cheese, figs and peaches and wild cherries. You want every bit of it. But as you're led through the paneled, art-filled second room, full of those politicos, you feel like you're going into Dante's *Inferno*. "Abandon hope, all ye who enter here." You think once you're seated the staff will send out for a Big Mac and fries and a giant Coke for you, and forbid you from getting the *real* stuff.

As you're waiting and wondering if you'll be served, you can't help but notice the decor of politically incorrect vintage posters of the Moro (or Moor, as in *Othello*) theme. Typical is a Fernet-Branca *affiche* of an intrepid white explorer on an African, or Caribbean shore, surrounded by restless natives, cannibals maybe. You can't help but notice all the other Americans, English, and Japanese being herded into the room. You take some comfort that most of them are extremely stylish and slender, taking a break from their Via Condotti shopping sprees. It's definitely not a tour-bus crowd, but what they share is a discomfiture that, all the Prada and Armani armature notwithstanding, they're still being sent into exile.

Then the food starts arriving and you quickly forget the status snubs. The waiters are friendly even though the host is not, and they help steer you through the dauntingly long menu. Not that you need help. You know exactly where you're going, first to the *spaghetti vongole*, which lives up to all the foodie hype about being the best in Rome. Great olive oil, the freshest, grit-free clams, the right balance of clam broth, white wine, garlic, parsley, and a tiny blast of *peperoncino* to send you into pasta heaven. Next stop is the *abbacchio al forno*, which for many is an excuse to get the sublime rosemary potatoes cooked in the lamb fat. The lamb is achingly tender, but there's not much of it; it's mostly bone, and a lot of work. But you're stuffed from the spaghetti and the potatoes anyway. You drink the house carafe wine, which is fine. If you insist on getting fancy and order a bottle, the waiters will place some finer crystal on the starched white tablecloths. You finish with a homemade tangerine *sorbetto*, so smooth and rich that you can't believe it's dairy free.

Despite all the carbo loading, you keep watching the other outlanders eat the things you had to pass up, and somehow, you get hungry again. It's not the Chinese restaurant syndrome; it's the greed and gluttony syndrome—you've gotta have it. You fake several trips to the refined wood-paneled bathrooms just to see what the elect Italians are eating. There are almost no women in the front rooms, just tycoons and politicos, and, mirabile dictu, they, too, are on the clam-lamb meal plan. There are no fat men here. How they eat this way and cut such dashing figures is more challenging than the French Paradox. Call it the Italian Conundrum.

The huge, glowering blow-up in the main room, with a smaller copy in the second room, is "Moro" himself, Franco's father, Mario Romagnoli, who was cast by his customer Fellini to play Trimalchio in *Satyricon*. Papa is dark and brooding. And while *figlio* is sleek and streamlined, he's still a chip off the old block, certainly in the intimidation department. As you leave, you see Franco conversing animatedly with the new denizens of the A-room. They're older men, and they're playing cards, like in the old social clubs of Little Italy. Apparently the A-room at lunch is the card room. You gather your courage and ask Franco for another reservation. This evening. He gives you a that's-impossible roll of the eyes, and deigns to readmit you three days hence. You're lucky you have a lot of sightseeing to do to keep you in town, luckier that he's letting you come back at all.

You end up coming back a few times. You find that the pastas are always wonderful, better somehow than any you get even in the best places outside

Italy. Is it the pasta, the water, the tomatoes? Whatever, you swoon over the *bucatini matriciana* and the dish that made Al Moro famous, its spaghetti carbonara, made without cream and black pepper, just eggs and Italian bacon. If you could eat three meals a day here instead of two, this would be the perfect breakfast. The vegetables here are Lucullan, baby arugula salads, baby peas stewed with prosciutto, broccoli *in padella*, sautéed to a near puree and mixed with garlic, olive oil, and peppers, a dish that could make vegetarians of us all.

Not everything is perfect. Al Moro has a heavy hand at the deep fryer. A touted dish of fried zucchini flowers is a leaden attempt at tempura. A fritto misto is even soggier and greasier. A lot of dishes have too much salt, enough to raise your blood pressure more than your exclusion, no matter how many times you come, in the *sala americana*. Furthermore, the simple grilled fish tends to be dry and overcooked. Poor Tom Cruise could have used that lemon. Give the guy a break! But for the most part, the food is great, particularly if you like the frequent daily specials of entrails, sweetbreads, tripe, brains, oxtail. This is great Roman grandma food, and it tastes as good as it sounds bad.

You even get to know Franco Romagnoli and begin to pierce his medieval battlements. "This is a *serious* restaurant," he says. You don't say, eh Franco? "We are very serious here," he reiterates. "If you are serious you will obtain success." Convinced that you are a serious diner (hell, you've spent serious money here, meal after meal), Franco then tells a little about Al Moro's roots. The family came from Ariccia, a small village in the hills outside Rome near Castel Gandolfo, the summer home of the pope, and hence a serious place. This is wine country, and Al Moro was founded to sell wine from the region. At first there was only the A-room, with a small kitchen in the back that turned out three pastas and three meat courses a day. That was the menu, no menu. There were only Italians eating here, regular Italians, no stars, until Orson Welles, filmdom's biggest eater, stumbled into the place in the 1950s, when Rome was a major colony of Hollywood *(Roman Holiday, Ben Hur,* et al., followed in the 1960s by *Cleopatra* and the spaghetti westerns). Welles liked to show off what a worldly palate he had, and scored points with his Italian friends by bringing them to a restaurant they didn't know about. In came Vittorio Gassman,

Vittorio De Sica, Anna Magnani, Fellini, and the world followed suit.

Today the restaurant is run, very seriously, by Franco and his sister Elisabetta. The same chefs have been in the kitchen for over thirty years. Franco scours local and regional markets for the best produce, the best fish (hold that lemon), the best meats. He gets his wonderful chewy, dense bread from the family's ancient baker back in Ariccia. He goes to a tiny town in Lazio for olive oil. "Vegetables are fundamental," Franco asserts. "If you begin good, you end better." Above all, he insists, "You must maintain tradition." Including, you ask boldly, the tradition of sequestering foreigners in the Little Black Sambo room? It's not snobbery, he insists. It's practical. The waiters of that room speak English. Even the stars sit there, unless they come in with Antonioni. "We decide where you sit," he says, closing the subject, Caesar-like. "You come here for eating, not seeing. If you want other things, there's the door."

Speaking of the door, what about the Cruise ejection, as well as others that have gotten Franco the reputation as the Gordon Ramsay of Italy (Ramsay throws everyone out)? He rolls his eyes, intones the atrocities: butter on bread, cheese on clams, lemon on fish. "If you want to die, you can dive from the bridge" is all he will say, like an ancient oracle. Although Franco has traveled throughout the United States, he said he didn't find one good Italian restaurant among the many he sampled. "Americans are not demanding." He's no kinder about French food. "Too elaborate, too much sauce," he says, with a grimace. Despite the endless raves from all over the world, Franco is indifferent to the food press. "I don't care of guides. I want the grandsons of my customers coming back. That is the best review." ★ ★ ★ ★ ★ ★ ★ ★ ★ ★ ★ ★

Hollywood on the Tiber:
Hostaria dell'Orso

Hostaria dell'Orso (Inn of the Bear) is the premier wanna-eat-at restaurant in Rome. To begin with, how many chances do you have to eat in a Renaissance palace overlooking the Tiber? The building dates from the fourteenth century; in the sixteenth, it became a hotel. Rabelais, Montaigne, and Goethe all stayed here. In the 1950s, when Rome became Hollywood for a decade, the Hostaria dell'Orso became Rome's answer to Paris's La Tour d'Argent and Castel all in one, a superchic restaurant-nightclub that the world's elite made their headquarters in the Eternal City. This was the favorite of the paparazzi, who were spawned in Rome, camping out along the riverbank to get a shot of Jackie Kennedy or Clark Gable getting into a limo after a hard night of *puttanesca* and Watusi-ing. This is where Gregory Peck and Audrey Hepburn hung out when they made *Roman Holiday.* And now, after years of decadent corruption and lying fallow, the Hostaria has been taken over and lovingly restored, in 2002, by Italy's preeminent celebrity chef, Gualtiero Marchesi, the first Italian winner of three *Michelin* stars. Now, in record time, the Hostaria has its first food star, one of only four restaurants in Rome to be so honored, and the only one that is a registered national landmark.

Rome is a dead nightlife town. The Eternal City's biggest business, the Vatican, isn't known for hard partying. Most visitors are tourists, too worn out by debilitating walks through hard cobblestones and high culture for nocturnal high jinks. Aside from the local kidocracy, the grandchildren of La Dolce Vita, who have their own places that you wouldn't know about and wouldn't get into even if you did, there's been no demand for neo-jet-set—or more accurately private jet-set—nightclubs. But in recent years the stars have come back to Rome, with Tom Cruise and Matt Damon among others filming their action spectacles around the city and at Cinecittà, the Mussolini-built Roman film studios near the Appian Way. Despite early-morning calls, the stars like to eat, they like to play, and they like Hostaria dell'Orso, which is all things to all stars.

Even without the ghosts of Jackie and Clark, or the prospect of sighting Matt and Tom, Hostaria dell'Orso would demand your attention because of Gualtiero Marchesi, the Paul Bocuse or Alain Ducasse of Italy. He's a big-time gourmet must, the father, or godfather, of modern Italian cooking, the man who put gold leaf in risotto Milanese, who muscled the old-fashioned grandmother out of the kitchen and replaced her with the camera-ready superstar. Marchesi grew up in Milan, where his family owned a restaurant. He went away to a top Swiss hotel school, and then worked in the grand hotels of the Alps and some of the grand restaurants of France: Ledoyen in Paris, Troisgros in Roanne. With his three-star French education, he came back to Milan and quickly was holding court in a three-star restaurant, the darling of the world food press. Operations in Japan and London followed, then in the Italian Lake District an elegant country inn, and now the Hostaria. Marchesi has had an enormous influence on Italian restaurants around the world, particularly in cutting-edge gastro-hubs like London and New York, where the young male chefs continue to muscle grandma away from the stoves.

Naturally, not everyone is pleased about that. There are a lot of grandma nostalgists who decry Marchesi as a traitor to tradition, a French pawn. Many worldly foodies regard *Michelin* stars in Italy, in fact anywhere outside France, as a reverse barometer. They feel that the stars are awarded by a French company based on the degree to which a restaurant's *cucina* approximates French cuisine, *la vrai chose*. Accordingly, purists tend to stay away from starred restaurants in Italy the way that Dracula would steer clear of crosses. So it is perhaps with some trepidation that you enter the Hostaria, not the least of which is getting a reservation. But they're extremely nice, in contrast to frosty Al Moro, and the menu seems to have lots of old-time goodies. Besides, you want to eat where Rabelais did.

Wherever you're staying, you should walk at least part of the way to Orso (let's get familiar). Rome is the greatest of all walking cities, so every wrong turn will be a history lesson, a blast from the past. Gastronomically, one of the most enticing streets is the Via della Scrofa, where you'll pass the original Alfredo (as in fettuccine), which was the most famous Italian restaurant in the world at the time that Orso was the most fashionable. The golden forks of Alfredo, the ones that mix the pasta with all the butter, cream, and cheese (this dish may have contributed mightily to President Eisenhower's massive heart attack), still mark the spot, and the place is still packed with tourists, many Japanese who have a filial and spiritual respect for great names, even when the reasons for greatness have long evaporated. You pass the glorious Piazza Navona, with its Bernini fountain, and another big Roman name, Tre Scalini, the progenitor of the *tartufo* chocolate ice cream delight. It was "da bomb" in the 1950s, and still may be, judging from the mob of tourists, many Japanese, who don't realize that the current reigning gelateria, Giolitti, is just steps away.

Finally you reach the Tiber and the Big Bear. You can't miss it because of the uniformed valet parker overseeing a thundering herd of Ferraris and Lamborghinis. Shades of Spago. You stand at the massive Renaissance doors and ring a bell, half expecting Steve Rubell to materialize out of the grave and tell you that you're not cool enough to get in. Instead a courtly man in a tuxedo opens up and gives you the warmest welcome. You enter the bar, tended by a rangy model, which is as eerie and empty as the bar in Kubrick's *The Shining*. It doesn't look like a palace. It looks like the cheesy Via Veneto disco Jackie O, the sole survivor of Rome's last days of disco in the 1970s.

The greeter leads you up a stairway into the main dining area. This is the Renaissance, all right: beamed ceilings, faded frescoes, Roman arches, huge fireplaces, candlelight. The rooms are as full as the bar is empty, glamorous people, aristocrat types, lots of black, mostly Italian spoken. These are the noblest Romans of them all. There's also a table of Arab-looking men and big blond models. Later you learn that this is Qaddafi and sons' favorite hangout when they're in from Libya. The most discordant notes are the hideous bright orange chairs, something not at all Renaissance but more out of another Kubrick, *A Clockwork Orange,* in more ways than one. Sensing your visual horror, the Armani-clad captain, also totally accommodating as if you were an oil sheikh, steps up and tells you that these are serious designer chairs by Poltrona Frau, and that they cost a thousand euros each. Luckily you're sitting in the chairs, not looking at them. You're in the prime position in the house, on the glassed-in terrace overlooking the Tiber, with Hadrian's Castle on the other side. You're in Rome, and location-wise, it doesn't get better than this.

What about the food? What about Gualtiero Marchesi? It turns out that he's not in the kitchen tonight, or many other nights. He's seventy-six and a food lord. Does Paul Bocuse work the stoves? Manning the kitchen is one of Marchesi's trusted acolytes from his country restaurant by the Lakes. Not to worry, the captain assures you, and hands you one of the most appetizing menus you've ever encountered. This isn't the typical Marchesi *alta cucina* of foie gras, truffles, caviar. This is classic Italian fare, not as entrail-y and down-home as Al Moro, but totally accessible. There are multiple choices: a vegetarian menu highlight-ing white-and-green asparagus soup, and a broccoli and olive risotto; a "Roman tradition" menu with anchovy salad with chicory, *maccheroni amatriciana,* roast baby lamb; a creative menu that starts with poached and pan-fried eggs with almonds and scares you off; and a fish menu, which you jump at.

Everything reads better than it tastes. The first course of eggplant stuffed with squid and Swiss chard is lukewarm and doesn't meld. A pasta, *tonnarelli* with scorpion fish ragout, is also tepid, in heat and flavor; it needs fire, and it's not there. Ditto the tiger prawn kebabs, with fried chickpea sticks and olive sauce. The food all sounds lusty, but it has all the courage of a cruise ship, and not even a Tom Cruise-ship. The prawns need some lemon. You ask for it. You get it. With a smile. The bread is great, as are the sorbets and gelati, nearly as many flavors as Howard Johnson, which was big in the fifties, too. Who would have ever thought Howard Johnson could disappear? It happened here once. Could it happen again?

On your way out you notice a Dalí-esque surreal portrait of the great Marchesi, surrounded with naked women and fallen columns. You won-der if he's been here lately, or at all. The bar is still empty, a side room set up for live music and dancing, but there are no dancers. It's midnight on Saturday. Maybe the aristos from upstairs will come down and shake their pedigreed booty. Maybe the Libyans. Maybe not. Is it a matter of late, or never? You wanted Hollywood, and here it is. In the battle between *Michelin* and grandma, this round must go to the little old lady. ⋆ ⋆ ⋆ ⋆ ⋆

The Italian Diet

There are four classic Roman *trattorie* that are most favored by the international food set—the stars, tycoons, and fashion elite—who seek out great Italian restaurants wherever they are, whether Tokyo, New York, or Sydney. These Roman restaurants provide the delicious gold standard that the restaurants in the other cities can somehow never attain. They share the same glittery clientele. But they're anything but glittery. They're old-fashioned, unpretentious, classic. They're nowhere as *serious* as Al Moro, but they're seriously great.

Checco er Carettiere ("Checco the wagoneer") is the only restaurant in Rome that Franco Romagnoli of Al Moro will recommend, and that's a major rave in this city. Checco was founded in the heart of bohemian Trastevere (the "left bank" of Rome) in 1935, and is nearly as old as Al Moro and every bit as traditional, if a lot more lighthearted. The restaurant is a warm, two-story affair with a big fireplace that makes it feel like a raffish country inn. In season (a long one in sunny Rome) there's also a lush garden filled with fragrant orange trees. The walls, up and down, are festooned with the fraying photos of people who seem totally anonymous, sort of like the failed thespians whose mug shots dominate dry cleaners in New York and Los Angeles. But if you come with an Italian, you'll learn that these are the people who really matter to the Romans: soccer stars, race car drivers, local singers and actors. Cameron Diaz may be at one table and Sean Connery at another, but if one of these holy Romans comes in, it is he or she who will get all the attention.

That is, if the diners bother to look up from their plates. Checco is the quintessence of the lusty peasant kitchen. They spice things up even more than grandma might, and the food is great indeed. The biggest star in the room is the cornucopian antipasto *vegetale,* a vast groaning table of perfect marinated vegetables: five varieties of zucchini, six eggplants, three kinds of broccoli, artichokes, peas, fennel, endless varieties of beans, you name it. It's a total meal in itself, but no one stops just here. Most people do take at least a few servings of Checco's pièce de résistance, a fabulous cold puree of potatoes, tomatoes, onion, garlic, and hot peppers. Called simply *puree rosso,* it's categorically the best mashed potato dish on the planet, alone worth a trip. There's also wonderful pasta here, and great fish. The *orata,* or *coda di rospo,* or *soglia* are perfectly undercooked, much better than Al Moro's, which is more a meat house than a fish one. Whatever, you won't even think about the lemon. Service, by the way, is casual, friendly, and obliging. Anything goes at Checco, and everyone comes.

Piperno is Rome's most famous Jewish restaurant, but the most Jewish thing about it may be the raving accolades of Mel Brooks, which has *tutto il* Great White Way making pilgrimages here. Piperno is one of the most common names in the ancient Roman Jewish community. The restaurant is located in a hidden square right in the center of the Jewish ghetto, but the Pipernos sold the place in 1961. Its days of fame came under its new owners, the non-Jewish Mori family, who still operate the place with familial care and love. Even though one of their signature dishes is a shellfish risotto, and they do a mean pork roast, the chief rabbi of Rome is an ardent regular, which says a lot. As does the patronage of such Semitic galloping gourmets as Brooks, Woody Allen, and Henry Kissinger, not to mention such eminent converts as Madonna and Liz Taylor. But paraphrasing the old Levy's rye ads, you don't have to be Jewish to love Piperno. The showbiz Italians—De Niro, DiCaprio, DeVito, Scorsese—are here in force, making it kosher for Hollywood's *cosa nostra.*

Piperno is famous for one dish, its "Jewish artichokes," which are often imitated but never duplicated in the E.C. (Eternal City). The whole globes are seasoned and deep fried—twice—in olive oil, resulting in crispy, crunchy, golden brown outer leaves and a melting-hot nutty interior. In Piperno's hands, this dish is one of the glories that is grease; in other hands, and there are lots of heavy hands in the Roman fry pits, it can be a soggy, leaden disaster. But everything is good here, as is the place. The British racing green dining rooms are elegant and homey without being too clubby, and the effect is heightened by large families of real Romans savoring large Roman meals. Outlanders who've never been to Piperno like to think of it as Rome's answer to New York's late and lamented Second Avenue Deli. It would be a *shonda* (shame), as they say in the ghetto, to sell the ecumenical Piperno that short.

Then there is Nino, Rome's ultimate model restaurant, for those who want their *penne* with a side of pulchritude. The models are here—for nearby Valentino and other designers, for the frequent fashion shows, for the endless photo shoots in this most photogenic of cities—and this is where they eat. If Nino has a New York analogy, it's Gino. Nino, too, is in the heart of its own Bloomingdale's Country, the Via Condotti shopping mecca at the foot of the Spanish Steps. This simple, high-ceilinged, brass-chandeliered, wood-paneled Tuscan trattoria was founded by the Guarnacci family in 1932. The Guarnaccis still hold court, with the elegant grandchild, now a stylish dowager, sitting at the cash register in media res, settling accounts by hand. This isn't a computerized operation, front or back. The waiters look as if they've been here from the 1930s. In fact, the place could be a stage set for *The Garden of the Finzi-Continis.* Its director, the great Vittorio De Sica, loved Nino, as have most of the great Italian—and American—directors. Tom Cruise and Katie Holmes had their pre-wedding dinner here. Now, *that's* entertainment.

Everything from the kitchen is close to perfect. The *penne arrabbiata* here is as famous as Piperno's artichokes, but let the kosher nostra be forewarned that it is made with a touch of *pancetta,* which adds a wisp of smoke to the fire of the peppers. The *fettuccine al ragù* has a Bolognese meat sauce that has no superior anywhere. Nino being a Tuscan restaurant, it is deeply proud of its *bistecca alla fiorentina,* grilled over an open fire with olive oil, salt, pepper, and lemon. Per Al Moro, lemon is okay on grilled meat, but not on fish. Go figure. Of course the models and the skinny chic shoppers have none of this animal protein. For them it's salad days, and no one makes better, fresher salads than Nino—dandelion greens, radicchio di Treviso, baby fennel, the best marinated zucchini in Rome. Oddly enough, for all the weight watching here, there are only decadent ice creams for dessert, and no sorbets. Everybody has it, so you should, too. It's a Nino tradition, and tradition is what Nino is all about.

The newest member of Rome's Classics Club is Costanza, in the aptly named Piazza Paradiso. The restaurant is located in the oldest spot of them all, built into the entrance passage of the 53 B.C. Theater of Pompey, who was the son-in-law of Julius Caesar and one of the bloodiest of Roman emperors; this is the spot where Caesar was stabbed by Brutus. Costanza, carved out of these bricks and stones, is enormously appealing—archaeologically, aesthetically, and above all, gastronomically. With its vaults and arches and faded glory, it's a true blast from the past, the most romantic great restaurant in the city. There are a lot of loving couples here, holding hands in the candlelight. They tend to love each other even more by the end of the long meal. Good food can be the greatest aphrodisiac, though being in the heart of ancient Rome doesn't hurt.

Although Costanza began as a kosher restaurant, like Piperno, specializing in fried artichokes, its new owners cut the Hebrew ties in the late 1970s. While Hollywood had pretty much left Cinecittà by then, visiting stars, led by Woody Allen, discovered Costanza and made it a prime stop on their culinary mystery train. The Jewish artichokes are still great here, but so is everything else. Costanza may be the best trattoria in all Rome, which is saying a lot. It has a monumental vegetable antipasto, a wall of hams and sausages, an enticing Tuscan grill, a market of fish. Its *fritto misto mare* takes frying, usually leaden in Rome, to an astral plane. Not only can Costanza give Al Moro a close run in the pasta sweepstakes, but it is also the rare restaurant in Rome that can stir a risotto with the stalwarts of Milan. Costanza's risotto *verde* is a vegetarian tour de force. Costanza thus pulls off the hat trick of being all things to all Italophiles, which is everyone. There's no particular patina here, no slick waiters, no attitude, other than that the customer is emperor. You'd think they'd be unable to resist offering a Caesar salad here, but Costanza is way too pure for that. ★ ★ ★ ★ ★ ★

Bice, Bagutta,
Paper Moon
Shopgirls

If you're a world traveler, the last place you probably want to go in Milan is Bice. Been there, done that, bought the T-shirt, you think, because just about every place you've been, from Vegas to Dubai, Palm Beach to Houston, Montreal to São Paolo, has a Bice. You've tried them, and they have highly variable, serviceable Italian food but are not in the forefront of whatever city they're in. Except in Milan. Bice should be the *first* place you think of here, because it's the best. It's not that Bice doesn't travel well. It's that Bice in Milan is the most chic, most classic, most delicious restaurant in the city, and it doesn't leave its dominant position in the heart of the world's most glamorous shopping area. Only the name travels. The diminution of that name is an object (if not abject) lesson in the pitfalls of licensing.

Bice is short for Beatrice, as in the heroine of Dante's *Inferno*, which is how hot Bice is with celebrities whenever Milan is having a fashion week: all the designers, all their models, and all the stars who like to buy the clothes or look at the girls. Typical regulars are the Agnellis, Calvin Klein, Naomi Campbell, Madonna, Queen Rainia of Jordan, Eric Clapton, George Clooney. That's the mix. The restaurant is a warren of intimate dining spaces, pale walls, paintings of old Milan, a veddy English red tartan carpet and tiny shaded wall lamps. The main dining room, for those who want to flaunt their new finery from the adjacent high-gloss Vias Spiga and Monte Napoleone, is flooded with sunshine (on rare good days) from an overhead skylight and with even more flower arrangements than La Grenouille in New York. It may be gray outside in industrial, fog-belted Milan, but inside Bice, it's eternal *primavera*. At lunch there's no more glamorous crowd anywhere, including Mortimer's of yore in New York. And unlike Mortimer's of yore, the food here is great. It has to be; there's too much competition. Milanese cannot live by chic alone.

But getting back to Beatrice, the original: Beatrice Mungai came to Milan from Tuscany to start a little café with her husband in 1926. He died, but she remained at the stoves, firing up such Florentine classics as bean soup and tripe. The haughty veal-choppers and risottophiles of Milan came to embrace Bice's southern hospitality and rusticity, and several of Beatrice's Tuscan relatives came north to work beside her. Bice stayed at the stoves until she was ninety-one, a commanding presence in a demanding town. Despite the grandeur of her clientele, the charismatic Bice kept it homey, coming up to the prime minister's table, giving him a kiss, and asking him sweetly if he'd get up and make room for the nice family from Peoria. Actually, there aren't that many Peorians in these precincts. But Bice, who lived above the restaurant until her death in 1997, was totally egalitarian. Her diners were far more starstruck with her than she with them.

Even before Bice died, her children were taking different positions about the potential of their mother's name. Bice had remarried a Signor Ruggeri and had three children, Roberto, Beatrice, and Roberta. The family had opened a highly successful New York outpost in 1987, followed by others in Chicago and Tokyo. However, once Bice and her husband died, within a few years of each other, the brother and sisters went separate business ways. Roberto moved to Beverly Hills and has stayed there, despite the failure of the Bice he started on Canon Drive. One flop in a string of triumphs—Atlanta, Mexico City, Dubai, Singapore, Miami. The sisters are more than a little abashed about their brother's successes, which can involve mixing and matching chefs and ingredients from throughout his empire, some mole sauce on the fettuccine, some Thai peanut glaze on the osso buco. Roberto may be a citizen of the world, the world of fusion. But little Bice, who is married to Bice's chef of twenty-five years, and Roberta are purists, chips off their mother's block. "We love America," Roberta explains about not wanting to join Roberto in becoming the Julius Caesar of licensing. "But for us America is here in Milan. We don't change anything."

That resistance to change is the glory and the essence of Italian cuisine, and what keeps the Milan Bice such a bulwark of tradition. The long, long menu is a trip back in time to Tuscany: *insalatina di funghi, culatello, ribollita con cavolo nero, tagliatelle Bolognese, costata di manzo alla griglia.* The most ordered dish is *pappardelle al telefono,* a mix of tomatoes, cream, and mozzarella that sounds heavy but tastes light. What it has to do with the telephone is that the stringy hot mozzarella looks like telephone wires. Bice's idea of fusion is to add delicious Milanese saffron risotto and *cotoletta alla milanese* to the Tuscan *carta.* And for the models? Yes, there are some offbeat *insalata* daily specials: mangoes and shrimp; a *tropicale* hearts of palm and Parmesan; octopus and arugula. But Roberta insists that's more for the Four Seasons–lodged foreign shoppers at lunch than the models, who tend to come late after the shows. "They're starving by then, and they eat like pigs," she observes. Tuscan pigs, to be sure.

Another shoppers' dining paradise in this paradise of shopping is the nearby venerable Bagutta, founded in 1927. While Bice feels like a sedate club, Bagutta feels like a country inn in the middle of the city, albeit a surreal country inn, for under the wooden beams and soaring ceilings, the plaster walls are festooned with more cartoons than the Palm. There are caricatures of famous artists, writers, musicians, though not the designers who have now become the biggest stars in this capital of fashion. Toscanini makes it, Armani does not. Aside from the notables, there are real cartoons of fat satyrs passing up young female angels in favor of wheels of massive mortadella, of a young boy looking up the short skirt of a salesgirl in a bookstore. She is climbing a library ladder to retrieve a book wrapped with a ribbon announcing "Premio Bagutta." The Premio is Italy's most important book prize, created in a pool many decades ago by the creative habitués of the restaurant, and it has kept

Bagutta in the minds of Italy, great and small, ever since. Bagutta is Milan's version of Elaine's, with models thrown in. That's another reason the brain trust loves it. Beauty has its rewards.

Even without the Premio and the literati, Bagutta would be a must because of its wonderful food, which more than lives up to the country ambience and the huge springy garden, a testament to Milanese denial over the worst weather in Europe. Critics may trash Elaine's for its food, one explanation being that starving artists never could afford to develop tastebuds. Not in Italy, where food is of central importance to life. That centrality is reflected in Bagutta's endless antipasto table, which dominates the long entranceway and is clogged with a subway-rush-hour throng of *fashionistas* and *artistas*, the latter claiming pride of place in this tavern of creativity. A third of the table is devoted to marinated vegetables, Milan's largest selection, with multiple mushrooms, squashes, chicorys, greens—and yellows, reds, and golds—you never saw before. Another third is marinated seafoods: four kinds of anchovies, baby octopuses straight out of Jules Verne, squids, shrimp, lobsters, clams, so bountiful a catch that you'd never know Milan is landlocked. The rest is sausages. Bagutta could grant a degree in sausages.

After the antipasto most diners order an espresso and call it a day. This is three meals in itself, and, at under twenty euros, one of the major bargains in this city of stratospheric prices. Habitués who have run the antipasto table for years can graduate to the wonderful pastas, grilled fish and meats, whose large-for-Italy portions are a meal in itself, just as the antipasto is, and a fairly priced one at that. If you have room, end the feast with Bagutta's celebrated *macedonia di frutta,* winner of the *premio* of world's best urban fruit salad. You'll think you're in the Garden of Eden, or the garden of the Finzi-Continis, not in smoggy Milan.

Completing the triumvirate of superb consumption for conspicuous consumers is Paper Moon. Paper Moon? What kind of Milanese name is that? Wasn't that a song from the 1930s? Yes, and it was also the favorite movie—the one starring Ryan and Tatum O'Neal as Depression con artists—of Enrica

Galligani, who started this most trendy of all the Via Monte Napoleone eateries in 1977 and has expanded with branches in New York and Moscow, with more soon to come. While Bice and Bagutta are of the true Paper Moon vintage and actually survived the real Depression, Paper Moon has known nothing but boom, never bust. It came of age just as the Milanese designers were conquering the world, evolving seemingly overnight from tailors to tycoons.

"Modern, quick and informal, that's our formula," says Enrica's daughter Stefania, who runs Paper Moon with her mother, kissing all the regulars, welcoming the new faces, complementing all on their new purchases, but always sincerely, without puffery. Father Pio died at only forty-nine in 1992. The Galliganis are country girls, with country warmth. The family is Tuscan, like the Mungais of Bice, and they offer a similar deep, classic menu, plus the thin-crust pizzas that have developed a worldwide reputation. Basically what makes Paper Moon is that it offers delicious fast food, old-time cookery in a hurry, though you could stand in line outside for an hour if you haven't booked. It also was the first restaurant in Milan to offer the grandmotherly fare in a strikingly modern, hard-angled glass-and-steel architectural decor, a place that had the look of the "new" Milan, not the Sforza Castle. The retro food and cutting-edge looks was a one-two punch that proved to be a knockout.

The walls of the two-level Paper Moon are covered with large photos of dead movie stars—Swanson, Hayworth, Monroe, Gable, Power, Grant— rather than the live ones, like Connery and Clooney, who eat here now. It's part of the black-and-white look of the place, and part of the Galliganis' cinephilia. The tables are so close together, the mood so festive and friendly, that it's impossible not to talk to your neighbors, and make new friends, particularly with the Galliganis running interference for you. They've got a lot of the O'Neals' insouciance of *Paper Moon* in them, hardly con artists but matchmakers to be sure. The food here may not be as exquisitely turned out as Bice's or as long-cooked and deep-rooted as Bagutta's, but that's not Paper Moon's mission, which is, like that of longtime customers Dolce and

Gabbana, cheap (relatively) and chic (awfully). With its speed, its style, its modernity, and its nonstop vegetables, Paper Moon is actually the perfect LA restaurant, though the most popular nonpizza dish is *pappardelle* Paper Moon, sauced with tomatoes, bacon, and cream. Italian women don't get fat, do they? At least not Paper Moon Italian women. ★ ★ ★ ★ ★ ★ ★ ★ ★ ★ ★ ★ ★

Dal Bolognese
Social Register

MILAN

Americans somehow don't think of Italy as a snobby, society place. England, yes, with its clubs and queen. France, yes, with its linguistic hauteur and its châteaux. New York, yes, with its Park Avenue Masters of the Universe. But despite all its *palazzi*, Italy seems like a nation of goodfellas, happy-go-lucky friendly types. How nasty can any populace be that subsists gloriously on the peasant fare of pasta? Very nasty, very snobby, very aloof. Just try getting invited into someone's *settecento* home in Milan. Italy has a very high, very closed society that rarely comes out to play, and even more rarely with outlanders—even a George Clooney, who had to buy his own villa on Lake Como rather than wait to be invited to *theirs*. And when Italy's elite do step out, it's not to Bice but for a walk on the wilder side, like the promenade taken by Gianni Agnelli's Fiat heir grandson Lapo Elkann, who nearly died of a drug overdose in the muscular arms of a Milan transsexual prostitute.

Milan's *alto mondo* does have its own public clubhouse in the new branch of Rome's Dal Bolognese, which since 1961 has been packing in the Parioli blue blood set to its picturesque location on the Piazza del Popolo, just next door to social Rome's favorite bar, Rosati. The Roman original also caught on with the jet set in the late 1960s, after the titanic failure of *Cleopatra* triggered an exodus of American filmmakers from Rome (the excesses symbolized by Liz Taylor having Chasen's chili flown in) and a resultant seedification of the Via Veneto. The Veneto thus gave way to the Popolo, but skeptics doubted whether severe Milan would welcome anything from provincial Rome, much less embrace it. Northern and southern Italy are two different countries, the north being almost Swiss in formality and precision, and the twain rarely meet.

But anyone who underestimated Dal Bolognese was making a bad bet. It's packed every night, with the most glamorous, fancily dressed crowd that Italy can offer. The ladies who lunch at Bice look swell, too, but the majority of them are contessa wannabes from Bel Air to Beirut. At Bolognese, the women are the real thing, and the dashing men are the owners, or the playboy sons of the owners, of the great northern Italy industrial entities that make Milan the *colossus urbis* that it is. You can wear your best duds and still feel underdressed, outchic'ed. You can *never* be this rich or this thin, so don't try. But if you're not too insecure, it's good fun to watch the show.

The money factor is apparent from the location in an annex of the Hotel Principe de Savoia, recently taken over by the Sultan of Brunei and Dubai'd to the max. You've never seen such a crush of Bentleys outside, so much gold and marble inside, so many billionaires in burnooses and worry beads in any lobby this side of the gulf. If this is Italy, you wouldn't know it, not until you step into the portals of Dal Bolognese, and the Arabs, and virtually all other non-Italians, mysteriously vanish. While the room in Rome's Dal Bolognese is very simple, very 1960s *moderno,* with the prime seating on the outdoor terrace overlooking the square and the obelisk, in Milan's the modern feel is Dubai designer showcase: hardwood floors, marble counters with displays of vegetables, a paneled "library" room with no books. The feel is a fancy tract-house golf-condo development near Vegas. There is a vast bar/lounge, with plush sofas and deep leather chairs and giant mirrors to sate the needs of the rare narcissist who might stumble in. There are more freshly squeezed exotic fruit concoctions than at any health bar, or any Trader Vic's, which this evokes. What the connection is to Emilia-Romagna (the province that Bologna is the capital of) is unknowable, but the lounge is one of the best pickup spots in Milan, assuming you've got the Right Stuff. But the bar is high in every sense, so be forewarned.

Of course, the nouveau decor couldn't matter less to a clientele whose bloodlines go back to the first popes, if not the Caesars. An ethereal blond model enters. An Italian points out that this isn't just some goddess from Brazil or the Czech Republic, but rather a Contessa Borromeo, as in the idyllic, exclusive Borromean Islands in the Lago Maggiore. Even the goddesses here have pedigrees. If the men look like bankers, they probably are. Because there are no bad people here, there are no bad seats. And no bad food, either. What's offered here is the hearty Emilia-Romagna fare that won the palates of Rome, if only because it was in short supply in the fish-intensive capital city. The Emilian classics are all here: definitive lasagna, cheese ravioli, meat sauces, a kingdom of hams and salamis. The most popular dish of all is *bollito misto,* an artery-clogging assortment of boiled brisket, tongue, and *cotechino,* a rough-textured sausage that you'll never see a model eat. Don't expect a lot of vegetables here, nor a lot of fish. This is meatland, "big deal" guy food, not for the faint of heart or diet.

It may seem a bit like carrying coals to Newcastle to be serving this Emilian cooking in nearby Milan, but the popularity speaks for itself. Besides, for all its proximity, there really aren't many Emilian restaurants in Milan, so the opportunity actually did exist to fill a niche in the currently sushi-crazy metropolis where the other "hottest" restaurant after this one is Nobu in the Armani superstore. Consider Dal Bolognese sort of a backlash restaurant, a return to roots. The owner, Alfredo Tomaselli, commutes between Milan and Rome, where his wife, Michi, and mother, Elena, hold the original fort. The Tomasellis are a major food dynasty in Rome. Not only is mama Elena a legendary cook, but her late sister Cesarina had an eponymous, celeb-filled trattoria off the Via Veneto that for decades was considered one of the finest Emilian restaurants in the country, honored with every gastronomic prize.

167

Elena and Cesarina were Rome's double-barreled answer to Bice Mungai. Sisterhood was powerful.

So was the challenge of taking on a new city. "I'm a megalomaniac," says the seemingly easygoing, always smiling Tomaselli. "I love challenges." A Milanese friend who never ate anywhere but Dal Bolognese when in Rome had once jokingly suggested trying a northern transplant, an idea that stuck in Tomaselli's head. "I thought that being in Milan would only make Rome better, not diminish it." So, leasing from the sultan the space where another fancy restaurant had failed, Tomaselli brought three of his top cooks from Rome and took the plunge. He's more than merely afloat; he's swimming. "Milan is much more fashionable, more snob," the un-Milanese Tomaselli says, marveling that all it took was two weeks for his upstart restaurant to be booked two weeks or more in advance. "Rome is much more casual, more a show-business, politician crowd. This is business, banking, money. They spend much more money on fine wines here. The expense-account dinners are great for us." They're great for you, too, even if you don't get any inside tips on Armani stock or get invited to the Borromean Isles. ★ ★ ★

Da Giacomo
Fashion Café

The restaurants of the Via Monte Napoleone are geared to shoppers. But where, you ask, aside from Bice and Paper Moon, do the designers eat? They tend to get out of the neighborhood and head across Milan to what has become their "local": Da Giacomo, a Tuscan trattoria that has become famous not for the usual Tuscan specialties of salamis and *bisteccas* but rather for seafood. In case you've forgotten your geography, Tuscany has a seacoast. Just think about Livorno, La Spezia, Porto Ercole, and the most stylish beach resort of all, Forte dei Marmi, which spawned all the *branzino*-grilling trattorias of Los Angeles. Yes, Tuscany is a piscatorial paradise, and nowhere, in Tuscany or out, is its bounty more enticingly presented than at Da Giacomo. This is Giorgio Armani's favorite restaurant in Milan. And Jil Sander's. And Miuccia Prada's. And Domenico Dolce's. And Stella McCartney's. Who could be more particular than the great designers? The only problem is getting in, so book far in advance.

Decorated by the famed Milan designer Renzo Mongiardino, the restaurant's new (since 1990) quarters look far more like a fin de siècle Paris brasserie than anything in Milan, with pale green and yellow walls and mosaic floors and white fluted columns and cherubs on the ceiling. Plus all the flowers that Milan restaurants put out to simulate April (in Paris, here), flowers that battle for display space with the just delivered sea urchin and cuttlefish. There is, however, absolutely nothing French about the food. But before you can get it, you have to wait. And wait. Even if you have that months-in-advance booking. Because there's no bar or anywhere to sit, you'll probably end up being told to wait outside, probably in the rain. You look around at all the empty tables and presume you're being dissed. What can you do? Take Armani's table? So you shrug it off. When you go outside to cool your heels, you'll see that the tables aren't empty at all. It's not a labor strike, all the people ringing Da Giacomo. The customers at the empty tables are all out in the drizzle, puffing away between courses. The Draconian Italian no-smoking laws have emptied the place out.

Why they would let nicotine dull their palates for what awaits them is a mystery. When you finally get seated in the elbow-to-elbow din, a waiter brings you a slice of the best pizza you have ever tasted. This upper crust is cracker thin, but not cracker friable. It's not a crumbling cookie but something beautifully chewy, topped with a thin smear of piquant tomato sauce, a hint of mozzarella, and slivers of tangy anchovies fresh from the sea. You ask for more and more, slice after slice, and could easily make your meal of this. But stop while you are ahead. There's terrific *spaghetti allo scoglio* (on the rocks), with tomatoes and more superfresh mixed shellfish, and then the sweetest simply grilled *langostini* you've tasted, making it impossible to eat the invariably frozen scampi in even the best American *ristoranti* without looking back here in jealousy. For dessert, even the models take the "dolce mamma," a *semifreddo* of zabaglione and hot chocolate that finally gives in to the reality of cold, damp Milan and provides a sumptuous antidote.

There are a lot of top-dollar wines for the free spenders who populate the place, but the ultimate super-Tuscan is Giacomo himself. Giacomo Bulleri is in his eighties now, and the only thing he cooks is the pizza. But from that pizza, you know what a master he is and must have been. Tall, sleek, with a twinkle in his roving eyes for all the 10s who adorn the rooms ("Women keep me young," he says), Giacomo is a bubbling presence that brings his restaurant to life. The heavy lifting is done by his daughter Tiziana, who must keep the hungry and angry waiting hordes at bay, and her husband, Marco Monti, who is the chef. Born in Tuscany, Giacomo moved to Torino with his family as a boy, with seven siblings. He gives all credit for his food talents to his mother, who cooked three square formal meals, with home-baked bread even, for the big family.

In the restaurant business, even the mighty can fall, as did Da Giacomo in its recent New York incarnation on East Sixty-fourth Street. It fell quickly, in less than eight months. That was a failure that Giacomo Bulleri, who had never been to New York, blames on the terminal illness of one of his American partners. The famed Sirio Maccioni, the Superest Tuscan of them all, has begged his landsman to try again, but Giacomo is holding out. Berlin is strongly beckoning, and Moscow has just opened, right near the Kremlin. The Moscow connection explains the presence of so many six-foot-tall Russian blondes and five-foot-tall Russian "financiers" in the Milan restaurant. Odd couples perhaps, but Giacomo Bulleri ignores the men and the money and brings some more of his heavenly pizza to the girls, always hoping that the way to their heart will be through their camera-ready concave stomachs. If anyone can get through, it is he. ★ ★ ★ ★ ★ ★ ★ ★ ★ ★ ★ ★ ★ ★ ★ ★ ★ ★ ★

Casa Botín
Hog Heaven

MADRID

Where restaurants are concerned, Spain is said to be the new France, at least in terms of cutting-edge gourmandise, what with El Bulli, in Roses, and Arzak, in San Sebastián, and any number of other three-star winners that even the French have to admit are determining all the big trends in food today. In Madrid, however, which may be the coolest, most happening of all European capitals, the restaurants that rule the roost are the oldies but goodies. None is older than Hemingway's beloved Casa Botín, which the *Guinness Book of World Records* lists as the oldest restaurant in the world, La Tour d'Argent notwithstanding. *Guinness* also says that Goya, in his starvation days, worked here as a dishwasher.

Whatever. The building housing Casa Botín goes back to the sixteenth century, when the spectacular Plaza Mayor, home of countless auto-da-fés, was built and the Spanish court moved to Madrid. The auto-da-fés have been replaced by autos, making these ancient streets impassable, so walk down the charming street called Cuchilleros, or cutlery row (street of utensil makers). This street of knives and forks leads to Botín, where you'll eat—Hemingway's Jake and Brett did in *The Sun Also Rises*—one of the world's great roast suckling pigs. It's the total opposite of cutting edge: pure tradition, as good as it ever was. That consistency, so rare in the world, is why everyone, from the king of Spain to Bend It Like Beckham to Vlad Putin to Natalie Portman to Jack Nicholson, keeps coming here.

When Botín was first opened for business as an inn, by an émigré Frenchman named Botín in 1725, it was considered a tavern, and guests were required to bring their own meats to roast in Botín's still functioning evergreen-oak-burning oven. In the next century it graduated from a BYO to serving pastries in addition to home-butchered grills, but it still wasn't allowed to be called a "restaurant," a term reserved in Spain for the most fancy, Frenchified establishments. Instead, Botín was classed a house of meals (*casa de comidas*), which sounds a bit like House of Pies, which it actually was. In 1925, Spain was on hard times, and so was the Botín family, which sold its casa to an ambitious private chef named Antonio González, who befriended Hemingway during the Spanish Civil War, and even invited him into the kitchen and challenged him mano a mano to a paella-cooking contest, which Papa lost ignominiously.

Botín at this point was still a very casual place. Hemingway made his own drinks, basically just hung out here and ran a long tab. He made it up to González by featuring Botín not only in *Sun* but also in *Death in the Afternoon*.

He also introduced his bullfighter friends Dominguín and Ordoñez to the place. A buzz began, which mushroomed when Hemingway became world famous. Everybody *had* to try Botín, and it never failed to deliver. A star was born, and it finally could begin calling itself a restaurant.

After World War II, Antonio González's son Antonio expanded Botín's heady sphere of influence by courting the Hollywood crowd that had been lured to Madrid as a second Rome, where epics could be filmed at a fraction of the cost of Burbank. Hence such films as *El Cid* and *The Pride and the Passion* made Botín regulars of Charlton Heston, Cary Grant, and Frank Sinatra, who became even more regular when his one true love, Ava Gardner, split from Hollywood permanently and made Madrid her new home, and Botín her prime hangout. Sinatra often came here alone when Gardner would refuse to see him. One for my baby, one more for the Plaza Mayor. The second Antonio González was a highly charismatic host, an accomplished artist who spoke five languages fluently. People came for Hemingway, for the food, for the stars, and for Antonio. Just as La Tour d'Argent became "The Duck Joint," in the 1950s, Casa Botín became "The Pig Joint." The González family was truly in hog heaven.

Today the third Antonio González, as courtly as his father, is continuing Botín's formidable tradition, though he grimaces at the notion that Botín is a one-dish wonder. Although González serves more than fifty whole hogs a day at Botín, and a like number at his also historic and idyllic Hotel Cardenal, built right below the Arab walls of nearby Toledo, he's rightly proud of everything on his enticing menu. González's one moment of failure was his Casa Botín in Miami, which lasted for six years in the 1990s. He claims to have gotten pigs from the Kentucky equivalent of his *primo* porkers raised in Segovia, but it didn't matter. "The Jews of Miami wouldn't eat pig," he laments, noting that the Jews of Hollywood sure eat it in Madrid.

You're already deep in the past as you walk to Botín through Old Hapsburg Madrid and the vast Plaza Mayor. But once you're inside there's no trace of the present at all. You're greeted by the sweet aroma of a display of white apples on the tiny bar where Hemingway stirred, behind which is one of the earliest known cash registers. A wall of sherries and vermouths stands at the ready. The tiny ground-floor dining room is covered in Mudejar tiles evoking the time when Spain was ruled by the Arabs from Granada. The ceiling is low and crooked, the windows are stained glass. You want to sit here, but González either takes you up or down, in either case pointing out the vast furnace filled with the fragrantly roasting carcasses of little pigs and haunches of lamb. You get hungrier than you ever thought you could be, atavistically hungry. You think you should be ashamed, but then you remember you're in macho Spain, home of bullfights, Hemingway country, and you let yourself give in to the savage impulses.

Up is where Hemingway sat, back to the wall in a corner, like a Mafia capo. There are low-beamed ceilings, white stucco walls, old paintings of game and fruit, wooden tables filled with the only clue you're in the current century: lots of sleek, chic women incongruously devouring big plates of meat. Maybe they're Atkins dieters, you think, but the platters of roast potatoes beside them put that theory to rest. Note that, given what you're about to eat, the time to come to Botín is lunch (the main meal in Spain), but the time for lunch in Spain is three o'clock. Actually, Spain is a good place to lose weight: a late breakfast at the hotel of wonderful omelets (*tortillas*) cooked in olive oil, then a vast lunch, which you can blissfully walk off, then a tiny sandwich or plate of Jabugo ham late at night, in the unlikely case your stomach is stirring. You can literally pork out and still come out ahead, or rather behind (on the scale). Try it.

If upstairs is a day in Segovia, downstairs is a night at the Spanish Inquisition, a dark, vaulted, brick dungeon that nonetheless is considered *the* place to sit at Botín, perhaps because it is such a giant step back in time. You won't be depressed, because of the festive packed house of glam diners, and especially when the food arrives. If this is your first visit, you must start with the house clams, tiny, tender mollusks steamed in a rich broth of tomato, garlic, and parsley. One taste and you'd think that you were sitting by the Mediterranean in Sitges, not in a subterranean dungeon in landlocked Madrid. Next is the house salad, nothing but perfect lettuce and sweet farm tomatoes and private-label olive oil. There's great chewy country bread to scarf up that clam broth and the olive oil. But watch it, or you won't have room for the pig.

Oh that pig! The skin is fat free, parchment golden and crisp, the underlying meat tender and juicy. It's a taste matched only by North Carolina–style pit barbecue (see page 256), except in Madrid there's no vinegar and spices to give heartburn for days (not that it's not worth it). Here at Botín it's pure pig; washed down with the same *rioja* that Jake Barnes drank, it's pure bliss. You look around, and just about everyone is eating the pig, and you may be reminded of Harvard's most exclusive club, the Porcellian ("the Porc," to the überpreps). Botín is Madrid's Pork Club, and the great thing is that it's easy for you to become a member. You can't help but notice other nonpork dishes: grilled sole, stewed partridge, platters of fried squid. Everything looks great, and it is.

175

You finish, if you can finish, with homemade lemon sorbet with house *cava*, which tastes like an alcoholic lemon milk shake. You get the bill, and you're amazed at how inexpensive it is. This is not a meal to have often, but a meal that you will never forget. It's already six o'clock and just the time for a sherry at an outdoor café in the plaza. Time travel is great, isn't it? Casa Botín could be the world's worst tourist trap and get away with it, but the González family is way too proud for that. Spain is all about pride and face, and the beneficiary here is you. ★ ★ ★ ★

Bulli Boy

So you've had enough of Old Madrid, enough roast suckling pig, enough scrambled eggs, enough of the past. What about New Madrid, the vanguard city, the Spanish London, the place the Tribeca crowd looks to as the pacemaker of hip? Then you must really try La Broche. Here in the trendy minimalist Hotel Miguel Angel (Michelangelo, señor), the hip, Cruise-ish, motorcycle-riding, electric-guitar-playing rock chef Sergi Arola will provide a two-*Michelin*-star simulacrum of the alchemy of Arola's mentor Ferran Adrià at El Bulli, rated by most food journals as the greatest restaurant on earth. It's well worth sacrificing that extra star in return for not having to make the dizzying three-hour cliff drive north of Barcelona to The Bulldog, assuming you can get a reservation, as the place is tiny and only open six months a year. On the other hand, La Broche is a five-minute cab ride from the center of Madrid, the Puerta del Sol, albeit light-years from a city suspended in many charming ways in the amber of Don Quixote.

Given his thirtyish studliness, his guest appearances with such bands as Franz Ferdinand, his selection to design the business-class menus for Iberia Airlines, Sergi Arola is a Player in Spain, and in Europe. Wanting to become one in America, he opened a La Broche in Miami, but his timing was lousy. The restaurant debuted in September 2001. Despite its ambitions and pedigree, it tanked. If Botín can fail in Miami, so can Arola. No *problema*. Arola did not lose face. He kept his friendship with such American superchefs as Charlie Trotter, David Bouley, Jean-Georges Vongerichten. He's playing in their league, which is Major. He's a star, but in general he doesn't get the stars in La Broche. Then, again, neither does Ferran Adrià. "Gastronomic restaurants are not for the famous," Arola observes, though he admits having fun serving the likes of Kevin Costner and Morgan Freeman. Just as gentlemen prefer blondes, stars prefer pigs, or at least pigs from Casa Botín.

Arola himself, for all his power biking and rock and roll, prefers subtle delicacy, the artists' way. He grew up at the feet of his Catalan grandfather, a rich man before the Spanish Civil War and forever an epicure, who regaled little Sergi with tales of his gourmet travels, to Maxim's in Paris, to Pyramide in Vienne, to Crocodil in Strasbourg. Sergi has traveled himself now, in grandfather's footsteps and beyond. Japan, the most delicate place of all, made the biggest impression upon him, the eight-seat restaurants "where the chefs are priests." And bankers, too, as the prices make New York's biggest biller, Masa, seem a bargain. Only stars can afford this, but stars are too impatient for such delicacy. Bankers, the big ones who can also pay the freight, seem more patient.

Arola draws as attractive a crowd of foodies as there can be, not the fat Falstaff lawyers nor the superserious Ruth Reichl cookbook obsessives nor the Berkeley-Cambridge brainy Escoffiers who look like the sick people who ironically seem to dominate "health food" restaurants. No, what Arola draws are globe-trotting, deep-pocketed post-yuppies who are unflagging in their pursuit of quality trend. So here you are. The tiny, white, thirty-five-seat room couldn't be more austere. It looks less like a dining room than an art gallery, decorated with a few abstract mobiles and a Day-of-the-Dead Mexican portrait of a chef surrounded by six deadly sins, avarice omitted. When you see the prices, you might get the joke, laughing all the way to Chapter 11. You sit in leather Eames-type chairs, attended to by punkette waitresses in black leather bomber jackets and pretty-boy captains much more soberly turned out in Armani suits.

Once the food starts coming, it doesn't seem to stop. Prepare for a French Laundry–style marathon of at least a dozen courses, and at least four hours. Lunch always affords more breathing room. Whatever time you come, after the Armani'd sommelier has chosen a few major Spanish wines that you've never heard of, the leather girl comes with a tray of flatbreads and three dips: guacamole, aioli, tomato. All yummy, not foamy, and totally accessible. Then the weirdness starts. Three different salts arrive: smoked, pink-peppered, oregano-thyme'd, along with sweet butters, four olive oils, and seven home-made breads (soy, sunflower, wheat, olive sourdough, more) to mix and match and confuse yourself. You invariably take too much salt and nearly choke to death. The idea is a smidgen, but even a smidgen takes away from the delicious breads and fats. So you give the salt a rest.

Next, the "Arola moment," as the punkette announces a selection of tiny tapas: fried baby squid in its ink; a microsandwich of pureed chanterelles, blue cheese, and spinach; bright red baby (as opposed to the oxymoronic jumbo) shrimp that live up to their name, in a caramel sauce; the smallest cockles you've ever seen. The whole show is more an exercise in miniaturization than in taste. Plus all the tinies are lukewarm, which perhaps is how Arola intended, but all the "moment" does is make you yearn for another moment in a full-size, fractionally priced tapas bar. Next you get an unnamed "Adrià moment" with a demitasse cup of what seems like a cream of mushroom soup, but may well be foamed-up peanut butter and jelly. They don't tell; you don't ask. This is Gerber baby food for billionaires.

Things return to normal, and goodness, with a "flight" of local seafood: grilled baby sardines with the world's smallest green beans (from Kenya) and wild trumpet mushrooms; oven-baked *merluza in salsa verde,* a delicate version of the same dish from Lucio, but with fresh peas and a nut-based vinaigrette; grilled red mullet with a lasagna flecked with Iberian ham and black sausage, as hearty as something this small can be. You switch from white wine to red, and the meats begin. There's a Christmas-in-July roast venison with Granny Smith apples and chestnuts. Then marinated wild boar with something scarily called "cocoa air," a kind of foamy mole, weird, yes, but also good. And then, for all you animal lovers, a blood-rare steak of horse meat, served with vanilla-flavored mashed potatoes and tomatoes stewed with olives. If you don't think about it, you could love it. Drink a lot. There are lots of little desserts: pumpkin ice cream and "cheese soup," forest fruit "acid" with Campari and Martini, popcorn-dusted chocolate. There's a huge choice of teas in test tubes, something out of *Little Shop of Horrors.* You try to imagine Keith Richards sitting through all this, and you understand why the stars all go to Lucio. ★ ★ ★ ★ ★ ★ ★ ★ ★ ★

Casa Lucio
The Host with the Most

MADRID

A few narrow, winding, crumbling blocks away from Casa Botín is another *casa de comidas*, the unmarked, unsigned Casa Lucio, founded in 1961 but looking centuries older. Lucio lacks Botín's illustrious history, but not its clientele. In fact, Casa Lucio probably has the most celebrity-studded clientele in all Europe. At any meal, on any day, you are likely to see more famous people here than anywhere in the Old World, except Harry's Bar in Venice, or its offshoot Cipriani in London, or maybe Davé in Paris. But Davé gets mostly movie stars and fashion luminaries. It is unlikely to get heads of state or serious royalty, as well as all the three-star chefs, as Lucio does. And the Cipriani restaurants are horribly expensive, cruelly snobby, intimidatingly stylish, and everybody is putting on the dog, of some bark. Lucio is none of that. This casa is very cheap, very funky, very down-home. It feels like a diner, and its most famous dish is scrambled eggs mixed with French fries. How fancy can such a place be? Yet scarfing down those eggs may be Bill Clinton at one table and King Juan Carlos at another, with a truck driver and his family in between them. Anybody can come to Casa Lucio; what makes someone cool here is simply *knowing* about this hidden gem, like a speakeasy in the Roaring Twenties.

Lucio is all about Lucio, Madrid's favorite host, or at least insider's Madrid. When he enters the room, the waters part. He's a little pixie, midseventies but still an impish boy, resplendent in a white dinner jacket, blue checked shirt and navy tie, a lesser version of which all the waiters wear. He's full of quips and puns in Spanish and, hardly a linguist, has fans on every continent. Lucio knows how to make you feel at home, because, at heart, he's just like you. A poor boy from the medieval walled city of Ávila, Luciano Blázquez came to Madrid as a twelve-year-old and worked as a dishwasher (shades of Goya) at a student dive called the Meson del Segoviano, which is where Casa Lucio is now; child labor laws were not being enforced. Lucio grew up and left the Meson to be an apprentice waiter a few doors down at El Schotis ("The Scottish," named for a highland fling of a dance popular in Old Madrid). When he was the ripe age of twenty-seven, in 1961, the Meson del Segoviano went up for sale. It was cheap. Lucio used all his savings to buy it. Already the area's favorite waiter, Lucio had a big following, which followed him to his own place. Eventually one of those followers brought a famous bullfighter, who brought a tycoon, who brought an aristocrat, who brought more aristocrats, who brought the king. The chain letter worked, and Lucio was "made."

Lucio will make you wait, an hour, sometimes two, even if you've booked months ahead, which isn't a bad idea. When you start waiting two hours for an 11 P.M. reservation, you're looking at a real midnight supper. No problem. Midnight is prime dinnertime in Madrid, especially among the social set. Lucio stays open, and stays full, till dawn's early light. So belly up to the bar, which is hung with dozens upon dozens of aging, fat-dripping Jabugo hams, and order a plate of this beloved local delicacy. Then have a plate of wonderful fresh anchovies, and a plate of fat pimento-stuffed olives, olives you can only get in Spain. Take a few lessons in sherry, and you'll start getting in the mood. Waiting with you might be a Rockefeller, or Michael Douglas and Catherine Zeta-Jones, or the Almodóvar film crowd, or Beckham and Posh, Ronaldo, Russell Crowe, Lenny Kravitz, maybe even Ferran Adrià. Everybody comes to Lucio; everybody waits. You'll be amazed at the mix of chic people and freak people. A lot of clochard types from the streets save up for one long drink here, and they are welcome. There are cops, and firemen, and street sweepers, and ambassadors, and high priests. Lucio is a culinary democracy.

The mix continues when you're led to your table. Upstairs is considered Siberia, or Portugal here in Spain. But if you like pretty models, there are far more of them than down below, where the women are either bejeweled, bedesignered dowagers or hippie gypsies. How the latter get in and get prime seating is beyond you, but they are obviously friends of Lucio, and Lucio goes way back, though multiple strata of society, low to high. The decor, such as it is, is mixed as well. White tiled walls, odd portraits of bulls, horses, penitent priests . . . actually, more bulls than anything else. The place looks like a thrift shop. People are drinking heavily, having a wonderful time, the dowagers happily mixing with the gypsies, stirred along by Lucio, who makes a pass through the room every fifteen minutes or so, aided by his sons and daughters. It's a family affair, one big endless party. People break out spontaneously into song, and sometimes into dance. The *rioja* flows like rivers.

The food is puzzling. The bread, which comes out like a giant bagel, is as hard as a three-day-old bagel. You have to try the *huevos* Lucio. You do. Maybe it's an acquired taste. The fries are limp and greasy. You send them back, asking for crisper ones. You seek but do not find. The new fries may be more cooked, but nobody drained them, so they're soaked in grease, not that you can tell much, as the lumpy eggs are greasy, too. This is Denny's fare, you think the sacrilegious thought, the kind of stuff they serve at Doe's Eat Place in Little Rock, Clinton's favorite restaurant. That's why he comes here, old home week. You can take the boy out of Doe's, but you can't take Doe's out of the boy, not even after bypass surgery.

A more conventional famous dish here is the *merluza in salsa verde,* a fine, firm-fleshed fish from the Bay of Biscay in a green sauce. The sauce is good enough, but the fish is a little too firm, as in dried out, and the peas are straight from a can. Lucio, like Bill Clinton, isn't big on veggies. How many bullfighters actually like veggies? You get the idea. Another dish of kings here is the steak on a sizzling platter, the steak of the toreadors. Alas, the platter sizzles so mightily that a rare steak becomes medium in the course of your eating it. For dessert you try the also famous caramelized rice pudding, sort of a cross with a crème brûlée, which is so sweet you order a very dry sherry to cut the sugar. In fact, you order a lot more sherry, and some powerful house *cava,* and you try to join the party, if you could only stay awake at 3 A.M. These Spaniards have gusto, all right. Perhaps the best plan here might be to do the raw thing at the bar, then turn in at a "northern" hour. But if Lucio lets you in, he won't let you out. The host with the most hates nothing more than a party pooper. ★ ★ ★ ★

Franco-Philes

When stars who come to Madrid are willing to dress up, they go to Jockey. Founded in 1945, Jockey was the postwar jet set's headquarters in Madrid, the place where you'd find the Duke and Duchess of Windsor, Barbara Hutton and all her swains, Oleg Cassini, the Greek tycoons, the Kennedys, even the Nixons, not to mention the Stones and Beatles in their prime. Their successors are still there. This is still the most glamorous, most exclusive, most high-society of Madrid restaurants; and Madrid society, with all its *condes* and *condesas,* can be as high as it gets. The Jockey was originally called The Jockey Club, and no restaurant anywhere is clubbier. Nevertheless, in the 1980s, when the original jet set started dying off, the management, not wanting to lose good business, dropped the "Club." But face it, the Jockey is still a club, albeit one that will let you in. Join it, for at least one meal, as it's a time trip back to the bad old macho days of the male prerogative of Generalissimo Francisco Franco, whose dictatorial spirit haunts the place.

The Jockey is in the heart of official governmental Madrid. The law courts, the ministries, the embassies are all around it, in a lovely, leafy precinct of converted town houses and mansions. The restaurant is barely marked, but you know it's there by the phalanx of Guardia Civil officers stationed outside guarding the bigwigs within. Within is a truly beautiful L-shaped room with deep green walls and rich wood paneling, duck presses, countless prints, bronzes, statues of horses, and little effigies of jockeys at every table. Just as Lucio is an ode to the bullring, Jockey is a shrine to the turf. At lunchtime, the room is almost all men, and almost everyone is smoking cigars, including the few female *Devil Wears Prada* types keeping these Masters of the Universe company. The menu is retro as well, so retro it might be in Paris in the 1950s, lots of foie gras, truffles, oysters. The one thing you will not find on this menu is a horse steak, *pace* Sergi Arola. They don't shoot horses here, do they?

There may be lots of France on the menu, ancien régime France, but there's plenty of Spain: the roast partridge with grape sauce, the *merluza* in *salsa verde*, the state-of-the-art gazpacho. They make a wonderful roast baby chicken, with a nod to Louis XIV in the form of the accompanying *pommes souf-flés,* the dodo of labor-intensive potato dishes, fast becoming extinct. Wines are noble, as are cognacs, which you have with one more cigar and the wonderful house-made orange *pâté de fruits* and a variety of chocolate truffles. The wait-ers, who barely speak English, have all been here since Franco's time. If you order what they say, they may like you well enough by the end of the formal meal, once the ministers have left, to start telling stories. Stories like the time three kings were at the Jockey simultaneously, at three tables: Spain, Italy, Bulgaria. Stories like the time Sinatra came in and caught Ava Gardner, not with the mas-ter Dominguín, whom the Othello-jealous Chairman was expecting to find, but rather a young toreador who wasn't even a star. Imagine, for Old Blue Eyes to lose his love to a below-the-line performer. He was so depressed, he didn't even smash all the horse art. He just slunk out, a stranger in the night. ★ ★ ★ ★ ★

Club 55
Le Freak, C'est Chic

Sometimes you just want a freak show. If that particular jones happens to strike when you're in the south of France, hie thee to St. Tropez for the greatest restaurant show on earth, the Club 55, or "Cinquante-Cinq," which has the same breathlessly anticipatory etymology as *soixante-neuf* in this sunny, sexy clime. Club 55 is a circus, far more so than Le Cirque could ever dream of being. In the last few decades, the only place that has ever approximated its energy, glamour, and fun was the seminal Ma Maison in Los Angeles. Like 55, Ma Maison was basically an outdoor garden shack serving fine French food to the most stunning and famous people in the world. Unlike 55, at Ma Maison these same people were not basically almost naked, which definitely changes the vibe and turns up the heat. Club 55 is right on the world's most famous topless beach, La Plage de Pampelonne, and the beachy-peachy abandon attendant to that location makes 55 the most erotic serious restaurant in the world.

Don't try to come in winter, because 55 is closed. If you have to wear *clothes*, what's the point? But in summer, the six-mile drive from the center of the world's most imitated and badly plagiarized fishing village can resemble the hellish *confiture* from Godard's *Weekend*. The real players come by yacht and anchor in the bay, like P. Diddy. And the even realer players come by helicopter *from* their anchored yacht, like Microsoft's Paul Allen, who remains discreet enough to garb his loins.

So just accept the fifty-dollar cab fare, and don't get intimidated when the Hollywood-handsome valet parker, who combines the worst of LA snobbery and Paris hauteur, sneers at your rented Renault. The guys who have the Ferraris and Bentleys are just as intimidated by Diddy and Allen, not to mention the likes of Jack Nicholson, Bruce Willis, Sly Stallone, Pamela Anderson, French stars like Jean Reno and Alain Delon, international fusion couples like Johnny Depp and Vanessa Paradis, any and all of whom might be making grand entrances here at any given time. Elton John and Bono and Beckham and Kate Moss and so many other Sceptered Isle stars come here that the boardwalk leading to the restaurant is the real "Promenade des Anglais," not the beach boulevard in Nice.

As exclusive as Club 55 may seem, it's not really a private club, and it's not hard to get in. Just call and book, or have your hotel do it. The place, a *déjeuner sur l'herbe* on flower-bedecked tables set with festive blue and white linens and spread out under white umbrellas and shady overhangs, is sprawling and infinitely elastic. In addition to the wonderful sea breezes, there are shady tamarind trees and umbrella pines and Evian spritzers to keep things cool. Very cool. The whole place feels like an Elysium, an earthly Eden, and for the sinners here, it's as close to heaven as they are likely to get. Lunch goes from noon to six (prime time is three o'clock), and it may be the longest lunch you'll ever have, but you won't want to leave. Club 55 feels like a chic party where no one knows anyone else, but you feel special just for being there. Before long, you'll be chatting up your neighbors. And before longer, and after a few bottles of chilled Domaine Ott rosé, you'll be peeling off some of those layers of Prada that you thought were necessary. A Gypsy Kings–like band of beach troubadours serenades the guests and adds to the party feel without being obtrusive.

Other than time of arrival, it's hard to tell what's Valhalla and what's Siberia at 55. The stars are scattered about, and everyone else looks rich or important if they're guys; and if they're not, they are young and impossibly beautiful, or aging and trying to do the impossible, which is to capture and cage the sweet bird of youth, either by extreme dieting or extreme plastic surgery. There is a lot of leathery skin here, of the pre-skin-cancer generation, and bronze is still beautiful, melanoma be damned. The under-twenty-five supermodels and superhookers cavort about as though there is no tomorrow. Perhaps they should take cautionary note of the supermodels and superhookers of yesterday who are still here. Perhaps they have. Maybe that's why they're cavorting so hard, to snare one of the Havana-chomping fat cats before hard tomorrow sets in.

Whatever their age, the women are all in the tiniest bikinis, with the occasional diaphanous shawl thrown over them. The men are either in white linen or in bathing shorts. Legend has it here that the bigger the belly, the bigger the portfolio. Club 55 is like the United Nations: a cacophony of all languages are spoken here, though increasingly Russian, as the oligarch crowd has taken mightily to the French Riviera. There are a lot of North African casbah types speaking French. Their former casbahs are only a Jet Ski across the Mediterranean. The Côte d'Azur for these Moroccan and Algerian and Lebanese jeans-and-stuff moguls is both a fresh-air fund and the promised land. They're loving it flat out, and their sense of wild abandon is what sets the party tone at 55, symbolized by the ritual anointing of deathly expensive champagne all over the deathly expensive bodies of the playgirls. There's money to burn and the flames grow higher by the hour, even as the sun begins to set.

Because 55 is fifty boardwalked yards deep in from the naked burning shore, you won't get sand in your food. At most beach restaurants, the food is so bad that sand would be a welcome condiment, but not at 55. The food is simple and perfect for the setting, just what you want on a hot day. The first thing you get when you sit down is a sprawling wooden platter of crudités, the freshest, ripest tomatoes, cucumbers, radishes, carrots, celery, mushrooms. And a big bowl of aioli to dip the veggies in. You could do this, sipping your rosé and munching on the toothsome baguettes for hours, and you may well, as the service is leisurely. Have steamed *moules* to start, or the refreshing salad Pampelonne, which is tomatoes, mint, and chèvre, then a right-from-the-Med *dorade*, or, if you're feeling macho, a big Charolais *entrecote* from the open grill, *au poivre* if you're in the mood for more heat. It may not feel like potato weather, but everyone loves the house potatoes, sliced thin and roasted crisp in a pan with olive oil and fennel and just enough sea salt to make you down another bottle of Ott. You'll have room for dessert, if only because you'll wait an hour more to get it. The *tarte aux fruits rouges*, a mix of raspberries, giant strawberries, and tiny *fraises des bois*, is worth both the wait, the calories, and the price. A hundred dollars a head for the food and the spectacle isn't bad in these moguls-only times.

The handsome, weathered man table-hopping in a djellaba who looks like a refugee from *The Sheltering Sky* is Patrice de Colmont, whose parents opened the place in 1955, hence the name. The year 1955 may have spelled darkest Eisenhower in the USA, but in France it marked the beginning of the sexual revolution, whose first cinematic Molotov cocktail was thrown right here on these premises. Playboy-auteur Roger Vadim had come to St. Tropez with his young discovery Brigitte Bardot to film the quasiporno art flick *And God Created Woman.* The elder de Colmonts were aristocratic beachcomber types living a Robinson Crusoe existence in a rough cabin on this then deserted strand. When Vadim, Bardot, and Tringtinant stumbled across the de Colmonts having a big outdoor feast with friends, the French New Wavers thought they had discovered the coolest offbeat restaurant. They asked the de Colmonts to cater for the cast and crew, the de Colmonts played along, though they nearly gave up the charade when they found they would be cooking for eighty. By filming's end, they had become de facto restaurateurs. And when the film became a global smash and Bardot a world-famous sex kitten, St. Trop and 55 became prime destinations on the map of the emerging jet set.

St. Tropez and 55 have been hot spots ever since, though not without their hills and valleys of popularity. Like that other long-running trendery, Mr Chow, Club 55 has benefited immeasurably by having been embraced by the high-rolling hip-hop aristocracy—Monsieur Diddy, Jay-Z, Beyoncé, Russell Simmons, and all the rest. Because the French aristocracy—the let-them-eat-cake crowd that survived the revolution—has its own obsession with all things *Africain,* even *Africain-American,* the arrival of the music stars made 55 a must destination all over again, with Beyoncé becoming the new Bardot. Meanwhile, the English, who had never really gone away, began coming back in droves. Don't forget, St. Trop was the site of the Mick and Bianca royal rock wedding in 1971, which assured the town its hot-spot permanent iconhood. Jerry Hall is still a regular. Another development that ensured 55's survival was its recent renovation of its formerly medieval bathrooms, which, for all their Stygian-ness, may have seen more action than the notoriously coed facilities at New York's Mudd Club.

Even though every trendy port, from Porto Banus to St. Bart's, has tried to ape the St. Trop yachts-croissants-designer labels-quaint stucco formula, no restaurant anywhere has successfully replicated Club 55's exclusive beach bacchanalia. Los Angeles, one would think, would embrace at least a dozen Club 55s. But it has none. Maybe LA's excuse is that topless cars take precedence over topless women, and that the Pacific Coast Highway's location so close to the sea prevents any restaurant from having a deep enough plot to be a complete beach "club." Other cities have the land, but they lack the touch. Maybe it's just the second generation of the de Colmonts (Patrice runs the show, sister Veronique runs the *caisse*) keeping this a true family business and tending the eternal flame of Bardot. Whatever, Club 55 is way too cool for *Michelin* ratings, *hors categorie*. But where a scene is concerned, there's no place that is more *vaut le voyage*. ★ ★ ★ ★ ★ ★ ★ ★ ★ ★ ★ ★

Food Festival

The three most glamorous events of the Hollywood year are the Golden Globes, the Oscars, and the Cannes Film Festival. For Hollywood foodies—and few Hollywood denizens are not—Cannes is by far the grandest of these *grande bouffes*. For one thing, the Globes and the Oscars are weekend blowouts, but Cannes lasts two decadent weeks. For another, the awards shows are winter affairs, and winters, even in LA, can be chilly. Cannes takes place in May on the French Riviera, springtime in paradise. And most important, Cannes is in the heart of food country, the Med in all its glory, with great restaurants everywhere and expense accounts to burn. For agents, studio executives, and producers, the measure of the festival has less to do with the often anemic films on display than with the gargantuan restaurant bills that are run up in the name of networking and "development." Even though the pictures, in Norma Desmond's words, may have gotten small, the tabs have not. And because the new generation of blingy stars and flashy agents hasn't experienced Cannes for decades on end, they know the legend and they all tend to come, as a matter of pleasure in the name of business, even if they have nothing to do with the small arty films that are featured in the festival.

There are four restaurants that are "musts" on the Cannes circuit. First is Tetou, on the water in Golfe-Juan, which makes if not the best then certainly the most expensive bouillabaisse in the world. Follow in the soup stains of Cary Grant, Grace Kelly, Gregory Peck, the whole Hitchcock crowd, with Matt Damon and George Clooney and the other bon vivant stars of today. Although it is nothing more than a glorified beach shack, Tetou is very snobby and almost impossible to get into during the festival. A call to Yanou Collart in Paris might help. Most people get the big "B" but the grilled fish is also perfect and the tomatoes Provençale are state-of-the-art. Tetou, around since the Roaring Twenties (the Fitzgeralds and Cole Porter came here), is where the late Marvin Davis's limo caravan was headed when jewel thieves held them up. It was a testimony to Tetou that the brazen multimillion-dollar heist did nothing to quell the Davis party's appetite; they pressed on and ate the night away.

In the old town of Cannes itself is Le Machou, which may be the definitive Provençale restaurant, and certainly the most star-studded. Michael and Catherine Zeta-Douglas hold court here, and the homier Brit stars like Kate Winslet call it home at festival time. But the flashers and splashers come, too, Joan and Jackie Collins, Mel Brooks, all the CAA boys. Machou is very farmhouse-y, with low-beamed ceilings and stone walls. The effect is that of a cozy cave, wherein you are assaulted by the wonderful smells of roasting beef, lamb, and chicken from the ancient oven, all seasoned with *herbes de provençe, la vrai chose*. Start with the huge platter of garden-fresh crudités and grilled bread dipped in Machou's famous sauce of white cheese, green onions, and more of those divine herbs. Finish with the lemon tart or cassis sorbet. Drink sangria. And be prepared to be booted out, as Machou has three celebrity seatings a night.

Then there is the amazingly beautiful Moulin de Mougins, a sixteenth-century mill in the hills above Cannes, which under the legendary chef Roger Vergé was for decades one of France's preeminent three-star dining shrines. In 2004 Vergé retired, and the toque was passed to Alain Llorca, chef of the also legendary Negresco Hotel on the Promenade des Anglais in Nice. Whether or not the Moulin will regain all its lost *étoiles* is pretty much beside the point at festival time. Sharon Stone conducts her celebrated AIDS auction here, and on any night the guest list for the rose- and prune-colored dining rooms, filled with sculptures by Cesar and Arman, is a virtual Promenade des Anglais: Hugh Grant, Ralph Fiennes, Jude Law, Michael Caine, Judi Dench, the omnipresent Naomi Campbell, who's like a movie star here even though she's not. The wine list is one of the grandest anywhere, and the stars drink like they never drink back home on Sunset; the cellar needs to be restocked by festival's end. Llorca has jettisoned most of Vergé's French classics in favor of his own fancified Spanish-heritage fare, like salt cod on a bed of pureed chickpeas with a *jus* of cod tripe. It tastes great, even though the stars and agents are usually too drunk to notice the difference.

With all the deals to do, who has time for romance during the festival? Still,

190

as long as there are starlets to be courted, there is no more romantic place to ply the love trade than La Colombe d'Or in that most picturesque of hill towns, St. Paul de Vence, which is also the artiest of all hill towns. The Foundation Maeght is here, and La Colombe d'Or is beyond well hung, with works of Picasso, Braque, Miró, Chagall, and many more of its famous patrons filling every wall. For all the art, the dreamiest place to sit is still on the outdoor rampart-terrace. Don't expect art on the plate, however. Order simply, very simply. While not a tourist trap (too many stars for that), La Colombe d'Or is proof that you can't expect to eat royally everywhere on the Riviera, even if you are surrounded by royalty. This was one of Lady Di's favorites, and those love doves Hugh Grant and Jemima Khan billed and cooed, after Liz Hurley, another Colombe-ian, had flown this nest.

Wherever you dine, drive your rented Ferrari (distances on the Riviera are short, driving times are long) to the Hotel du Cap (d'Antibes) for fifty-euro fresh-peach Bellini nightcaps in the marble and tapestry lobby or on the vast moonlit terrace overlooking the glimmering sea at this, the grandest of all the Côte's grand hotels. This is where the highest and mightiest stars and moguls hang at festival time. Harvey Weinstein is the self-appointed ringmaster of this celebrity circus. The Cap used to be cash only, a hardball policy that separated the true high rollers from the merely leveraged. Recently, the Cap began taking plastic, lots and lots of it, judging from the plastic molls on the arms of the Russian oligarch (polite for something worse) types who have taken a shine to the joint. One never hears French anymore. Word is that the Cap may soon fall into Russian hands. No, the Riviera ain't what it was when Cary and Grace innuendoed it up in *To Catch a Thief*. But it's still the gold standard where fame and fortune reign, and it never reigns harder than at Cannes-time. ★ ★ ★ ★ ★ ★

Night Flight
Café Sex

MOSCOW

It is a wild and crazy commentary on the anything-goes license of the gold-rush metropolis that is post-Communist Moscow that one of the city's very best restaurants is also one of its very best brothels. With more casinos than Vegas, more clubs than New York, more whores than Bangkok, and more sushi than Tokyo, Moscow has, out of nowhere, become the nightlife capital of the world, and that's not even counting the Bolshoi. The Russian women, who run a short but Olympian-Amazonian gamut from Veruschka to Maria Sharapova, are widely considered to be the world's most beautiful, and most mercenary. Money talks here, louder than anywhere else, because money is a voice that had been silenced for nearly a century, and absence had made Russian hearts grow ravenous.

There's a lot of lost playtime to make up for, and nowhere do people play harder than at Night Flight, a Swedish-owned pleasure dome right on Tverskaya Boulevard, Moscow's Fifth Avenue, a short walk from the Kremlin and Red Square. You can't miss the place: there is a small army of burly bouncers in black designer suits outside, opening doors of Bentleys and Hummers and stretch Benzes to greet rather smaller men in black designer suits. Down the street, Lenin is turning over in his tomb.

Join the crowd, and you are shown into a large vestibule with two check-rooms. One is for your coat, or coats, because in winter, baby, it's cold outside.

The other is for your weapons, because, winter or summer, heat is packed in Moscow. There are several bigger men with metal detectors, and at least one with an Uzi, so don't try anything cute. If you're going to the downstairs bar, there's a cover charge of around fifty dollars. If you're coming upstairs, there's no cover. Upstairs looks like a fancy Ikea store, all blond woods and angular furniture and Marimekko prints, plus a great view over the palaces and fin de siècle czarist luxury shops of Tverskaya. The restaurant may look like a designer sauna, but in terms of heat, it's nothing like the downstairs bar, which is as florid as the restaurant is subdued. The bar is hellishly red, and hotter than Hades, lined with at least one hundred distaff temptations, beckoning languidly with subtle come-hither smiles from a long, long mirrored wall of banquettes.

All diners stop at the bar first to whet their appetites, though for the unattached, or unvirtuous, it may be very hard to concentrate on the food after a visit to this inferno. There's a disc jockey playing everything from Sinatra to technopop, even at nine, when the place opens (it closes at 5 A.M.). The demoiselles are nothing like those of Picasso's Avignon (not the papal French town, but the Spanish brothel of the same name), but are more like *Vogue* fashion spreads. Bedecked in designer finery, speaking professorial English, these are girls you could take home to Mama, but even the proudest mama wouldn't believe her boy could score like this. In the Communist era, these ladies would have surely been KGB spies, modern Mata Haris. But today the KGB is gone, and so are most respectable paying jobs. When doctors in Ukraine are making only $300 a month, it's not surprising that these knockouts have joined the underground economy here at Night Flight, and at dozens of other playpens in Moscow, where rates start at $300 an hour (women of this caliber could command ten times that in London or Dubai; just give them time).

Unlike Vegas, what goes on at Night Flight does not stay at Night Flight. Everything here is to-go, and often upstairs to a "courtship" dinner, if you've been prescient enough to book space for newly found companions. Although there are so many big businessmen and international diplomats here that Harvard Business School alums treat Night Flight as their Moscow club, the upstairs space is so proper and the food so raved-about in the local press that plenty of wives are in evidence. It's not bimbotopia by any means, though there are plenty of red-faced moments when family men get caught in flagrante by friends.

When confronted, say you're only here for the reindeer steak and that your consort works for "the ministry"; she's likely smooth enough to help you finesse it. Simpler still, just *come* for the reindeer steak, or the elk one, or a bloody T-bone. The meat, grilled over an open hearth and served on oak platters with big baked Idahos or golden Swiss *rosti,* is the best in Russia. In fact, though the chef and owners here are all Swedish, the menu is as all-American-wholesome as the bar scene is not. Fish here is great, fresh and fine, straight from the icy Baltic. Only the starters can be exotic: excellent foie gras, with a black-currant-strawberry gelée, elk carpaccio, hearty borscht, and white asparagus in season. It's amazing what grows in the far north.

For the fat cats, there are five different kinds of caviar; and for the trendoids, there's a page of sashimi and Japanese specialties. For reasons of hipness and thinness, Moscow has gone sushi crazy. Most restaurants, whether Italian or Uzbeki, have a sushi bar, though most of the chefs are North Koreans (the Kim Jong Il old Communist connection) pretending to be Japanese, because very few Japanese live here. When Nobu opens here (it's in the works), prepare for lines as long as that of the first McDonalds's in nearby Pushkin Square. For dessert everyone has the "New York" cheesecake, though don't expect anything on the order of the dense Bronx S&S classic served at Peter Luger and the Palm. Made with two layers of sweet cheese, each whipped to a different consistency, Night Flight's cheesecake is as light as the willowy models downstairs.

There's a deep, deep wine list, with many great French vintages, but also lots of finds from South Africa and Portugal. Once you start drinking, you probably won't stop, and few diners can resist the call of the wild for a downstairs *digestif.* Service, up and down, is impeccable and smiling, never leering or smirking "you bad boy, you." The Swedes who run Night Flight are the souls of discretion.

In Sweden, land of free love, ironically, prostitution is highly illegal and punished severely, both buyers and sellers. Apparently, the land of free love doesn't want you to pay for it. But here in Russia, not so far away across the Gulf of Finland, there's a sea change in attitude, and the Swedes of Night Flight have ridden the wave all the way to the bank. When Night Flight opened fifteen years ago, its unique combination of great food and deluxe commercial sex made it a must on the itinerary of every international businessman harboring a hedonist playboy wanting to break out. The boys in the suits are still here in force, but so are a lot of ladies, who want to see not only the Kremlin, but also why their boys want to be boys. The refreshing thing about Night Flight is its total lack of hypocrisy, and the fact that any woman can dine alone or with friends here and be treated every inch the lady, and not the lady of the night. ★

195

Galereya, Café Pushkin, Palazzo Ducale
Face Control

MOSCOW

In the mythology of Moscow restaurant czar Arkady Novikov, the defining moment in his career was when he was rejected as a fry cook at the first McDonald's on Pushkin Square, the one near Night Flight and the first Western restaurant in the Soviet Union. Fry cook was the dream job, and Novikov reached for it and lost it. Now he has the dream job in the exploding Russian restaurant world, with sixty establishments, including all the "coolest" venues in Moscow. He is the Ian Schrager, Nobu Matsuhisa, Wolfgang Puck, Michael Chow, David Tang, and Arrigo Cipriani of Russia, all in one. Yet he is unlike all the others in that he was neither a chef nor an epicure nor even an artist, but an angry young man with a McDonald's rejection slip. The forty-five-year-old multiple-cell-phone wielding, T-shirted, go-go Novikov is actually most similar to Japan's restaurant impresario Kozo Hasegawa. But Novikov's top restaurants have much more of a monopoly on Moscow's high end than Hasegawa's do in Tokyo.

Novikov is famous for his policy of "face control," wherein powerful doormen, like those of Studio 54 in its nastiest heyday, pass judgment on your state of cool when you arrive at one of his elite restaurants. Even if you have a reservation, if you don't look elite, you don't eat. It is unlikely that the unprepossessing Novikov could get into his own places, particularly his current flagship Galereya, which boasts the most drop-dead female clientele in the world, including Cipriani and Chow. What makes Galereya so master-race is that while Cipriani, for instance, will let in the rich and titled and famous, in Russia there aren't that many "stars," and many of the famous oligarchs are in prison and hence not on the food scene. Thus who gets in are the women, who are all of major model stature, even if they are merely shopgirls or call girls, and the often ugly or scary-looking men who come with them. Galereya is as sexist and chauvinistic and as politically incorrect, if not downright rude, as it can get. But that's Moscow for you. There is some comfort that there are far fewer guns here than at Night Flight, but Night Flight is a guy place, and Galereya is a chick place, and therein is the difference.

Galereya looks like a contemporary Montparnasse brasserie in the heart of old Moscow. Across the street is a crumbling ancient walled monastery with fabulous Byzantine architecture and icons that date back to the ninth century. Go see it before dinner. It gives you some perspective, for when you cross the street, and if you are turned away, at least you have seen something of enduring cultural relevance. Luckily, Galereya likes Americans, so if you've booked from a cool (translation: enormously expensive) hotel like the Baltschug Kempinski, you'll probably make the cut. Lots of men dine alone here, in hopes of getting lucky with the large number of unattached females dining in groups, although unlike at Night Flight the beauties here are not up front and personal about being for sale. The possibility, the grand illusion perhaps, but the divine hope of true romance thus fills the rooms.

And what rooms they are. Galereya is a study in plush leather, chocolate brown chairs and sofas, jet-black lacquered tables, high ceilings. A gallery of photos (hence the name) of wonder women lines the walls. Wait a minute, is that . . . , you wonder, as you scan the room, thinking that the women on the floor, both guests and waitresses, are the women on the wall. Close, but no cigar. Actually, lots of cigars, as smoking seems to be de rigueur. Moscow does not regulate very much, not sex, not smoking, not discrimination.

There are a number of seating areas: a big main room, a bar lounge, a library, an outdoor terrace with a rock garden and waterfall, very Japanese, and a perfect place to have your sushi appetizers, also de rigueur in a Novikov restaurant. Despite its emphasis on looks, by no means is the bill of fare at Galereya restricted to things raw or *minceur*. Yes, there are lush salads in the dead of winter for *les girls*. But Novikov doesn't forget that Russia is a man's world, so there are lots of meat, steaks and stews, plus updated czarist (or is it really Russian Tea Room?) classics like beef stroganoff and chicken Kiev. There is *basta* pasta, which tends to be overcooked and oversauced in the American-heartland Chef Boyardee manner. But the new Russians have learned to undercook the good Baltic fish, and there is an entire bakery devoted to voluptuous chocolates and creamy sweets that would have sated Catherine the Great.

A few blocks away, Novikov has another similarly themed operation, Vogue Café, which is a joint venture with Moscow's Condé Nast licensee. The formula is the same as Galereya's, with face control at the door, *Vogue* covers on the walls, *Vogue* models at the tables, a menu of international greatest hits, with a little borscht thrown in. For all the worldly glamour of his establishments, Arkady Novikov is still a borscht homeboy, as proud of his down-market chains like Kish-Mish Uzbeki grills and Yoli-Palki peasant cafeterias as he is of his Paris homages. Novikov grew up poor and hungry in the Communist projects, lucky to eat bad pierogi when the bad fried meat ran out. He loved the *idea* of food and dreamed of becoming a cook in a Soviet embassy, somewhere, anywhere but here in Moscow. He would have settled for McDonald's, but that, too, was a pipe dream.

But when communism imploded, money (questionable money, but what venture capital isn't?) seemingly overnight appeared in Russia, and pipe dreams suddenly became reality. In the early 1990s Novikov had his first restaurant, a fancy fish house called Sirena, whose gimmick was a glass floor with an entire aquarium underfoot. After a century of starvation, Russia didn't know from good food at that point, so gimmicks were the way to draw a crowd, and Sirena was a hit. Novikov's next gimmick was to create a restaurant based on a hit Russian film called *White Sun of the Desert*, with Uzbek decor, belly dancers, and raucous cockfights. Another smash. Despite his catholic offerings, he likes to cater to rich men. "To understand food, you need money," he has said. Novikov has recently opened a branch of the Italian chain of Cantinetta Antinoris and is learning to make al dente pasta. Can authentic sushi made by real Japanese masters, not Pyongyang impostors, be far behind?

Speaking of gimmicks: if you want to take a time trip to imperial Russia, go, like every famous visitor to Moscow does, to the elegant Café Pushkin, right around the corner from Night Flight, but completely devoid of Night Flight's whores and Galereya's face control. Café Pushkin is Moscow's historical Disneyland dining theme park, and is the most wholesome place in the city. It's the one place that's correct in every way, though such correctness would have struck Stalin as imperialist porn and earned Pushkin's creators Siberian exile or worse. When you consider how perfectly the bombed-out palaces of St. Petersburg were restored, you'll appreciate that no one can beat the Russians at replicating the past. All that skill has gone into the creation of Café Pushkin, which, while totally ersatz, seems totally authentic, a palace in the city.

Café Pushkin is the creation of Arkady Novikov's chief rival, Andrei Dellos, a Russian émigré from France who returned home to cash in on Moscow's restaurant boom. But while Novikov is selling sex to businessmen, Dellos is selling history to tourists. To both restaurant Barnums, food seems secondary, though for Dellos's newest project, an opera fantasy called Turandot right next to Pushkin, he has enlisted London's Alan Yau to create exotic Oriental menus to match the far-out Venetian fantasy of Asian decor. Meanwhile at the twenty-four-hour Café Pushkin, the Bushes, the Clintons, the Spielbergs, and other first families have dined in splendor in three different venues: a downstairs apothecary (that bars the drug lords omnipresent at other big-ruble Moscow scenes); two floors of paneled and frescoed palace (where the stars sit), one a ballroom, the other a vast library with string quartets; and a terraced roof garden overlooking all the skyscrapers of Moscow, most notably the "seven sisters," identical wedding-cake high-rises that were the apogee of Stalinist architecture.

The food is supposedly nineteenth-century Russian, what the aristocrats ate that made the peasants want to kill them. Pushkin is the converse of the restaurant that made Dellos's fortune, a farm fantasy called Shino, that served poor-folk specialties like pig rib baked in cabbage and featured a central (glassed off to prevent smells) *tableau vivant* of babushka women milking cows, with chickens and pigs scurrying about. Here's what you might eat at Pushkin off the vast eight-page menu: "salade russe," with shrimp, carrots, peas, and mayonnaise; cold salmon with dried mullet roe and roasted pears, mangoes, and strawberries (the czars liked it sweet); a whole page of pickled cucumbers, tomatoes, mushrooms, and sauerkraut that would be the envy of the Lower East Side, pre–Wylie Dufresne; "petite pâtés à la Russe" (the czars had lots of French pretensions), or meat pies (stuffed with veal marrow, lamb, mushrooms, or cabbage, all great for a snowy Moscow night); *pelmeni*, or dumplings, stuffed with salmon or minced pork, or mushrooms (again, delicious); borscht with smoked goose breast (the goose is what separates the tsars from the serfs).

If you aren't stuffed on starters (it's totally cool to stop at any time here), you can continue with even heavier main fare: baked starlet (not the Night Flight kind, but a Baltic fish) in a rich, czarist caviar sauce; a "lasagna" of cod and snails in a creamy, Frenchy *sauce d'ecrivisses;* venison in a red wine sauce with juniper berries; wild boar "thick hoof" (sic, no mad cow implications, but a Russian term denoting prime cut) with mashed potatoes and chestnuts; definitive beef stroganoff; duck stew with buckwheat and liver. Desserts are surprisingly light, particularly the homemade sorbets in ten different flavors, the best in the city, and the fruit terrines. If you need to load up, go for the sweet rice dumplings with fresh cherry sauce or the apple strudel. Service is by waiters in black tie and serving maids in plunging wenchy outfits. It's a little sexist, yes, but compared to Night Flight, where everyone is on sale, Café Pushkin is as innocent and G-rated as the Pirates of the Caribbean ride.

For the best food in Moscow, hands down, and an even more ornate interior than Andrei Dellos could conjure up, head for Palazzo Ducale, which may be the world's most kitschy Italian restaurant. It also, believe it or not, may have some of the world's best (and most expensive) Italian food, prepared by master chef Agostino de Montis, who caters many of the most important banquets at the Kremlin. So fond is Vladimir Putin of de Montis's *cucina* that insiders say that the specialty pasta of the house should be called "spaghetti Putin-esca." As much as Russia's nouveau riches seem to love the south of France, they love Sardinia even more, and the richest of the rich have bought monster villas there. Accordingly, the Sardinian chef has become the ultimate status symbol for the oligarch who has everything. De Montis is reputedly the best of all Sardinian chefs and unwilling to work for just one family, whatever the rewards, and thus had no problems getting backing for Palazzo Ducale.

The restaurant is basically a re-creation of Carnavale in Venice. You sit on plush silk cushions in the prows of gondolas, on thrones, on pulpits, in choir stalls, surrounded by masks, fine antiques, and presumably fake Canalettos (though with the money spent here, they may be real). The waiters are dressed as the doge's courtiers, and not one speaks any Italian, or English. None is necessary, as the clientele is all Russian. There is a parking lot of Ferraris outside, and phalanxes of bodyguards. The women here are spectacular, Night Flight types who hit the jackpot, decked out in Paris couture and New York jewelry; they glitter as much as the interiors. The men are far more somber and scary, billionaire businessman types who could be assassinated by rivals the minute they step out the Murano glass doors (reputedly bulletproofed). If this is the price to have trophy consorts like these, you may not covet them so much.

The food is as serious as these oligarchs are, no sushi, no nonsense. It starts with the bread, five varieties, homemade and better than any you will have in Italy, hot out of the oven. All the fruit juices for mixed drinks are squeezed to order by hand, which gives you another idea how meticulous the place is. Expect long waits, and don't push: for one, you won't be understood; and two, looks can kill, and so can the lookers. The prosciuttos and mortadellas and *parmigianos* are Italy's finest, and make the best appetizers, though go slowly and be prepared to eat a lot of courses. Everything is that good.

The pastas, both the most expensive imported dried varieties and the hand-made ravioli and lasagna, are all fine, the sauces deft and light and perfect for dipping the toothsome bread in. All the fish and shellfish are flown in daily from the Mediterranean, and thus sparkling and pristine. The linguine with razor clams is something you might have on the Costa Smeralda, if you were the Aga Khan: a perfect balance of the al dente pasta, the freshest crustaceans, the best olive oil, the ideal balance of broth, red pepper, garlic, parsley. Fish is equally sublime and perfectly, simply prepared. If it's a sea bass, or any bony item, it is dissected with surgical skill. Oligarchs want to go out in a blaze of glory, not undergoing the Heimlich maneuver. The little things, like garlic rapini and rosemary potatoes, are state-of-the-art, prepared with the kind of care you take when a potential assassin is looking over your shoulder. There is wonderful osso buco, and veal chops, and Tuscan steaks. And mangoes and papayas flown in from India and Burma for dessert, because the oligarchs like their fruit, and they like it to be the best that all the money on earth can buy. Wines are staggeringly expensive, as befits this clientele. Be prepared to spend no less than $200 a person here, and possibly a lot more. This is the kind of food Las Vegas ought to serve to its highest rollers, but Vegas generally does food in name and price only. Too bad Frank Sinatra wasn't around to enjoy this, as he loved great food, he loved Italy, and he loved mobsters. At Palazzo Ducale, even though it's not quite Hoboken on the Volga, the Chairman, surrounded by other chairmen, would have had it His Way. ★ ★ ★

r East

The China Club
Not Simply Red

David Tang is an unlikely savior of the upscale Chinese restaurant. But that once revered institution desperately needs him, and he has stepped into this unexpected breach like a knight of the dim sum, hot and sour, moo shu realm. His China Clubs in Hong Kong, Beijing, and Singapore, and his China Tang in London, are models of elegance, wit, and above all, gastronomy. While Alan Yau's London restaurants are supertrendy riffs on Chinese peasant (Communist) food, David Tang takes the very high road to China, feasts for the last emperor, the taipan, the fat cat, served imperially. Tang is catering to the "exploiters" of "the people," and he's doing it unabashedly. And brilliantly. Fat cats have to eat, too, don't they? They can eat fancy French and fancy Italian and fancy Japanese, so why not fancy Chinese? Tang wants to replicate this model, Nobu-style, all over the rest of the known world, or at least the beau monde that is *his* world. The odd thing is that there aren't already dozens like it. Somehow, Chinese food has fallen off the celebrity food map. It seems preposterous, but look around, and the void is obvious.

In the 1970s and early 1980s there was no hotter cuisine than Chinese, and, specifically, the hot Chinese fare of the Szechuan and Hunan provinces. The imperial and all-powerful *New York Times* critic Craig Claiborne had anointed Chinese food as the equal of his beloved haute French when he gave four stars to Shun Lee Dynasty at a time when no Italian restaurant in Manhattan got more than two. Claiborne was thus instrumental in taking Chinese food out of Chinatown as gourmets and nascent foodies in all the big cities flocked to newly stylish "uptown" Chinese dining shrines. New York had the Shun Lees and the David Keh spice palaces. San Francisco and Los Angeles had their Mandarins. London had the lavish Zen chain, Paris the ornate Tse Yangs. Mr Chow was, as always, right on the spot, but Chow was less a Chinese phenomenon than a metrosexual one. Wolfgang Puck's Chinois in Santa Monica was his own *hommage* to how "hot" Chinese food had become. Suddenly Hong Kong had nearly as many food pilgrims as Paris.

But by the time of the handover of Hong Kong to Beijing in 1997, the elegant Chinese restaurant revolution seemed to have run its course. The fancy restaurants remained, but the heat had dissipated. There was a kind of Marco Polo effect, as when the explorer brought Chinese noodles home to Italy. Now the trattoria boom seemed to have stolen the Chinese restaurants' mojo, not to mention the effect of the rise of the sushi bar. On New York's Upper West Side, where *everything*, from shoe repair to beauty shops, seemed to be Hunan or Szechuan, the vaunted Empire Szechuan Gourmet added its own sushi counter. Talk about bastardization. Talk about Rodney Dangerfield and respect. It was as if Katz's Delicatessen on the Lower East Side had added a pork barbecue counter. Could the world's most venerable, most elaborate cuisine be reduced to a fad?

Not with David Tang keeping the faith. The Hong Kong "lifestyle" entrepreneur had the unusual combination of Asian wealth and heritage combined with British education and acceptance. A member of the top Pall Mall clubs, Tang knew about class and exclusivity. But with his wicked sense of humor, he couldn't take it all that seriously. And unlike his clubby British peers, he knew all about fine food. The Brits may have seen Tang as a wily Oriental gentleman, but given his brains and resources, they couldn't *not* take him seriously. The result was his first China Club, a multimillion-dollar Shanghai 1930s fantasy founded in 1991 atop the Beijing-owned Bank of China building, which looks totally deco but was actually constructed after World War II.

In 1967, the Communist Chinese had stood atop this edifice and used megaphones to urge the locals to rise up against their British colonial oppressors. Those entreaties had fallen on deaf ears, but once the Chinese took control of the former Crown Colony, skeptics wondered how long they'd tolerate Tang's monument to capitalistic hedonism. The China Club is still thriving, and Tang has another one, in a former Buddhist temple not far from the Forbidden City in Beijing, as the new China embraces capitalism as fervently as does the new Russia. Tang's big cigars, fine leather, and live lobsters have an allure that even Mao would have found seductive. "The whole idea of luxury is not marble and chrome," Tang has declared. "Luxury is when you feel a hundred percent comfortable." And so you do at the China Club.

In Hong Kong, the Club is located at ground zero of the Central Business District, convenient to the offices of all the city's power brokers and politicians. At lunch it feels very Wall Street, Eastern version. At night, it's pure Hollywood, Eastern version as well, with all the Chinese stars from Gong Li to Jet Li, and all the visiting foreign ones as well. This is by far *the* place in Hong Kong, so dress to the nines. Half the crowd is East, half West. This is where the twain meet. Tang, known to his friends as Tango, is the twain himself. He is often around, sometimes looking like the chancellor of the exchequer in his Savile Row suits, sometimes like the last emperor in his black silk pajamas and cloth slippers, in either case Cohiba always in hand.

It is slightly ironic that Tang had chosen a Shanghai theme for the club, with Shanghai currently about to overtake Hong Kong as the go-go business center of China. Nothing, however, can overtake Hong Kong's spectacular location in the South China Sea, and the China Club's view of its harbor—the world's most colorful, with junks, ferries, yachts, and tankers crisscrossing at every angle, framed by architecturally notable skyscrapers shooting out of the flat Kowloon plain—may be the best view of any club anywhere. Not long ago the two quintessential Sino-Anglo Hong Kong experiences were, first, to be picked up at the airport by one of the Peninsula Hotel's liveried Chinese chauffeurs in a British racing green Rolls-Royce, and, second, to have drinks overlooking the water, colonial style, on the tropically shaded veranda of the sprawling Repulse Bay Hotel. Today in Hong Kong there are as many Rolls-Royces as Lexuses, and the Repulse Bay has been razed for a mall. If you want a taste of Hong Kong's past, you have to go to the China Club.

The decor is less a bankers' sanctuary than a good-old-days MGM set designer's fantasy of an opium lord's pleasure dome. All is mahogany and rosewood, with plush antique chairs and wooden floors and hanging lanterns everywhere. There's lots of Communist kitsch: Warhol prints of Chairman Mao, a yellow star, which is the club's symbol, yellow being the color of the emperor, obscuring a red Communist star below it. Hostesses in cheongsams look like Gong Li herself, and mandarinized waiters are dead ringers for John Lone. Service is perfect, totally attentive, punctilious but never groveling. Even if this is your first time, the staff seems to know exactly what you want.

Have a drink at the Long March Bar, and have something tropical, like a Singapore sling or a mai tai or a suffering bastard. For unlike at the old Trader Vic's, here the juices are all squeezed to order, and there's a huge difference in the taste. While you're boozing it up, enjoy all of Tang's witticisms, which make this club anything but stuffy. There's a big library with five thousand volumes on China, all of them in English, that includes a lot of pulp fiction like Sax Rohmer's tales about Fu Manchu. Tang loves to *épater les chinois*, because, as he feels, it takes one to know one. Birds chirp from gilded cages, competing with Chinese opera on the sound system, but the result is pure harmony, especially after a few Planters punches.

If you weren't too distracted by all the powerful men and stunning women floating through, you may have perused the huge menu. While the food might easily be secondary in such exotic, almost theme-park-y surroundings, it actually takes precedence. The menu is a compendium of Canton's Greatest Hits, and you want to bring a gang of more than four to take advantage of the endless array of temptations. What's remarkable about the food is that while a lot of it is stir-fried and deep fried, it's never even vaguely greasy or oily. The vegetables are fresher than you've ever seen, and most of the seafood is live, not merely fresh, caught right outside of those deco windows.

Start with smoked vegetable bean curd skin rolls, which has only one downside: you'll never want to eat a spring roll again. Next try some Cantonese barbecue, which again will wean you off that hanging red fowl you see in Chinatown. The marinated chicken flavored with conpoy (dried scallops) is an exercise in elegant subtlety. The chicken tastes as if it were just slaughtered and is moist and tender beyond belief. This is as good a place as any to experience shark's fin soup, here flavored with salty Yunnan ham, fresh crabmeat, and mushrooms; it's totally delicate and totally delicious. If you need a punch at this point, try the hot-and-sour soup, which is more vinegary than you're used to. You'll see why it's called hot and "pungent" around here.

The China Club is also a fine venue for trying exotic fish, which you can later brag to your explorer friends about: coral leopard trout, humpback grouper, humphead wrasse, all simply steamed with soy and scallions, and sublime. For the less subtle, go for the fried squid slices topped with mashed shrimp and spicy salt, then have another strong drink to neutralize the yummy saline. Returning to land, the club does a definitive Peking duck. This deep-fried boned duck, "Shanghai style," has lots of spicy flavor and is more lustily gratifying. If you need some veggies, take the edible crispy bird's nest filled with lotus root, sweet pea pods, fresh water chestnuts (like you've never seen back home), celery, and assorted exotic fungi.

There's so much more that you'd have to dine here for weeks to cover it: sea cucumber in many ways, tofu, fresh-water prawns, pigeon, quail, even sweet-and-sour pork, the platonic ideal of the "one from column A" cliché. There's a page of noodles and rice, exotic stuff like egg noodles served with red vinegar and caster sugar, fried rice with shrimp roe, and foie gras wonton soup. There's also a page of "Old Hong Kong Favorites": quail congee with bird's nest, poached corned ox-tongue, oxtail soup, all of which might be too "real" for most outlanders. Desserts, always the Achilles' heel of Chinese cuisine, are here as good as they can be: fresh mango pudding, chilled ginseng jelly in red date syrup, sweetened green bean soup. Just pretend they all have aphrodisiacal qualities, like rhino horn, and the sweets will taste a whole lot sweeter. For compensation, Tang offers an encyclopedia of great cognacs to end the evening, or as a prelude to the great Havanas the club stocks.

The biggest problem with the China Club is that it is indeed a club, so you can't just call and book. You have to know someone to get in. And though anyone who's anyone in Hong Kong is likely to be a member, if you're just coming here for the first time, unless you have global connections, you may be out in the heat, or dining at the floating seafood palaces in Aberdeen Harbor. Some resourceful concierges can "fix you up" with a member who can get you in. By all means, don't be too shy to ask, because the China Club will make your visit. Most of old Hong Kong, especially the Anglo-colonial white-man's-burden stuff that may have been insufferable but was great on atmosphere, has fallen prey to the wreckers' balls. So before the former Crown Colony becomes nothing more than a Vegas for shoppers (to say nothing of nearby Macau becoming the Vegas of the East), don't miss the endless retro charms of the China Club. As David Tang described his inspiration for this blast from the past, "Wouldn't it be nice if there was a club that tended all the desires of gluttons and hedonists like me?" Jolly good idea! Let's hope Tang keeps taking his pleasure show on the road to your city. Sunday takeout somehow just isn't the same. ★ ★ ★ ★ ★ ★ ★ ★ ★ ★

Kyubey
King of the Sea

You might well find yourself eating sushi between Tom Hanks and Tom Cruise at the counter of Matsuhisa in Beverly Hills, or at any one of its Nobu progeny around the world. You also might find yourself in that same position, the fever dream of any tabloid reporter, at Kyubey, the celebrity-mogul sushi shrine in the Ginza, Tokyo's luxe shopping district. The main difference between Kyubey and Matsuhisa is that Kyubey's sushi is better, a *lot* better. Matsuhisa's sushi would taste great to any mortal palate; rating Kyubey's as better is saying a mouthful. It's the difference between Lucullan and sublime. Kyubey's fish is fresher; the cut of the sushi is smaller, more elegant; the rice is fluffier; the ambience is more templar, more serene.

You know you're in sushi heaven the moment you enter the place. But this is not to say that Kyubey is stuffy. This was the favorite restaurant of John Lennon, who obviously had a thing for Japan. Mick Jagger loves Kyubey, and Harrison Ford, and Tom Ford. Every film star, rock star, or runway star who does a show in Tokyo makes at least one pilgrimage here. At any given meal, you will see the world's most beautiful, most famous, and most demanding gourmets at the twenty-seat counter on Kyubey's ground floor. This tower of sushi has five floors, but the Poseidons of this universe prefer terra firma.

The Ginza has a split personality: the main drag is a vast in-your-face neon fantasyland of fancy department stores and every big-brand chain in the world; but the side and back streets are unmatched in intimacy, taste, and price. It's like going from Broadway to Rome's Via Condotti in the turn of a corner. Kyubey is on one of these mewslike passages, where all the signs are in discreet neon, with nothing in English. The effect is dreamlike, something out of *Hiroshima, Mon Amour*, and it only enhances the mystique that you are going to the greatest sushi restaurant in the world. Of course, if your driver doesn't take you to the door, you won't be able to find it, unless you ask a hundred people, none of whom speaks English.

Finally you arrive at a sign-less bamboo-shrouded pathway that leads to a sliding screen that somehow opens electronically. You are greeted by beautiful bowing geisha types in regal pink silk kimonos who somehow know your name. (Don't think about not booking; the Japanese seem to organize their lives decades in advance, especially events like this one.) If your concierge has promoted you properly, you will get a ground-floor perch, maybe next to one of the Toms, but surely next to a Japanese tycoon and one of his stunning Chanel-clad, Harry Winston–bejeweled mistresses (brands are as big a turn-on here as looks), for whom the sushi interlude is merely one expensive stop on a long slow evening of seduction.

If you prefer seeing family rather than concubines, come for lunch, when the wives and daughters of the plutocracy take $200 shopping breaks here. But the nighttime is the right time to see the aphrodisiacal effects of the best fish that money—lots of money—can buy. The Chanel girls, by the way, are usually short-termers from the nearby unmarked hostess clubs, which don't allow Americans in for fear of spoiling the mood. They cost upward of $5,000 a night, so the few hundred for the fish is cheap by comparison. The Japanese tax laws let the corps deduct it all as "entertainment."

The room is all pale woods, white screens, and rare flowers tastefully arranged. The room has a golden hue. There are no fluorescent lights here, only incandescent ones. But the thing you notice most is the five-man team of white surgical-coated sushi chefs, one for every four diners. They smile and bow, a supremely confident team of young and old, tall and short, highly professional in their demeanor, a Japanese version of the Rembrandt painting *Syndics of the Cloth Guild*. Your palate will be in their hands, and you feel blessed. So you bow and sit down, and a geisha brings you some emerald iced green tea if it's hot outside, and vaguely sweet rare sake. You don't ask the cost, because you don't want to know.

And then your chef will begin his magic, and again, don't ask, but let him do his *oma-kase* (chef's choice) thing. He may ask if there's anything you don't eat, but do try to be open-minded. And never ask for anything with avocado, like a California roll, or, worse, anything with mayonnaise, like a spicy tuna hand roll, or these purists might just commit seppuku (suicide) at the westernized horror of it all. This is purity, ground zero, so have it their way. Please. You won't be sorry.

Here's a typical fishing trip: First they give you a little palate-cleansing salad of deep green seaweed spiked with baby ginger. It's bracing, as is that green iced tea whose caffeine punch is cocaine-ish. You'll be started with one sushi piece (never two) of chu-toro, or medium fatty tuna. It's a pink, striated revelation of voluptuous flavor that literally melts in your mouth, a Pritikin version of foie gras. Note that at Kyubey, the fish is draped over the rice. You never see the white sidewalls as you do in America. The next bite is tai, local red snapper, that has the brine of the sea. Don't be disillusioned to learn that most of the fish you eat, here and at Nobu, is caught far from home and frozen on board the fishing fleets. What makes the fish at Kyubey so great is that it comes from Tsukiji, Tokyo's great fish market, the biggest and best in the world, where if the fish can be fresh it is, and if it's not, it's frozen for the shortest possible time.

As entr'acte, you're next served a gossamer sea custard with baby shrimp, octopus, and scallop. Its sweetness is instantly offset by ika sushi, squid tender enough to warm the heart of Jules Verne, accented with coarse sea salt. At Kyubey, they don't give you dipping bowls of soy sauce. The chefs have a medicine chest of soys, *ponzus*, salts, garlic, radishes, whatever, to flavor the fish, and they give it to you as it must be. Don't ask, just eat. Then comes the freshest, tangiest *uni*, or sea urchin, you've ever tasted, wrapped in the crispest nori, or seaweed. Kyubey's fame is founded on inventing, nearly a century ago, *gunkan,* or wrapped sushi, as opposed to fish atop rice, which is the progenitor of today's ubiquitous hand rolls. The wrapped uni is so delicious you could reorder a dozen, but less is more is the Kyubey way.

The next thing you get is a tiny deep-fried shrimp head, which looks like some Jivarro shrunken-head treatment of a fierce Japanese warrior. You welcome the sizzle of oil, the glory of grease, after all the nonfat virtue that has come before. Still, it's only a whisper, followed by the shout of the still wriggling live translucent gray shrimp body, accented with some fine sea salt. No shrimp cocktail will ever do after this. Next is some local striped jackfish with a dab of soy. It tastes like cold, rare, prime steak, Peter Luger steak, and it's good. Then comes *akagai,* a pink, clammy Japanese mollusk, which could be the poster child for Greenpeace, so pristine and unsullied is its deep ocean flavor.

Next you get a tiny bowl of unsalty miso soup with the tiniest clams you've ever seen. Then it's time for light pink, full-fat toro, and all you can do is revel in the fish oil you're consuming. Your palate is primed for big tastes now, so your chef, who somehow may remind you of the smoked-fish countermen at Zabar's, treats you to deep red bonito topped with a wallop of freshly pressed garlic. Bam! Emeril's got nothing on these guys. Still, what strikes you is what you're eating, not who's serving it. For all their precision and quiet charm, and often striking good looks, the sushi men fade into anonymity. This is the cult of fish, not personality. Wolfgang Puck would die here.

The Kyubey experience is that of explosions of flavor punctuated by moments of reflection and repalatization. More cleansing now, with a radish "sandwich," two slices of baby white radish around a *shiso* leaf, sprinkled with sesame seeds and splashed with soy. A Japanese Big Mac? Why not?

The new explosion is tuna "prime rib," grilled toro on the bone, never seen in the USA. You're expected to gnaw, even amid the high decorum here. The geishas bring new hot towels to blot up the mess. It's a fish-pickin', and it's as down-home as you will get on the Ginza. This is beer food now, and they bring you an icy draft Ebisu, the champagne of Japanese brews, to wash down the pleasure.

Then it's time for *anago*, or sea eel. Two fire-grilled chunks of it are served, one with a candy-sweet mirin soy sauce, the other with that crunchy sea salt. You could mainline endless amounts of both, but *no!* Eating Japanese is all about control, which is too bad, with decadence like this to lapse into. Some delicate pickled eggplant, which puts to shame anything in the pickleworks of the Lower East Side, then more *gunkan*, in the form of a heavenly cut tuna roll, dotted with miniature scallions. Now you're done, except for Kyubey's coup de grâce, its *tamago*, or omelet, which takes the egg to a different universe. This golden flanlike delicacy is served in two thin slices sandwiching a bite of rice. It's like a French pastry but far lighter, sweeter. Escoffier would have been moved.

You finish with a sliced, honey-sweet Japanese pear, accented with sprigs of mint, the platonic ideal of fruit. You've been so engrossed in your food that you didn't notice that the Chanel girls and the Sony boys have stolen off into the night for God knows what expensive pleasures. You're all alone at the sushi bar, with the Rembrandt boys and Proustian memories and a bill that your accountant may never understand. Kyubey has "shops," as branches are called, all over Tokyo, and they're all fine, though nothing tops the original. Kyubey has been in the same family for generations. These are the Meiji of sushi, the royal family, the aristocrats. This is as close to heaven as food gets, which may help you justify the price. ★ ★ ★ ★ ★ ★ ★ ★ ★ ★ ★ ★ ★ ★ ★ ★ ★ ★ ★

Forbidden Fruit

As undeniably magnificent as Kyubey's sushi and Ten-Ichi's tempura are, the most amazing thing you are likely to taste in Japan is the freshly squeezed nectar of the Kyushu mango that you can imbibe at Lemon, the world's ultimate juice bar. Lemon, or Lemon Fruit Parlor, was founded in 1969 in the basement food halls of the Takashimaya department store in Nihonbashi, Tokyo's Wall Street, about a mile from the Ginza. The elegant Takashimaya, a shopping palace with Frank Lloyd Wright overtones built shortly after the 1923 earthquake, which destroyed most of Tokyo, can be said to be the Harrods of Tokyo. But Takashimaya's food halls make the much vaunted ones of Harrods and Selfridges seem like 7-Elevens by comparison. Not only will you find the ultimate in Japanese food and produce—from Kobe beef to rare rice crackers to soba noodles to recherché candies, at wonderful, spotless stands to take out or eat in—but you will also find all the great foods of the world, branches of Peck of Milan, Dallmayr of Munich, Fauchon of Paris, Godiva, Leonidas, Maison du Chocolat, Iberian *pata negra,* Strasbourg foie gras, Iranian caviar, Maine lobster, and on and on. You could have the greatest food journey of your life by never leaving this endless basement, a theme that is repeated in all the major Japanese department stores, but never quite iterated like this one.

But the top stop of all is the veritable garden of eden that is Lemon, where the same stars and statesmen you may have seen at Kyubey and Ten-Ichi sneak in (everybody's so obsessed with the food here that celebs go unnoticed) for a tiny, perfect glass—or five or six—of juice. No one can stop at one, and because each juice costs about ten dollars, it's quite easy to spend fifty dollars for the world's healthiest breakfast, which isn't so bad if you consider that's about the same price as an (also perfect) egg white *fines herbes* omelet at the nearby Four Seasons Hotel.

Lemon is a ten-seat counter, very 1960s-ish, *Leave It to Beaver* in cheery pastel shades. But there's nothing vaguely casual about it. Three intense fruit men in white coats and natty soda-jerk hats stand at the ready. Behind them is a glass wall of fruit, the most gorgeous exotic fruit you've ever seen, all individually wrapped in shock-absorbing crisscross padding. You see all kinds of mangoes and papayas, as well as the hundred-dollar honeydews and yellow watermelons and white peaches you've read about, rare stuff like lychees and durians and passion fruit. If Adam and Eve had this stuff to tempt them, they would have ignored each other. The customers, mostly beyond-chic women, are almost as beautiful as the fruit, a great advertisement for Lemon.

A fruit man hands you a menu, which is a seductive all-color affair, with photos of the fruit and flags indicating the countries of origin. The mangoes are from Kyushu, Philippines, Mexico; the pineapples from Taiwan; the raspberries from Australia; the kiwis from New Zealand (where else); the lychees and purple grapes from China; the stinky durian from Thailand; the cherries, à la George Washington, from the USA. You can have the fruits in a salad, or in a sandwich with the crust trimmed that would be the dream of any high-toned women's club, or squeezed. For first-timers, squeezed is the way to go, and what a way it is.

Take the mango. The fruit man tells you that the Kyushu variety is "number one," a universal phrase meaning the best. In this land where so much can get lost in translation, "number one" is foolproof. He then carefully peels the mango, slices it around its thick core, hand crushes it in a squeezer, then strains the juice into a blender. He runs the blender for a moment, then pours the ambrosia into a cocktail shaker, adds a few filtered ice cubes, then shakes it, martini-style (never stirred), and then pours it into a little chilled six-ounce glass, not wasting a drop. The fruit men never seem to waste a drop. They're like magicians, and you revere them all the more once you taste the mango juice. It's the sweetest, most delectable taste ever, and it's gone in a second. But that may be one of the best seconds you'll ever have.

You'll probably order at least two more, just like pinching yourself to make sure it's all real. But then you'll also want to go for the hard stuff. Lychee juice is the most labor intensive. First the tricky skins must be peeled off, then the interior pit removed. To get even a little glass of juice, dozens of the critters must be operated on. But it's worth the work and the twenty bucks for it. Nothing could be sweeter, but you'll have trouble ever again settling for a canned-juice Trader Vic's–style tropical cocktail at your local bar, or even the Ritz. Passion fruit, with all the seeds, is likewise a labor of Hercules, as well as Croesus. You'll never taste anything like the Hawaiian papaya in Honolulu, much less the purple grape in your Welch's bottle, *pace* Larry King, who hawks the stuff so effectively.

Even the juice of the California-import Sunkist oranges is better than anything you'll ever get in the Golden State, mainly because the fruit men don't squeeze every last cent out of the oranges by pressing them down to the bitter rind. To those who know their fresh juice from chains like Jamba Juice, whose only fresh offerings are basically orange, carrot, celery, and beet, Lemon will be both an epiphany and a finger of shame to Americans to step up to and embrace their garden bounty instead of processing it to death. Think how hard it is to get a fresh, really fresh (not squeezed by machine hours if not days before) glass of OJ in even our best hotels. France is even worse. Ask for *jus d'orange* at any bar in Paris and they'll give you some swill from a bottle or can. *Orange pressé* is the magic phrase, but unless you add *sur commande,* that "fresh" juice may have been standing in the fridge for days, and while touted as "Jaffa" it may taste more like it was stored in a Nablus fallout shelter.

There's a telling poster on the wall of Lemon. It's an old ad for a long defunct California company called Boyhood Grapefruit. It depicts a Huckleberry Finn–ish boy driving a donkey cart transporting a giant mutant grapefruit. The slogan is "Eat Me and Grow Young." Judging from the beautiful people eating and drinking the beautiful fruit at Lemon, this is one case of total truth in advertising. ★ ★ ★ ★ ★ ★ ★ ★ ★ ★ ★ ★ ★ ★ ★

Ten-Ichi
O Tempura

Statesmen don't eat sushi. Sounds like "real men don't eat quiche," and surely Prime Minister Koizumi ingested deep-fried peanut butter sandwiches and the like when he visited his beloved Elvis's Graceland. But in general sushi and other recherché Japanese fare is a little much for the likes of world leaders. So they come to Ten-Ichi, where frying is the universal language, and they are happy indeed. Ten-Ichi, also in the Ginza, is the world's most famous tempura restaurant. Connoisseurs may argue that there are better, but at the top of this hot game, where the oil is spotless, the temperature is max, the ingredients are perfect, and the chef is a master at taking the grease out of frying, it's almost pointless to cut distinctions. Ten-Ichi is wonderful. The montage photograph at the entrance, of Chirac, Annan, Sinatra, Clinton, and Helmut Kohl, all resplendent in white Ten-Ichi bibs, says it all. There's another photo of the Gorbachevs, and another of Henry Kissinger, and a Chagall in the rock-garden waiting area that the artist presented to this, his favorite Japanese restaurant.

Lunch is less bedlam than dinner, because tempura is "guy food," and the ladies who lunch need to eschew deep fat, however little there may be here, because the frying is so flash, to do justice to Hanae Mori and Jil Sander. At night, Ten-Ichi is like Mike Milken's predators' ball, where the big players on the Tokyo exchange come to celebrate their gains or drown their losses in the snap, crackle, and pop of Ten-Ichi's fried fare. Like Kyubey, Ten-Ichi, which was founded in 1930, has branch shops all over Tokyo, but there's no place like home, a five-story temple of tempura right near Hermès and Chanel. Outside may be like Vegas, with all the neon and the billion-dollar logos. But inside is pure Zen, lovely flowers, recessed lights, sliding screens, pale woods, ancient paintings of trees, rocks, mountains, and, yes, fish and more fish. But you don't need any subliminal seduction. The classic, atavistically alluring smell of what's frying does it all. There are tempura bars on each floor, none of which seats more than ten people. The statesmen and stars reserve private tatami rooms, each with its own fry pit and fry master, so no one can observe the celebrity gluttony.

And, oh, what food these morsels be! Your geisha ties on your white bib and starts you with a little green salad with a ginger-soy-tomato dressing, and a plate of superfresh baby string beans and squares of homemade tofu, both marinated in soy milk. But that's as light as it gets. Then come some deep-fried baby shrimp heads, not as fierce-looking as those at Kyubey, but not so demure that you can resist crunching down on them. The depth charge of heat and salt and oil and shrimp carapace is overwhelming. You're hooked now. You've gotta have it.

And you get it, with three of the bodies of those fine heads, barely coated in a filigree batter that provides only texture and allows you to taste the shrimp within, which literally explode in your mouth. What shrimp these are! Caught that day in Japan's southern Inland Sea, they will be a revelation to most Americans, who have probably never tasted a truly live shrimp, but rather variations on the all-you-can-eat Sizzler and Red Lobster frozen variety, even in the top tables of New York and San Francisco. A fresh shrimp, much less a live one, is a *rara piscis* in the West. So eat up here, landlubbers.

The aroma of the frying oil, combined with the sizzle of whatever's being dropped into it, continues to make you ravenous. Everyone starts out with beer at Ten-Ichi, then decompresses later into sake. Put yourself into your geisha-waitress's delicate hands. The chef feeds you; she hydrates you. This is the opposite of self-service. It's more like the Old South, being waited on, fed, hand to mouth, *Mandingo* minus the slavery. Of course, the joke's on you, wage slave, who must pay for this cosseted pleasure. After the shrimp, you get more live seafood, piece by piece, conger eel, butterflied *ayau*, or sweet-fish, which literally melts in your mouth.

With each bite, you have the choice of a *ponzu* sauce with freshly grated radish; salt and lemon; or a curry powder. With the fish, the lemon-salt is the way to go, to enhance but not mask the fragile fresh flavors. With the veg-etables, the *ponzu* hits the spot: asparagus, gingko nuts, wild mushrooms, baby eggplant, *shishito* peppers, all homegrown, all fresher and better than any-thing that the famed Chino Ranch, supplier of Puck and Waters and Keller, can put forward. The best veg of all is the sweet potato, not orange like our Thanksgiving staple, but pale yellow, dense, Idaho-y, a great vehicle for fry-ing. Some fast-food chain could make a fortune out of these if they weren't so damned expensive, for these may be the best fried potatoes on the globe.

Men with yen may mount an entire deep-sea expedition, ordering aba-lone, oysters, scallops, flathead, whatever. But you don't have to go the Thor Heyerdahl route to fill up. At the end of the repast the chef will make you *ten-don*, which is a bowl of tempura'd shrimp and fish pieces in a sort of fried omelet, served on a bowl of rice, over which you pour the *ponzu*-radish sauce and scarf down the whole thing in five seconds. The geishas then remove your bib and take you to a cozy booth, where they serve you rare fruits and fine tea, and let you decompress. A tempura dinner can run anywhere from a hundred to three hundred dollars, depending on how exotic you want your stomach aquarium to be. The only consolation is that tempura is cheaper than sushi. But at least you will have gone to the mountain and seen the other side. Who would have ever guessed that a wokful of oil would be some-thing to strive for? But it is, because Ten-Ichi will grab you, hook, line, and sinker. You'll be back. ★

Cheap and Chic

You *can* eat stylishly and well in Tokyo without breaking the bank. You just have to know. What better avatar to follow than Eric Clapton, the most gastronomically savvy of all rock stars. When he and his brethren play Budokan in Tokyo, they always take their postconcert vittles at Maisen, a supercool 1950s roadhouse that would not be out of place in Clarksville, Mississippi. Actually, Clarksville would be a better fit than its actual location in trendy Aoyama, which is the Chelsea or SoHo of Tokyo. In keeping with the Japanese fashion of restaurants specializing in one dish, Maisen's fame and fortune rest on *tonkatsu*, breaded and deep-fried pork cutlets, served with rice and shredded cabbage and a dipping sauce that strongly resembles A.1. Note that Maisen is also the favorite hangout of Nobu Matsuhisa, who has a hot, coals-to-Newcastle Nobu branch here in Roppongi.

Maisen has its own pig farms, black pigs that yield the tenderest loins, from which these nearly fat-free cutlets are taken. So famous is Maisen's tonkatsu that sandwiches of it—plain white bread encasing the golden crispy pork—are sold in train stations throughout Japan and at all the city's elegant convenience stores. (Its stateside equivalent would be the fried chicken sandwich of Georgia's Chik-Fil-A chain, which is the unequaled aristocrat of American fast food.) The mother ship, formerly a bathhouse, has a long counter that could be a classic American diner, and a big paneled room with whirring ceiling fans that is very evocative of Hollywood's Musso & Frank Grill, where Faulkner and Fitzgerald, among many others, drank away their screenplay frustrations. But what Clarksville roadhouse has koi ponds and moss gardens and waterfalls and tatami rooms? Maisen has all of these. So if you want to go the Zen route with your holy hog, you can easily do so, lolling on the floor and drinking sake while porking out, all for under thirty dollars a head.

For the same price, you can also treat yourself to a sushi feast at Sushi-Bun, the best of the many funky fish stands at the legendary Tsukiji fish market, a twenty-minute stroll from the Ginza into another world and another decade, the 1950s, when Japan was still recovering from World War II, selling "made in Japan" junky toys whose paint your parents worried would poison you if you put the toys in your mouth. That was before Sony and Toyota ruled the world. Now what you put in your mouth can only bankrupt you, after bringing ecstasy.

You can have that ecstasy on a budget at Tsukiji, whose prime time for fish haggling may be the crack of dawn, but which stays open for lunch until two in the afternoon. The most famous sushi stand, Dai-Wa, has hour waits at all hours. Local cognoscenti pick Sushi-Bun, which costs a few yen more but has far shorter waits. Great-looking Japanese gourmets, male and female, throng this place, a seven-seat counter with a set lunch of ten or so pieces in succession of whatever's freshest that particular day. It's pretty much the same bill of fare as at Kyubey—tuna, uni, anago—but everything here is cut far bigger, American (or Linda Lovelace *Deep Throat*) style. Hence you're getting even more fin for your yen, but your jaw muscles will get a workout. The only elegance is in the clientele. Lots of visiting stars of the Bruce Willis ilk are spotted here, if only for the reverse chic of it all.

And then there's Tableaux, the haunt of action heroes Willis and Stallone and Pierce Brosnan, the Tokyo fave of Jack Nicholson and Drew Barrymore, as well as unofficial headquarters for the Rolling Stones whenever they come to Japan. The underground boîte is an odd choice for such a lusty crew, because with its da Vinci–style Sistine Chapel murals of falling angels and its deep red leather decor with lots of florid ecclesiastical touches, Tableaux reminds you of a gay New Orleans bordello, something sinisterly beyond *Easy Rider.* Furthermore, it has a similarly explosively decorated sister restaurant in West Hollywood, La Bohème, which is one of the musts of LA's Boystown. But here in hip Daikonyama, the closest thing Tokyo has to an artists' village, Tableaux is the hottest spot in town for hetero networking, rather than leather cruising. Maybe what's gay in West Hollywood is straight in Tokyo; maybe the place just appeals to the Japanese inner Liberace. And we all know how perverse Mick Jagger is.

Much of Tableaux's masculine charm comes from its manager, Scott Lawther, an expat former Hollywood actor who does most of the Marlboro-man rugged English voice-overs for Japanese television commercials (not Dandy House), and from its studly owner, former marathoner and Ferrari racer Kozo Hasegawa, whose company Global Dining owns fifty-six restaurants in Japan, plus more in Hawaii and Los Angeles, with New York on the horizon. In his mid-fifties, he's the Ian Schrager, the Gilbert Costes, of Japan. A university dropout, he went to Sweden for the babes and became an illegal-alien dishwasher at a Stockholm coffee shop, where he saw that the way to a woman's heart was over the counter. So he came back to Yokohama and started his own coffee shop, which led to an antiques shop, which eventually got fused into the kitschy La Bohème, and then the ultrakitsch, fairly priced Tableaux, which has been mobbed since opening in 1991. Now married to an American former model, Kozo is still the heartthrob, and lots of single women, foreign models on the prowl, and local social types come here to hang with him.

What they eat at Tableaux is a fusion cuisine as mystifying as the fractured English slogans on Japanese T-shirts. Talk about being lost in translation. Going one hog higher than the New York Grill, Tableaux tops its Caesar salad with *pata negra*. There's a Zuwai crab and red shrimp spring roll, with ginger, coriander, spring onion, *yuzu*-lime pepper mayonnaise, and sweet chili sauce. There's a broad bean soup with tarragon, cream, and chives. Pastas are as exuberant as the decor: smoked chicken linguini with *caciocavallo* cheese, black olives, capers, fried eggplant, and tomato sauce. Stop, you scream. Stop in the name of too many ingredients. Small wonder that Kozo is a great fan of the Cheesecake Factories. But then again, so is Alain Ducasse, who modeled his Spoon chain after them. The safest things here are the simple fish and meats cooked in the wood oven. Just ask them to hold the sauce. Tableaux is the diametric opposite of the classic Japanese approach to cooking. If Aoyagi and Kyubey represent perfect simplicity, then Tableaux represents total anarchy. And guess which the new generation of hipsters prefers? So come here to see the New Japan in all its convoluted glory. You may be clueless, but, as Bill Murray proved, being clueless in Tokyo has a cool all its own. ★ ★ ★ ★ ★

Joel Robuchon,
Antica Osteria del Ponte,
Aoyagi
Brand Names

In some ways, Tokyo feels like an outdoor Las Vegas, or at least an outdoor version of the Caesar's Palace Shops. Every famous label on earth is right here. Where restaurants are concerned, there's a Tour d'Argent, a Maxim's, a Joel Robuchon, a Pierre Gagnaire, an Alain Ducasse. And that's just France. From Italy come such *Michelin* superstars as Enoteca Pinchiorri from Florence, Sadler from Milan, and Antica Osteria del Ponte from the Lombard country-side. From Spain comes the three-star Sant Pau, outside Barcelona, with lots of talk of a Tokyo El Bulli in the works. From America there's Spago, Nobu, even Lawry's Prime Rib, a big chunk of the LA dining experience, turning the Pacific Rim into one homey neighborhood. In Vegas these temples often exist in brand name only. But in Japan, land of precision, respect, and intense shame at failure, the branches always equal and usually outstep the original. The Japanese are the world's greatest travelers. They have been everywhere, tasted everything, and are total sticklers for authenticity. Hence when you're in Tokyo, you can "be" in Paris or Milan or anywhere your palate desires.

If you want to "be" in an over-the-top other world, nothing can touch the Joel Robuchon "château" smack in the middle of a huge shopping center in Ebisu, formerly home to the brewery that makes Japan's finest beer. The château looks like the home of one of the American robber barons, or William

Randolph Hearst, who transported the stones to build his San Simeon all the way from Europe. Robuchon's Xanadu has been similarly constructed. It used to be called Taillevent-Robuchon, a joint venture of two of the grandest names in French gastronomy. But in Japan's economic meltdown of the last decade, Taillevent gave up the ghost and left Xanadu to Robuchon alone, who is making his own global comeback, in Paris, Vegas, and recently New York. The interior is a cross between Versailles and a Gianni Versace boutique, gilded yellow halls of mirrors and crystal with chandeliers worthy of Marie Antoinette. With its liveried waiters and chained sommeliers, the place reeks, figuratively, of excess, of foie gras and truffles and heavy cream in this land of culinary minimalism and restraint.

If Japanese had bar mitzvahs, the Robuchon château would be *the* place for them. As it is, there are so many special events here—weddings, retirements, graduations, birthdays—that coming here just for a $500 dinner seems out of place. You feel as if you need a reason. Then again, Marie Antoinette didn't need a reason. What you'll eat is a seasonal menu with a few nods to local simplicity amid a cornucopia of excess. You might start, for instance, with a local lemon, like those prime ones that make ten-dollar lemonade at Lemon Fruit Parlor (see page 215), turned into a vanilla-scented ice cream, in a pool of licorice cream. Then comes the foie gras course, in a napoleon puff pastry served with smoked eel in a "sauce orientale," which means soy and ginger. Sounds bizarre, but the chefs pull it off. Next comes a soufflé of sea urchin in a fennel-cream sauce. More Tsukiji fine fish, a bass grilled on one side, with a green vinegary *verjus* sauce. The highlight is billionaire's Kobe beef with shallots and asparagus, followed by a wow mille-feuille dessert of rhubarb and wild strawberries with rosemary-raisin ice cream. Sounds like a Häagen-Dazs concoction, and it kind of is, but super-pumped-up. Amazing petits fours and baby candied fruits and other party favors complete the *bouffe*, and even if you had nothing particular to celebrate, by the time it's all over, you'll think you have.

A less demanding Robuchon option is offered in another gargantuan shopping center called Roppongi Hills, adjacent to one of Tokyo's elaborate red-light entertainment districts, Roppongi. There's nothing naughty, however, about Roppongi Hills except the prices, and at L'Atelier du Joel Robuchon, even the prices are manageable. L'Atelier, a strictly counter restaurant with no reservations taken, is the master's French take on the sushi bar. It has been a huge hit in Paris and New York, and it's huge in Roppongi Hills, especially at lunch with the sophisticated women shoppers who are as au courant with Paris as they are with Ginza. You never see men here during the day; they're all working in those endless office towers to pay the wifely bills. But the glamorous women look as if they're worth it. And so is the food, simple French country fare served almost sushi-style, tiny course by tiny course, at a beautiful long black-and-red lacquered counter before an open kitchen by superattractive young black-clad male and female model-types. What everyone is eating is perfect gazpacho, baby lamb chops, grilled coquilles St. Jacques, *poulet roti*, lots of wonderful baby vegetables from Japanese farms, and, always, a plate of Robuchon's trademark *puree*, or mashed potatoes with more butter and cream in one dish than most traditional Japanese will ever ingest in an entire lifetime.

The kitchen is totally suggestive of the farm, hearth and home, with displays of oranges, lemons, asparagus everywhere, baskets of the best chewy authentic French baguettes, hams hanging from the ceilings. However, an order of orange juice as an opening thirst quencher brought something not off the pile of citrus but, at best, out of a Tropicana carton. When this was pointed out to the model-server, she abjectly bowed in deep apology, then ran to the back and returned with a manual squeezer, took a few of the lovely globes from the pile, and juiced them herself, by hand. The result was as it should be, and as it should have been, but you almost have to smile at the old French try to cut corners, which doesn't happen in this culture.

Perhaps the very best of the imported *Michelin* restaurants is the Antica Osteria del Ponte, which in Italy is an old farmhouse inn by a bridge, and in Tokyo is none of the above, but the food is superb. Housed atop the Maru skyscraper in Nihonbashi, across from the red-brick late-1920s Tokyo Station, Osteria is part of a luxury food court of French, Chinese, and Japanese top-dollar feederies that offer spectacular views of the futuristic Tokyo skyline as well as of the verdant expanse of the centuries-old, off-limits-to-the-public Imperial Palace complex. Nothing could be further from the Italian *campagna* or from the seventeenth-century viscount's villa that houses the original Osteria.

That original restaurant was founded by a Milanese grocer and passionate self-taught chef, Ezio Santin, who turned his passion into a business in 1976. Santin went to France to learn "presentation," then sent his son Maurizio there to learn how to make fancy desserts in apprenticeships at Taillevent, Robuchon, Ducasse, and Lenôtre. This French respect was the stuff that thrilled *Michelin* inspectors, who gave Osteria three stars in 1990 (only the second restaurant in Italy to win that distinction, after Gualtiero Marchesi). And those stars were the stuff that thrilled Japanese investors who were building the Maru tower and were looking for *Michelin* catnip to lure tenants, all of whom are foodies in this country.

Like most famous restaurateurs with outposts in Tokyo, the presence of the Santins is in name only. The "stars" may visit Japan a few times a year but rarely to cook. They come to eat sushi and tempura and be cosseted by their Japanese partners. Osteria actually has a French resident chef, which does not bode well for those seeking real Italian food under the rising sun. Nor does the modernity of the room inspire confidence. There is a Roman mosaic tiled floor at the entrance, and an Old World dark-wood-paneled hallway with vaulted arches. But the main dining room might well have been Windows on the World, full of fat-cat hedge funders and currency traders, with those knockout Chanel consorts, surely from the superexclusive hostess clubs that you see at Kyubey. These ladies do not look like wives. Not yet, at least, but maybe in time.

You see only one Italian in the place, a handsome captain, and you may want to run off to the nearby Takashimaya basement food halls, but hold your ground. It gets better and better, beginning with the perfect rolls and focaccias and bread sticks that come out, actually much better than most of the bread you get in Italy. It's light and crusty and supremely chewy, so good you won't even dip it in the beyond-extra-virgin olive oil the smooth tuxedo'ed Japanese waiters bring with it. The deal is sealed with an *amuse* of a fat Japanese anchovy atop an eggplant puree on delicate puff pastry, Italy meets France meets Japan, totally felicitously. Then comes some wonderful buffalo mozzarella with incomparable Japanese summer tomatoes and you're right on that Lombard bridge, if not the Bridge of Sighs, it's so good. The final *amuse* is a recently alive giant-shrimp marinated *crudo* with tiny spring onions and a dollop of imported Italian sturgeon caviar from Alto Adige. You know now that you're in the right place. Order a top-dollar bottle of Italian wine from a noble list, and settle in for treat after treat.

For your main meal here, you can stay gourmet, go grandma, or mix it up. There's a fine peasant pasta dish of *paccheri,* huge *pappardelle*-like noodles, perfectly al dente, with fine slivers of gold and green zucchini and the earthy salty tang of pecorino cheese. With a grind of black pepper and a splash of olive oil, this is the pure *sapori d'Italia,* or taste of Italy. Or go the risotto route. The Japanese sous-chefs have all the patience in the world to stir and stir the rice for the half hour it takes to get it exactly right. Try the classic Milanese risotto, yellow with the finest saffron, and vegetized with the tenderest, greenest baby asparagus, the essence of spring. There's hardly any butter, just olive oil and broth to give the rice a lightness that's rare even on home turf. The dish is a triumph of taste and appearance. As Donovan once sang, "Mellow yellow, quite rightly."

If you have room, try some of the Frenchified but not bastardized Osteria classics that won it its Gallic stars: the totally original corn bread of mille-feuille of goose foie gras and porcini mushrooms; a lemony red mullet stuffed with rare olives and topped with a pancetta-cream sauce that sounds far heavier than it is, and further levitated by a chicory salad with an orange vinaigrette; a filet of deer in a pepper sauce with marjoram-flavored onion preserves, great with a big Barolo. The desserts live up to the pedigreed French provenance, the specialty being the giant *millefoglie* (the Japanese are deeply impressed with puff pastry techniques) of Piedmont chestnut cream.

You may have room only for the smooth-as-silk sorbets—melon, strawberry, raspberry, lemon, each served in its own tiny cup, each capturing the essence of the fruit. On the side, your waiter will bring you some baby strawberries in balsamic vinegar and custard cream that will make you swoon. Have some grappa to cushion the bill of it all, for it will be huge. At least you don't have to tip. Service, which is always superior, is always included in Japan. Again, we could learn from this. A lot.

If you want to see the genesis of all these multicourse "tasting" dinners, you should shoot the moon and go to Aoyagi, which is where the Santins, Ducasse, Robuchon, Gagnaire, and all the other star chefs (plus the likes of Clinton and Chirac) like to eat when they come to Tokyo to survey their Eastern empire. Aoyagi, in a nondescript neighborhood and unfindable except by a smart cabdriver, may be the most unassuming great restaurant in the world. Across the street is the Peter Pan Sandwich Shop, and aside from the chauffeured Bentleys outside and the distinguished greeter who looks like an ambassador, you would never guess that you were at a major gastronomic shrine. There are four tables, a six-seat counter, and a single undecorated tatami room. The staff is Mister Hirohisa Aoyagi, his wife, daughter, and a couple of aides in simple kimonos. But Aoyagi, who is a giant of a man at six foot four with great charm and charisma, has a major weekly food column in Japan's most prestigious paper, *Asahi;* he operates a renowned Japanese cooking school in Paris; and he is the author of several famous and beautiful cookbooks that have become bibles of their kind. You need to book months in advance to eat here, and your meal will run into the thousands. But it will also run there at Masa in New York. So if you want to indulge yourself in the highest end of the Japanese culinary spectrum, why not just follow the *Michelin* stars right here?

The only choice you need make is beer or sake. The rest is done for you. The kimono girls start you off with a tiny ceramic bowl (each bowl is unique and a work of art itself) of the creamiest tofu with a dot of green wasabi that is more sweet than hot. Hot is easy; sweet is hard. You know you're in masterly hands right at the get-go. Next is a plate of baby red shrimp and spinach in a reddish, slightly salty jelly flecked with shredded shark fin. The pearls of this jelly slip through your chopsticks like mercury, and you stab away for every sliver, like gold in a prospector's pan, because you know what this is costing you. You don't see the other diners, because the tables are shielded by shoji screens, and all you see are the backs of the men at the counter, and a counterman dutifully grinding wasabi with a mortar and pestle. This isn't communal dining in any way. You're left alone to commune with the delicacy, not to stare at tycoons.

The great specialty of Aoyagi is *hamo,* an eel-like freshwater fish that is the great delicacy of Tokushima, the chef's home region near Osaka. What Aoyagi serves is country cuisine in the big city. He's been here only a decade, but he's the king of country in Tokyo now, and the *hamo* is his trademark. You get it first steamed in a silver bowl, in a broth flavored with lime rind and a local vegetable named *jim sai* that has no Western equivalent. The fish is dense, meaty, and full flavored, but not at all "fishy." This is spa food that makes you feel virtuous, light, and healthy, not like Thomas Keller's thirty-course cream-and-butter orgies, which make you feel like you're ready for coronary bypass surgery. If you're going to have thirty courses, Japanese is the way to go, if you really want to keep going.

What follows is more fish, an elegant tiny sashimi platter of halibut, and supertender squid, decorated with slivers of white radish. Afterward comes charcoal-grilled freshwater eel in a sweet soy sauce, four bites of sheer sweet-sour heaven. And then there are "mixed appetizers" of figs in a sesame cream, wood-grilled baby green pepper, octopus with red beans, a salad of lotus root and seaweed, and a fried *hamo* backbone that could be a very addictive snack, if you were prime minister or head of Mitsubishi. In Aoyagi's first cookbook, entitled *Windborne Flavors,* the master sets out his precepts: "1. Let the material speak out for itself. 2. For the ultimate in cooking, the chef must kill his own ego. [Hear that?] 3. Listen to people other than yourself. 4. There is a golden ratio for each good flavor."

Now it's meat time. The women bring you a hundred-year-old duck egg, almost as a symbolic act, because the taste is so evanescent and indecipherable. Then a platter of Aiwa beef from the Tokushima prefecture. This may be the best beef ever, not dissolving in fat like Kobe, but filet mignon with sirloin flavor, charred and bloody and accentuated by a mustard soy sauce. Peter Luger, move over. Then, it's Mr Chow's turn to move over, when you get a plate of fried seaweed, greaseless and crunchy, that makes Chow's famed "*gambei* with goodies" seem like a plate of greasy fries at Denny's. And then it's duck time, a rare breast slice that separates instantly from its perimeter of toothsome fat, steamed in a broth with melon, turnip, and eggplant. Move over, Michel Guerard, who should add this page to his book of *cuisine minceur.*

The pièce de résistance is the bowl of piping-hot *hamo* porridge, flavored with pickled eggplant and radish and soy. This is hearty 49er Gold Rush food, and while you may need a strike to pay for it, you suddenly feel supermasculine, like the world leaders who may be seated near you but whom you cannot see. Macho man, in Japan. Wash it down with barley tea, which adds to the adrenaline rush, then cool off with a series of desserts: silk-smooth ginger sorbet with sliced mangoes; watermelon juice flan; sweet tapioca; and three more kinds of tea to send you into the Tokyo night. Poorer, yes. But richer in the experience of having eaten the best that the ultimate food nation can offer. ★ ★ ★ ★

New York Grill
Cost in Translation

Complaining about the brutal prices in Japan is akin to complaining about the heat in Singapore or the water in India: futile. Suck it up or get out. A fact of life is that a great meal in Tokyo costs two to three times more than one in New York that simply won't be anywhere as good. So you do want to have your *anago* and eat it, too. Foodies don't like price to come between them and something wonderful to eat. They whine and dine, but dine they must. The whining lets them feel slightly better than simply taking the prices lying down.

The prices are staggering indeed at the restaurant that always tops the Tokyo Zagat poll as the most popular dining venue in the city, the New York Grill of the Park Hyatt Hotel, which served as the backdrop for much of the lack of action in the Sofia Coppola–Bill Murray ode to anomie, *Lost in Translation*. The Park Hyatt Tokyo, in its Kenzo Tange (famous for rebuilding Hiroshima) skyscraper, with its remote control bidets and views of Mount Fuji and impromptu bar concerts by Billy Joel and Elton John and deep sleep beds that celebs like Arnold Schwarzenegger buy and ship to Brentwood, is considered by many to be the coolest hotel in the world, and has spawned an entire new global brand synonymous with the ultimate in lodging. And its New York Grill, with spectacular views, cathedral ceilings, and Lichtenstein-style blow-up posters of the glories of Gotham, is a glamorous homage to the Rainbow Room. Or, more accurately, to the Rainbow Room crossed with Spago, for the food here is very Puckish (most of the head chefs have come from California) and the wine very Napa-ish, which is only just, for a venue embraced by so many Hollywood stars. Homesick New Yorkers of all nations love it, though not as much as the Japanese. For them it's the coolest "date" restaurant in the whole country.

It certainly shows commitment. Dinner at the New York Grill can set you back far more than breakfast at Tiffany's. The taxi alone to Shinjuku, a new development that is a cross between City Hall and Times Square, where the hotel is located, can cost $75 and take an hour. Once you arrive, you must take three elevators into the clouds to arrive at this room at the top, full of cozy booths and widely spaced, seduction-friendly tables whose best view is of an illuminated high-rise designed as a knockoff of the Empire State Building. Ladies' menus have no prices. Too bad you can't show off, but they *know*. Here, for example, is one set menu, the "Madison Avenue," priced at around $200 a person, without wine, which at the least is $25 a glass, $150 a bottle. A lobster and tomato salad, and, oh, those unmatchable Japanese tomatoes. Seared foie gras with a cherry tartlet and balsamic sauce. Pan-roasted John Dory with fresh peas. Yonezawa rib eye with corn risotto. And more risotto, this one sweet orange with passion fruit sauce, for dessert.

These are tiny portions, mind you. You won't gain weight here. Then again, the last thing a date restaurant should do is make you fat. What you do see here are lots of lecherous older corporate types dining with two or three much younger distaff "associates," whom he is plying with luxe food and drink. Most of these older gents look like they're clients of Dandy House, Japan's preeminent chain of plastic surgery clinics for men, whose spokesman is Richard Gere, in endless subtle television spots featuring the American Gigolo cruising in a con-vertible. Up to now, sexual harassment is not a corporate concept in Japan; but if it ever becomes one, this will be ground zero. Also dining here are lots of very rich young kids, teenagers with platinum cards. Tokyo has more millionaires than any city on earth, and more restaurants (300,000, compared with 180,000 in New York, and a scant 50,000 in LA). It seems like most of their progeny have made the New York Grill their clubhouse.

À la carte is much, much more, but it lets you run the show. Start with the raved-about Caesar salad, which veers from orthodoxy by adding crisp strips of bacon, which is otherwise rarely seen in Tokyo. Bacon, which is viewed as quintessentially American, is thus considered culinarily "cool," even if it doesn't quite work in the otherwise pungent and garlicky Caesar. Whatever. It's nice that the Japanese like us so. The gazpacho with fresh crab also harks back to California, more Mexican than Spanish, with lots of cilantro and a garnish of tortilla chips. But France does get its due, after a Napa fashion: there's a fine cold confit of goose liver with a yummy grape jam.

Because of the rampant Yankophilia at play, everyone at the New York Grill seems to want a steak, cooked on the open grill. Top-of-the-line is the Miyazaki "Koyama" Sirloin, which costs about $140, and is tiny—maybe six ounces at most, all of which is marbled fat, which the Japanese love. Cholestophobes may opt for the much leaner grass-fed New Zealand imports at half the price and a tenth the fat. The Kiwi beef tastes great to American palates, as do the wonderful hand-cut skin-on fries, and the sautéed organic garlic spinach, all of which is washed down well by whatever your selection of California red from the 1,800-bottle glassed-in cellar in the sky.

Take your dessert in the bar where Bill Murray drowned his sorrows. If Billy Joel isn't there, a good American combo will be, belting out standards as those tycoons stuff their underlings of desire with macadamia nut tarts topped with banana rum ice cream, or hot chocolate and churros, depending on how hot it is, though it's *always* hot in the New York Grill. If Tokyo ever gets too much for you and you want to "take Manhattan," this is the place. ★ ★ ★ ★ ★ ★ ★ ★ ★ ★ ★ ★ ★ ★

The Inn Crowd

For all the sophistication of Tokyo's cosseting amenities, it is still the most relentlessly urban of all cities, a place where the emperor controls all the chlorophyll and where you have to find the rare cemetery to get a patch of green. You've got to get out, way out, to get back to nature, to regain your sanity. Just as New York has Central Park as its pressure valve, Tokyo has Kyoto. Although Kyoto is 250 miles away, the trip takes only two and a half hours by *shinkansen,* or bullet train: the trip, along the sea with Mount Fuji looming in the distance, is part of the relaxation process. Kyoto is the spiritual capital of the country, with verdant rolling hills filled with some of the world's most beautiful ancient temples and elaborate gardens, which the Japanese do better than anyone. To walk in beauty, to savor antiquity, is the perfect yin to Tokyo's clanging yang. While Kyoto itself is a huge city, with a population in the millions, somehow it doesn't feel like one. Lacquered geishas in kimonos pad about the Gion, the centuries-old red-light district, and even when they're passing a McDonald's the sense of blast from the past is palpable.

A key part of the Kyoto escape is to stay in a *ryokan,* or inn, those serene screened, bamboo-and-wood affairs with stone lanterns and interior rock gardens and moss forests and waterfalls and babbling brooks. Here, beautiful geisha types bathe you three times a day. Wearing a robe and slippers, you are fed the most delicate *kaiseki* feasts, on the prettiest dishes, that you have ever experienced. A *ryokan* is kickback to the max. You sleep on the floor, on lush futons, and you'll never sleep better or more silently, the sleep of angels, or of shoguns. Trying to choose or distinguish among *ryokans* is fairly inscrutable, like choosing between great sushi bars. They're *all* wonderful.

But the three best *ryokans* in Kyoto are all a few blocks from one another in the heart of the city, though once behind the tatami screens, you'll swear you were in the depths of the country. The most famous is Hiragiya, built in the early 1800s and the redoubt of the princes of the imperial family ever since. Charlie

Chaplin stayed here, and all the top French designers, who would be the perfect sorts to appreciate the couturelike efforts taking place here. The flagstones at the entrance are always wet, a symbol of hospitality, and every room is filled with antiques and has a *tokonoma,* or flower alcove, worthy of a master florist. The food is perfect but very recherché. The most famous two-century-old specialty is *wagashi,* little dumplings filled with sweet bean paste. That may sound simple, but here it is raised to an art.

Next door is Tawaraya, which dates back to the 1700s, but, like most of Kyoto's wooden structures, burned down and has been lovingly and seamlessly restored. Tawaraya is an artists' retreat—Leonard Bernstein, Saul Bellow, Alfred Hitchcock, those types of creative legends have filled the guest register, though you can't imagine Hitch coming up with a murder maguffin in a setting so peaceful and mellow. Tofu is emperor here, prepared in a multiplicity of delicious ways, and you may feel after your stay that meat, even Kobe beef, is too barbaric for you.

A block farther is the most "Hollywood" of the lot, Yoshikawa. Buddhist Richard Gere, beloved in Japan because of his Dandy House male plastic surgery ads, stays here, as does Paul McCartney. Mellow George Harrison came and loved it, as have far noisier types like Christina Aguilera, and even famous kids, like *Harry Potter*'s Daniel Radcliffe. One of the lures, aside from the shoji-screened privacy of it all, is Yoshikawa's renowned tempura, reputedly the greatest in Japan, and to the *gaijin* palate certainly the equal of Tokyo's nonpareil Ten-Ichi. Actually, the sizzling tempura experience might seem a little bustling, given the silence factor, and this is maybe why the Western fry-babies are drawn here. The touch of fat will only make you sleep better, not that you need to worry about sleeping amid the babbling brooks and rustling leaves. The only thing that *might* keep you awake is anxiety over the tab, which can run up to a thousand dollars a room in these places. Silence is golden. Literally. ★ ★ ★ ★ ★ ★ ★ ★ ★ ★ ★

Rockpool, Tetsuya's, Machiavelli, Tropicana
Oohs and Oz

SYDNEY

The great thing about Sydney is that as a harbor-beach metropolis it is *almost* as fabulous-looking as Rio yet *nowhere* as dangerous. While a Carioca has to worry that a drug gang the size of an army might decimate the entire Rio police force, a Sydneysider's idea of an urban problem is that a Vietnamese family has moved into the neighborhood. Having forgotten its rough-and-tumble convict roots as a British penal colony, Sydney has become the LA of the Antipodes, a sun-bleached, palmy, laid-back surf city full of movie stars and cutting-edge fusion restaurants. The Wolfgang Puck of this new gastrocapital is a ponytailed butcher's son named Neil Perry, whose restaurant Rockpool is the heart and soul of the Australian food revolution. Not renaissance, mind you, since there was nothing to resurrect or renew. Perry and his cohorts in the last two decades have created a new cuisine of their own out of the whole cloth of formerly xenophobic Australia's change of heart and immigration policy toward Asia.

Sydney, which used to be true Brit, with an underclass of post–World War II Greek and Italian peasant immigrants, is now a true melting pot of more than a hundred nationalities, and Neil Perry seems to draw from every one of them. Rockpool, in the heart of tourist Sydney in the "Rocks" area of Circular Cay overlooking the iron-age Harbour Bridge and the space-age

Opera House, is the leading temple of local gastronomy. But because Sydney is even more casual than LA, it hardly feels like one. Rockpool's stone-and-timber building is ancient history by local standards, going back to 1860. It was once a hotel called the Shipwrights Arms, then the Hotel Chicago, until Perry bought and gutted it in 1989. Today it is sleek and modern, with two levels around an open kitchen, with lots of stainless steel, designer chairs, track lights, sea blue carpet, and running-water effects. But the most effective effects are the platters of food streaming out of the United Nations of a kitchen with its confidence-inspiring wall of live fish and shellfish tanks, like a spotless version of a Chinatown seafood palace. It looks good, smells good, is good.

There are few neckties at Rockpool, except those belonging to the suits from the nearby office towers. This may be a temple, but it certainly isn't La

Tour d'Argent. The dress code is basically that of Disneyland; rarely have superfoodies (and they must be, to be here) seemed so down-home as here Down Under. Yes, there's a slanted catwalk in the center of the restaurant for grand entrances; and yes, Nicole and Russell and Mel and Naomi and Kylie and all the big Aussie stars do come here. But this place is for chow, not Mr Chow. The waiters are young and smart and "g'day mate" unpretentious for such an ambitious temple. All in all, Rockpool looks like a shrimp-on-the-barbie crowd, except that the shrimp on Neil Perry's barbie will be Margaret River marron tails, Balmian bugs, or some other fancy local crustacean pedigree.

There are so many exotic (to you) local ingredients at Rockpool that you'll have no idea what to order, so put yourself in Perry's hands for a tasting menu, and these are some of the works you will shoot: live scallop with pea puree; tartare of kingfish with green beans and avocado; salad of live king prawns with tomato sorbet and gazpacho sauce; hand-picked crab with hazelnut and zucchini salad and lime caviar; goat cheese *tortelloni* with pine nuts and raisins; shiitake and *enoki* wontons; stir-fried squid with squid ink noodles, chili, and coriander; onion and eggplant pastilla with spicy carrot dressing; bass grouper with garam masala and coconut milk; snapper crumbed "El Bulli" style with green olive butter; lobster *en vessie* with green curry sauce;

roast suckling pig with white peach and black pepper salad; Australian cheeses from the hills above Perth; almond-milk jelly with plum soup and rose sorbet. And that's Rockpool, all over the map: French, Italian, Spanish, Moroccan, Indian, Thai, Chinese, Japanese, and a touch of the old sod, all there "on the Rocks," and all deftly executed in perfect fusion and never *con*fusion. Plus there is an education to be had here in Australian wines, from the vaunted Hunter Valley and beyond.

How did Perry learn to do it, you will marvel, turning a certain disaster high-wire act into a daily tour de force? The way Perry cooks, you'd think he had gone to the Cordon Bleu and apprenticed at El Bulli and Paul Bocuse. But he's just a Sydney homeboy, a butcher's boy, whose father had befriended a group of Chinese refugee students who would cook all the exotic fish that dad, an obsessive angler, would catch on his days off from the meat market. For all his Chinoiseries, however, Perry had never been to Asia when he opened Rockpool with his cousin Trish Richards in 1989. Instead he had been working like a coolie in a lot of local restaurants, just grilling fish mostly, no lemongrass. Until he opened his first place, the little Blue Water Grill in Bondi Beach, where he turned a cursed (thus cheap) location into an unexpected success that led to the increasingly ambitious and exotic Rockpool, and then took those long delayed trips to Asia and the rest of the world as the ambassador of Australian cuisine. Today, Perry masterminds all the first- and business-class food on Qantas, which, along with Sergi Arola's menus for Iberia, is way up there as the best food in the skies.

Like much of Sydney, Perry got ahead of himself when Sydney hosted the 2000 Olympics, by opening too many spinoffs, such as the perhaps overly witty Wokpool, when the expected post-Olympic tourist hordes never quite showed up. Marshaling his forces back at Rockpool, the mother ship is better than ever, especially with the local seafood. Perry, who uses only fishermen catering to the elite Japanese market, adheres to what he calls a "stress-mini-mizing catch methodology" practiced by Japanese seafarers for centuries, in which the fish are line caught, brain spiked (sounds like something from *The Godfather*, or maybe codfather), and ice slurried. The fish are then dry fileted, because Perry decries the normal practice of doing it under running water, which leaches out the flavor. The meticulousness turns up on your plate.

Possibly even more meticulous is Perry's chief rival as Sydney's superchef, Tetsuya Wakuda. If Perry is Australia's Wolfgang Puck, then Wakuda is its Nobu Matsuhisa. Unlike Nobu, who had been a highly trained chef in Japan, Tetsuya washed up in Sydney at twenty-two in 1982 with no kitchen experience, only a desire to live in a brave new world of kangaroos and koalas. His first job was as a dishwasher in a place called Fishwives, but he worked hard and upward. A local restaurateur who wanted to add growingly popular sushi to his "continental" offerings made Tetsuya his sushi man only because he was Japanese. Again Tetsuya rose to the occasion, paying particular attention to the French techniques the rest of the restaurant was employing. By 1989 he had

scrimped and saved enough to open his own tiny place in the distant suburb of Rozelle. But because of the success of Neil Perry and other chefs, Sydney went foodie, developing an obsessive food press that discovered Tetsuya and sent waiting lines into the suburban road. Soon he was a superstar. In 2000 he moved his operations into a grand Japanese shrine of a place, with pagodas and rock gardens and koi ponds, as well as Tetsuya's ceramics collection, in the heart of Sydney's Central Business District. Despite the space, you still have to book about a month in advance.

It's worth planning for. But because stars don't plan, and don't seem to be patient enough to sit still through the three- to four-hour tasting experience at Tetsuya's, you're less likely to spot Cate Blanchett or Heath Ledger than at more casual venues. Tetsuya is the star here, but he's shy and modest and doesn't work the room like a Puck. Though dining here is an Australian version of *Teahouse of the August Moon,* no one dresses up in beachy Sydney, even in templar respect, and the waitstaff are gorgeous but anything but formal surfer girls. And while the mood is very Kyoto, the food is more Berkeley, Pac Rim delights with French accents served in a succession of tiny portions that will leave you hungrier at the end than the beginning.

There's no menu, as the kitchen is market driven, but here's a sample of what you might get: tea and tomato soup. A scallop in the shell with lemongrass. Baked octopus on a *rosti* potato cake, garnished with wakame. Scampi with deep-fried leeks. Crab sushi. And those are just the warm-up—each plate is no more than one or two bites or swallows. Tetsuya's signature main course, which is five or six bites, is his confit of Tasmanian ocean trout, a salmonesque game fish, served with unpasteurized trout roe, in a sauce of green parsley and olive oil. Then there is filet of spatchcock, a local baby chicken, cooked in a broth with fresh soybeans, spring onions, peas, and bok choy, Tetsuya's answer to "Jewish penicillin," minus the matzo balls. You end the main courses with a rare bite of meltingly tender Kobe beef with *sansho* and shiitake mushrooms. Then head for home with dessert, which might be light, an apple sorbet atop apple jelly, or less light (nothing's heavy here except the bill), a flourless chocolate cake with bitter chocolate sorbet and blood orange ice cream. It's all great, but still hungry gourmet Aussies are known to stop on the way home at a local institution called Harry's Café de Wheels, a harbor stand famous for its disgusting—but very filling—"pea floaters," greasy meat-filled pies with lumpy mashed potatoes and mushy frozen peas on top, which are the stars' hangover cure.

About the only public restaurant (as opposed to private Anglo clubs) where you can see Aussie men (men at work) in suits is Machiavelli, the aptly named home of the Sydney power lunch, the city's answer to the Four Seasons, an authentic white-walled, Mediterranean-evocative trattoria deep in the heart of financial Sydney. You will do an interesting double-take here, for the tycoons, like the Murdochs and the Packers, and the politicians, who you probably won't recognize though you can feel their heat, are both at the tables and up on the walls, in huge three-by-five black-and-white blow-ups of these power brokers. No "power" restaurant anywhere is quite so upfront about Who Matters. But then again, Australia is that kind of straightforward place.

Machiavelli was founded in the 1950s by the Toppi family, who were part of a wave of postwar flight from the devastation of the boot. Australia, desperate for manual laborers, promised the equivalent of twenty acres and a mule, and millions of Italians and Greeks snapped at the bait. Alas, most of the transplanted Italians left everything behind in the Old World, including their *cucina*. While the Greeks, who mostly settled around Melbourne, never forgot how to make moussaka, the Italians, eager to be good mates, Anglicized their dishes, drowning everything in cream and cooking their fish and pasta to death. Even today, in the era of Perry and Wakuda, Italian food is still largely stuck in a 1950s time warp. Maybe Italy is simply too far away to make its gustatory truth be felt.

But luckily for Sydney, and you, Machiavelli has kept the faith. The new generation of the family still runs the place, and it's as close to home as you can hope for this far away. Have the huge vegetable antipasto, which takes full advantage of the Australian harvest and marinates it in the best imported olive oil. Have the baby arugula salad. Have the *calamari fritti*, which are never frozen and always tender and crisp and lemony. Have the house spaghetti with live prawns, mushrooms, garlic, and chili. Have any grilled fish. And finish with the tiramisù, as all the moguls and politicos do. It may be déjà vu for an Italo-jaded Yank, but after you've been Down Under long enough you'll be more than happy to see this déjà vu over and over again.

But forget about Rupert Murdoch. Where are his stars, you ask? Where? The one place you can *always* count on seeing stars, directors, models, the beautiful people of all stars and stripes is the sprawling indoor-outdoor Tropicana Café in Darlinghurst, Sydney's Greenwich Villge. It is directly adjacent to King's Cross, which is its Times Square, pre-Giuliani cleanup. So you may have Elle Macpherson at one outdoor table and a transsexual hooker at another, Baz Luhrmann making a major film deal and a pusher making a major drug deal right next to him. It's wide open in every way, and that's why the stars like it. Beware, however, of the thick fog of cigarette smoke and the discordant symphony of cell phones. There's more networking done here than the Polo Lounge ever saw in its heyday.

The Trop, as it is known, also has the distinction of being the only coffee shop that has its own film festival, Tropfest. Tropfest was started in 1992 by actor (now hot director) and Trophanger John Polson just to show the short films of his friends in this movie-mad city. They set up a projector and a screen, and in Sydney the weather always obliges, and an event was born. Tropfest now is a Big Deal, a movable feast of films that plays not only on the sidewalk of the Trop but also in parks and public spaces all over Sydney. And even New York now. When Polson directed Robert De Niro in *Hide and Seek* in 2005, the raging bull was so taken with the Tropfest concept that he made Tropfest a part of his own Tribeca Film Festival.

The weather's still better in Sydney, just like the strong coffee, focaccia sandwiches, and hearty soups. The Trop is run by a Machiavelli-like family from Italy that didn't go English, and it has some of the best quick fare you'll eat outdoors this side of the Piazza del Popolo. The *passato de verdura*, a pureed vegetable soup made only in Sydney's short winter, is Neil Perry–worthy, and the spaghetti *bolognese* is Bologna-worthy. The Trop's model-friendly salads have won food-mag awards as the best in Sydney. And while the scrambled eggs and ricotta pancakes might not be the match of the world-famous Bill's breakfast nook across the road, seeing Russell Crowe here on his cell phone and not throwing it at anyone is a frisson that makes up the difference. ★ ★ ★ ★ ★ ★ ★ ★

The Am

HOMINY GRIL
Grits ar
Good fo
you
Rosie
BREAKFAST
LUNCH DINNER

ericas

Fasano and Figueira Rubaiyat
Dead Man Eating

The first thing foreigners think about in São Paolo is getting killed or getting kidnapped, or both. That's a huge mistake. They should think about urban pleasure rather than urban pain. Yes, São Paolo has a terrible crime rate and brazen, vicious gangs that challenge law enforcement to a perennial duel in the sun. But São Paolo is also the New York of the Southern Hemisphere, with shopping, nightclubs, and restaurants that can put Manhattan's to shame. There are lots of superrich people here, people who are the kidnap targets of these gangs, people with walled villas and helipads and private armies. But these rich people like to shop and party and eat like there is no tomorrow (there may not be), and São Paolo caters mightily to this epicurean mentality.

The best caterer of all in this *Blade Runner*–ish pleasure dome is a dashing, dapper, fortyish bon vivant sportsman named Rogério Fasano whose family are the Ciprianis of Brazil. The Fasanos own four of the best and most fashionable restaurants in São Paolo, the equal of any in Milan, as well as the most exclusive restaurant in Rio, and now what is arguably the best hotel in the entire world, the Fasano in São Paolo, which is saying a chic mouthful. The mastermind behind all this perfection is the perfectionist Rogério, who went off to London as a young man to become a film director but was transfixed by what he saw at Claridge's and the Savoy, not to mention the Ritz and

La Tour d'Argent on Channel hops to Paris. He realized that he had the mission to go home and become a prophet in his own country. After all, he had the name, he had the base, and now he had the vision. The high life you will live in his establishments is a testament to the genius of his execution.

The Fasano experience requires total immersion. To do Brazil right, you must eat, drink, and sleep Fasano. It begins at the airport, a *Touch of Evil* sinister third-world touchdown where you are rescued by a charming Italian-suited driver who whisks you into a cool black-windowed (you see out; *they* can't see in) PT Cruiser for the ride into the miasmic megalopolis, whose fortunes began as a coffee exporter. Today the place is like downtown Detroit during its riot era, mile after mile of scarred and hideous tenement blocks, factories everywhere, clusters of angry unemployed youths glaring at your natty chariot with covetous eyes. But your driver is playing a samba tape that puts an Ipanema lull over the Harlem fear.

And, suddenly, the hellish city turns heavenly. Big trees turn the gray industrial blight into an emerald forest. Architectural high-rises erupt. Chanel, Vuitton, Cartier, Armani logos beckon. All the women look like Gisele Bundchen. You are in Jardims, which is what it sounds like, "gardens," São Paolo's Upper East Side. It's the most chic, elegant urban pleasure zone you've ever seen, especially in contrast to the endless combat zone you've passed through.

Then you arrive at the Fasano, a towering brick-and-marble spire that has no sign, naturally. This place has no need to broadcast itself. The lobby is totally, architecturally high-Milanese: plush dark leather couches, modern-museum-quality armchairs, burnished woods, flashing steel. You feel like you're in an Agnelli living room. There are elegant men smoking cigars, and more Bundchens flashing tanned designer thighs, sipping tropical nectars being squeezed to order by a battery of expert bartenders, and nibbling seductive-smelling toasted panini. You thought you were dead, from the flight, from the city, but now you're ready to party. The fear is gone.

As a hotel, the Fasano is a vertical palace, seventy-five rooms on twenty-five floors. With its parks and towers, São Paolo looks far better from above than down below. The rooms are out of a millennial James Bond, great art, great gadgets, great views, great beds. There are tubs and showers and screens and music everywhere and special toiletries and mirrors, mirrors, mirrors, mirrors. The London and Paris grand-hotel-trained staff bring you a deft omelet *fines herbes* and Paris-perfect croissants and a big glass of fresh papaya juice to stave off hypoglycemia, and a book of menus from all the Fasano restaurants so you can chart your gastronomic course for the days ahead. No cocoon could be more reassuring than this one.

You'll want to eat at all the Fasano restaurants. Start at the hotel on your first night with the flagship, which is what you think you're supposed to get at Gualtiero Marchesi in Italy but never quite do. The room is grand and sleek and gleaming, like the Ferrari executive dining room might be, the clientele so glamorous you can see why there's a huge kidnapping problem here. These folks *have* it, and they *flaunt* it, baby. Diamonds are forever. But don't count on it, unless your armored Hummer is waiting outside. But you won't have to brave the mean streets. You're an elevator ride away from Nirvana, so relax and chow down.

Chef Salvatore Loi, who's won every award in the Southern Hemisphere, offers three tasting menus: Fasano in Umbria, Fasano in Piemonte, and Fasano Mare. Or you can chart your own course down the boot. Everything is divine. Take the Umbria trip, for instance, and you'll start with *fegatelli salsa pervada*, which sounds better than chicken livers in a vinegar and anchovy sauce, and tastes great; then a saffron risotto with black truffles; a main of puff pastry filled with quail, garnished with more of those black truffles and green beans; finish with a pine nut torte. As you can see, this is top-dog gourmet fare for the kidnap clientele. Wines are major league, the best of Italy, as you would expect.

If you want to go peasant, Fasano has an answer for you, right across the well-guarded street. This is Gero, the nickname for Rogério, a brick-walled, skylit, soft-jazzed, chicly casual loftlike trattoria where you can choose from multiple carpaccios (octopus, tuna, lamb), multiple salads, multiple polentas (squid ink, *taleggio*, mushroom) to start. Then you'll take a classic pasta: green lasagna, *pappardelle* with duck ragout, *tagliolini* with squid and arugula sauce, fish ravioli *alle vongole veraci,* proof that there are plenty of fish in the sea, and it doesn't have to be the Mediterranean to be Italian. If you have room, the veal Milanese may be even better than the best of the grandmotherland. Because of Brazil's unequaled tropical fruits, Gero's gelati and *sorbetti* may be the best on earth.

You could eat at Gero every day and night in São Paolo, but Rogério Fasano won't let you, because he has still another restaurant, Parigi, where he proves he can do French as well as he can do Italian. Parigi is near Fasano in São Paolo's booming Wall Street–like financial core, where the bankers somehow have far more dash and flash than their brethren at Salomon Brothers; if you're a woman on the prowl, Parigi is a happy hunting ground. Parigi is Rogério's homage to the legendary fin de siècle brasseries, and he gets art nouveau exactly right: the curved woods, the banquettes, the chandeliers, the mirrors, with no trace of nouveau whatsoever. But the food here is the thing, and what makes Parigi special and true to its name is that there are two menus: "French Classics" and "Italian Classsics." So you can have garlicky, buttery escargots or a *soufflé au fromage* to start, or *spaghetti chitarra al sugo di baccala,* a rustic Abruzzi feast of homemade wheat spaghetti with a peppery, tomato-y codfish sauce. For mains, the French side offers an Ami Louis–worthy *pintade roti sauce morilles,* while the Italian *carta* offers an Amico Luigi–worthy *piccata al limone;* homages abound, like *canard à la presse Tour d'Argent.* But the very best main course is the self-homage of *gigot à la Parigi,* a luscious leg of lamb roasted for seven hours. For dessert it's a toss-up between the French *tarte Tatin,* the Italian *crema di mascarpone,* or the Brazilian mango flambé with vanilla ice cream. The only solution is to come back the next day.

And if all these offerings weren't enough, Rogério Fasano has also built the world's ultimate panini parlor. The Forneira (oven) São Paolo has a whole wall of wood ovens belching forth the most amazing sandwiches of home-cured meats, home-baked breads, rare imported cheeses, all to be devoured by endless lines of São Paolo's *jeunesse doré,* the sleekest bunch of sandwich eaters you've ever seen. Nothing, not even panini mavens 'ino and Via Quadronno in New York, come anywhere close to this.

Perfectionists tend to be born, not made, and Rogério Fasano comes from a long line of them. The Fasanos came to São Paolo from Milan in 1902, part of a huge wave of Italian emigration to the New World that turned the coffee port into a very big Little Italy. The patriarch, Vittorio Fasano, began a century of Franco-Italian fusion by opening the Brasserie Paulista in the city center. A series of bakeries, teahouses, restaurants, and dinner theaters, featuring songs by Nat King Cole and lectures by Fidel Castro, would follow, as would lucrative liquor distributorships and publishing houses. The Fasanos have an empire, and Rogério is the newest emperor, whose imperial plans include a new innkeeping venture with Philippe Starck in hotel-deprived Rio, right near Rogério's superhot branch of Gero, which serves all the girls from Ipanema.

Just in case you get to thinking there are no non-Fasano restaurants in São Paolo, do venture a few steps from the hotel and try one of the world's best steakhouses, La Figueira Rubaiyat, which was founded long ago by Lebanese immigrants (São Paolo is as much of a melting pot as New York, hence the Omar Khayyam reference) under a primeval block-long brontosaurus of a fig tree. In this garden of eden outside the gates of hell, under the tree, and under a Plexiglas roof that is as unnoticeable as the ubiquitous armed security guards, the kidnap set enjoys fig-tree-size baby beef from the owners' *fazenda* in the grasslands of Brazil cooked on vast wood grill pits. The meat is succulent and tender and sizzling, but the grilled fish is equally fine, and the homemade, puffy, hot cheese bread is so addictive you'll be full before the main courses come. There are offshoots in the bodyguard-unnecessary metropolises of Buenos Aires and Madrid with more being planned.

Speaking of getting supersized, Figueira has a Sunday buffet featuring *feijoada*, the national dish of Brazil, which Figueira does better than anyone else. The name of the dish comes from *feijao*, Portuguese for "bean," and black beans are the heart of this heart-stopping stew of thinly sliced pork and pork entrails. The stew is served with fresh collard greens and *farofa*, or toasted local manioc flour. This is slave food of a high and filling order, gone gourmet but without losing its soul. With the buffet comes an equally fattening dessert buffet, as rich in tropicalia as the Amazon itself. Do it once and then go back to the Fasano designer gym in the sky. Rogério Fasano is waiting to feed you again tonight, and you better make room, because, like most things in São Paolo, it will be to die for, one way or another. ★ ★ ★ ★ ★ ★ ★ ★ ★ ★ ★ ★ ★ ★ ★

Copacabana Palace and Cervantes
Fred and Ginger Revisited

RIO DE JANEIRO

Until Rogério Fasano opens his new hotel in Ipanema, the only place to stay in Rio is, has been, and may always be the Copacabana Palace. Constructed in 1923 for an international exposition that never quite materialized, the Copa Palace was a bit like the Dakota apartments when New York's Upper West Side was still a frontier outpost, all dressed up with no place to go. A tunnel had just been built connecting civilized Rio with a very empty Copacabana (Quechua Indian for "luminous place") beach, whose pounding surf and gale-force breezes were not considered at all salubrious at the time. But these were the Roaring Twenties, and people around the world had money to spend and imaginations to capture, and the Copa Palace quickly became a rich-and-famous travel fantasy.

The white and truly palatial Copa Palace looked and felt like the grand hotels along the French Riviera, the Carlton in Cannes, the Negresco in Nice. But Rio was even more beautiful than the Côte d'Azur, and far more exotic. Europe in the tropics was the idea, and it was irresistible. The hotel was built by Otávio Guinle, whose family were the Rockefellers of Brazil, having built the port of Santos that linked São Paolo and its coffee—the black gold that made it a metropolis—to the sea. What put the Copa on the world map, more than anything else, was the movie *Flying Down to Rio*, which introduced the world not only to the hotel, where much of the action took place (although most of the film was actually shot in Malibu), but also to Fred Astaire and Ginger Rogers. It was released in 1933 at the height of the Depression, when the world sorely needed an impossible dream. The movie's "Carioca" became a dance craze, and the Copa Palace became a hotel craze.

Copacabana itself was further fetishized as the backdrop for the romantic intrigues of Cary Grant and Ingrid Bergman in Hitchcock's Nazis-in-Brazil thriller *Notorious*. But what turned the Copa Palace into Hollywood's overseas beach club were the playboy escapades of Otávio Guinle's nephew Jorginho ("Little Georgie" was only five foot five, but partied like a giant). Young Guinle was Brazil's "ambassador to Hollywood," a lightweight official PR post that involved making the country look good in films like *Notorious* and Carmen Miranda's *The Gang's All Here*. Unofficially, he shared a villa with Errol Flynn and bedded even more stars than his Tasmanian Devil bunk mate. Among his highly reported "romantic interests" were Lana Turner, Rita Hayworth, Veronica Lake, Jayne Mansfield, Kim Novak, Anita Ekberg, Zsa Zsa Gabor and Marilyn Monroe, all of whom were his pampered guests at the Copa Palace.

Eventually Jorginho dissipated the family fortune, and as Brazil's urban crime rate went out of control and Copacabana went into lockdown, with machine-gun-toting policemen outnumbering surfers on the sand, the aging, un-air-conditioned Copa Palace hit its own skids. In 1989 the Guinles sold the grande dame to Orient Express Hotels, which sunk a fortune into it and gave Jorginho a roof over his bankrupt head until his death at eighty-eight in 2004. He had been in the hospital, waiting for surgery for an aortic aneurysm, but he decided he had had enough. So he went back to the hotel's Pergula restaurant, by its fabled swimming pool, had his favorite meal of chicken Stroganoff and raspberry sorbet, and died that night in his suite overlooking the Rio sand and Atlantic surf.

Today the Copa Palace, lovingly restored and cooled off, remains a mighty fortress in the sea of sleaze and danger that is Copacabana. Ipanema and Leblon, a few miles farther away along the shore, are where the rich people live, although they, too, ride in armored cars with armed drivers. It's a shame, because Rio is still by far the most dramatically beautiful of all beach cities, and the Copa Palace is still the most romantic of all beach hotels. It's also still the nerve center of Rio, where all the big Carnaval balls are held, all the society weddings and debutante parties. To *stay* at the Copa Palace is to *be* in Rio. And that's why the stars still come, and not just to hide out while getting a nip and tuck from ultimate plastic surgeon Dr. Ivo Pitanguy. Plus they can afford the bodyguards.

The Pergula, where Jorginho Guinle had his last supper, remains, along with Rogério Fasano's local branch of Gero, *the* place to eat in Rio. The hotel also features a Cipriani restaurant, with chefs from its Orient Express outpost in Venice. But the locals don't go there. Pergula is their spot, for breakfast, for tea, for drinks, for anything when they're in Copacabana. Yes, being part of a chain, even a superchain like Orient Express, has taken away some of the family touch from Pergula. But you can't take away the pool (Lady Di swam here) and the beach-club feel of sipping rum and freshly squeezed exotic tropical fruit concoctions (ask for mangoes in anything) and watching stunning women in shocking *tangas* frolicking about in the water.

The food may not be great, but it won't spoil the view. The salads, as you might expect, are outstanding, especially the mix of local greens with cauliflower, potatoes, olives, green beans, and anchovies. Both the roast guinea fowl with an olive and celery sauce, or the just caught grouper with crayfish sauce, sound fancy, but they are clean, simple, and not hotelish at all. The shrimp in Rio tend to be among the freshest and best anywhere in this frozen-shrimp world, and Pergula will stir some up for you in a hot-as-voodoo "bobo" stew with *dende* oil and manioc flour that will have you ready for Carnaval. Even if you're here in fall.

253

But the most delicious thing you'll eat in Brazil is a seven-block walk (if you're brave, reckless, or packing) inland from the Copa Palace. Beachfront in Rio is a string of elegant art deco high-rise apartments, but behind that façade of glamour is a treacherous Tijuana-like tacky commercial zone filled with the angry residents of the *favelas* (slums) in the fog-shrouded hills above. It's totally to-have-and-have-not, and the rage is palpable.

That's why you'll see so many fancy cars double-parked at a funky open-air sandwich stand called Cervantes, and you'll see everyone there from soccer great Pelé to plastic man Dr. Pitanguy to all his famous patients (he'll never tell) to Mick Jagger to Rod Stewart. What they're all lining up for at Cervantes is no Quixotic wild-goose chase but the Real Thing: the best sandwich on earth, succulent, hot-from-the-oven thinly sliced roast pork topped with a freshly grilled slice of the sweetest pineapple on the crustiest, chewiest, most perfect sandwich roll ever baked. The combination of salty, starchy, hot, and sweet is a speedball of taste. It's unlikely you can stop at one, or even two, and it's unlikely that fear of this combat zone next to the beautiful sea will transcend your hunger to come back again, and again, for this platonic ideal of a snack. It's much more Dagwood than Fred and Ginger, but that sandwich will keep you flying down to Rio in your gustatory dreams. ★ ★ ★ ★ ★

Hominy Grill
True Grits

CHARLESTON

Even without the canals, Charleston is the Venice of America. It's an incredibly beautiful city on the sea, perfectly preserved, a living museum, but not at
all Disneyfied like Colonial Williamsburg. There is an aristocracy here that
both founded the country and then tore it apart, and their descendants are the
doges, the ruling class, of the Carolina marshland. People live and work here in
total splendor, notwithstanding the brutal summer heat and humidity. Nobody
goes to Venice for the weather, either. They do go to Venice for the food, if
only to witness the daily spectacle at Harry's Bar. And while Charleston in the
post–Civil War century was never known for its food, it is now, and it has its
own Harry's in the Hominy Grill. Actually, analogizing Hominy to Harry is a
bit unfair to the former. Yes, "everybody" goes to both. But Harry's is a social
experience, while Hominy is a gastronomic one. Perhaps a fairer description
would be to say that Hominy Grill, with its glorification of the most traditional
southern cooking with the finest, freshest, most artisanal southern ingredients,
is the Chez Panisse of the Low Country.

Hominy Grill looks straight out of *Porgy and Bess*. The restaurant occupies
the ground floor (a former barbershop) of a shotgun three-story wooden dwell-
ing in a Catfish Row–ish dodgy neighborhood called Cannonborough, perhaps
because of all the shots fired around here. Still, the unpaved parking lot next

door is filled with Rollses and Aston Martins as well as pickup trucks. There's nothing snobby here, just an obsession with perfect food that cuts across class lines. Moreover, Hominy Grill, which modestly bills itself as "Charleston's Favorite Neighborhood Restaurant," is one of the cheapest great restaurants in the world. You can eat breakfast, lunch, or dinner for under ten dollars, and rarely more than twenty, so it's really a case of y'all come, hear. Many foodie visitors to Charleston take all three of their meals here, every day. Though there is plenty of other good food in town, nothing comes close to this, so total immersion is not a bad strategy. Inside Hominy's glass-windowed storefront is a big, sunny, tin-ceilinged room with polished pine floors and comfortable Windsor armchairs and three big paddle fans above. You could be in a diner in *To Kill a Mockingbird*, except for the Arctic air-conditioning, the one touch of modernity. For those who like it hot, there's a mossy, lush patio out back. Sugary iced tea is the coolant of choice, though some people bring noble wines. Either will do. You can book or you can wait in line, diner style, and get excited, very excited, about the plates passing before you.

For breakfast, there are homemade granola, and banana breads, and spicy sausages, and fluffy biscuits with even fluffier free-range eggs and golden hash browns. For lunch, there is Hominy's signature shrimp and grits, a vinegar-laced, bacon-tinged, scallion-greened confection with rarely seen fresh (never frozen) crustaceans that ranks with any seafood risotto in the Veneto. There is a sublime version of the southern pimento cheese sandwich, this one gentrified with homemade whole wheat bread and arugula. And a dazzling array of fresh fruit cobblers and pies and other dessert treats, the most famous of which is the key-lime-ish buttermilk pie. Dinner is hog heaven. The chef, from North Carolina, has an oak smoker in the back and fires up perfect North Carolina barbecue: crackly minced pork with vinegar and spices, with mouthwatering vinegary coleslaw. The South Carolina version of barbecue uses mustard, a sacrilege to Tar Heels, and hence banned here. Antiporks are well served with sesame-crusted farm-raised catfish with sautéed okra and "geechee" (from the Gullah Islands) peanut sauce. Even vegans are catered to, with a black-eyed-pea croquette with avocado relish, jasmine rice, and a roasted tomato sauce.

Southern fried is never done more greaselessly and deftly, be it hush puppies, fried green tomatoes, or perfect hand-cut French fries. There are at least half a dozen boardinghouse sides: collards, corn bread, cheese grits, fried eggplant. And these examples merely scratch a glistening, cornucopian surface. Every day at Hominy Grill seems like Thanksgiving.

The force of nature behind Hominy Grill is an unassuming, very thin, late-thirtyish young man in a white coat and a red do-rag who only occasionally is seen outside the kitchen. Robert Stehling doesn't work the room like Wolfgang Puck, or any other star chef. Then again, Charleston isn't Beverly Hills. Stehling owns Hominy with his wife, Nunally Kersh, a producer of the Charleston Spoleto Festival, thus the kind of star you will see here tends to be Jessye Norman rather than Lindsay Lohan, Peter Cincotti rather than Jay-Z. But you never know who might show up. Amazing home cooking like this is a magnet for all.

Stehling's home was Greensboro, North Carolina, from whence a local stone mill grinds all his famed grits. Stehling didn't intend to become a grit-meister. He was studying art history at Chapel Hill when he took a student job as a dishwasher at Crook's Corner, the one good gourmet restaurant in that charming but food-challenged university town. At Crook's, Stehling fell under the spell of Bill Neal, one of the fathers of the "new southern" cookery, though there was nothing at all precious about it, drawing from the Dixie holy trinity of pork, corn, and fat to create a soulfully satisfying repertoire.

Bitten by the food bug, Stehling went north to Yankeeland, cooking at several trendy New York restaurants until he learned that Gotham-trendy was not his mission on earth. Thus to Charleston he and his wife came in 1996. In xenophobic Charleston, a Tar Heel *chef* coming down from New York would have normally been looked upon with the deepest suspicions. But Stehling's food conquered all. The Dixiecrats all loved him, but so did the Yanks, won over by a series of raves in *The New York Times*. Soon Charleston was on the map not for its plantations and poinsettias and Fort Sumter, but for Stehling's plantation cuisine, which includes slave dishes, such as "purloo," a pilaf cross between paella and jambalaya, as well as master fare, like his big-house fried chicken (with a spicy peach sauce) Sunday dinner.

Hominy Grill's success is evocative of *The New Yorker* cartoon juxtaposing four restaurants, each with a different marquee. The first says "Best in the World," the second "Best in the Country," the third "Best in the City." Each of them has a couple of customers drifting in. But the fourth, whose marquee reads "Best in the Block" has a line running off the page. Stehling isn't trying to be General Sherman marching through the South, obliterating all in his path. What makes his food so wonderful is its rootedness, its respect for tradition—except for that stupid mustard in the barbecue. ★ ★ ★ ★ ★ ★ ★ ★ ★ ★ ★ ★ ★ ★ ★ ★

Ta-boo
Totem and

PALM BEACH

Ta-boo, which is basically Maxwell's Plum Revisited with palm trees, is arguably the sexiest restaurant in the United States. In the heart of Worth Avenue, Palm Beach's more luxurious answer to Rodeo Drive, Ta-boo is packed night and day with gorgeous, stop-at-nothing-and-at-no-plastic-surgeon women wanting to marry (or already married to) a billionaire. It is also full of Palm Beach billionaires trying to trick these same women into a close encounter of the third kind, the kind that will not result in alimony. The result is a new chapter in the battle of the sexes, love Palm Beach–style, and this mating-and-baiting game is a highly amusing show to watch. Moreover, the food is delicious, far better than it needs to be.

Ta-boo was frequently mentioned in the notorious 1991 William

Kennedy Smith rape trial. The Kennedy family has been coming here since the 1940s. The priapic Old Joe was supposed to have had a fling in the Ta-boo cupboard with his not-so-secret love Gloria Swanson, and the priapic JFK was hardly averse to cruising the bar, which habitués claim was the real inventor of the Bloody Mary, not Harry's in Paris (no relation to Harry's in Venice). In fact, Ta-boo can best be said to be the Harry's Bar (Venice, of course) of Palm Beach. It is action-central in a fairy-tale village otherwise devoid of action.

Ta-boo is always mobbed, particularly at lunch. You give your Rolls to the valet on Worth and fight your way down the long black granite bar to the handsome bronze maître d', or, if you're really lucky, to the owner, Franklyn De Marco, who is a preppy Danny DeVito, if such a hybrid is possible. If you're a woman with a great tan and great legs that you're showing off, De Marco may seat you well, best being by the roaring fireplace, winter or summer; second best being the rattan garden room, with its skylight and tropical ceiling fans. A pianist plays "Almost Like Being in Love." De Marco is an awful flirt, commenting on your outfit and most notoriously on your panty hose, or lack thereof. De Marco has a well-publicized bête noire about panty hose, which he deems unnatural, just as he has a thing about men's T-shirts, which are forbidden, even if they're Armani. A Lacoste tennis shirt is fine, because it has a collar. In any other city, De Marco would be deep in sexual harassment litigation. In Palm Beach, he has the droit de seigneur; ownership has its privileges.

De Marco, a Jersey-born, University of Virginia–polished mortgage broker in the D.C. area, bought Ta-boo, which first opened in 1941, in 1988 when it was down-and-out. He partnered with his then girlfriend, Nancy Sharigan, who had owned several restaurants in the Philadelphia area. She had the experience; he had the chutzpah. Together they rode the Clinton prosperity wave that made Palm Beach into Wall Street's favorite second home, and Ta-boo PB's fave venue. Of course, they broke up, for bachelor De Marco scorns marriage more than panty hose. But Ta-boo was too hot to cool down, and the two of them are there every day, rarely speaking, like a sit-com; *Cheers* with money.

259

You might see anyone here, from old-guarders like Dina Merrill, whose mother Marjorie Merriweather Post (Toasties) owned Mar-a-Lago, PB's grandest estate, to The Donald, who turned it into a club for *les plus nouveaux riches*. Rod Stewart, who now has a home here, obviously loves it, as does Tommy Lee Jones, who plays polo nearby. Almost everyone old is superrich, from all around the world, while everyone young, and blond, and thin, and enhanced is likely on the make. The tall, willowy blondes you see working the tables are not the hookers you think they are. They are floor models from the Worth Avenue boutiques doing an informal lunch show and handing out cards from the stores. It's an old Palm Beach tradition, plus De Marco likes the ladies.

You can order high or low at Ta-boo. The huge rare filet mignon burgers on homemade brioche buns with hot waffle potato chips are outstanding guy-food, while the ladies go for the huge salads, the most popular being the warm steak salad with a garden of local greenery; they take maybe two bites and put it aside. The Old Guard tend to order mutant-shrimp cocktails, whole live lobsters, or big-bucks platters of stone crab claws with a mustard mayonnaise dip that is almost indistinguishable from that of Joe's Stone Crab down the turnpike in Miami. What's amazing is how many of these platters are sent back, with the claim that one of the claws was "off." Locals say that is an Old Guard ploy, to get more goodies for nothing. (One way the rich are different is that they love to eat for free.) For dessert, the tour de force is a chocolate walnut brownie in a sauce of decadent hot fudge. Everyone orders it, no one takes more than a taste, but it fits the sybaritic mood here. The creamy, puckery key lime pie, given the locale, lives up to expectations.

Don't get the idea that Ta-boo is only about rich men and climbing women. This is one of the rare places you can find that dodo of masculinity, the gigolo, who seems to have gone out elsewhere about the time of Rudy Vallee. Here you see a number of society grande dames in the walkers, propped up by their liveried butlers or chauffeurs, sitting alone and drinking Trader Vic's–style cocktails. These old broads are ready for Freddy, and Freddy tends to be very George Hamiltonian here: tanned to leather, blazered, pink-shirted, smooth as silk. Love at first bite. Not that all these playboys are looking to become the male equivalents of Anna Nicole Smith by finding a foot-in-the-grave nonagenarian. A lot of the men are social climbing as well and want nothing more than to graduate from Ta-boo to the Everglades Club across the street. Imagine New York's Swifty's on acid, and you may get the Ta-boo picture. But you really have to see it to believe it. ★ ★ ★ ★ ★

Joe's Stone Crab
Waiting for the Joe

MIAMI

Speaking of cartoons, there is a locally famous Miami parody of a Roy Lichtenstein tableau showing a distressed young blonde saying, "The stone crabs were lovely, Brad. But we didn't get served for 3 *hours!*" Her worried boyfriend has a balloon over his head with the thought, "Gulp . . . I've *failed* her!" A sign JOE'S STONE CRAB glows behind them. That's the story of Miami's most legendary restaurant, which opened in Miami Beach in 1913 before Miami Beach was even incorporated. The founder was the Hungarian-born Joe Weiss, who came from New York to this deserted tropical sandbar for his asthma. Joe had been a waiter, his Hungarian wife, Jennie, a cook in little restaurants. They knew food and little else, and began their Florida life running a lunch stand in a bathing casino near Collins Avenue, which was not paved at the time. Eventually, they bought an adjacent bungalow to live in and began serving fish sandwiches on the front porch. They put out a sign: JOE'S RESTAURANT. And later another sign: SHORE DINNER.

What transformed the Weisses from mere red snapper fryers to tycoons was the lunch visit of a Harvard ichthyologist who was helping to set up the new aquarium. The Harvard man asked Joe if he served the local stone crabs. Nobody will eat that junk, Joe told him. Joe had fresh crayfish on the menu. Who could ask for anything more? But the Harvard man persisted, showing up a few days later with a sack of live stone crabs. Nonplussed on what to do with them, Joe ultimately threw the critters in a vat of boiling water. Not only were the claws, which held all the meat, hard to crack open, but they had a nasty iodine taste. Case closed. But the waste-not, want-not Joe couldn't throw food away. He put them on ice overnight, to give to the help, or to some desperately hungry soul. But lo and behold, refrigeration gave the crabs an entirely different, lobsterlike taste. The iodine was gone. The thrill was there. Joe spiked some mayonnaise with mustard powder and created a dip. He served the claws with his already perfected *mitteleuropa* hash brown potatoes, and his Hungarian sweet-vinaigrette coleslaw. The ichthyologist smiled. A tradition was born.

As Miami Beach became a major destination, with its string of art deco hotels, so did Joe's. Al Capone and his bodyguards ate there every night at 5 P.M. Al Jolson was a regular, as were Will Rogers, Amelia Earhart, Sophie Tucker, George Jessel, Tommy Dorsey, and his young crooner Frank Sinatra. That great restaurant buff Joe Kennedy would drive down from Palm Beach with Gloria Swanson, and J. Edgar Hoover would arrive with his inamoratus Clyde Tolson. But the two people who really emblazoned Joe's in America's consciousness were the columnists Walter Winchell and Damon Runyon, who decreed that the Florida stone crabs were "too good for visitors" and advocated that a certificate of four years' residence be required of any stone crab eater. The legend was thus burnished. When Joe died, the torch was passed to his lawyer-trained, seven-times-married son Jesse. There was only a slight flicker during World War II, when Jesse went into the service. A hurricane hit one summer, and the place was nearly destroyed. Plus Jesse had major gambling and alimony debts. In the legal maneuvering, to thwart one of his exes, Jesse changed the name from Joe's to Joe's Stone Crab. As always with the Weisses, it was a smart move.

The stone crab's Harvard name, *Menippe mercenaria*, couldn't be more apt, as it has become one of the great cash cows of the sea. Today Joe's bungalow has become a sprawling Spanish stucco Alhambra, serving as many as two thousand dinners a night. Joe's has its own fleet of crabbing boats in the Keys, its own processing plant. Joe's is high on the list of America's most successful restaurants, even though it is only open during crab season, October to May (who needs the hurricanes?). There are licensees in Chicago and Vegas, and Tokyo and Osaka, where the Japanese revere the Joe's name in the same hungry breath as La Tour d'Argent. But Joe's has not devolved into a tourist trap, simple as that might be. The Weiss progeny still own it and still run it with eagle eyes and iron fists, and lots of pride. Joe's may be the greatest big restaurant anywhere.

The only problem is the wait. Reservations are not taken. You arrive, and it looks like a warehouse sale at Barneys or a Depression-era bank run. People are mobbed in the street. You'd never know you were a block away from the cool of South Beach and Ocean Drive. You fight your way into the imperious old-pro tuxedo'd maître d', and give him your name. You don't dare slip him a twenty; he'd surely be insulted and ask you to leave. He gives you an ETA, never less than an hour, and you retreat to the bar for mojitos that make you so drunk by the time you're called that you may not taste the glories that are Joe's. You see stars, lots of them, from Madonna to Gloria Estefan to J Lo to Shaq and Pat Riley, and you wonder if *they* had to wait. You hear rumors that if you—or your PR firm (hah!)—knows one of the top black-tie guys (there are an army to pick from), one with juice, and if *they*, not you, "take care of him" (no money is to be seen changing hands) to the tune of several C-notes, you can play celebrity leapfrog. But mind you, these are only rumors. And for some famous people, especially politicos like Bill Clinton, the wait is part of the Joe's experience: it provides even more time to press the flesh.

You finally sit down. It seems like years. There are a warren of black-and-white-tiled rooms with plain wooden chairs and tables, classic Roaring

Twenties simplicity. You can just imagine Capone at the next table. But would he have waited? Maybe that's why he and the boys came at five o'clock. The noise, bouncing off the hard surfaces, is deafening, Grand Central at rush hour. But when the food starts arriving, you'll see that all the misery was worth it.

Everything is the platonic ideal of what it *should* be. The only problem now is making room for it. The Manhattan clam chowder is redolent of fresh clam broth and the slight smoke of salt pork. The coleslaw, with the added fillip of sweet relish and a touch of mayonnaise to richen the Old World vinaigrette, has no equal, nor do the hash browns, crisp on all sides, melting inside, the potato cake to end all potato cakes. There are huge portions, and any side dish is enough for a full meal, plus you're famished. Prepare to atone at the gym for the next month.

Finally, the main course, the stone crab claws, piled in a neat pyramid, all the black tips perfectly lined up, their shells ("harder than a landlord's heart," as Damon Runyon said) cracked and ready to devour. Don't be dainty. Use your fingers to claw out the meat, then dip it in the mayo-mustard, or in the melted butter, if you want a hot-cold sensation. You'll feel totally atavistic by the end, and in need of a Biscayne Bay of finger bowls to clean yourself up.

You won't have any room by the end, but you'll still have to order the key lime pie, an orgy of tart sweetness, made the way it always was, before cholesterol awareness, with egg yolks, heavy whipped cream, condensed milk, butter, sugar, and, yes, real and rare key (not Persian) lime juice in a graham cracker crust.

The good news is you're finished and can retreat to your hotel and sleep it off. The better news is that you have to come back tomorrow, because you've missed the very best thing on the menu, which is also the cheapest: the five-dollar Maryland fried chicken platter. Joe's fried chicken, created by its all-black kitchen staff in the 1920s, is the greatest fried chicken in Dixie, and that means anywhere. It is also a big secret, not even appearing in the Joe's cookbook, which gives away the key lime pie recipe as well as the mustard-mayo formula. It is said that the chicken is Joe's gift to Miami, so that anybody can come here and eat like Al Capone for next to nothing. The crabs, by comparison, depending on the size you order, can easily run well over one hundred dollars per person. The five-dollar chicken is a huge half bird, a cousin to the great auk of Ami Louis in Paris, and crispy, crunchy, golden brown, the glory that is grease.

But how can you stand the wait? Easy. You don't have to. Next door to Joe's is Joe's Take Away, which opened in 1987, to address the queue problem. You can get anything to go. And since they send the stone crabs around the globe in their trademark crab boxes, you can rest assured that you and your fried chicken can make the ten-minute ride to your suite at the Setai or the Shore Club without losing anything in transition. An even cleverer solution is to go to Joe's Take Away on Sunday afternoon, when the restaurant is closed for lunch. You have the whole patio and the endless Miami sunshine all to yourself, and you can order the chicken and the claws and the hash browns and the coleslaw and the pie and spread out and have the feast of a lifetime right on Joe's otherwise overwhelmed premises. And you won't have to worry about tipping a soul. ★

Shore Club, Casa Tua, the Forge
Hip, Hip, Oy Vey

MIAMI

The coolest thing about the Shore Club, South Beach's supercool hotel, is that it pulled off the astonishing feat of taking the driving out of Los Angeles. Los Angeles? Aren't we in Miami? Not really: the Shore Club is Hollywood on the

Atlantic, having assembled three of LA's most exclusive venues—Ago, Nobu, and the Sky Bar—under one roof. This roof looks so much like the Schrager-Starck Mondrian on Sunset (they're both, along with the nearby and also similar Delano, part of the Schrager-founded Morgans Hotel Group) that, after a few drinks (and nobody has less than a few here), you won't know where you are. But at least you don't have to drive.

Just as no one sleeps at the Mondrian, no one sleeps at the Shore Club, even if they want to. This may be the noisiest grand hotel anywhere, from the rat-tat-tat of Manolos on the hard sandstone corridors to the all-night disco thump of the bars and restaurants overlooking the dreamy pool, which may be the only dreamy thing in this REM-deprived caravansary. This Starck look-alike was actually designed by the Brit David Chipperfield, for whom style is obviously more important than silence. Yet even if you can't snooze, you can eat very well here.

Ago, which has a splendid outdoor terrace evocative of St. Tropez's Club 55, had the best Italian chef in Miami in the Sicilian Mario Maiffia, who, alas, left in 2005 to open his own place in Palm Springs. Maiffia had divided his time between the two coasts and the two Agos, though the one here is even more bedlamic than the West Hollywood venue (see page 325), which may be LA's noisiest star restaurant, so bring your earplugs. But don't fret about the food, since owner Agostino Sciandri, a great chef himself, has a pipeline into Italy's restaurant scene, and what cool young Tuscan wouldn't want to cook for stars under the stars of South Beach? No, you won't need to come with an owner like De Niro to get al dente pasta here.

The Nobu at the Shore Club is more crowded than any of the three mob scenes in New York. That's okay, because the decor, unlike the New York branches, is so minimal as to be nonexistent. There's nothing to miss. The people, young and perfect, are the decor. The sushi and all the Peruvian-Japanese fusion creations are just like all the other Nobus, whose greatest pride is their consistency, the hardest thing to pull off in any chain. Wherever you go at the Shore Club, the dominant leitmotif is one of fatal beauty, impossibly tall and gorgeous models with clipboards asking if you're on "the list." Whose list? That is the question. If you don't know, you ain't on it. So scram.

If you stay in a room here, they can't toss you out; so even if you can't sleep, you can eat all night.

If the din of the Shore Club proves overwhelming, the quietest place in South Beach is just two blocks, and a century, away. This is Casa Tua, housed in one of the few remaining once private mansions from the era when Joe Weiss was starting his crab dynasty down the beach. There's a high wall of ivy and an iron fence around the property, creating a Casa Refusa effect. It all makes sense when you learn that Casa Tua is a public restaurant *and* a private club, whose members pay nearly $3,000 a year to get priority on reservations and an always warm welcome at this incongruous iceberg of Miami privilege.

Casa Tua is the brainchild of Italian construction and horse-breeding heir Miky Grendene and his Chicago-born Latina model wife, Leticia. The membership roster is headed by fellow Venetian Giuseppe Cipriani, who accords Casa Tua-ites reciprocal privileges at his oh-so-private club atop Downtown (Cipriani) on West Broadway in New York, and Lapo Elkann, the Agnelli grandson ensnared in the transsexual-prostitute-drug scandal in Milan in 2005 (shoulda stayed in Miami). Other members include stars from every sphere: Boris Becker, Roberto Cavalli, George Hamilton, John Cougar Mellencamp, Elle Macpherson, and Ricky Martin.

But there's no Vida Loca in Casa Tua, which plays out like an aristocratically sedate house party in proper Barbados, not raucous St. Bart's. If you want raucous, don't leave the Shore Club. Silence reigns here in the preppy plush striped-cushioned multiroomed interior, filled with books and flowers and perfumed by scented candles as well as the alfresco bougainvillea. A tiny planter of rosemary decorates each linen-covered table. The soft music is totally Euro. There is a pristine open kitchen with an antique eighteen-seat communal table covered in rose petals, shades of *American Beauty*. This is where members, and you, can just drop in and join the sedate party, if there's a space. Somehow you feel Martha Stewart overseeing the whole operation. It's her kind of place.

The gatekeepers here are a phalanx of fabulous, giraffelike South American models, though minus the offensive clipboards. You didn't realize there were so many tall people in South America, but here they are. And they're very nice, too. The stonewall is on the phone. You come here only if you've scored the res. You may go upstairs to the members' lounge for a cocktail before, or after, dinner. Again, it's very preppy, very clubby, and filled with the kind of decorous people you don't expect to find in South Beach. They look as if they've driven down from Palm Beach, or flown up from Rio, and they may well have. There's a lot of Chanel, and a lot of blue blazers; gold chains are a rarity.

While the Amazon goddesses seat you and get your drinks, your waiters will be men, in preppy white button-downs, men who look like members themselves. The menu is enticing, and the food, prepared by an all-Italian kitchen, delivers. It's mostly northern Italian, more delicate than the gutsier southern Italian fare over at Ago, but it fits the mellow mood here. There's an olive oil menu, the wines are only from "boutique" vintners, and your waiter will share with you that the prosciutto comes from only free-range pigs, in case you didn't know that Italian pigs can get the humane chicken treatment. On a hot night (most are) start with some of that pampered pork, plus some buffalo mozzarella just flown in from Puglia. Or get fancy with marinated yellowtail carpaccio (*crudo* is big here) with sugar snap peas, candied lemon zest, and *osetra* caviar. Pastas are outstanding. The house special, simple and sublime, is the ricotta *cavatelli* with organic cherry tomatoes. But again, you can put on the dog with a *tagliolini* with more of that *osetra* and crème fraîche, or shoot the moon with the seventy-dollar risotto Parmigiana with truffles from Alba. The best main course is the roasted veal tenderloin marinated in key lime juice. You *are* in Florida, so don't snicker; it *tastes* totally Italian. A very Venice-meets-Miami dessert is the frozen champagne soup with a fresh fruit salad, which is *almost* as good as the garden of delights offered by the myriad Brazilian fruit and juice vendors on the nearby Lincoln Road Mall, which is the very best thing, and the cheapest, you can taste in Miami.

When you go to the Shore Club, or to Casa Tua, you are transported to Somewhere Else other than the real Miami, which may be fine with you.

But if you've got a *Miami Vice,* or *Scarface,* or *Godfather* fantasy percolating in your mind, get thee to the Forge, which is pure Miami Beach. Its founder, Al Malnik, used to be Meyer Lansky's lawyer (and Michael Jackson's; what a clientele), while his son Shareef, also a lawyer and who now runs the Forge, is the confidant of Russell Simmons and other hip-hop moguls. So the Forge is thus the favorite of gang*sters* and gang*stas,* as well as every other sports and movie star who hits the Beach and wants to luxuriate in a heady, psychedelic *nouveau*-something Alice-Cooper-in-Wonderland ambience that could play this well only in Miami Beach.

Part of the Forge's mystique was established by a bloody 1977 shoot-out between Lansky's stepson and the scion of another gangland dynasty, followed by the patronage of Frank Sinatra and his own *Ocean's Eleven* gang. But Richard Nixon and Bebe Rebozo came in as well, so the Forge had them all, the outlaws and the in-laws, plus Beatles and Stones. Another part of the mystique is the decor of the former blacksmith shop, in the crumbling heart of fast-vanishing Old Jewish Miami Beach. The façade is that of a grand nineteenth-century Paris *hôtel particulier* in a souk of delis, thrift shops, and chiropractors. Inside are five out-of-control salons, each with a name, like a hall at Versailles. The Main Salon, where most of the big names go, has twenty-foot ceilings and a huge crystal chandelier. For romantic bibliophiles, the Victorian Library Room has cozy love seats and original Tiffany stained-glass windows from Wall Street's Trinity Church. The Dome Room has murals of naked Greek goddesses, illuminated by a chandelier from the Paris Opera and a collection of French art deco mirrors for the narcissists to admire themselves. There's an iron-gated Wine Room, an aptly named Nouveau Room, and a Wine Cellar with two full-time sommeliers that houses one of the most important collections in America.

"I have taken the best of the most decadent pleasures—champagne, caviar, cognac, cigars—and created my own version of safe sex for the millennium." Thus speaks Shareef Malnik, who says he changed his name from Mark "for spiritual reasons." Shareef is a race-car-driving, ski-racing, hard-partying globe-trotter who, when he's not married (there have been three ex-wives so far, while Joe Weiss had seven; maybe it's a Miami restaurateur thing), is always ranked among South Florida's most eligible men-about-town. In 1991 he took over the Forge from his father, another multiply married food man who has eight-year-old triplets and a one-year-old baby, in addition to a grandson, Yaseen, from Shareef's marriage to a Saudi princess. The Malniks, for all their antiques, can be avant-garde and open-minded, as seen in their restaurant and their lives.

Shareef quickly won over the Don Johnson crowd with his special Wednesday nights, where blue-haired ladies in furs and jewels would mix with transsexuals in fur and jewels, plus the Madonnas and the models and the Euros. Realizing how the international set, especially the rich kidnapper-fleeing South Americans, were making Miami their second home, Shareef then brought in club doyenne Regine to work her global magic at Jimmy'z at the Forge. Regine has retired, but the Euros and polo players still abound at the Forge's endless party.

The Forge, at its blacksmith's hearth and heart, is a steak house. Because of its Mafia associations, it is often compared with Sparks in New York, where Paul Castellano was gunned down. But Sparks is like the Union Club in comparison to the wild and crazy Forge, whose menu is as eclectic as its decor. The specialty of the house is the "Super Steak," a sixteen-ounce behemoth marinated in herbs and grilled over live oak. The *Wine Spectator* rated it the best in America. The Super Steak is for superstars: Michael Jordan and Shaquille O'Neal both love it. If you have less than an NBA appetite, there's much, much more.

Shareef, whose father gave him his first glass of Château Lafitte at the Plaza Athenée when he was fourteen, is a total globalist. He serves a Paris-worthy platter of escargots, and a Nobu-worthy tuna tartare, along with a Forge-worthy appetizer of the four largest shrimp, as big as lobster tails, you'll ever see in a cocktail. Then he'll play Sirio Maccioni and do his homage to Le Cirque's spaghetti primavera, and then do another homage to LA's La Scala's original chopped salad. As with his antiques, Shareef scours the world for the best and brings them back to the Beach.

While it is said that the Forge's double-barreled beef servings of saturated fat have killed more Mafiosi than Eliot Ness, Shareef atones with his simple, perfectly oak-grilled pristinely fresh Gulf fish. The real guys and dolls here finish with one of the Forge's chocolate or Grand Marnier soufflés, then try in vain to boogie it off in Shareef's disco rooms. Whatever you eat, be forewarned that all portions are grotesque. Shareef Malnik may have an Arabic name, but he has the soul of a Jewish grandmother. ★

Chez Panisse
Yuppie Nirvana

BERKELEY

The waitress calls it "Hillary's bathroom," the new loo opposite the fabled wood-fired open kitchen on the ground floor of America's ultimate yuppie dining shrine, Chez Panisse. Off the record, for this shrine is way too serious for celebrity gossip. Chez Panisse is the once and future yuppie-in-chief's very favorite restaurant on earth, and the bathroom was supposedly built to spare her highness from the treacherous stairs (and stares) en route to the regular facilities on the second floor of this very glorified brass-and-wood Craftsman bungalow.

The first floor, Hillary's floor, is the "A" Panisse, the five-course, dinner-only, book-months-ahead tiny dining room, where *everybody*—from the Clintons to the Dalai Lama (sans Richard Gere, who comes on his own) to Metallica—has paid edible homage to the true birthplace of California Cuisine. The second floor, with its own open kitchen, is the "B" Panisse, a café with wonderful pizzas and the best salads in America, where you can be more spontaneous and book only a week in advance, and sometimes not at all. In neither section need you dress up. This is Berkeley, after all, casual country. Both Levi's and the Gap, founded across the Bay, have dressed the baby boomers, and Chez Panisse has fed them, even if they've physically never eaten here.

A pilgrimage to Chez Panisse is a trip every boomer should make, like a Muslim to Mecca, a Christian to Bethlehem, a shopper to Milan. The anchor of what has become known as "the gourmet ghetto," a few blocks from the verdant and regal Berkeley campus, with more wonderful and recherché restaurants and food shops than any *endroit* of Paris, Chez Panisse will turn you on to food like no other restaurant. Its founder and guiding light, Alice Waters, may be the most influential Berkeley alum since Mario Savio shook up a generation leading the Free Speech Movement here in the 1960s.

Although the image of Waters is that of Lady Bountiful, the closest thing in her past to being to the garden born was being born in the Garden State, in 1944. With no ambitions of becoming a chef, this Jersey girl was simply a brainy yuppie who went west for college at Berkeley. There she majored in French cultural studies, which is where the food comes in. A junior-year visit to France and its homey, rustic bistros in 1964 was an epiphany to Waters, who began preparing "authentic" French dinners with her college friends. Although she believed that she could never find at home the glorious ingredients she had sampled in Provence, Waters discovered, mirabile dictu, that, fish, fowl, and produce-wise, Berkeley actually wasn't as far from Avignon as she had thought. There were lots of little farmers, ranchers, and fishermen in the area producing wonderful stuff, stuff that never made it to the supermarkets.

In 1971, after myriad communal dinners that had made her the Pearl Mesta, hostess-with-the-mostest, of the Berkeley activist set, Waters left her job as a Montessori schoolteacher and mobilized these suppliers into a business team in order to found Chez Panisse. The restaurant was named after a Marseilles sail-maker in the great Marcel Pagnol film trilogy—*Marius, Fanny,* and *César.* (Waters's daughter is named Fanny, and her Berkeley breakfast shrine is Café Fanny.) Chez Panisse began the way it is now, serving only a prix fixe multicourse dinner that changed daily, in short, a Waters dinner party every night. Waters had a partner, Paul Aratow, a brainy comp-lit instructor who had spent *beaucoup de temps* in France and was a gifted cook. But brainy as he was, Aratow couldn't resist the lure of Hollywood, and sold out his interest to become a film producer. Pagnol he was not. After the megaflop *Sheena, Queen of the Jungle*, Aratow went back to his true love, the range, and the free range, and translated one of the classic French cookbooks, *La Bonne Cuisine de Madame Saint-Ange*.

Meanwhile Alice Waters, heavily aided by Chez Panisse's charismatic chef, Jeremiah Tower, had created her own *bonne cuisine*, which became known as California Cuisine. Some credit this to Wolfgang Puck, but Waters was first. What Puck was doing was an amalgam of designer pizza and complex *haute-français*, plus a big side of stars. It was totally original, but Puck's razzle-dazzle was far removed from the essential purity and simplicity and sheer country-ness of the Waters kitchen. Michael McCarty came closer, yet the Michael's compositions were much busier than those of Chez Panisse, as though McCarty had been inculcated with the LA blockbuster mentality. Waters's stars were the amazing ingredients on her plates, not the characters at her tables, and things haven't ever really changed here, other than her 1980 opening of the upstairs café, which serves lunch as well as dinner.

Getting into Chez Panisse for dinner downstairs can be harder than getting into Berkeley, so plan far ahead. And don't expect anything templistic like Paul Bocuse or Troisgros. Chez Panisse is almost unnoticeable from the street, hidden by a fence and foliage. There's no valet parking, so you might have to find a spot blocks away, which is fine, because you'll have the gastro-foreplay of passing all the enticing markets and cafés. (The one next door is called Cesar—no relation.) The place is amazingly quiet, not solemn, but definitely serious. The lightest touches are the beautiful flowers everywhere and the vintage Pagnol film posters that decorate the walls. There's a no-nonsense, dark-suited French maître d', but the rest of the white-shirted, khaki-panted, and white-aproned staff seem like summa cum laude grad students who can explain the night's menu the way they'd defend a thesis.

Speaking of theses, many of the clientele are very academic-looking,

Ivy League Americans, the men in Brooks Brothers tweeds and khakis, the women in Talbots. The older ones could be the parents of the waitstaff, the younger ones think-tank types, doctors, lawyers, all very white-collar. The biggest contingent, however, are glamorous Hermès and Chanel-wearing Japanese, young and old, in their endless, brand-obsessed, shrine-hopping quest for "number one." And then there are the stars. There's always at least one star table here, though the star may be from the cabinet, or from the Bolshoi, or from the Spanish royal family, rather than from Hollywood. You've really entered the pantheon at Chez Panisse if they allow you to smoke on their balcony, as have Baryshnikov and Juliette Binoche, who had her fortieth birthday *fête* here.

Don't expect to see Alice Waters working the room. Chez Panisse is not a cult of personality, but one of ingredients. Nor is it likely that you will

see her in the kitchen. Waters is an impresario, not a cook, and she hires great cooks, many of whom have become star chefs, like Jeremiah Tower, Paul Bertolli, Mark Miller, Mark Peel, Suzanne Goin, and Judy Rodgers (see page 277). But no chef is a star at Chez Panisse; only the food is allowed to shine. As for Waters, she's often traveling the world supporting noble food causes: the Slow Food movement, sustainable agriculture, feeding our children fresh food, food like she serves to you at Chez Panisse.

The menu, which is presented to you as a souvenir booklet with a color engraving of a red-and-green tomato plant on the cover, changes every night. Early in the week, it's cheaper (sixty-five dollars) and more rustic. Weekends, for twenty dollars more, they trade you up from pork to lamb. Whatever, it will be the best simple food you can eat in this country, and, as such, in the age of the Alain Ducasse three-hundred-dollar dinner, it's one of the deals of the century. Although there's a definitive *carte* of California wines, you can also bring your own, at a reasonable corkage fee of twenty dollars a bottle. While most restaurants in America (and France, for that matter) tend, even at the top end, to be profit-obsessed defrosting-and-reheating operations, Chez Panisse is all about the finest ingredients most lovingly prepared.

You always start with an aperitif, such as fresh melon juice with some rare Napa white. You devour the *pain au levain* from the nearby Acme bakery, founded by Panisse alumni, and it's better than Paris's Poilâne, denser, springier, with that only-in-San-Francisco sour tang, and perfect with the sweet creamery butter that tastes straight from Normandy but is actually straight from Sonoma and a testament to Cal-Yankee ingenuity. A first course of *insalate caprese* takes you straight to the Italian *campagna*, proof that Panisse isn't solely French but wholly Med, except that the tiny yellow heirloom tomatoes are even better than what you might find in Naples, even with its Vesuvian prime-tomato-growing volcanic soil, and the homemade mozzarella is up to the Neapolitan par. The best of Italy is also apparent in the next course, tender-as-the-night Monterey-caught fresh squid, *alla veneziana,* in a piquant sauce of its own ink, tomatoes, and saffron, on a square of polenta that's as corny as Kansas in August, rare in America, where most polenta is so tasteless that you forget where it came from.

The main course is a grilled rack and loin of Cattail Creek Farm (Panisse always gives credit where credit is due) lamb, served with a ragout of romano beans and shell beans, along with torpedo onion rings. The lamb, rare and succulent and nearly fatless, will evoke that legendary lamb restaurant Les Oliviers, in the hills above Cannes, where drivers were always waylaid by the sights and smells of whole lambs roasting outside on open pits. The onion rings will evoke the great drive-ins of your misspent youth. If you have room, you can finish your wine with an optional California artisan cheese course. But if you don't, the dessert of a Gravenstein apple tart with champagne sabayon and wild blackberries will take you to Provence and back, and set you up for the sweetest French dreams you've ever dreamt. ★ ★ ★ ★ ★ ★ ★ ★ ★ ★ ★ ★

Zuni Café
Top Brass

At first blush, Zuni Café looks like a clone of Chez Panisse. The two restaurants do have a striking similarity. Both are the creations of brainy boomer women from culinary wastelands who were gastronomically transformed in their girlhoods by summer trips to France. Both are obsessive about the provenance and eco-correctness of their ingredients. Both cook these ingredients with the most elaborate simplicity. Both are totally casual, yet totally serious in their mission. Both are filled with the country's most demanding epicures, and with whatever notables come to this foggily romantic tourist Mecca. Visits to Panisse and Zuni are as de rigueur here as riding the cable cars. And neither will ever let you down. So if this is cloning, send in the clones!

Still, Zuni Café is every bit its own restaurant. To begin with, it is *in* San Francisco, and very much *of* San Francisco, albeit not the classic old-guard Nob Hill San Francisco that Hitchcock captured in *Vertigo*. Zuni is the opposite, located in a glass-walled two-story flatiron building that allows you to see the amazing freak show on seedy Market Street outside. There are panhandlers, fire-eaters, street magicians, and mean muggers, a scene evocative of Djem El Fna, the anything-goes central square of Marrakech. The only thing missing here are the camels. It's too cold, or they'd probably join this urban circus as well. Not that the seediness scares anyone away. Quite the opposite.

It's part of the draw. Tony Blair loves this place, as does Martha Stewart, who you might think would find it all de trop. All the Hollywood stars who live in San Francisco—Robin Williams, Nicolas Cage, his uncle Francis Coppola, Sean Penn—call this their food local, and they bring their famous pals from down south whenever they need a quick city fix. In major denial about the chilly weather, Zuni puts tables outside, but if you want to do alfresco, bring a down jacket and a bodyguard. Or two.

Unlike Chez Panisse, which houses two intimate entities, a restaurant and a café, Zuni Café is much less a café than a sprawling brasserie, like the ones in Paris but far higher in quality than anything Paris currently can offer. There's a long zinc bar and an oyster counter, and you can come in here from morning to night and order anything from a fresh-squeezed lime juice Patron Margarita to a plate of briny Tomales Bay oysters to the city's best hamburger to the country's best roast chicken. The latter is Zuni's most famous dish, a giant golden bird, brined for days in advance for total succulence and always cooked to order and served with homemade *pommes allumettes*. It takes an hour, but it's worth the wait. You can always watch the show outside and stuff yourself on Acme bread, wonderful rabbit *rillettes*, wood-oven pizzas, and sublime local-farm salads that make the time fly.

No matter how much you've pigged out, you'll manage to find room for the divine French desserts, like a white peach and raspberry tart, or fresh strawberry ice cream, made from pedigreed local strawberries that you never believed could be so sweet in this processed-till-the-taste-is-gone country of ours. Because the menu changes daily, retaining certain classics like the house-ground burger and the chicken, you could easily eat here every day, and because of the size and the long opening hours, you could probably get a table on relatively short notice. Service, by a Panissian Ph.D. corps from every conceivable country, is as knowledgeable as it gets. The waitstaff will also refer you to the best new restaurants in town, and they're generally more reliable than *Michelin*.

Zuni is the masterstroke of chef and cookbook author Judy Rodgers, a decade younger than Alice Waters and a follower on the Waters path of culinary enlightenment. In 1973, when she was sixteen, Judy left her food-challenged home in St. Louis to go to Roanne, France, for a high school year abroad. To her great good fortune, her St. Louis neighbor arranged for her to board at the home of the Troisgros family, arguably the greatest restaurant family in the world. Her first real *sandwich de jambon* was made for her by Jean Troisgros in the middle of the night to atone for the cottony industrial sandwich Judy had eaten at the *autoroute* snack bar, and to show his guest how wonderful simple food could be—perfect bread, thin slices of perfect ham, country butter, designer mustard, tarragon-spiked cornichons. That sandwich was Rodgers's Proustian madeleine, and it changed her life. Although she went on to Stanford, she began making road trips across the Bay to Chez Panisse, where she eventually got a job cooking. In the 1980s she made her own name at the little Union Hotel in Benicia, a country inn north of San Francisco, winning hosannas for her chicken from Ruth Reichl, then critic for *New West*. She came to Zuni in 1987 and never looked back, nor ever diluted Zuni's essence by trying to spin it off in the time-honored chef-turns-mogul mode of Ducasse, Puck, and Vongerichten. Judy Rodgers, tall, towering, and eternally Bohemian, has kept the Waters faith. Her devotion is your reward. ★ ★ ★ ★ ★ ★ ★ ★ ★ ★

Down Nob Hill

San Francisco was for a long, long time America's gourmet restaurant capital. People from all over the country would come here for a "food vacation," even more than they would New York, mainly because San Francisco was so beautiful, romantic, and charming, everyone's favorite city. The Tony Bennett song didn't hurt. In 1971, the year Chez Panisse opened, with its then communal tables laid out with peasant fare, *Holiday* magazine, then a major arbiter of taste, gave 17 of its 142 highly coveted restaurant awards to San Francisco showcases whose only connection to the peasantry was their dishwashing staff. These were legendary haunts like the Blue Fox, Alexis, the flagship Trader Vic's, Ernie's, where James Stewart courted Kim Novak in *Vertigo* and whose beef Wellington may have been the most-fantasized-about rich dish in the country. Everybody dressed to the nines and ordered noble French wines; Napa stuff was for the winos on Market Street. These shrines were a reflection of San Francisco's extremely stratified, gold-rush-based high society, which was as blue-blooded as Boston's. There was a reason they called the pinnacle of this caste system Nob Hill.

All those restaurants are gone now. What's left of high society has retreated to its clubs, the Bohemian, the Pacific Union. The great hotels of Nob Hill—the Fairmont, the Mark Hopkins (as in Top of the Mark, America's most storied bar), the Stanford Court, and the Huntington—are full of package tourists in Bermuda shorts. And Herb Caen, that great chronicler of this society and cheerleader for the city (he led a lifelong attack on the appellation "Frisco"), has entered that *Blue Book* in the sky. The new royalty of this princely city, Baghdad by the Bay, as Caen called it, are dot-com titans like Larry Ellison, who came from Brooklyn and rarely goes out, and Danielle Steele, who entertains mostly at home in her palace in Pacific Heights. The only ties you tend to see are on hotel clerks and Montgomery Street bankers. In general, this once formal city has become almost as casual as Los Angeles, which it is no longer fashionable to despise up here. The lines between Northern and Southern California, once as belligerent as antebellum North and South, have become completely blurred.

The "hottest" restaurant in town is the Slanted Door in the restored Ferry Terminal, a foodie paradise of farmers and artisans and oyster breeders. The Door may have the best Vietnamese food outside of Hanoi and Saigon, the triumph of the house being its *masala-dosa*-like giant golden rice-flour crepe exploding with the freshest shrimp, pork, bean sprouts, and onions, which will make you rethink these prosaic ingredients anywhere else you go. The Meyer Ranch "shaking beef" with garlic, watercress, and organic red onions has become a modern classic here, as are the green papaya salad and the spicy Dirty Girl Farm haricots verts (provenance revelation is nearly statutory in San Francisco). But for all its palate-expanding fare, there's nothing vaguely exclusive or chic about the Door. The bare-bones giant room seats hundreds and is more crowded and deafening than BART at rush hour. Yes, there's Jake Gyllenhaal, and Sarah Jessica Parker, and, wow, Charlie Watts, and, double wow, Bill Clinton, but they're cheek by jowl with the Bermuda shorts and warm-up-jacket tourists from Keokuk. The views of the Bay Bridge provide the only ambience. Again, food is king in this foodiest of cities. Even at the area's most expensive restaurant, Napa's four-hour-dinner (way too long for most itchy celebs) French Laundry, no one dresses up. Where's the glam of yesteryear?

You can see what you're missing if you take the elevator to the top floor of the Empress of China in the heart of Chinatown, one of the rare *Holiday* award survivors. In its day the Empress was considered the best and grandest Chinese restaurant in the country. Alas, that day has passed. Now is the day of the Slanted Door. Only the then original Szechuan-Hunan menu and the now tattered imperial decor remain, along with the wall of stars: photos of Tony Bennett, Sammy Davis Jr., Peter Lawford, Lana Turner, Jeanne Moreau, Marcel Marceau, Mick Jagger, the Ronald Reagans, the George Bushes, all in their primes, all dressed to the hilt, all clearly psyched to be in Foodville-by-the-Bay. The most recent pictured celeb is Jackie Chan. Where oh where is Danielle Steele?

She's probably at Plump Jack Café, the last redoubt of what remains of San Francisco coat-and-tie society. Located in Cow Hollow, down the hill from

Pacific Heights, where most of its clientele lives in Gold Rush splendor, Plump Jack, which opened in 1994, is the Mortimer's (of New York) of San Francisco, the current home of the ladies who lunch and of the men who support them and dine. And drink. Plump Jack began as a wine store, and its wonderful list of California's best is priced closer to the retail bone than any other restaurant in the city, an economy with great appeal to these oft Scroogian WASP aristos. Providing even greater appeal is the fact that Plump Jack was founded and is owned by Mayor Gavin Newsom, probably the country's most dashing, handsome high-level politician and a very potential Kennedyesque presidential candidate.

Newsom, a fourth-generation San Franciscan, named Plump Jack in honor of the opera of the same name written by his best friend, billionaire Bohemian Gordon Getty. "Plump Jack" was Queen Elizabeth's pet name for Shakespeare's greatest and lustiest comic character, Sir John Falstaff, from *Henry IV.* Newsom wanted a Falstaffian operation, and he got it. The Plump Jack group has gone on to acquire the next-door Balboa Café, famed for the city's best "society burger," like J. G. Melon's in New York, as well as Plump Jacks in Squaw Valley and the ritzy Carneros Inn in Napa. The only problem with Plump Jack, which has a cozy fireplace, English shields as chair backs, and a comforting menu of simple, clubby food (tomato soup, roast chicken) made with artisanal ingredients (shades of Alice W.), is that its last two chefs have been hired away by Pacific Heights families who don't *really* want to go out. Hence consistency, the premier virtue in this elite world that abhors change, has been a problem.

For the best food *among* the most glamorous people, the young rich set has embraced the nearby A 16, on San Francisco's answer to West Broadway. The name refers to the *autostrada* linking Naples to Bari, and nowhere outside the boot will you find better, gutsier southern Italian fare that is cooked by a kitchen of non-Italian, globe-trotting Alice Watersites (maybe they should be called Alicians) who have clearly done their homework. There's a foosball table to break the ice, a wall of unusual wines, wonderful chewy pizzas, spicy pastas, home-cured *salumi,* and more Hollywood-gorgeous women than at lunch at the Ivy, and all this without a Kitson in the neighborhood. The City by the Bay may have taken off its starched shirt, but it still knows how to put on the dog. ★ ★ ★ ★ ★ ★ ★ ★

The Hitching Post
Wild West

If you saw *Sideways,* that filmic paean to pinot noir, you'll know about the Hitching Post, the steak-and-wine restaurant in the Central Coast of California where much of the film's imbibing took place. But there are two Hitching Posts. The one in *Sideways* is in Buellton, near Santa Barbara, and is actually called Hitching Post II. Hitching Post I, the original, is an hour north, in the stunning rolling hills of Casmalia, an unreconstructed Wild West town. It serves the best steak dinner in America to everyone from Leonardo DiCaprio and Gisele Bundchen (or whatever supermodel or goddess the star is courting, unless she's vegan) to the joint chiefs of staff. Generals, and other top brass and senators, have been known to schedule state visits to nearby Vandenberg Air Force Base as an excuse to dine at the Hitching Post. It's cowboy food, he-man food, all-American food, and it lives up to the signs on the deserted road that winds through the cattle pastures leading to it: WORLD'S BEST BARBECUE.

Casmalia has a population of two hundred people. There's a general store, with a bunch of burly, weathered men in sombreros on the porch, swilling beer from longnecks. Big, scary dogs run freely and bark ominously at strangers. Across the street in a red frame building that looks like the Last Chance Saloon is the Hitching Post. There are lots of cars that line Casmalia's one dusty street, everything from pickups to stretch limos. But don't let any intimations of Hollywood put you off. Those cowboys at the general store look as if they would have shot any highfalutin agents putting on airs here in this little Dodge City.

You step inside and into the past, something out of *Gunsmoke*, a real live saloon. It's dark, but you can't miss the densely packed long, long bar, above which are stuffed animal trophies, bison heads, several varieties of deer, lots of antlers. There are wonderful, old, scale models of the stagecoaches that used to serve this town as well as saws, hoes, watering cans, and other farm implements that were the basis of its economy. Now the Hitching Post is the main basis—as butchers, waitresses, drivers, janitors, handymen. Aside from the animal heads, what really grabs you is the aroma, the irresistible aroma of steaks sizzling over the huge, glassed-in open iron grill that dominates the center of the restaurant. You can see the beautiful red meat on the grill, and you want it. Badly.

But first you go up to the bar to drink some house-bottled pinot noir, just like Paul Giamatti and Thomas Haden Church did in *Sideways*, which has now added a new generation of younger wine-ies and foodies to the Hitching Post's historical mix of generals and ranchers and in-the-know epicures, as well as locals who simply want to eat great beef. There are a lot of families here, extended families at the big red-cloth-covered tables, celebrating birthdays, anniversaries, IPOs. The Hitching Post is a special-event kind of place. If you're here in summer, take your pinot outside and sit on the huge lantern-lit terrace, surrounded by mountains, breathing the bracing salty air of the nearby Pacific. There are cow skulls and buckboards and wagon wheels and other western detritus; it all seems natural, authentic, not at all "decorated."

The Hitching Post is old, one hundred years old. It began life as the eleven-room Casmalia Hotel, built when the region was prospering from an oil boom, and railways were being built. There was a long tradition of good food here, beginning with the Veglia family, who bought the hotel in 1920 and offered bountiful family-style Italian meals to the guests. In 1944 the booms had gone bust, and lodgers were no more. New owners came in and converted the inn into a steak house and gave it its current name. In 1952, the place was sold once again, to another Italian-American family, the Ostinis, who have now become a steak dynasty. The basic set meal has not changed from that time: shrimp cocktail, tossed salad, steak, French fries, garlic bread, ice cream—America's meal. But a menu from 1957 shows the price was $3.75. Today, depending on how big your steak is, it's only in the $30s, one of the deals of the century. But this is country steak, not hundred-buck Peter Luger or Dan Tana city-steak, with infinitely less overhead to pass through.

And this country steak is even better than those wonderful, legendary city-steaks. In fact, *everything* is better here in the country, cowboy country, God's country: the velvety, fruity pinot noir is perfect steak wine. The cocktail of sweet baby bay shrimp, in a pumped-up ketchup sauce, is just like you used to get on Fisherman's Wharf when Joe DiMaggio's family ran the place, before the tourists ruined it, retro-gourmet. Ditto the salad, with its voluptuously creamy homemade blue cheese dressing. It's iceberg, all right, but it's right off the farm down the road, and therein lies the difference.

And then the steak. The steers aren't local: they're corn-fed cattle from the Midwest. The meat, which the restaurant doesn't claim to be USDA prime, is aged and butchered on the premises. It's leaner than the city-steaks, but somehow more flavorful, akin to the "baby beef" of Argentina, which is similarly cooked on live red oak grills. True to its billboards, the Hitching Post barbecues its steaks. It doesn't incinerate them the way Luger and Tana do on gas grills that leave a supercharred crust and a bloody center. Here there's no outer char. But the flavor is intense, surely due to the house seasoning mix of red wine vinegar, garlic, salt, pepper, and vegetable oil, which sounds simple but is actually an elixir whose formula is as closely guarded as that of Coca-Cola. The chef, a local boy named Louis Meza who has been here for a decade, working his way up from busboy, is like a shaman with his beloved fire. He sees steak-cooking as both art and science.

Although you have a choice of top sirloin, New York strip, and T-bone, the thick twelve-ounce filet is the way to go, because it's the best filet mignon on earth. You had no idea that a filet, usually girl food, could have this ruggedly macho flavor. Leave it to these cowboys. And, for a Cal-Mex local touch, try some of the delicious house-made spicy salsa with it. The super-fresh French fries, cut every day from Idaho russets, have been anointed by *The Los Angeles Times* as the best in all Southern California. They put to shame all the august places from Spago to Mortons that use frozen spuds, and you'll order at least one extra helping. You finish with Dreyer's vanilla ice cream with homemade chocolate sauce, and you'll swear you're back in the I-Like-Ike fabulous 1950s.

When Hitching Post patriarch Frank Ostini died in 1977, his two sons, Bill and Frank Jr., took over the business. The latter spun off his own Hitching Post in 1986, a fancier, red-carpeted place, where they shot *Sideways*, but there's no sibling rivalry here. Both restaurants share the same meat source, the same pride in old-fashioned perfection. But Post II is a restaurant, and Post I is a legend, so drive the extra hour into the West, the Wild West, and be an Eisenhower cowboy for a night that you will not forget. ★ 285

Los

Angeles

The Golden Age of
Hollywood Restaurants

For all its name and face power, there is still something of a letdown that a current temple of celebrity like Toscana is as Shawnee Mission–ish as it is. Especially when you compare it to its counterparts during Hollywood's Golden Age, back before, as Gloria Swanson put it in *Sunset Boulevard,* "the pictures got small." Ever since Hollywood became Hollywood, at the dawn of the Roaring Twenties, Los Angeles became the world capital of celebrity dining, since its dream factories were in the business, the very big business, of creating celebrities. And where better for the studios to show off their stars than where they ate.

Because the flowering of Hollywood coincided with the advent of Prohibition in 1919, the earliest celebrity haunts combined the forbidden exclusivity of the speakeasy with the spectacle of the Ziegfeld Follies, and the public was instantly hooked. Culver City's Washington Boulevard, near MGM and other studios, became LA's Great White Way, a bordertown of illegal booze, drugs, gambling, and prostitution, all to the jazzy beat of "colored" orchestras straight from the hearts of Harlem and New Orleans, at a plethora of restaurant-nightclubs with names that say it all: the Doo Doo Inn, the Hoosegow, the Monkey Farm, the Midnight Frolics, the Sneak Inn. Duke Ellington, Cab Calloway, Louis Armstrong all played there, for the likes of Pickford and Fairbanks, Keaton and Negri, Mack and Mabel, and the hardest partier of all, Charlie Chaplin, with Scott and Zelda furiously taking note, and notes, on the sidelines.

The hottest of all show-business spots in the 1920s was Fatty Arbuckle's Plantation Club, in Culver City, housed in an actual, or Hollywood actual, plantation mansion. Adding to the naughtiness of the enterprise was the fact that Arbuckle had been acquitted, amid violent controversy, in one of the trials of the century over his involvement in a fatal sex orgy in San Francisco. But Hollywood, then and now, always forgives its own, and the stars came out to the Plantation in droves. Still, the studios, mindful of their image and fearful of powerful federal smut detector Will Hays, began orchestrating their creations' public image. To that end came the rise of the Hollywood grand hotel. None was ever grander or more glamorous than the four-hundred-room Ambassador, where Bobby Kennedy was assassinated by Sirhan Sirhan in 1968. In its prime, the Ambassador, and its great nightclub, the Cocoanut Grove, were every night the red-hot center of the celebrity world. The Grove was like a jungle, with a rain forest full of tropicalia. Only the monkeys scaling the palm trees were fake, operated as puppets by a huge staff of animators. The place was a triumph of Hollywood set design, with most of the foliage left over from the filming of Valentino's *The Sheik*. There were weekly Charleston contests, generally won by either the town's best dancer, Lucille Le Sueur, before she became Joan Crawford, or the second best, Jane Peters, before she became Carole Lombard.

There was lots of talk about the secret booze at the Grove, but no one ever mentioned the food. Gastronomy was the province of the Montmartre Café, right on Hollywood Boulevard near the Musso-Frank Grill, today the atmospheric sole survivor of those glory days, but no competition for the giants at the time. The Montmartre had a kitchen full of French chefs, and the quality of its cuisine was validated by its being the favorite haunt of the Marquise de la Falaise, otherwise known as Gloria Swanson. On his first visit to California, Winston Churchill came here to stargaze, as did the king of Sweden and multiple pages of *Burke's Peerage*. Hollywood, from its beginnings, had always held a special allure for privileged Europeans.

Swanson would have yet another essential connection to the annals of Hollywood gastronomy: her next husband, after the marquis, was an entrepreneur named Herbert Somborn, who built the Brown Derby, in the shape of said hat, on Wilshire Boulevard right across from the Ambassador Hotel. Aside from his architectural inspirations, Somborn grasped the role of sex in creating a hot restaurant. Accordingly, he hired only waitresses, no waiters, and he only hired ex-Ziegfeld girls for the jobs. He also took most of the starch out of the "continental" food previously served to the film colony by offering a menu of all comfort food. Before the Cobb salad was invented here in the 1930s by subsequent owner Bob Cobb, the Somborn Derby was renowned for its corned beef hash, its pot roast, and its pies. And, yes, its ham sandwiches, which the folksy, destarched menu described as "made from pleased pigs that have made perfect hogs of themselves." If Somborn liked to "ham it up," how could he help himself? This was Hollywood.

The stars were anything but gourmets. One fan magazine reported some of the celebrities' favorite dishes: Marlene Dietrich devoured mixed chicken-and-pork burgers drenched in melted butter. Katharine Hepburn's favorite dish was a plain lettuce and tomato salad. Joan Crawford doted on prunes stuffed with cottage cheese, even when she went to the Montmartre. The Brown Derby captured the winning formula of scintillating simplicity that has characterized the Hollywood restaurant to the present day.

Aside from its showgirl servers and its down-home fare, the Derby established a number of show-business-oriented "firsts." It began the custom of paging customers, then bringing a phone to their table. You hadn't "arrived" in Hollywood until you had been paged at the Brown Derby. And to make sure the world knew you had arrived there, the Derby was the first restaurant to hire its own in-house public relations firm, headed by none other than the cousin of gossip queen Louella Parsons, who would hold court, like J. J. Hunsecker in *Sweet Smell of Success,* at the second Brown Derby on Vine Street. Then, just to make sure nobody forgot that they were in the high temple of celebrity, the Derby festooned its walls with black-and-white caricatures of all its famous patrons.

In 1933, the year Prohibition was repealed (as if it were actually enforced in Hollywood), Billy Wilkerson, the owner of the trade bible *The Hollywood Reporter,* accomplished a feat of PR synergy by opening the Vendome across from *Reporter* offices and reporting in the *Reporter* all the stars who graced his portals. Unlike the Brown Derby, the Vendome was conceived as a damn-the-Depression gourmet paradise, with its own luxe delicatessen offering take-out Russian caviar, French foie gras, Westphalian ham, Scotch salmon, and vintage wines. There was a whole section of cheeses, jams, and teas imported from Fortnum & Mason in London. In fact, Vendome for years served only the midday meal, and it became legendary for Tinseltown's first power lunch. It was at the Vendome where Louella Parsons got the scoop that made her career, when Mary Pickford told Louella that she was divorcing Douglas Fairbanks. Rather than despise Hollywood for such high-profile extravagance during the country's hard times, America, on the contrary, sought escape in the gossipy escapades. Just as it sought escape in the deco fantasies of Astaire and Rogers, Powell and Loy, all of whom were Vendome regulars.

Given the success of Vendome, Wilkerson began looking for other venues. He wanted a nightspot, and where better to put one than on the Sunset Strip. Of course in 1934, Sunset Boulevard in what is now West Hollywood was an empty expanse of fruit orchards, with very few sidewalks and no one to walk on them. Yet Beverly Hills had displaced Hancock Park as the new home of the stars, and Sunset was the main route home from the studios. Hence if Wilkerson built anything on this stretch, the stars couldn't help but notice it. And so he did. Francophile Wilkerson christened his new venture the Cafe Trocadero. It was a *très* swank black-tie venue, with murals of the Eiffel Tower complementing drop-dead views of the twinkling Los Angeles basin from the Sunset heights, with a menu of heavy Ritz-y classics like *boeuf forestier* and *ris de veau Toulousaine*. There were two big bands: one was Harl Smith and his Continental Orchestra; the other Ramon Litee and his Parisian Tango Orchestra. Immediately, the Troc became to the Hollywood night what Vendome was to the day, *the* place to be seen. And according to studio edicts, stars *had* to be seen. None of that "Garbo stuff" would be tolerated in other luminaries.

But Hollywood couldn't be glamorous all the time. The stars may have feasted on foie gras, for the benefit of the studio publicists, who wanted to give them "class." But, left to their own devices, they wanted then, just as now, to keep it simple. To that end, a failed transplanted New York vaudevillian named Dave Chasen was staked to three thousand dollars by Harold Ross, the editor of *The New Yorker.* A lot of the Algonquin Round Table wits like Dorothy Parker had come out west looking for easy screenplay money, and they needed a canteen. Thus in late 1936 Chasen's Southern Pit Barbecue on Beverly Boulevard near Doheny became It, and stayed It for over fifty years, until it became a fancy supermarket, but no Vendome. Chasen's invented the Shirley Temple non-cocktail for Little Miss Marker herself, and in time the place got fancier, grilling steaks in flaming saucepans tableside and adding a sauna and a barber who became the favorite of Humphrey Bogart, Bing Crosby, and Errol Flynn. In the early 1960s, Chasen's became even more famous for the wretched excess of Twentieth Century-Fox's airfreighting its chili to the Rome set of *Cleopatra,* for the delectation of lovebirds Elizabeth Taylor and Richard Burton. When the film became the biggest fiasco in the industry's history to that point, the chili was Exhibit A in What Went Wrong.

In the 1940s, the indefatigable Billy Wilkerson opened still another show-place on the Sunset Strip, Ciro's, where the Comedy Store is now. Down the Boulevard, the director Preston Sturges opened the Players Club, which also had a barbershop. The Players was a favorite of the artier set, led by Orson Welles. Another booming genre was the Polynesian fantasy restaurant with lethal rum concoctions. The original was Don the Beachcomber, which was the young John F. Kennedy's favorite showbiz haunt whenever he stepped out west in the footsteps of his father, who had once owned RKO Pictures.

These seminal Hollywood restaurants were spectacles worthy of Louis B. Mayer and often concealed criminal activities worthy of Bugsy Siegel, the town's favorite mobster. There were secret gambling dens, with roulette wheels and slot machines, not to mention massive money laundering. Eventually the law got wise, and a new, less spectacular dining enterprise came into being that was less nightclub/dinner theater than pure restaurant.

The prototype here was Romanoff's, which opened on Rodeo Drive in Beverly Hills in 1940. Mike Romanoff was a total mountebank-hustler who pretended to be "the cousin of the late czar," whatever that meant. Everyone knew he was a ridiculous liar, but Hollywood, as well as high society, loved his audacity. Romanoff's backers included Cary Grant, producer Darryl Zanuck, tycoon Jock Whitney, banking heir Harry Crocker, and Algonquin raconteur Robert Benchley. They all called him "Emperor." Bogart had his own meal plan at Romanoff's, often sitting with the Emperor and his two imperial dogs, Socrates and Confucius. Romanoff, who traveled with Frank Sinatra on some of his world tours, became the archetype of the Hollywood restaurant patron-as-star. He has never been equaled. ★ ★ ★ ★ ★ ★ ★ ★ ★ ★ ★ ★ ★ ★ ★ ★ ★ ★ ★

Toscana
Spaghetti Western

BRENTWOOD

"Is that all there is?" This is the question you might be asking yourself upon your first glimpse of Toscana, which ranks close to the pinnacle of Tinseltown celebrity eateries. Like the Hollywood agents to whom its pasta is manna, Toscana is known to be xenophobic, exclusive, powerful, and intimidating, at least to those outside the business, making it all the more alluring to the anointed ones therein who regard it as their own little *circolo*, or club. As Dante wrote in *The Inferno*, "All hope abandon ye who enter here," especially if ye don't have a major studio deal.

The exclusivity is apparent right from the start: nobody who hasn't been to Toscana before can find it. There is a tiny sign, but it is totally obscured by shrubbery. "Across San Vicente from the Hamburger Hamlet" are the best directions, and even then you're not sure; the valet parkers are around the corner. So only after you've seen a few too many Aston-Martins and Benzes making an obscure turn into a Brentwood lane do you know you've hit the spot. There's a huge crush of people in jogging suits and sports club mufti, in windbreakers and jeans, at the door of the plain brick-and-glass room. They don't look like Hollywood stars and moguls. They look like suburbanites from Shaker Heights or Shawnee Mission.

Your second question is, "Is this really an Italian restaurant?" The deafening roar is straight out of the lowest *loggia* of Dante's hell, and the wood-burning pizza oven near the entrance emits blasts of heat and flame that recall the old AGIP dragons at the rest stops along the Italian autostrade. There are some hanging beaded lampshades that some decorator might say came from Milan. But that's about it for the physical plant. It's bland, generic, and so noisy you might think about crossing the median and settling for a burger and a side of silence.

But then you notice a big guy sitting across the room. It's Michael Eisner, the former head of Disney (as if you need to be told), the most highly paid man in movie history. You may not recognize him in a non-Mouseketeer context. But you can't miss Warren Beatty and Annette Bening two tables away. Plus Aussie heartthrob Heath Ledger. And, wow, Scarlett Johansson. Director Oliver Stone. Legendary screenwriter Robert Towne—"It's Chinatown, Jake." And there's Don Henley of the Eagles. Hotel California indeed. And those are just the marquee names, all cool, all street-casual. Remember that no one dresses for dinner in LA.

When your industry friend arrives (without an industry friend, you might as well not be here, because Toscana has the highest ratio of VIPs to total seating in town, and the fewest tourists), and he's been obligatorily grazed on both cheeks by the ebullient maître d', Francesco, he'll point out the high-leverage, low-visibility heavy hitters, people like Brad Grey, the new head of Paramount, and Ned Tanen, an old head of Paramount. Record czar Irving Azoff, who cut his teeth—or fangs, as that business requires—managing the Eagles. Wendy Stark, daughter of the late superproducer Ray, and one of the city's reigning social arbiters. And, in the back of the room, Mike Ovitz, who went from being the most powerful agent in Hollywood to the most denigrated studio executive in his disastrous brief tenure under his erstwhile best friend Michael Eisner.

That the two men are both here under the same roof is either a testament to the sirenlike lure of Toscana's *cucina* or an indictment of the intelligence-gathering skills of the two tycoons' advance men. Whatever. In palmier days, Eisner and Ovitz invariably ended the weekend with a Sunday dinner at Toscana. When Eisner had his quadruple bypass surgery, Toscana altered its already Mediterranean offerings by reducing the salt and oil content. Overnight, *tutto* Hollywood, mortified that its most powerful figure could be mortal after all, began flocking to Toscana and ordering self-concocted cardiac-friendly variations on the Italian theme. Off the menu, of course. Only a rank out-of-towner would ask for a bill of fare.

Most of these people live right here in Brentwood. Toscana is their neighborhood local. O. J. Simpson, when he was a neighbor, loved the place. There are no bad tables, because just about every table is filled with equally famous or powerful diners. Aside from the stars and the star makers, there are political heavyweights like First Republican Brad Freeman, who brings Laura Bush here. (They won't let her sit in the window tables.) Arnold Schwarzenegger is a regular, as is rising politico Bobby Shriver, who often came in with cousin JFK Jr., making Toscana the unofficial clubhouse of Camelot West. The only people who get more respect than all this Hollywood royalty are European royalty. Even Tom Cruise gets left in the lurch when a Ruspoli or a Caracciolo, or even a Hanover or a Bismarck, comes calling from the Old World. For the suave, skilled waiters at Toscana, who are rare birds in this town for not being actors-in-waiting, nobility trumps fame any day. Lady Di never made it here (Fergie did), but she would have loved it.

The awful din might explain why movies are so bad. The power players are making deals that none of them can clearly understand. They're also too busy checking out who else is coming in, leapfrogging tables to meet, greet, and network. Francesco has kissed more people than any president on a whistle-stop. The waiters, all Italian, all either superhandsome or supercharming, do the Italian stereotype proud. Without a star chef like Wolfgang Puck or Nobu, without a star mystique like the Ivy or Mr Chow, Toscana holds its own with its waitstaff. These waiters are actually what make Toscana unique. The crowd loves them and is seduced into thinking it's in Capri. Everyone starts yammering to the waiters in Italian. The room sounds like a really bad Berlitz class.

The language of the kitchen, however, is Spanish. Most of the staff are Mexicans who have been recruited and trained by the original chef-owner, Agostino Sciandri. Agostino, after a nasty dispute with his partner, accountant-to-the stars Michael Gordon (the prime investor in Toscana was Johnny

Carson's bandleader Doc Severinsen), decamped for West Hollywood a few years ago to start the equally star-studded Ago, backed by Harvey Weinstein, Robert De Niro, and Ridley Scott, and thus commencing the Tuscan Wars that are still raging today (see opposite). Why it's hard to fill the kitchen with Italians, most of whom come out of the womb knowing how to cook and all of whom seem to be born with dreams of living in Hollywood, seems incomprehensible. But it's probably because the Italians all want to be out front charming the stars rather than splashing around vats of *sugo di pomodoro*. There is usually one Italian head chef, who changes with some frequency, depending on the chef's Hollywood ambitions, but he's often away from the stoves, preparing private dinners in the separate wine room for the likes of Rob Reiner and Arianna Huffington. The ultimate luxury of Toscana, aside from being kissed by Francesco and cooed to by a waiter, is to have that chef take the long time to stir up one of Toscana's risottos, particularly the virtuous all-vegetable *risotto primavera*, the best version of this slow dish in the fastest city on earth.

If the chef is otherwise engaged, what should you eat? The best bet is to keep it very simple, or go for the classic stuff that the Italian capo has had a hand in preparing in advance, such as the *spaghetti bolognese,* which may be the most authentic in Los Angeles. Toscana is famous for its *pollo al mattone,* or chick under brick, a grilled chicken dish served with olive-oil-and-rosemary roasted potatoes that spawned an entire luxury fast-food spin-off called Rosti (now a casualty of the Tuscan Wars). It also makes a succulent *bistecca alla fiorentina* in that Dantean pizza oven, not to mention a mean gossamer-crusted pizza itself. Do ask that the roast potatoes be cooked to order, or else you might get a plate of little grease sponges. In fact, be as demanding (not to say obnoxious) as you never dreamed you could be. If your waiter likes you and you're not calorophobic, you will likely receive a sampling of the cornucopia of homemade cakes and cookies that greet you at the door, or if there's been a run on sugar, at least a plate of flaky, starship-shaped biscotti.

There are countless noble wines on the menu. But where the food is concerned, keep it simple and be fussy, fussy, fussy. This is have-it-your-way central. If you pretend you're a star, they'll probably treat you like one. ★ ★ ★

The Tuscan Wars

If you want to see famous people in Los Angeles, Brentwood beats Hollywood, Beverly Hills, even Malibu, by miles. And it's not just because a lot of celebs live in this safest and grandest of LA neighborhoods. Just because celebs live somewhere doesn't mean they go out. When you're as rich as they are, the world comes to you. The one thing that will, however, smoke a star out of his gilded cage is a great Italian restaurant, and Brentwood, suddenly and inexplicably, has more of them than any neighborhood this side of Parioli. Italian food is an aphro-disiac to Hollywood, and here it is, in nearly a dozen trattorias splayed out over less than a mile of the medianed, coral-treed San Vicente Boulevard, historically (if one dares speak of history in LA) a thoroughfare so suburban that Hamburger Hamlet was as good as food got.

No more. The vast success of Toscana has spawned one rival after another. You can't call them imitators any more than you could call Paper Moon in Milan an imitator of Bice. Like the restaurants in Milan, they're mostly all good, and they're all packed with the same famous faces, who love having the option to not only table-hop but to trat-hop, a *penne arrabbiata* to start at one place, a *branzino* at another, a *torta alla nonna* at a third, and an Amaro at a last one before packing it in (in the Bentley). Who do you see? Eastwood, Stallone, the Beattys, the Spielbergs, Kennedys and Shrivers, the Hiltons of several generations, Blake Edwards and Julie Andrews, the *Sex and the City* girls, the Italy-obsessed Clooney posse.

Which is "the best"? Impossible to say, as the situation is so fluid, as seen in the recent departure of Toscana's gifted chef Piero Toputti to Caffe Roma in Beverly Hills, recently acquired by ousted Toscana founder Agostino Sciandri (Ago), whose growing empire also includes Sortino in Brentwood (A-plus lasagna classica). Now the old Mexican hands are doing the pasta at Toscana, albeit with no loss of customer loyalty. But for *vera cucina italiana,* best to stick to chef-owned places, like Palmeri, with the brilliant Sicilian Ottavio Palmeri, and Osteria

Latini, with the equally inspired Triesteian Paulo Pasio. Two different experiences, one deep-southern, one high-northern, both great. Palmeri probably makes LA's best thin-crust pizza and salt-baked fish, while Latini tops the city for his spaghetti Bolognese and multiplicity of veal chops. You can get hearty and exotic Abruzzi fare (lots of lamb and pig) at Pecorino, run by a former Toscana waiter, and inventive vegetable-based pastas at Pizzicotto. And for LA Italian classics, there's La Scala Presto, a branch of the old Sinatra Bev Hills favorite, which invented one of Hollywood's most emblematic dishes, the salami-provolone-garbanzo chopped salad.

Although all the trattorias remain packed every night, celebrity alone is no guarantee of longevity. Before the current pasta rush began, one of the hottest restaurants in the show-business world was Mezzaluna, right on San Vicente in what is now LA's Via Veneto. But that was where Ron Goldman worked, and where Nicole Brown Simpson had her last supper. Today, O.J.'s nearby Brentwood mansion has been razed, and Mezzaluna has become a Peet's Coffee. Sic transit glorious gnocchi. ★ ★ ★ ★ ★ ★ ★ ★

Spago

Starcissism

The Chasen's-Romanoff's chili-meets-flambé post–World War II Hollywood restaurant scene didn't really change much until the 1980s, aside from the later emergence of the wildly popular Polynesian fantasies that were (the late) Luau and (the still Singapore-slinging) Trader Vic's. The old restaurants were like MacArthur's old soldier: they didn't die; they just faded away. Yes, there were the newcomers that became classics, like the Bistro, the brainchild of director Billy Wilder, who assembled a group of epicure expatriate showbiz types homesick for Parisian home cooking: the resulting restaurant looked like a stage set for any joint in Les Halles, before it was demolished to become a shopping mall, something out of *Irma la Douce*, which Wilder directed. The Bistro was immortalized in the film *Shampoo* for Julie Christie's under-the-table fellatio of Warren Beatty at a Nixon fund-raiser; its pâté, *soupe à l'oignon*, and coq au vin became Hollywood's versions of soul food.

And then came Puck. Or more accurately, first came Terrail. Terrail, what a name. Claude Terrail was the owner of La Tour D'Argent, the most famous, most glamorous restaurant in Paris, and hence the world, for Paris then *was* the world when it came to food. Patrick Terrail was Claude Terrail's nephew, and so could not avoid dreams of grandeur. He had recently graduated from Cornell's prestigious School of Hotel Administration and was looking to follow in his uncle's footsteps. But uncle had little to do with nephew. They rarely spoke. Hence nephew got the bright idea to make his fortune in the brave new world—or the Wild, Wild West, as most Frenchmen regarded anything west of the Hudson River. Young Terrail was starstruck, as had been his uncle, who had not only had romances with Marilyn Monroe and Ava Gardner, but had actually married, and later divorced, the daughter of Jack Warner. Claude Terrail was thus Hollywood royalty. His name was magic, and nephew Patrick milked it for all it was worth.

Thus it was fairly easy for Patrick to assemble, in the late 1970s, a group of on-the-outside-looking-in Los Angeles doctors and lawyers to invest in his new restaurant, a place called Ma Maison, in an open-air former garden-supply store on then torpid Melrose Avenue. The idea was to serve authentic French food in a casual alfresco atmosphere, as opposed to the Bistro's stuffy quasiformality. The place was hideous, with no decor whatsoever, and a patio covered in *Exorcist*-green AstroTurf. It was as far from the superelegant La Tour d'Argent as a restaurant could be. But nobody in Hollywood realized that. They all thought that Ma Maison was La Tour West, and that Patrick had not only Claude's name but also his imprimatur, which was as far from the truth as "La" was from "Ma."

What the two restaurants did have in common was outstanding food, though Ma didn't emulate La's most celebrated dish, its pressed duck. In fact, Terrail's original formula, when he opened Ma in 1974, was to create a brochette, or French shish-kebab, house that would be the flagship of a chain. That was Cornell thinking, furthered by a corporate stint at Restaurant Associates in New York, which, in addition to the Four Seasons, was in the chain business. It took several failed chefs and several failed formulas before Patrick met Wolfgang, an inspired French chef who just happened to be from Austria. Wolfgang Puck had the perfect Hollywood, Romanoffian name, with evocations of Mozart and Shakespeare. He had a great résumé, having left home at fourteen to apprentice in the kitchens of France, culminating in the then three-*Michelin*-starred L'Oustau de Baumanière, one of the great tables of Provence. He was said to be "*le prochain* Bocuse," because of his gifts with *nouvelle cuisine,* whatever that was. (A quick definition would be to mix Escoffier with raspberry vinaigrette.)

Despite Puck's skillet skills, what truly made Ma Maison was its *haut snobisme,* in which Patrick took every French cliché about restaurant arrogance to its most illogical extremes. He delisted the phone number. He made reservations impossible. He seated anyone who wasn't famous at dreadful tables. He hired the most pretentious French-speaking captains and waiters. He even rented exotic sports cars to decorate the entrance and instructed the valet parkers to hide anything less than a Rolls or Bentley in a side lot. The formula was straight out of the period best-seller *Winning Through Intimidation,* and it worked. For all its power trips, Hollywood may be the most masochistic of all societies. If it's painful, they will come. More stars filled Ma's AstroTurf than had ever jammed the booths at Chasen's or the Brown Derby. From 1977 to 1982, this garden shed was the most exclusive restaurant on earth.

It might have gone on forever had Puck and Terrail not fallen out. But they did. Puck had become Tinseltown's first celebrity chef, and he had no trouble putting together his own consortium of starstruck doctor-lawyer investors for his own enterprise. That starship was called Spago, Italian slang for you-know-what, and it wasn't what anyone expected from this supposed heir to Bocuse and Troisgros. Forget it, he told *The Los Angeles Times* on the eve of his grand opening in what had been the funky Armenian kebabery Kavkaz atop the Sunset Strip, whose former glamour had morphed into teenybopper rock heaven. "Nouvelle cuisine is a dead-end street. Everybody doing the same thing, beurre blanc everywhere. Only the decor changed. Nicer flowers. A little raspberry vinegar, a little soy sauce, a little hazelnut oil. . . . That's not really food. Who needs truffles on a good piece of fish?"

Puck may have been inspired by one of Hollywood's favorite haunts at the Cannes Film Festival, a place called Le Pizza at the old port. There, glamorous folks in Lacostes and espadrilles would get off their yachts to eat delicious salads, grilled fish, simple pasta, and pizza from a wood-burning oven. There was zero atmosphere, other than the A-list crowd itself, and the A-level views over the harbor and the Bay of Angels. Why not transport the exact concept to LA, where the crowd, the views, and the snob quotient were roughly analogous? After all, weren't Beverly Hills and Cannes officially sister cities? You bet. On Spago's opening night, reporters counted twenty-one Rollses in the parking lot. A star was born. As was "California Cuisine," a concept that was almost as amorphous as nouvelle cuisine. It had to do with wood grills and local produce, but it wasn't at all healthy, ladling on the butter and cream with a lavish hand. Basically, California Cuisine, LA version, was French Provençal served in a different longitude. Above all, it was *star food*.

Today Spago remains the most famous restaurant in Los Angeles, and in the known show-business world, but it's nothing like the little shacks that were Ma Maison and the original Spago itself, both sadly departed. Instead it's a grand, Vegas-y temple of gastronomy, a three-hundred-seat dining room and banquet hall of *salles privées* encircling an open garden of ancient (for LA) olive trees. In clement weather, which it usually is, the garden is the seating Valhalla of this culinary Olympus. Wolfgang Puck, for all his empire that extends to Tokyo, Maui, Vegas, San Francisco, Chicago, all the way to the endless supermarkets that sell his frozen foods, is almost always, miraculously, here: hugging, kissing, signing cookbooks, providing an unforgettable frisson to the pilgrims from all over the globe who have made this obligatory pilgrimage to the Lourdes of designer pizza.

Ironically, Spago has become so grand that pizza is not even on the menu. But what is, in this town? The kitchen will treat anyone from Dubuque like an insider if he or she whispers a secret craving for Puck's famed "Jewish pizza," with smoked salmon, crème fraîche, and caviar—Zabar's goes to Hollywood. For all his Austrian-ness, Puck has a way with the Old World Jewish culture that created the movie business. His first wife and business partner and restaurant designer, Barbara Lazaroff, was defiantly from the Bronx. In her honor, Puck made national headlines when he instituted the Spago Seder, featuring cayenne-spiked gefilte fish, arugula as the bitter herb, and olive-oil-fried matzo topped with garlic and chili flakes.

But today, what makes nights at Spago different from all other nights is that Wolfgang Puck has more than lived up to his buzz of three decades before. He has become the next Paul Bocuse. The trip to his shrine in Beverly Hills is similar in countless ways to its counterpart in Lyon, and to Puck's *Michelin* roots. Bocuse, for all his globe-trotting and global reach, is also always there, and the place is huge and full of private parties. Yet the food and service at both are of the highest order for any places so vast. The problem with Spago, for those in search of the stars and moguls who made it famous, is that they tend to get lost in the crush. Sure, you might see anyone from Tony Curtis to Paris Hilton, Al Gore to James Baker, blasts from the Reagan past like Betsy Bloomingdale, for whom this place was the Republican local in its previous incarnation as the Bistro Garden. (A colossus that folded after the owner was accused of making an anti-Semitic remark to a lady who didn't lunch enough. Bring on the seders, fast.) Stars and legends, there will be. But only in a tiny ratio to the vast dressed-up crowd of reverential, mortal foodies. What made the old, tiny, supercasual Spago so exciting was the thrill of catching your idols *in flagrante ristorante*.

No place in the world could make a normal diner feel more insecure, not New York's Le Pavilion at its 1950s heyday of snootiness, not Mirabelle when it ruled 1960s London with the pomp of a Buckingham Palace social secretary, not even La Tour d'Argent. To begin with, you could never get a reservation, maybe at the loser hours of six or ten (it's early to bed in LA) a month in advance. And say you did score an eight. That's when the real humble pie began. The valet parkers would suppress a sneer at your new Beemer and hide it behind the lesser Benzes. The small army of paparazzi camped on the steep hill leading to the pearly gates wouldn't even look up. Their sixth sense, the scent of celeb, told them that you Didn't Matter. Nor did your reservation, and the beautiful but unfeeling hostess would herd you to the tiny bar with the rubes from Dallas and Detroit. No kisses for you from Wolf or wife Barbara. Tough luck. An hour later, if you were lucky, you might get a table—in Vladivostok, around the corner, near the back, so you couldn't see the Chosen, and the Chosen couldn't see you.

But, oh, the Chosen. Although superagent Swifty Lazar made Spago the locus of his annual Oscar party, the A-est ticket of the A-list, every night at the old Spago seemed like Oscar night. You were always awed at the assemblages. One night, all the superheroes—*Terminator, Rocky, Road Warrior, Die Hard, Death Wish*—were there, at separate tables along the "Murderers' Row" by the windows, overlooking Sunset billboards with the stars' magnified countenances staring right back at them. Narcissism, or, better, starcissism, had no limits, and Spago played it to the hilt. Another night all the Traveling Wilburys would be there, Harrison, Orbison, Petty, Lynn, a living rock-and-roll hall of fame; only Dylan could resist the Spago siren. Another night might see a coven of television's supervixens—Morgan Fairchild, Heather Locklear, Farrah Fawcett, Joan Collins, with Sally Field across the way for a dose of syrup. And some nights legends strode the boards—Kirk Douglas, Gregory Peck, James Stewart—and the earth moved.

The food was *très simple:* pizzas with Santa Barbara shrimp or goat cheese or homemade duck sausage, pastas with the same, wood-grilled chicken and fish adorned with lots of baby vegetables from the soon-to-be famed Chino Ranch near San Diego. Plus some decadent French desserts created by Nancy Silverton (who went on to make a carbo fortune by founding La Brea Bakery), like the warm apple tart with caramel ice cream, for those who had given up on thin, if not rich. The party lasted until 1997, when Puck spotted the Bistro Garden space and announced that, despite all his innovations in molding the California Dream, it was high time for "people to take me seriously as a chef."

And so they have, albeit at the expense of the exquisite torture of the favoritism of yore. The end of Spago as we knew it and feared it may have been symbolized by the 2004 death of arguably Puck's best customer, the oil tycoon Marvin Davis, who had once owned Twentieth Century-Fox as well as the Pebble Beach golf paradise, and lived in perhaps the grandest estate in Beverly Hills. Davis was a behemoth who used to have his bodyguards bring his own thronelike chair into Spago to accommodate his grandeur. He always traveled in a stunning entourage that included such luminaries as Sidney Poitier, Michael Caine, and Jackie Collins, who got much of her *Hollywood Wives à clef*-isms from her Spago nights. Davis and company were regulars at the old Spago, and they brought their exclusive ebullience to the new one. Alas, they don't make high rollers like Davis anymore. So when he died, some of the power and the glory of Spago died with him.

The new Spago's menu is as ambitious as anything at Baumanière, where Puck dispatched his second in command, a cherubic Jersey boy named Lee Hefter, to acquire classical spit and polish. The menu is huge and always enticing, the must-have triumphs being the Chino Ranch chopped salad, the sweet white corn and mascarpone *agnolotti* (to which even an Italian master like Gualtiero Marchesi has tipped his toque in awe), the tempura soft-shell crab, the steamed wild striped bass Hong Kong–style, and the grandmotherly classic wiener schnitzel. It doesn't sound very French, but neither do a lot of Paris menus today, and for Franco-purists there are always inventive specials with foie gras and truffles, not to mention the award-winning desserts of the aptly named Sherry Yard. Whatever you do order, you'll invariably eat too much, for Puck and Hefter are always passing out freebies, such as the famous tuna tartare in a sesame cone, as well as Lucullan petits fours— fives and sixes . . . And it's not just the celebrities who get the treats. The new Spago is an exercise in democracy, gourmandise for everyone. "Let them *all* eat cake" might well be Puck's new motto. ★ ★ ★ ★ ★ ★ ★ ★ ★

The Pickiest Eater

"If you can satisfy Arthur Sarkissian, then light a candle for yourself," says Wolfgang Puck about the man who every top restaurateur in Los Angeles concurs is the pickiest eater in a town full of them. "Arthur is impossible," says a waiter at Toscana, who's had to take back pizza (too much cheese), pasta (too salty), fish (overcooked), and wine (white not chilled enough) from Sarkissian, on multiple occasions. "But we love him. He's one of our best customers. He keeps us on our toes."

"Oh God, it's Arthur," groans a veteran waiter at the Ivy, where Sarkissian frequently sends back Margaritas that have too much lime, or too much tequila, or two little of one or the other or both. He sends back the stone crab claws if he thinks they've spent a minute too long on the plane. "He'll send back San Pellegrino he thinks is too flat," the Ivy man says, yet greets Sarkissian with a big ready-for-anything smile.

They all smile, because Arthur Sarkissian not only is a big tipper and a serious player in the movie business, but also brings in a lot of customers, important ones. And LA hosts don't forget the rule that the customer is always right, even if he *is* impossible. Sarkissian, who has often called Puck on the table for fish that was undercooked or oversauced, is not afraid of taking on famous names, whether on or off the screen.

"Cowards!" Sarkissian says, dismissing all those who *don't* send food back. "They're intimidated by the stars around them, the star chefs. They're afraid to stand up for themselves. People in this town settle. They settle for bad movies, they settle for bad food. These restaurants would be a lot better if people sent things back." And it's not just LA. Sarkissian has sent back "old" oysters at Le Cirque in New York, "dry" sole at La Grenouille. In London, where Somerset Maugham said you could eat well if you had breakfast three times a day, Sarkissian can't seem to get a properly poached egg ("The yolk should *ooze, not run,"* he insists, "and the white must be semihard, not dry") anywhere, from the Dorchester to the Savoy. At least, not the first time. And you should see him in Vegas, at the ersatz foodie temples. "They're morons, these people who spend $300 a head for garbage and say this is great. Fools! I can't stand that."

One of the reasons Sarkissian, fifty, is such a tough customer is that he has been a seller as well as a buyer. Born in Tehran to a prominent pre-Ayatollah Armenian industrialist, Sarkissian was sent to a posh boys' school outside of London, and it was hard to keep him down on the farm after he'd seen the Kings Road. At eighteen he got his first Ferrari and opened a chic boutique called Vincci on Jermyn Street across from Wiltons, the Edwardian fish house, where the oysters were never old and the sole never dry. He spent a lot of time at Mr Chow in its miniskirted glory years. "I never had to send anything back. The waiters there were great. They asked precisely what I wanted and gave it to me." When London turned cold in the mid 1970s and Michael Chow relocated to LA, Sarkissian sold his shop and did the same.

A movie obsessive since childhood, Sarkissian decided to give the film business a shot. All he had was his Ferrari, a closet full of Italian suits, and the rights to Malraux's *Man's Fate,* none of which did him the slightest good in Hollywood. But he persevered and lowered his artistic sights. His first hit was the Sandra Bullock sleeper *While You Were Sleeping,* which cost peanuts and grossed caviar. Even bigger was the *Rush Hour* series starring Jackie Chan and Chris Tucker, which enabled Sarkissian to send back lots of dishes in Hong Kong for too much salt, MSG, lard, you name it. His next film, a remake of the Melville gangster classic *Le Cercle Rouge,* will either keep the *Michelin* stars of Paris on their toes or bring them to their knees.

While dismissing such LA food fetishes as the famed La Brea Bakery's croissants as "stringy and doughy," Sarkissian still thinks there's good stuff to be had here, as long as you ask for it. A few times. Like the chicken chili at Kate Mantilini. "It's excellent, but I won't eat anything else there." Sarkissian qualifies his endorsement. Nate 'n Al's is fine for breakfast, "but only for the dollar-size pancakes," Sarkissian specifies. While he often sends back the prime burger at the Grill for being overcooked, he loves the one at the Polo Lounge, "as long as they scoop out the bun."

Sarkissian has his favorites, and he gives them their due. He thinks Dan Tana is pretty great, "because I only order two things, the steak and the Tana salad, chopped fine, and I've only had to send back the steak a few times for being overcooked." Matsuhisa bats a thousand. "Nobu is great. He gets it." At Sarkissian's persistent urging, the chefs at Ago finally learned to cook fish *à point,* and those at Giorgio to grill a lobster to perfection. And he likes Osteria Angelini, now that they've cut down the noise. "I told them it was ridiculous. It killed my appetite. I couldn't stand it." So they insulated an entire brick wall. When Arthur Sarkissian talks, restaurateurs listen. As you see, it's not always about the food. It's about the customer. The LA customer is right indeed, particularly when he's number one at the box office. ★

Mortons
Burger King

WEST HOLLYWOOD

The other twin tower of Los Angeles celebrity dining is Mortons. If Spago was the favorite restaurant of the stars themselves, Mortons was the favorite of the moguls and agents who created them. And if Spago has grown up into a grander, kinder, and gentler version of its old nasty self, Mortons, which always had good manners and a certain *politesse,* has conversely run in place, barely changing. But since no business changes as fast as show business, Mortons, while still revered by its powerful loyalists, is no longer the red-hot center of the celebrity world. Except, that is, on Oscar night, when the annual *Vanity Fair* party, the most exclusive bash in the universe, reminds the whole world what Spago and Mortons in the 1980s were like just about every single night.

When Swifty Lazar died in 1994, *Vanity Fair* editor Graydon Carter and Loew's hotel heir and producer Steve Tisch stepped into the party void with their dear pal Peter Morton and created this extravaganza that out-Swiftied Swifty and preserved Mortons's position as an essential stargazing venue. Not that Peter Morton needs stars; he is one himself, as the cofounder of the global Hard Rock Cafes and of the Hard Rock Hotel in Las Vegas, institutions that have changed the face of how the youth culture, from boomers to Y-ers, entertains itself. Unlike Wolfgang Puck, however, Peter Morton shuns the spotlight.

Handsome, elegant, aloof, and obsessively healthy notwithstanding the burgers that built his empire and that he now eschews, Morton is considered by many to be the Howard Hughes of the hospitality business.

The Chicago-born Morton was restaurant royalty. Meat was in his blood. His father, who built the international chain of Morton's prime steak houses, also cofounded the Playboy Club with Hugh Hefner. His parents having separated, Peter grew up with his remarried mother in Bel Air and attended the University of Denver, one of the premier party schools of the 1960s. On a trip after college to Israel and Egypt in 1969, the meat heir was recuperating in London at the home of Victor Lownes, who ran Playboy in Europe. On his first day back from the Unholy Land, Lownes asked Morton what he was hungry for. His answer—a classic American burger—left Lownes short. There wasn't a decent burger in the UK, Lownes told him; this was Wimpy-land. Loving London at first sight, Morton got an entrepreneurial brainstorm: bring the real thing here. If you grill it, they will come. Lownes rained on Morton's parade, telling the young man that the whole thing could be a real disaster, but Morton, unperturbed, turned the negative into a positive. Hence the burger stand, the Great American Disaster, was christened.

Inspired by the prime charcoaled burgers of LA's Hamburger Hamlets, which were then America's most upscale coffee shops, Morton mobilized family support to start the first American hamburger restaurant in Europe, on London's burgeoningly trendy Fulham Road. The decor of the Great American Disaster was blown-up front pages of newspapers chronicling such tragedies as the Chicago fire, the San Francisco earthquake, the Wall Street crash, the Hindenburg disaster, Pearl Harbor, and such. The star was the burger, the likes of which London had never tasted, and a buzz began that spread all over Europe. Morton had caught two perfect waves here: the rise of Swinging London and the advent of baby-boomer foreign travel, both of which converged at the Disaster. Two years later, he and Isaac Tigrett, a rich Tennesseean dabbling abroad, married the quality burger concept with cool music and opened the first Hard Rock Cafe in a former car showroom on Piccadilly near Hyde Park Corner. It was a vast success.

Just as Wolfgang Puck wanted to be taken seriously as a chef, Peter Morton wanted more than being the world's burger king. So he went upscale, opening the elegant dining club Mortons on Berkeley Square. He married a very social British top model, Pauline Stone, the widow of actor Laurence Harvey, and thereby got connected to London's beau monde, the Annabel's crowd, as well as the film colony, all elements that can make a restaurant a hot spot. Mortons was as hot as anything in the city. But Peter Morton got homesick, and he transported the concept to West Hollywood in 1979. Just as Hollywood was loving Ma Maison as La Tour d'Argent West, even though it wasn't, it immediately embraced the new Mortons as another sophisticated European transplant, even though this transplant was as meat-and-potatoes all-American as nearby Lawry's Prime Rib, which itself began as a total knockoff of London's famed Simpson's-in-the-Strand. *Plus ça change* . . . Further inspiration came from the open kitchen of the Guinea Grill, the then famous steak house off Berkeley Square. Mortons became the first LA restaurant to let its hair down and show the stars who and what was cooking. Whatever young Peter Morton did seemed to work, and brilliantly. He had a mystique as a restaurant Midas, and that mystique became a self-fulfilling prophecy of success.

While Ma Maison was selling Euro sophistication, Mortons was selling expensive comfort. This was club food, and show business is nothing if not the most exclusive club. A perfect match was made. Monday nights at Mortons became an institution, with virtually every studio head in town in rapt attendance. The deal that created the late DreamWorks among Spielberg, Katzenberg, and Geffen was sealed at Mortons. The wake for Don Simpson, the bad boy megaproducer of *Top Gun* and *Beverly Hills Cop*, was held here.

Meanwhile, those preppy waiters who were among the most articulate in the city weren't just actors doing an Ivy League impersonation. Many were actual Ivy Leaguers, lured to the job by the six-figure paydays (not hay in the 1980s) that the press was reporting Mortons's waiters were taking home. Hollywood has some of the world's biggest tippers. In the early 1990s, Peter Morton moved his restaurant across the street into the space vacated by the once hip Trumps. The room was bigger, quieter . . . clubbier. There were towering palms, a giant Francis Bacon, an Ed Ruscha, a Julian Schnabel, all from Morton's art collection and long, long bar with some of the best drinks in Los Angeles.

Even with the huge buzz created by the *Vanity Fair* party, Peter Morton was ready to fry bigger fish than the swordfish on the menu. He put his twin sister, Pamela, in charge, sold his stake in the Hard Rock Cafes for nearly half a billion dollars, and turned his sights to his new hotel and casino in Las Vegas. Once again, he was ahead of a curve that would prove to be a magic rainbow leading to still another pot of gold. Don't expect to see him working the tables; he only recently began going to the *Vanity Fair* Oscar bash. Peter Morton is a genuine mogul who thinks stars are for tourists, or other stars.

But don't write Mortons off, especially on Monday. Hollywood has so few traditions that this one isn't likely to be discarded. Dine like a mogul, or mogulette. There is no gender divide here. Start with a Beefeater martini—straight up with olives—that's even better than the storied ones at Musso and Franks. Then have a Caesar salad, a prime New York steak, and a baked potato. Then pretend you have a big deal and indulge in a thick hot fudge sundae with coffee and vanilla ice cream, or the banana beignets drizzled with warm caramel sauce and crowned with whipped cream. You'll feel "big" in Hollywood, and that's the point at Mortons. And never forget to keep your high-concept idea in your back pocket. You'll never know whom you'll meet at the valet parkers. ★

Matsuhisa
Turning Japanese

BEVERLY HILLS

It's only fitting that this city of movie stars should spawn so many kitchen stars, none of whom blazes more brightly than the totally self-effacing Nobu Matsuhisa. Spago may be the most famous restaurant in the city, but Nobu may be the most famous chef on earth. No chef's name, short of McDonald, has a higher global recognition. Nobu has restaurants everywhere: New York, Aspen, Miami, London, Milan, Melbourne, the Bahamas, Mykonos, St. Moritz. And whatever the hot spot, Nobu is invariably the hottest restaurant there. Perhaps he is proudest of his success in his hometown of Tokyo, for selling sushi to the Japanese is like carrying coals to Newcastle. He's won *Michelin* stars in London, and lots of *New York Times* stars in Manhattan. But what lures the crowds in isn't so much the critical stars as the Hollywood ones. They follow Nobu like cultists wherever they may be shooting, or flogging, a film. The press invariably takes note, the paparazzi start shooting, the tabloids run the pictures, and the snowball of publicity turns into a perpetual avalanche. Everybody goes to Nobu. Where else is there?

It all started in 1987 here on La Cienega on tacky Restaurant Row, up from Benihana and the Stinking Rose. The mother ship is the least imposing spot in the entire Nobu empire. There's no David Rockwell interior, no flash, no glitz. There's a sushi bar, a little tempura bar, and a cramped table space between. Any noodle shop in a Little Tokyo strip mall has more ambience. But does it have Tom and Nicole, and Brad and Jen—all at separate stations, of course. Or Cameron and Drew, or Matt and Ben? Or Michael D and Catherine Z? They're all here, and they're in London, too, and Aspen and Mykonos. This is the millennial jet set, and Nobu has accommodated them by creating safe harbors for them wherever they may be. But LA is home, and Matsuhisa, as Nobu is called here, is most charitably called homey. The only decorative flourishes are lovingly autographed blockbuster posters and the silhouettes of chopstick-wielding diners painted on the plain walls.

For all its absence of panache, Matsuhisa is still the sexiest restaurant in Los Angeles, the eroticism enhanced by the cheek-to-cheek crampedness of the place. All those cheeks are chic indeed, lean and elegant, whether by God, Doctor Ray, or the Nobu diet. Matsuhisa's food—the impeccable multihued, gleaming raw fish, much of it flown in from Japan, as are the intense masters who slice and dice it—is considered an aphrodisiac. No restaurant in this city has more beautiful creatures—on the plates, at the tables, or at the sushi bar, where the biz's hottest agents and producers are trying to seduce the hottest new faces, into bed and into deals, and at the same time make time with the hottie sitting beside them. Thou shalt not steal thy neighbor's client is a Hollywood commandment honored only in the breach at Matsuhisa. Everyone is hustling, flirting, eating, drinking, spending. It's a whirlwind, a maelstrom, and it's great fun. For once in torpid LA, you feel totally wired, totally alive, as the movie business at its best—and worst—can do for you. The result is that this otherwise dead room is supercharged with the sexual energy you would expect, but rarely get, in usually strictly business planet Hollywood.

Below those silhouettes on Matsuhisa's walls are expensive platters of the highly original Japanese-Peruvian fare that made Nobu the Mikado of fusion. His genius was to take the delicate but demandingly subtle fare of Japan and kick it up, Emeril-style, with peppers, chili, and garlic (bam), and French it up, Puck-style, with butter and cream (yum). The result is a new cuisine that's much more accessible than classical, solemn, serious Japanese, and much more fun to eat. Decades before, Rocky Aoki pulled a similar trick by fusing the American steak house with Kabuki theater, and Benihana down the block is still packing them in, albeit not Harrison and Calista. Nobu's food is pure Hollywood, exalted yet entertaining, a blockbuster on a plate.

Nobu's beginnings are pure Hollywood, too, in a heartfelt *Rocky*-underdog-becomes-a-champ way. All Nobu Matsuhisa ever wanted to be, as a boy growing up in Tokyo, was a sushi chef. He had done a long apprenticeship and was working at a sushi shop in Shinjuku when one of his customers, an import-export guy, lured him to Lima with sugarplum visions of cornering a market in a city that had lots of Japanese, including the future President Fujimori, but only four or five Japanese restaurants. At the time, Peru had an economy that seemed about to break out, and a long Pacific shoreline full of wonderful fish. So Nobu took his wife and embarked for this brave new world, to partner with his client at Matsui, named in honor of the Tokyo sushi shop where they had met.

Originally intending to do in Lima precisely what he had done in Tokyo, Nobu quickly came under the spell of the local *comida china*. There was a huge Chinese population in Lima, descendants of coolies brought over to build a railroad over the Andes that ran out of steam and was never completed. Still, Lima was full of striking Chinese restaurants built as pagodas and palaces straight out of the Forbidden City in Beijing. But the Chinese food in Lima barely tasted Chinese at all, for with the local cilantro, chili, and oils, it had evolved into something uniquely local. Nobu was impressed, and radical food combinations began to seep into his classical mind. "I got a lot of ideas," Nobu reminisces, with an almost naughty grin.

The Lima economy turned out to be less booming than expected, and Nobu decamped for Buenos Aires for three years. Alas, the Portenos were such rabidly confirmed carnivores that sushi, even spiced-up sushi, didn't stand a chance. (It would probably work today, now that BA has gone so trendy.) So it was back to Tokyo for a year. However, the entrepreneur bug had bitten, and Nobu could not remove the stinger. Next stop was Anchorage, Alaska, which Nobu had gotten to know because he'd had layovers there on so many of his flights home. The pipeline still meant big business, and there were lots of fish in those pristine Alaskan seas. So Nobu tried his hand there, opening a sushi

315

place on Thanksgiving Day. Fifty days later, in the dead of winter, it burned to the ground. Nobu had no fire insurance. He was ruined, and he considered seppuku, the honorable way out of a life with no foreseeable future. Then he considered his wife and young daughter, and decided—to quote Dorothy Parker—you might as well live.

Unable to face the shame of failure in Japan, Nobu chose the world's last-chance saloon, the capital of reinvention, Los Angeles. He had one friend, a sushi man at the Imperial Gardens on Sunset, which had once housed Preston Sturges's Players Club. He lived in a tiny apartment on Sawtelle Boulevard, where a large Japanese colony had grown up around the many plant nurseries there. He was horrified by the racism, which he had not encountered in South America. People called him, "Hey, Jap." But he persevered.

After a series of counter jobs, he wound up at a little sushi place called O-Sho, across from Cedars-Sinai, the hospital of the stars, and worked there for seven years in the late 1970s and early 1980s. Sushi was just catching on, and there could be long lines at the thirty-seat restaurant. Despite the many celebrities across the street, "Stars didn't wait in line," Nobu recalls. The only one who did was Linda Evans, and that was before her *Dynasty* hegemony. They became friends.

In 1987, the owners of O-Sho put the building up for sale. Nobu had nightmares of being out of a job, of having to go back to Anchorage. Going back to Anchorage was his bête noire, a recurrent nightmare that woke him up in a cold sweat and still haunts him to this day, he admits. When he saw a FOR LEASE sign on what had been a little pita and souvlaki joint on La Cienega, Nobu jumped at it. He threw together a sushi counter and brought in two friends from O-Sho to work it with him. He claims he invented tuna tartare there, not to mention his black cod with sweet miso sauce, the classic that caused Robert De Niro to christen Nobu "the Codfather." He put together a thick notebook of fusion dishes, the best of which remains halibut cheeks in creamy spicy sauce, a concoction that combines wasabi, cream, oil, batter, and garlic into an irresistible explosion of flavors that takes fried fish to another level, if not galaxy. The fried rock shrimp in a similar creamy-spicy concoction is the fallback for those who aren't feeling cheeky. Whichever plate you choose, grease is the word!

The faithful Linda Evans was Nobu's first star customer, and she brought in lots of other televison stars, and a chain letter of hungry celebrities was launched, aided by foodie-producer Jay Weston *(Lady Sings the Blues)*, who had, and still has, his own restaurant newsletter with a big Hollywood subscriber list. The most fortuitous link in this chain was De Niro, who was brought in by his *The Mission* director, foodie Englishman Roland Joffé. De Niro, who was getting into the restaurant business at the Tribeca Grill, wanted to get into it some more, and he begged Nobu to take one of his spaces in downtown Manhattan. But Nobu was still on shaky ground and refused. It took four years of courtship by De Niro to win Nobu's brilliant hand. Meanwhile, he had become a star in LA and had begun taking that star on the road. He became friends with his clients, got cameo roles with De Niro in *Casino* and with Mike Myers in *Austin Powers*. He became partners with Giorgio Armani in Milan and got a heartfelt letter from Bill Clinton when his mother passed away. Nobu's proudest moment, though, may have been on the publication of his first cookbook, when the governor of Alaska sent Nobu an autographed picture of a giant salmon. "Please come back and try again," the governor wrote on the photo.

In addition to his La Cienega flagship, the crew cut, sporty Nobu also has Nobu Malibu, a deceptively casual outpost, again unlike his New York and other extravaganzas. But because it has the best food by far in Malibu, and because so many stars live there, it is packed with the most glamorous neighborhood crowd anywhere: Barbra Streisand, Pierce Brosnan, Kelsey Grammer, Dustin Hoffman. If they're at the beach, they're at Nobu. There are also far fewer tourists than at La Cienega, and because Nobu runs the tightest navy in fooddom, the food is pretty much identical at each. Do note that sushi purists might do better at Matsuhisa, where wannabe Nobus from the greatest sushi temples in Tokyo, like Kyubey in the Ginza, come to do their American apprenticeships. Wherever, don't miss the exotic fruit sorbets, especially the lychee, which brilliantly evoke Nobu's tropical years south of the equator. And whatever you do, don't mention Anchorage. ★ ★ ★ ★ ★ ★ ★

The Food Pack

"Mike Ovitz was my best customer," Nobu Matsuhisa says reverentially of the former superagent who introduced Tom Cruise, Dustin Hoffman, Goldie Hawn, and a host of his other CAA clients to Nobu's unique Latino-Japanese fusion dishes. The celebrity of these celebrities was what made Nobu himself a celebrity. Thus he doesn't hold it against Ovitz for going from customer to competitor: Ovitz loved sushi so much he now has his own sushi palace, Hamasaku, in Westwood. It was designed by the ultimate celebrity architect, Frank Gehry, who eats there all the time, thus attracting even more celebrities, until such a critical mass is reached that one day Ovitz might give Nobu a run for his monkfish.

Such is the nature of celebrity dining here in its Fertile Crescent. Stars can make a place, and stars can own a place, but the latter doesn't guarantee the former. For every De Niro, who exported Nobu to New York and into restaurant history, witness the troubles of Kevin Costner's Twin Palms or J Lo's Madre's in Pasadena. But, hey, what stars go to Pasadena? What were they thinking? Still, nothing sells a restaurant in LA, or anywhere, like a major Hollywood clientele, and there are certain Hollywood foodies whose restaurantitis is highly contagious. Although Hollywood people tend not to read restaurant reviews, or any newspapers for that matter, unless their pictures are on display, they do read the "trades." The *Hollywood Reporter,* whose founder Billy Wilkerson was a driving force behind the rise of "star" restaurants, for decades had a column by George Christy called "The Great Life" that chronicled where and what the stars ate. Christy, more than anyone else, "made" the Ivy and Giorgio, among others. But wanting to be more journalistic and objective, today's *Reporter* has discontinued the Christy column, which now appears in the private restaurant newsletter of producer Jay Weston. Now where the stars go is mostly by word-of-mouth.

Who, then, are Hollywood's "food pack"? A lot of the members of this hungry tribe have restaurants either in their blood or in their pasts. Take Steven Spielberg, whose mother, Leah Adler, owns the kosher Milky Way dairy restaurant on Pico Boulevard. Or Michael Caine, who owned London's once superhot Langan's Brasserie. Or Clint Eastwood, who still owns the Hog's Breath Inn in Carmel. Or Arnold Schwarzenegger, with his schnitzelry Schatzi in Venice, which he still owns but is run by a fellow Austrian. Schatzi is one of the Terminator's rare non-smash-successes. How, he must wonder, did his landsman Wolfgang Puck hit it so big? Blame it on the pizza. And Planet Hollywood was a stunt, not a passion. In any event, the Governator, Mister *ET*, Alfie, and Dirty Harry are all among the town's most avid restaurantgoers, creating a buzz that has a seismic ripple effect on the mortal foodie public.

Of course, you don't need a restaurant pedigree to be in the food pack. Nor do you have to be a star, as long as you're a huge enough cog in the star-making machinery. Like directors Rob Reiner *(A Few Good Men),* Harold Becker *(Sea of Love),* Mel Brooks, and Oliver Stone (you know). What they all have in common was growing up in the restaurant culture of New York City, where small kitchens and natural curiosity created a kind of territorial imperative that made Yankees quest for the next great place. Take Alan Grubman, the Brooklyn-born multicoastal king of the entertainment bar (Rod Stewart, David Geffen, Keith Richards, P. Diddy, Madonna, Graydon Carter, Martha Stewart). Grubman loves to eat out and loves to talk about it. His big mouth and big appetite have recently made the old warhorse Lawry's Prime Rib a go-to place here in veganland.

The money men—studio owners, studio heads, producers—all may be busy, but not too busy to eat. Of all the conglomerateurs, none seems hungrier for food in high places than Sumner Redstone, who has replaced the late Marvin Davis as the mogul most likely to be seen. And no studio head since Michael Eisner has been seen in more high-profile restaurants than Redstone's new chief at Paramount, Brad Grey, who is equally high-profile in Santa Monica's Palisades Park, jogging off all those Dan Tana and Ivy fat (cat) calories. But the most ravenous producer award surely goes to *A Beautiful Mind*'s ultralite Brian Grazer, who, as legend goes, can do three power lunches a day. After all, Mr Chow, Spago, and the agent-intensive The Grill are only a few Beverly Hills blocks apart.

Even writers can get into the influence act, like Robert Towne *(Chinatown),* who is from San Pedro but has a gourmette French wife. *C-town*'s director,

Roman Polanski, is the foodie king of Paris, along with Christopher Lambert of *Highlander* and *Greystoke* (also Towne), while Diane Lane, ex of Lambert, is one actress who eats out everywhere. So does Gwyneth Paltrow (New York roots again). And Paris Hilton (where *does* she put it all?). Other powerful writer-foodies are Steven Bochco and his *L.A. Law* spawn David Kelley, whose attendance at any table with wife, Michelle Pfeiffer, will make the night of any paparazzo or starstruck foodie.

Finally, no one has more authority to validate a place than the star restaurateurs themselves. Chefs Puck and Nobu work so hard that they're never sighted anywhere but their home places. But, conversely, neither Michael Chow nor Peter Morton, owners not chefs both, are ever sighted *chez* themselves. It doesn't hurt Mr Chow or Mortons, but it has done wonders for the Italian places these two highly fussy chowcoons love to discover and anoint. If these guys think a place is good, it's good. After all, who, even in the gratitude-free zone of Hollywood, would dare to bite, or to doubt, the hands that feed them? ★ ★ ★ ★ ★ ★ ★ ★ ★ ★ ★ ★

Mr Chow
The Last Emperor

If Nobu Matsuhisa is Japan's gift to the world of celebrity dining, his Chinese counterpart and predecessor—in fact the true progenitor of the field—is Michael Chow, whose Mr Chow in Beverly Hills is currently enjoying a renaissance as the very hottest restaurant in this city of heat. It's even hotter than Nobu Malibu, hotter than Toscana, and that's saying something. Especially since five years ago, Mr Chow was pretty much dead, a deco morgue. It opened in 1974 along with Ma Maison and had enjoyed a long run at the peak of the Los Angeles dining renaissance. But long runs are made to end, and Mr Chow was merely obeying the cruel law of nature that anything so hot *had* to get cold.

But soon after 2000 Mr Chow broke that law, plus the edict that there are no second acts in American life, particularly in Hollywood, whether you were a star actor or a star restaurant. Mr Chow made a comeback. Hey, John Travolta did it, and Joan Collins, and Candice Bergen, so why shouldn't Mr Chow defy the Tinseltown rule of once down, always out? But it was like defying gravity. The Brown Derby, Chasen's, the Bistro, even Ma Maison had all attempted comebacks and had failed ignominiously. Mr Chow beat long odds, and it did it with the aid of hip-hop. Hip-hop? Yes, the black record crowd—Sean (Whatever) Combs, L.L. Cool J, and the like, with their love of bling and unabashed luxury—took a shine to Mr Chow and its big-bucks bill of fare. Bicoastal as they were, they made the Bev Hills and Manhattan Chows their clubhouses. Once the hip-hoppers had anointed Chow as hip, Young Hollywood, which adores rap, came rapping at the doors. And once Young Hollywood came in, Old Hollywood, which wants nothing more than to be young again (*pace*, Doctor 90210), wanted back in as well. A star was reborn.

To arrive at Mr Chow at night is to see Beverly Hills come to life. This sunlit shoppers' paradise is the Dead Zone at night, except here on Camden Drive, where there are more paparazzi camped out than at a Tom Cruise film premiere, and more leg on display than in a Hanes panty hose commercial. This is one of the few places in Los Angeles where everybody dresses up like New York, so look your best. Not that it will matter. There's total bedlam as the bulbs flash, and the camera stalkers scream out "Paris!" "Lindsay!" "Jessica!" You feel even more out of it when you enter the black-and-white deco inner sanctum and are crushed into a tiny bar and splashed with lychee martinis and Cosmopolitans as angry agents and their dolled-up clients wave their arms like eager students with the right answer and scream "Chris" as loudly as the paparazzi were screaming "Paris" outside. Chris is the cool, wiry, Pete Townsend–ish Brit maître d' who is the gatekeeper of Michael Chow's Kingdom of Heaven. He promises he'll do what he can. It's a big lie.

The reason your reservation will rarely be honored here, and that you'll probably wait an hour or more and get very drunk, is that the stars are all in the seats you want, and Chris will never ask a star to get up. So look at them, marvel, stare. The show is free: Stevie Wonder and Eminem; Jay-Z and Beyoncé; the Hiltons and the Olsens and the Duffs and the Simpsons, all proof of how powerful sisterhood really is; as well as legends like Edie Wasserman, widow of Lew, who ran MCA, and Barbara Davis, widow of Marvin, plus generations of star families like Goldie Hawn and Kate Hudson, Blythe Danner and Gwyneth Paltrow, Lionel and Nicole Richie, Quincy and Kidada and Rashida Jones. They're all up against the power wall, on the left, just past the bar area, very reminiscent of Spago's Murderers' Row in the 1980s, and, because the world has changed, far more of an ethnic stew.

The celebs all eat what Chowers have been eating since Swinging London in the 1960s. The menu has not really changed, only the prices. The noodle master in the kitchen comes out every hour and puts on a Benihana show slinging, stretching, and noodling. The noodles come with a chickeny bolognese sauce, plus cucumbers, and are an homage to the fusion that was Marco Polo. The *har gow,* or shrimp dim sum, have become a cliché by now. But here clichés are classics, so order them. Then there are the "secret ingredient *gambei,*" a crispy, deep-fried mystery green that deeply denies being the shredded kale it looks like. And the pièce de résistance, the Peking duck. Or the crispy fried Gambler's duck, with even more fanfare. Don't forget that the stars like fanfare, and Mr Chow lays it on thick. Other celeb faves are the crispy orange beef, the chicken with walnuts, and the garlic-ginger lobster. There are enormously expensive champagnes and fine wines that everyone orders, and desserts flown in from confectioner Bindi in Milan. Marco Polo again.

Like Peter Morton, Michael Chow rarely visits his eponymous pleasure domes. He's too busy with his varied enterprises. He designed the Beverly Hills Giorgio Armani store, and many others call on him for his great eye. In his midsixties, he's timelessly chic, in Italian driving moccasins, jeans, black T-shirt, and big round Philip Johnson eyeglasses. "They give me instant recognition," he says. As if he needs it. He has a new outpost in Tribeca and is planning more in Miami and Vegas (who isn't, these days?). If you've got a name, exploit it. Chow is following Nobu into Morton's (recently sold) Hard Rock Hotel. Talk about Murderers' Row. What a lineup, and all LA.

For all its famous restaurateurs, "LA has no food culture," Michael Chow laments. "It has a movie culture, a house culture, car culture, but there is no passion about dining out." He estimates that there is a pool of only about fifteen thousand "serious" diners in the entire LA area who will support "serious" restaurants, a tiny fraction of the foodie pool in New York City. Small wonder that so few investors are willing to come up with the two million that Chow estimates is necessary for a start-up restaurant gamble. London, on the other hand, where the same start-up Chow estimate is four to six million, has money men lining up to roll the dice. "London has a great restaurant culture," Chow says. He should know; he helped create it.

"London in the 1960s was very much like LA," he recalls. "A lot of what made London swinging then were the Americans making movies there because it was so cheap," he says with a nostalgic laugh. London cheap? Ancient history. But it was. And for $50,000, the would-be actor, son of a Beijing Opera star, gutted a Knightsbridge hairdressing salon, installed a fire-house-style circular stairwell to showcase the area's miniskirted "birds," and began dishing up the most sophisticated Beijing fare ever served in the culinary wasteland of Wimpy Bars and Lyons Carveries that Peter Morton later mined with his prime burgers. Lured to LA by music mogul Jerry Moss (the *M* in A&M Records), who loved the London Chow so much that he invested half a million dollars to re-create it, Chow went on to open his New York branch in 1979. But he has remained in LA, despite its decried lack of sophistication. "The movies I loved, Billy Wilder, Fritz Lang, they were sophisticated. LA is provincial," he says, then adds, "if I'm living here, LA can't be *that* bad."

Today, more than ever, Mr Chow is a brand. "There are only four real restaurant brand names," he says immodestly. "Mr Chow, Nobu, Harry's Bar, and Jean Georges. They're all high end. They have the same clientele of VIPs." Chow then outlines his four requirements to become a brand: First, a high-low culture, which is appealing to an influential and admired focus group, like movie stars or artists. Second, being user-friendly, meaning the food must not be too complicated or intimidating, like Alain Ducasse. Third, a price point that is expensive enough to be exclusive, but not ridiculously so, again like Alain Ducasse. And, fourth, casual chic. "I was born to be a party giver," Chow declares, in his boy-can't-help-it mode. "Creative glamour is simply part of me." ★

Ago
The Ago-ny and the Ecstasy

If any restaurant fits Michael Chow's formula for joining the pantheon of
brands, Ago is it. Aside from the original on Melrose, just west of the old
Ma Maison, the Ago in Miami is the *re* of South Beach. There are plans for
Manhattan and for Vegas. And with backers like Robert De Niro, Harvey
Weinstein, and director Ridley Scott *(Gladiator)*, the juggernaut seems unstop-
pable. Ago is a casual, minimal-decor West Hollywood restaurant jammed
with movie stars, studio heads, and superagents, featuring a wood-burning
pizza oven, an open kitchen, and a parking lot jammed with Bentleys and
Ferraris. So you might think the place was simply the old Spago, drop the
Sp. But Spago was a serious French restaurant that happened to serve highly
inauthentic pizzas that acquired an authenticity of their own as the new food
form known as California pizza. Ago, quite the contrary, is a full-fledged
Italian restaurant serving highly authentic pizza, as well as everything else on
its Tuscan menu. Only the stars are the same.

Ago is Ago, or Agostino Sciandri, the Italian chef who is the longest
running act in a city that twenty years ago didn't know rapini from Fellini.
How Italy displaced France in the appetite of Hollywood is indicative of the
seismic shift in dining that transformed LA in the 1980s from Palookaville to
Firenze Novella. The unlikely apostle of the Tuscan gospel was a restaurateur

named Bruno Vietina who owned Maito, the primo *ristorante* in the primo beach resort of Forte dei Marmi, near Lucca. The richest Milanese—the Agnellis, the titled and monied—all vacationed there, at private beach clubs. At night they all went out to restaurants; Forte is consequently considered one of the most sophisticated food towns in Europe, and Vietina was at the top of the chain.

When Vietina visited LA at the height of Ma Maison, he had a Peter Morton moment. He figured that if Patrick Terrail could make a fortune selling *rillettes* and *canard* in a garden shed, why couldn't he, Vietina, do the same with pasta and *vitello*. Accordingly, Vietina found a shed on a dead residential street of Beverly Hills. Imitating Ma Maison to the max, he covered its floor with AstroTurf and fitted it out with the cheapest, clunkiest wrought-iron garden furniture. Fittingly enough, he named his shed Il Giardino.

Vietina then found his own Puck in Sciandri, who was raised on a farm and had a true feel for rustic cooking. He also had a top culinary education, having graduated from two of Italy's hotel schools, one in the north at Bellagio, the other on the Adriatic in Rimini. Sciandri thus knew a wide range of Italian specialties. Plus he spoke perfect English (Vietina spoke none), having spent ten years in Albion, gaining spit and polish at the Savoy and marrying a half-Italian, half-English girl from Derby. Sciandri was the ideal chef for the LA experiment, and, as he says, "I was ready for an adventure." He arrived in 1985.

Il Giardino took off immediately, aided immeasurably by what might be called "the oat bran crisis." The early 1980s saw America go cholesterol crazy. Medical researchers validated the long suspected connection between cholesterol and coronary heart disease; they also indicted saturated fat as the culprit. There were endless articles and books on good cholesterol and bad cholesterol, and the bottom line was that nothing seemed worse for you than French food, with all its red meat, organ meat, and dairy, dairy, dairy. *La vache qui rit*, or the laughing cow, all the way to the mortuary. Yes, there was the "French Paradox," which postulated that notwithstanding their deadly diet, the French lived longer than Americans because of all the red wine they drank. But Angelenos couldn't really test this hypothesis for fear of losing their driver's licenses. In LA no car, no life.

The easier way out—aside from mainlining oat bran, the "cereal killer" of bad cholesterol, which reigned for several years as a panacea—was to embrace the Mediterranean Diet. LA, unlike New York, had very few Greek restaurants, and almost zero Spaniards in the works. California Cuisine *sounded* healthy but was indicted by the new diet police for its major dairy content. Thus in LA the Med Diet meant one thing: get thee to a trattoria. Bruno Vietina's was the first and best of what would become a thundering multitude.

Il Giardino greeted its guests with an enticing *antipasto vegetali*, in effect a Lucullan salad bar, a cornucopia of marinated and grilled vegetables like you see everywhere in Italy but, oddly enough, never before in the farmers' paradise of Southern California. Then there were the olive-oil-based pastas, the *spaghetti alle vongole*, or the *penne arrabbiata*, penne from heaven, indeed, if you wanted to get there. And then there was the *branzino*, flown in from the Med itself, grilled on the fire, slicked with olive oil and herbs, served with olive-oil-sautéed spinach that would make a Popeye out of you, and succulent olive-oil-and-rosemary roast potatoes that would make you happy. Who could ever look at a fish in cream sauce again, even if Wolfgang Puck was making it? The end was homemade *sorbetto al limone*. To this day, this remains the standard Italian LA meal in LA, whether at Toscana, Ago, Giorgio, or their countless imitators. It always works. You left having no saturated fat and feeling very virtuous, plus you knew you were in good company, for you had seen every star in the world having what you were having.

In addition to Agostino Sciandri, with his instant success, Vietina brought over a host of other Italian cooks and waiters to give his celebrity clientele a totally authentic *dolce vita* dining experience. This merry band of Bruno's Apostles would go on to become LA's Italian restaurant mafia, minus any gangland tactics. They got their way with truffles, not bullets. Because sheds last only so long in Beverly Hills, the lease on Il Giardino was sold to an office park developer. But by then Vietina was off and running, with spin-offs such as Madeo, Maito, and Principe, while the cooks and waiters were spinning off on their own, Giorgio, Drago, Il Cielo.

Agostino Sciandri had an initially rocky road. He opened Rosso e Nero on Melrose Avenue only to see what had promised to become LA's King's Road devolve into its Brixton. He went on to cook at Chicco, an offbeat eight-table location in a little motel that had once housed LA's most exclusive breakfast hangout, a woody, boozy Irish pub called Sculley's, run by a chef from Chasen's. But the head waiter of Chicco got involved with the *real* Mafia, and the place collapsed. And then came Doc. Doc Severinsen, Johnny Carson's bandleader, had loved Il Giardino so much that he wanted one of his own. Doc talked to Bruno Vietina, who was game. Bruno couldn't miss at this point. He was an Italian Midas. Doc found a vacant pharmacy in then restaurant-challenged Brentwood, and got his accountant, Michael Gordon, involved. The pharmacy owner wasn't interested. He wanted to put a Penguin's frozen yogurt outlet on the spot. A trattoria in Brentwood sounded like a mad folly. This was Hamburger Hamlet territory, not the Via Veneto, for chrissake.

But the accountant Gordon persisted. He rounded up hungry neighbors like Michael Eisner and Richard Dreyfuss as investors, and in 1989, he opened shop. Bruno sent Ago to be the chef. A year later, Il Giardino's star waiter to the stars, Alberto, came aboard. The pharmacist ate his hat. Eventually, Bruno Vietina reached too far. He had Madeos in Beverly Hills, Santa Monica, San Pedro, even Manhattan. Plus he loved to gamble, and not just on restaurants. Recessions, fires, O. J. Simpson, and a major earthquake nearly killed Los Angeles. Its restaurant boom became a bust and is just starting to recover. Bruno Vietina folded most of his places and went back to Forte dei Marmi.

Toscana was recession-proof, but not ego-proof. A huge success results in multiple paternity claims, and to prove that he alone "made" Toscana, in 1997 Sciandri left his Brentwood redoubt and threw in his lot with De Niro, Weinstein, and Scott to start a new place. As if to flex his ego with an Iron Chef challenge, Sciandri picked the deadest location he could find, a former

All American Burger stand on Melrose that had been the graveyard of multiple celeb-backed eateries that had bitten the (star)dust there. It was pretty much a garden shed itself, with exposed pipes and zero decor. The lack of any soundproofing made it even more deafening than Toscana. That is, if anyone bothered to show up. Even with Weinstein and all his talent in frequent attendance, Ago didn't get off the ground for over two years.

What may have been the secret of Ago's success was not its Tuscan delicacies nor the patronage of all of Hollywood's "Big Os"— De Niro, DeVito, Pacino, Aiello, Tarantino, et alio—but rather the city's smoking ban. Unlike Toscana, Ago had a huge outdoor terrace, which became the smokers' patio. It was next to the parking lot, with its attendant fumes, but Ferrari exhaust is like perfume in these climes, and besides, these were smokers. These same folks wouldn't touch a creamy *steak au poivre*. They were at Ago to be healthy, right? How did smoking fit in? It didn't, but it was cool. For all its health-club attendance and personal trainers, most of Young Hollywood smoked. Healthy was cool, smoking was cool, Ago was cool. As Emerson said, a foolish consistency is the hobgoblin of little minds. Out of nowhere, Ago's patio was the coolest place to be in the entertainment world. Agostino Sciandri was vindicated. He had a hit.

Not that Toscana became a flop. But Brentwood was a different world from West Hollywood. Brentwood was family territory, and Toscana had no bar. Ago had a long one, subway-car-packed with aspiring MAWs (model-actress-whatevers, often fancy hookers, as need be) just waiting to be discovered by the famous smokers on the patio. The presence of all this seminaked pulchritude added something that Toscana couldn't match: sin. Penne, with a side of sex, is an unbeatable combination. ★

Giorgio and Dan Tana's
The Other Italians

There are no free women, nor even available expensive ones, at Giorgio, in Santa Monica Canyon. There is no bar here, no barflies, no smokers, not even many table-hopping agents, just a lot of "family" people from the neighborhood. But oh, the families; oh, the neighborhood. Santa Monica Canyon, often known as Rustic Canyon, lives up to its name. It's so lush, foggy, and verdant you'd think you were in Marin County. But once you saw the Spielbergs, and the Stallones, and the Hankses, and the Streisands, all of whom reside in adjacent Pacific Palisades, you'd know this could only be one place, and you were there. Il Ristorante di Giorgio Baldi (the restaurant's full name) barely has fifty seats, just a dozen or so tables. None are bad. Like LA's other Italian stalwarts, Giorgio's square room has basically no decor, not even a pizza oven, and a postage-stamp open kitchen. The celebs are the decor.

Unlike Toscana and Ago, however, Giorgio doesn't feel like a party. It feels like a temple. It's serious. People who wait, and all those without Oscars usually wait, do so respectfully, out on the sidewalk, breathing the sea air off the Pacific across the road. The waiters don't kiss you. Giorgio Baldi, who barely speaks English, and is quite shy, despite his impish grin, rarely leaves the kitchen, and that creates a mystique.

The stars believe Giorgio has the best Italian food in the city, and they treat it seriously. It's certainly the richest. No cholesterol-phobe he; Giorgio doesn't stint on butter and cream. His greatest dishes are his homemade ravioli, filled with lobster and porcini and asparagus in a sauce that would make Nathan Pritikin spin in his grave. Giorgio Baldi may be Tuscan, but he cooks like a Torinese, with lots of meat, lots of truffles, lots of dairy. It's cold-weather food, which doesn't necessarily suit these palm latitudes. But the stars, normally so health-conscious, lap it up. Despite the general air of discretion here, many stars, like Tom Cruise, prefer to do their lapping in Giorgio's private dining room across the Bentley-filled parking lot.

Giorgio is a huge favorite of the English film set—Jeremy Irons, Hugh Grant, Anthony Hopkins, Madonna and Guy Ritchie, Gwyneth Paltrow (honorary Brit for her *Shakespeare* Oscar)—who love to come here and drink from Giorgio's collection of very expensive Italian wines. These post–*Loved One* cine-Brits hail from a long and only recently challenged tradition of bad food and fine drink. Even if they couldn't eat well in Blighty, they could kill the taste of the kidney pies and toads in the hole with noble clarets from across the Channel. Today in Hollywood, when the English strike it rich, they still like to booze it up, high style, and Giorgio is their gastro-trat for so doing. And it's not only the tipple that wins the heart of the Commonwealth. Tea and sympathy work wonders. One night the Pierce Brosnans showed up after the kitchen had closed, and Giorgio reopened it for them, by himself. Word got out, and that sort of buzz helped to lock Giorgio in the firmament.

Thus you wait. And once you've finished waiting and you've stumbled over a few Oscar winners trying to squeeze into your table, the waiter will usually send you a peace offering of lightly fried polenta squares covered in a scrumptious sauce of tomatoes and porcini. The porcini are a leitmotif here. You may end up getting them on everything, whether the aforementioned ravioli or the homemade *pappardelle* with olive oil and fresh Parmigiana, or a prime white veal chop. Nonporcini favorites are the *penne simplice*, made with a tomato sauce that Giorgio now bottles and sells at LA's most exclusive markets, like Vicente Foods in Brentwood, and a sublime *lasagne al pesto*, which is straight off the dock in Portofino.

"I taught Giorgio how to make pasta," Agostino Sciandri says affectionately of his former acolyte in the Il Giardino kitchen, who bravely went off on his own in the early 1990s to this tiny beach cottage and never looked back. Of course, Giorgio believes it was the other way around, that he taught Ago all the tricks. Such is the posture of Italian chefs in Los Angeles; each thinks he is the king, that he alone was the culinary Columbus who brought *la vera cucina italiana* to this hamburger heaven. Now in his late sixties, Giorgio has brought his daughter Elena, a UCLA business graduate, into the house. She, too, is polite but totally serious. The stars like to be kissed, but sometimes they like to be left alone, and this is the place for it. Aside from the pastas, don't miss the warm lobster and cannelini beans, the fritto misto, served on butcher paper, and the grilled prawns, live that day from Santa Barbara. Those Tuscan dishes, plus the homemade coffee gelato and strawberry *sorbetto*, can make you feel you're at the most exclusive beach club in Forte. In many ways, you are.

There is real Italian, like Giorgio, and fake Italian, which was all LA knew pre–Bruno Vietina, and then there is New Jersey Italian, by way of Serbia, which is Dan Tana's, next to the Troubador on the border of Beverly Hills and West Hollywood. Despite its Italian menu, its red banquettes and checked tablecloths, its hanging Chianti bottles, Dan Tana's is the steak house of the stars, LA's answer to Peter Luger. This is a man's world, all right. There's Clint Eastwood. And Sumner Redstone. And Mick Jagger. And Kobe Bryant. Kobe beef. In their glory days under Magic and Kareem, the Lakers had a training table at Tana's every Sunday night. But there's Cameron Diaz, tucking in to a New York strip. And there's Sherry Lansing, the first femme studio head, with husband William Friedkin. Girls Who Kick Ass love this place.

So did Phil ("To Know Him Is to Love Him") Spector, who went here for a Caesar salad and two glasses of wine ($50 bill, $500 tip) before he took Lana Clarkson back to his château and allegedly shot her in the head. O.J. had his last meal before Nicole's death at McDonald's; Robert Blake had his, before Bonnie Lee got shot, at Vitello's in the Valley. At least Phil showed some class for his last supper, sayeth the wags. There is a real Dan Tana, a Serb soccer fanatic, who founded this roadhouse in 1969. He was the inspiration for the unreal Dan *Tanna*, the private eye played by the late Robert Urich on the 1970s TV series *Vegas*, created by DT regular Michael Mann, who went on to give us *Miami Vice* and many films, including *Heat*, which is what DT is all about. Just because LA lacks a Social Register doesn't mean it doesn't have roots.

Aside from the prime strip steak, charred on the outside, blood rare within, there are four other great things to eat here: the very Little Italy baked clams *oreganata;* the Spector Caesar salad, garlick-y, anchovy-rich, pungent with Lea & Perrins, which may be the best anywhere; the homemade French fries, an endangered species; and the sautéed whitefish in lemon butter, call it *pesce piccata*. The mixed drinks here are potent; have a few. All this is bad for you. All this tastes great. Go outside and have a cigarette afterward with the kids waiting in line for the Next Hot Thing at the Troub, and you'll feel young and carefree again. ★ ★ ★ ★ ★ ★ ★ ★ ★ ★ ★

The Ivy
A League of Its Own

Then there is the Ivy. The scene of the tacky power lunch of John Travolta and Danny DeVito in *Get Shorty*, the Ivy on Robertson is every tourist's fantasy of the LA celebrity restaurant. A block from Kitson, the world's hippest clothing store, and adjacent to numerous high-profile car wrecks caused by paparazzi chasing teen idols in their Mercedes SUVs, the Ivy is now working on its third generation of celebrities. "We're just a neighborhood restaurant," insists Richard Irving, the baker who founded the place in 1980 with his now wife, socialite–aspiring actress–turned antiques dealer Lynn von Kersting. He said this in refusing an interview, and the Irvings, in fact, are even scarcer in their temples of fame than Peter Morton and Michael Chow are in theirs. Yet the Irvings don't seem, like Morton and Chow, to have empire on their minds. Theirs is an empire of two, the Ivy here, and Ivy at the Shore in Santa Monica. With two colossi like these, certainly among the busiest restaurants in the country outside of the Cheesecake Factory, who needs an empire? Because of the Ivy's international reputation as a commissary of the stars, the crush of tourists here is just as heavy as that at Spago. The result is nothing like Giorgio or Toscana, where everyone is famous, but more like a Knott's Berry Farm for millionaires. Here even Oprah can get overlooked in the shuffle.

The restaurant is one of the rare ones in LA—home of the set designer—to look set-designed; but then again, Lynn von Kersting is an interior designer. You feel as if you're in an antiques shop in Santa Fe, with the adobe walls and fireplaces and endless bric-a-brac. Then, again, if you're inside, you *need* to have something to look at, because, whatever the weather, the stars are outside, on the ivy-covered (what else?) terrace. Despite its alfresco-ness, nobody seems to smoke out here. It's not raffish, like the Ago terrace, but very proper, very well behaved, very salubrious. The tourists are reverent, and the stars, conscious of being observed by the fans who have somehow made the cut to this outer sanctum, are on their best behavior.

The menu is one of the most enticing anywhere, a compendium of Americana's Greatest Hits: meat loaf, fried chicken, chowders, tostadas, burgers, omelets, pastas, pizzas, totally coast to coast, trend to trend. Their Caesar salad ranks with Tana's as LA's best, and the crab cakes may be tops in America, served with a tartar sauce that people spread like butter on the hot homemade

Anadama molasses bread, a recipe from the American colonies, whose name comes from a servant and great cook named Anna and her master who said "Damn her" for leading him into temptation and making him so fat.

There is a lot of mesquite grilling, which sounds like a blast from a past that appeals to all diners. There is another retro emphasis on Cajun, and many of the Ivy's most famous dishes—the soft-shell crabs, the blackened prime rib—have intimations of K-Paul in his 1980s glory years. The mesquite swordfish and salmon are served with addictive Mexican rice, with a confetti of minced veggies, and with a creamy puree of green squash. The most classic Hollywood plate is the chopped grilled vegetable salad, topped with mesquite shrimp or chicken. A lot of the veggies are grown in the gardens of the George Cukor estate, behind whose forbidding walls the never photographed Irvings lead their exclusive lives, almost as private as director Cukor's favorite actress, Greta Garbo. Given the daily tumult in their restaurants, they want to be alone.

All the seafood is supposedly flown in daily from the Gulf, which, given the dislocations from Hurricane Katrina, may explain the grumbles that things aren't as sparkling fresh as they used to be. However, no one complains about the legendary desserts, which, given Irving's roots as a pastry chef, is understandable. The restaurant actually began its life known as LA Desserts. The signature chocolate chip cookies with macadamia nuts, and the frosted chocolate brownie "baby cakes," as *Michelin* might say, are *vaut le voyage*, worth a special trip. There is a white chocolate lemon cake, topped with raspberries, blueberries, and strawberries, that is worthy of being the Ivy's own tricolor flag. And skinny Hollywood's favorite indulgence is the Ivy's hot fudge sundae, with roasted whole almonds, vanilla and praline ice cream, and the most decadent chocolate sauce. You might not fit into Kitson down the block afterward, and the stalkerazzi may ignore you, but the Ivy pig-out is proof that stars cannot live by fame alone. ★ ★ ★ ★ ★ ★ ★ ★ ★ ★ ★

Many Are Called,
Most Are Frozen

If you think it's hard finding a good movie in Hollywood, try finding a good French fry. The major restaurants of this town—Spago, Mortons, Patina, the Grill, Capo, Michael's—all use precut, frozen spuds. It may seem like small potatoes in a world of big problems, but then again, French fries are everybody's guilty pleasure, as American as apple pie (remember freedom fries?). And if you can't get great, fresh fries in LA, it's a sign that there's something wrong in a culture that increasingly prefers the fake to the real. Or maybe it's inevitable in a town that's the apotheosis of the ersatz. After all, Hollywood is the capital of plastic surgery, and here it seems that silicone breasts have replaced natural ones as the standard of feminine beauty.

Some chefs, like Patina's Joachim Splichal, justify their freezers on the grounds that frozen potatoes fry up crisper than fresh ones, and that the end of crispness justifies any means. Even food fanatic Arthur Sarkissian's favorite fries are the rice-flour-coated "freezers" at the Polo Lounge. "They're incredibly crisp and hot. I don't care how they get there. There's nothing worse than soggy fries," the maven says.

Try telling that to Keith McNally of Balthazar in New York, whose handcut, double-blanched Belgian *pommes frites* set the tuber standard in America. Alas, it's a standard to which Hollywood restaurants seem indifferent to rising. One would think that the way Hollywood loves France, with its endless trips to the Cannes Film Festival and the couture collections, they'd know and decry the *faux frite*. Then again, it's awfully hard to find a fresh French fry in Paris these days, either. The Gauls have embraced American frozen-food technology with a gusto once reserved for Josephine Baker and Jerry Lewis.

Everybody's favorite drive-in in LA, In and Out Burger, makes a virtual fetish of its fresh potatoes. Few sit-down restaurants seem to have taken In and Out's loudly trumpeted cue, but Los Angeles does have a few classicists. The venerable Musso-Frank Grill, which does everything from an earlier era, does lots of classic potato dishes and does them right, serving the same freshly cut fries (do ask for them crisp) that they did to Faulkner and Fitzgerald on their otherwise disastrous Hollywood sojourns. The Ivy hand-cuts their fries, but they sometimes get lost in the crush and come out flaccid; Sarkissian has sent them back. The best fries in town are at Hal's, a three-decades-old (Methuselahan here) art-world hangout (Ruscha et al.) in Venice, which cuts its potatoes just thick enough to taste the tuber, then immerses them twice in good old-fashioned boiling lard, which produces a crackling fine result, albeit one that would send Doctors Pritikin and Atkins spinning in their graves. When the chips are down, this is the place to go. ★

Kate Mantilini, Fountain Coffee Shop, Nate 'n Al's
Fast and Furious

For the stars, not every meal *has* to be special. It does, however, generally have to be simple, whether Cajun or Tuscan. The lives of the stars are complicated enough; their meals should not be. Stars are rarely foodies, for whom every restaurant should be a special event. The stars are their own event, and their restaurants should be there to either further their glory or make them happy. That's why places from the Brown Derby to the Ivy have focused on comfort food for the stars. They sometimes want this comfort food without the fanfare, but it's become a real challenge. LA, the world capital of the car, used to have a magnificent counterculture of drive-ins with roller-skating curb girls, Googie-style coffee shops, diners that looked like flying saucers. But these should-have-been landmarks are all gone, victims of predatory developers. The one survivor, or rather inheritor, of the stylish fast-food tradition is Kate Mantilini, a diner right between the grand private theaters of the Motion Picture Academy and the Writers' Guild, and it is as good a place as any to see stars and other players grabbing some comfort food on their way to an industry screening.

But what diner has comfort food that includes raw oysters, Dover sole, lobster bisque, and cherries jubilee? And what diner was designed by a winner of the Pritzker Prize, the Oscar of architecture? Thom Mayne conjured up the industrial-deco Kate Mantilini in 1987, long before he was in the league of Frank Gehry (who himself designed Hamasaku, Mike Ovitz's sushi bar in Westwood). But an even more important pedigree element than the designer's is that of the owners, Harry and Marilyn Lewis, who created the Hamburger Hamlet. That chain of glam coffee shops, which the Lewises sold for $33 million and celebrated by building KM, influenced not only Peter Morton, but basically created the entire celebrity comfort-chic dining ethos that lay the red carpet for Spago and the Ivy. Ronald Reagan, Sammy Davis Jr., Dean Martin, Cary Grant, and Warren Beatty were all Hamlet regulars.

Harry Lewis was a failed actor; modelly Marilyn, with her trademark orange hair, went on to create her own successful fashion line Cardinali. Their inspiration for the Hamlet was a burger palace in Cleveland, whence Marilyn hailed. The Lewises' inspiration was to top the charred meat burgers with exotic local ingredients, sort of what Puck did with his designer pizzas. The burgers at Kate Mantilini's, if you can persuade the counterman to get the grill cook to do them rare (lots of E. coli lawyers in LA), are among the best in this city that burgers helped build. That you may be sandwiched between Leonardo DiCaprio and Jodie Foster can only make them taste better. They used to have brains on the menu, if only for Billy Wilder, the only person in town who didn't have to wait in line. The young agents who run the town may not have remembered him, but the Lewises did. To them he was still big. The pictures had gotten small. When he died, the brains went.

On the subject of deluxe fast food, the best 1950s breakfast in the best 1950s atmosphere can be found at the serpentine counter of the Fountain Coffee Shop, downstairs at the Beverly Hills Hotel, where you can luxuriate with juices squeezed *sur commande,* sublime eggs, and towers of fluffy pancakes and crusty homemade hash browns in an atmosphere of the hotel's green-and-white banana leaf wallpaper. On any given day you can see stars lining up, with casually chic multimillionaire neighborhood types waiting ravenously for a coveted seat at the counter. The industry's power breakfast used to be upstairs at the Polo Lounge, but cell phones have made the rite of passage of being paged at the Polo obsolete.

The Polo Lounge still packs them in, particularly for its Neal McCarthy salad, which is the hotel's version of the Brown Derby's Cobb and is beloved by the Schwarzenegger-Shriver clan. But ever since the Pink Palace, as it is known, was sold to the Sultan of Brunei, it has become much less the Bev Hills clubhouse that it was when Darryl Zanuck, Howard Hawks, and their sporting friends used to hitch their horses outside and drop in for post-polo-match benders. Now the hotel, and the Polo Lounge, are big-deal, big-money legends. But in the little coffee shop, the neighborhood folks still drop in to perpetuate the tradition. Because the neighborhood is 90210, these folks are pure *Lifestyles of the Rich and Famous,* and that lifestyle begins with the sweet OJ at this counter.

Finally, completing this triumvirate of fast and famous, there is Nate 'n Al's, Beverly Hills's deli to the stars. Remember the award-winning Levy's Rye Bread ads from the 1950s and 1960s, showing Indians in saris, Englishmen in bowlers, Chinese courtesans in cheongsams, Irish policemen in blue, and other unlikely types, all taking a bite of a slice of rye, with the tag line "You Don't Have to Be Jewish to Love Levy's"? Well, that's Nate 'n Al's, which has fed bagels and lox and corned beef and latkes to the film industry since the days before the Goldwyns and the Mayers and the Warners, the dynastic Jews who "invented" Hollywood, sold their studios to the conglomerates.

The deli food at Nate 'n Al's is better than what exists in New York today, where the owners of the Stage and the Carnegie have ascended to that great counter in the sky, and their legacy has become touristized. Nate 'n Al's remains in the same Mendelsohn family that started the place. The fast-talking waitresses are unique and have had their own spread in *Vanity Fair.* These gals know everyone, and they play no favorites, and that means you, bub. The rye bread (forget Levy's) is finished being baked on premises, and is the crispest, chewiest excuse to have a smoked meat sandwich and double your Lipitor dose. The corned beef is a *fresser*'s dream, the roast beef blood rare, the homemade coleslaw and potato salad are sides of paradise. You *can* go home again!

Today, you're as likely to encounter Denzel Washington and Jack Nicholson and Gong Li here at Nate 'n Al's as you are Barbra Streisand and

Dustin Hoffman and Jerry Seinfeld. Just as you could see the last mogul, Lew Wasserman, eating *matzo brei* every morning with Larry King, now you can see Sumner Redstone, and Brad Grey, and whoever is next among the men who would be king of Hollywood. Join them. Wait in line with them, as all who enter here must do. It's as democratic a power haunt as you can find anywhere. If you're lucky, very lucky—and this is the town where luck truly counts—power may prove to be contagious. ★

Where Exactly
Does Everybody Eat?

NEW YORK

La Grenouille 3 East 52nd Street, 212-752-1495

Da Silvano 260 Sixth Avenue, 212-982-2343

Rao's 455 East 114th Street, 212-722-6709

Gino 780 Lexington Avenue, 212-758-4466

Peter Luger 178 Broadway, Brooklyn, 718-387-7400

Elaine's 1703 Second Avenue, 212-534-8103

Primola 1226 Second Avenue, 212-758-1775

The Four Seasons 99 East 52nd Street, 212-754-9494

Michael's 24 West 55th Street, 212-767-0555

Balthazar 80 Spring Street, 212-965-1414

Swifty's 1007 Lexington Avenue, 212-535-6000

Via Quadronno 25 East 73rd Street, 212-650-9880

LONDON

The Savoy Grill Savoy Hotel, The Strand, WC2, 44-20-7592-1600

La Famiglia 7 Langton Street, SW10, 44-20-7351-0761

Cipriani 25 Davies Street, W1, 44-20-7399-0500

San Lorenzo 22 Beauchamp Place, SW3, 44-20-7584-1074

The River Cafe Thames Wharf, Rainville Road, W6, 44-20-7386-4200

The Ivy 1 West Street, WC2, 44-20-7836-4751

Le Caprice Arlington House, Arlington Street, SW1, 44-20-7629-2239

China Tang Dorchester Hotel, 53 Park Lane, W1, 44-20-7629-9988

Hakkasan 8 Hanway Place, W1, 44-20-7927-7000

Yauatcha 15 Broadwick Street, W1, 44-20-0870-780-8265

Sweetings 39 Queen Victoria Street, EC4, 44-20-7248-3062

Mirabelle 56 Curzon Street, W1, 44-20-7499-4636

Gordon Ramsay at Claridge's 45 Brook Street, W1, 44-20-7499-0099

Connaught Hotel Restaurant Carlos Place, W1, 44-20-0871-332-8733

Harry's Bar South Audley Street, W1, 44-20-7408-0844

PARIS

La Tour d'Argent 15 quai de la Tournelle (5th), 33-1-4354-2331

Davé 12 rue de Richelieu (1st), 33-1-4261-4948

Chez Omar 47 rue de Bretagne (3rd), 33-1-4272-3626

Chez l'Ami Louis 32 rue du Vert-Bois (3rd), 33-1-4887-7748

Arpège 84 rue de Varenne (7th), 33-1-4551-4733

Le Restaurant de la Quai Voltaire 27 quai Voltaire (7th), 33-1-4261-1749

Le Relais Plaza 25 avenue Montaigne (8th), 33-1-5367-6400

Costes 239 rue St.-Honoré (1st), 33-1-4244-5025

Le Stresa 7 rue Chambiges (8th), 33-1-4723-5162

Le Cherche Midi 22 rue du Cherche-Midi (6th), 33-1-4548-2744

ZURICH

Kronenhalle Rämistrasse, 4, 41-44-262-9900

VENICE

Harry's Bar Calle Vallaresso 1323, 39-041-528-5777

ROME

Al Moro Vicolo delle Bollette 13, 39-06-678-3495

Hostaria dell'Orso Via dei Soldati 25C, 39-06-6830-1192

Checco er Carettiere Via Benedetta 10, 39-06-581-7018

Piperno Monte dei Cenci 9, 39-06-6880-6629

Nino Via Borgognona 11, 39-06-679-5676

Costanza Piazza del Paradiso 63, 39-06-686-1717

MILAN

Bice Via Borgospesso 12, 39-02-7600-2572

Bagutta Via Bagutta 14, 39-02-7600-2767

Paper Moon Via Bagutta 1, 39-02-7602-2297

Dal Bolognese Piazza della Repubblica 13, 39-02-6269-4843

Da Giacomo Via Pasquale Sotto Corno 6, 39-02-7602-3313

MADRID

Casa Botín Cuchilleros 17, 34-91-366-4217

Casa Lucio Cava Baja 35, 34-91-365-3252

La Broche Miguel Angel 29-31, 34-91-399-3437

Jockey Amador de los Ríos 6, 34-91-319-1003

ST. TROPEZ AND THE CÔTE D'AZUR

Club 55 43, boulevard Patch, Ramatuelle, St. Tropez, 33-4-9455-5555

Tetou Avenue des Frères-Roustand, Golfe-Juan, 33-4-9363-7116

Le Machou 15 rue St. Antoine, Cannes, 33-4-9339-6221

Le Moulin de Mougins Notre Dame de Vie, Mougins, 33-4-9375-7824

La Colombe d'Or St. Paul de Vence, 33-4-9332-8002

MOSCOW

Night Flight 17 Tverskaya, 7-495-629-4165

Galereya 27 ulitsa Petrovka, 7-495-937-4544

Café Pushkin 26a bulvar Tverskoy, 7-495-629-9411

Palazzo Ducale 3 bulvar Tverskoy, 7-495-789-6404

HONG KONG

The China Club 13/F Old Bank of China Building Central, 852-2521-8888

TOKYO

Kyubey 8-7-6 Ginza, Chuo-ku, 81-3-3571-6523

Ten-Ichi 6-6-5 Ginza, Chuo-ku, 81-3-3571-1949

Joel Robuchon 1-13-1 Yebisu Garden Place, 81-3-5424-1338

Antica Osteria del Ponte Maru Building F36, Marunouchi, 81-3-5220-4686

Aoyagi 1-22-1 Toranomon,
  Minato-ku, 81-3-3580-3456
New York Grill Park Hyatt Tokyo,
  Shinjuku-ku, 81-3-5313-3458
Lemon Fruit Parlor Takashimaya
  Department Store, Marunouchi,
  81-3-3273-0033
Maisen 4-8-5 Jingumae, Shibuya-ku,
  81-3-3470-0071
Tableaux 11-6 Sarugakucho, Shibuya-
  ku, 81-3-5489-2201

SYDNEY
Rockpool 107 George Street,
  The Rocks, 61-2-9252-1888
Tetsuya's 529 Kent Street,
  61-2-9267-2900
Machiavelli 123 Clarence Street,
  61-2-9299-3748
Tropicana 227B Victoria Street,
  Darlinghurst, 61-2-9360-9809

SÃO PAOLO
Fasano 88 Rua Vittorio Fasano,
  55-11-3896-4000
Figueira Rubaiyat 1738 Rua Haddock
  Lobo, 55-11-3063-3888

RIO DE JANEIRO
Copacabana Palace 1702 Avenida
  Atlantica, 55-21-2548-7070
Cervantes 335b Avenida Prado Junior,
  55-21-2275-6147

CHARLESTON
Hominy Grill 207 Rutledge Avenue,
  843-937-0930

PALM BEACH
Ta-boo 221 Worth Avenue,
  561-835-3500

MIAMI BEACH
Joe's Stone Crab 11 Washington
  Avenue, 305-673-0365
Shore Club 1901 Collins Avenue,
  305-695-3100
Casa Tua 1700 James Avenue,
  305-673-1010
The Forge 432 Arthur Godfrey Road,
  305-538-8533

SAN FRANCISCO
Chez Panisse 1517 Shattuck Avenue,
  Berkeley, 510-548-5525
Zuni Café 1658 Market Street,
  415-552-2522
Slanted Door 1 Ferry Building, Number
  3, 415-861-8032
Plump Jack Café 3127 Fillmore Street,
  415-563-4755
A16 2355 Chestnut Street,
  415-771-2216

SANTA BARBARA
The Hitching Post 3325 Point Sal Road,
  Casmalia, 805-937-6151

LOS ANGELES
Toscana 11633 San Vicente Boulevard,
  Brentwood, 310-820-2448
Spago 176 North Canon Drive, Beverly
  Hills, 310-385-0880
Mortons 8764 Melrose Avenue, West
  Hollywood, 310-276-5205
Matsuhisa 129 North La Cienega
  Boulevard, Beverly Hills,
  310-659-9639
Mr Chow 344 North Camden Drive,
  Beverly Hills, 310-278-9911
Ago 8478 Melrose Avenue, West
  Hollywood, 323-655-6333
Giorgio 114 West Channel Road, Santa
  Monica, 310-573-1660
Dan Tana's 9071 Santa Monica
  Boulevard, West Hollywood,
  310-275-9444
The Ivy 113 North Robertson Boulevard,
  West Hollywood,
  310-274-8303
Kate Mantilini 9101 Wilshire Boulevard,
  Beverly Hills,
  310-278-3699
Fountain Coffee Shop 9641 Sunset
  Boulevard, Beverly Hills,
  310-276-2251
Nate 'n Al's 414 North Beverly Drive,
  Beverly Hills, 310-274-0101

345

Acknowledgments

No book ever written could have been more delicious to research than this 347 one. Special thanks to Ronald Winston, global epicure extraordinaire, who helped take the inscrutability out of the Japanese restaurant scene and whose reminiscences of a gilded Manhattan childhood brought the Henri Soulé era back to life. Much appreciation to the trailblazings of galloping gourmet Alan Grubman, whose embrace of a restaurant will have half of show business beating down its doors. Barbara Kafka, whose eye is as keen as her palate, went beyoned the call of duty for a fellow writer. And all the rest: *New York:* Daniel I. A. Cohen, Pat Geoghegan, Susan Haar, Anita Cotter, Alice Marshall, Drew Nieporent, Karen Preston, Marian Goldberg, Giuliano Zuliani, Giuseppe Cipriani, Robert Caravaggi, Elaine Kaufman, Paolo della Pupa. *Los Angeles:* Agostino Sciandri, Nobu Matsuhisa, Michael Chow, Francesco Greco, Mori Onodera, Kate Stingley, Jay Weston. *San Francisco:* Isaac Cronin, John and Kim Balkoski. *Palm Beach:* Lanny Carew, Rodney and Peggy Dillard, Franklyn De Marco. *Miami:* Shareef Malnik, Brett Ratner, Sandro Sciandri. *London:* Isabelle Hotimsky, Helen Kirwan-Taylor, Oliver Maude-Roxby, Alvaro Maccioni, David Tang, Toby Young. *Paris:* Suzy Patterson, the late Claude Terrail, Sandy and Elizabeth Whitelaw, Dave Cheung, Gilbert Costes, Nello Di Meo, the Faiola brothers, the Picot family. *Zurich:* Vreni Gerhartz. *Venice:* Arrigo Cipriani.

Rome: Franco Romagnoli, Giulia Cosmo. *Milan:* Giacomo Bulleri, Enrica and Stefania Galligani, Paola Gradi, the Mungai sisters, Alfredo Tomaselli. *Madrid:* Antonio Gonzalez, Lucio Blazquez, Andrea Lowndes, Sergi Arola. *Tokyo:* Shunji Nohara, Kozo Hasegawa, Debbie Krisher, Pamela Mori, Tracy Mercer. *São Paolo:* Rogerio Fasano. *Rio de Janeiro:* Dr. Ivo Pitanguy.

The following hotels, amoing the most legendary lodgings in the world, extended the hospitality that dreams are made of: Claridge's and the Savoy, London; Lutetia, Paris; Ritz, Madrid; Gritti Palace, Venice; Eden, Rome; Excelsior Gallia, Milan; Baur au Lac, Zurich; Baltschug Kempinski, Moscow; Fasano, São Paolo; Copacabana Palace, Rio de Janeiro; Four Seasons Marunouchi, Tokyo; Hyatt Regency, Kyoto; Charleston Place, Charleston; the Breakers, Palm Beach; Mandarin Oriental, Miami; Four Seasons, San Francisco. Thanks are also due to American, Iberia, and Qantas airlines for stretching the limits of the sky.

Finally, it took a singular agent, Mel Berger, to sell a book that was so much fun it made publishers guilty, and it took a singular editor, Chris Pavone, and his colleagues at Artisan/Workman, to get the pleasure on the page.

—W.S.

This book was a dream come true for me. Cooking, food, and dining in great restaurants have been a lifelong pleasure and hobby for me ever since my parents coerced me into taking my first trip to France with them instead of summer camp. Ah, the first taste of Cavaillon melon and baby lobster while sitting at a table alfresco overlooking Lac d'Annecy in Talloires at the legendary Auberge du Pere Bise, where I reluctantly accompanied my patient and nurturing mother and father, Adleen and Richard. (He's the pickiest eater I know, yet still enjoys a martini and New York steak at the ripe age of eighty-six and can go out and play three sets of tennis the next day.) I am truly grateful to them for supporting my habit and giving me the freedom to choose my path.

I also owe much to the inspiration and support I received from my brother, Peter Morton, one of the greatest restaurateurs on the planet, and my sister, Pamela, who always believed in and promoted me whenever possible and runs one tight ship at Mortons restaurant in LA.

To Barry Fogel, whose advice has been indispensable. Judith Sidney, whose constant encouragement kept me going even when the going got tough; she really knows food and restaurants and isn't afraid to ever ask for what she wants. Paul Beirne, a galloping gourmet himself, who planted the seed in my head that a book about restaurants was something I should consider doing. Rick Reidy for insisting that I could do it whenever I doubted myself. My co-author Bill Stadiem. Alan Kannoff, for actually helping us to bring it all to fruition through his introduction to Mel Berger, literary agent par excellence, who just "got it" from the outset. Our brilliant editor at Artisan, Chris Pavone; his great taste guided this book to the finish line. Along with all his wonderful associates, especially Nicki Clendening and Jan Derevjanik.

My gratitude to the following people, places, and things that were all in some part responsible for shaping my palate and appreciation for food and restaurants: To the great house of Cipriani, including Arrigo and his handsome and generous son Giuseppe, who convinced me that New York was the place to be; I still celebrate every birthday at one of his grand eateries around the world. To Hassan, Sergio, François, and Milton, who extend the Cipriani brand of care and service; Dario Mariotti, who introduced me to all of New York City; the host with the most, Sirio Maccioni, his wife, Edgi, and his sons, Marco, Mauro, and Mario, of Le Cirque and Osteria del Circo; Maguy and the late great Gilbert Le Coze of Le Bernardin; Eberhard Müller, Jean-Georges Vongerichten, and Phil Suarez of the Jean Georges empire; Daniel Boulud of Daniel; Pino Luongo of many incarnations; Steve Tzolis and Frank Minieri of Il Cantinori; Aldo Bozzi and Paolo Casagranda of Mezzaluna; Philippe Delgrange and Lionel Deniaud of Le Bilboquet; and extra kudos to Giorgio Baldi, Robert Caravaggio, Vreni Gerhartz, Howard Kuo and Nobu Matsuhisa, Drew Nieporent (I could listen to his fascinating restaurant stories for hours on end), Paolo della Pupa and Casey Lam, and the dynamic duo of East Fifty-second street, Julian Niccolini and Alex von Bidder.

To everyone at American Airlines, especially Linda Almedia, Phyllis Bruno, Bernie Ladika, Kathleen Locke, John Stanich and their extraordinary partners in the American Airlines Admirals Clubs and Premium Services, who have been there for me as I traveled the globe. Sara Duffy, of New Act Travel, the travel agent that anyone who needs or just loves to travel should not be without.

My thanks to the following hoteliers, who cushioned me and made research for this book a delight; Anita Cotter of the Maybourne Group; Karen Preston of Leading Hotels of the World; Alice Marshall of the Dorchester Group; Raouf Finan and the hotel and spa La Reserve in Geneva, which can work magic on the effects of jet lag (I never knew Geneva could have such a sexy place!); Michel Rey and the Baur au Lac, where I exercised off the chocolate mousse of the Kronenhalle in the most sensational gymnasium in which I have ever broken a sweat; the regal Francesca Bortolotto Possati and the Bauer Hotel in Venice, whose hospitality is unparalleled; Thomas Citterio and the Four Seasons Hotel in Milan, as well as Daniela Bertazzoni and the Grand Hotel et de Milan in Milan; the Hotel de Russie in Rome; the Martinez in Cannes, where you have to go to hear Jimmy McKissic sing in the piano bar; the Hotel du Cap, where drinking the freshest peach juice with champagne poolside is de rigueur; Franka Holtmann and Celine Bataille at Le Meurice Hotel in Paris and all their concierges, each and every one of whom holds the key to dining out in Paris (I could move into this hotel if only to wake up to their spectacular petit déjeuner); Claridge's Hotel in London, especially the unique Martin, who will be my friend forever, as he is the concierge who can make just about any wish come true; the Connaught in London, where they make you feel that you are a guest in a grand English country home; James McBride and the Carlyle, home to the Bemeleman's Bar, where Ali and Jose will stir or shake you up the most elegant martini in the world to go along with those tasty little bar snacks; the Tisch family—if I could get myself out of bed earlier in the morning, I would be a regular at the Regency Hotel's dining room for possibly the best breakfast in Manhattan, with a who's-who clientele that can make anyone awake from a deep sleep.

A very special mention to the Canyon Ranch, by far the best place on this earth to recover and renew your body, mind, and spirit, especially after all of the dining out and traveling while researching this book.

To my dear friends Gael and Francesco Boglione, Marco and Enrico Boglione, *miei fratelli italiani,* who have always treated me as a member of

350

their own family and are responsible for introducing me to my first tastes of some of the finer things in life; Franco Martinetti, gentleman winemaker and my personal guide to Italian cuisine; Alessandra and Giovanni Borletti; Sarah Canet and Spoon PR; my little English treasure, Wendy Meltzer, a woman of style and grace, who is the expert on eating in the South of France; Evangeline and Alan Brinkley, brilliant scholars and culinary geniuses; Victoria Goldman, whose wisdon and experience has been invaluable; Alison Moore, who has been there from the conception of this book and stayed through thick and thin (she still makes the best roast chicken this side of the Atlantic!); Ann Lawlor at Warren Tricomi, who always makes sure that I am looking my best before venturing out on the town to do research; the illustrious Patrick McMullan, whose photos have memorialized those moments and more, and his trusted associate, Clint Spaulding. To the rest of my friends, you know who you are, and I thank you for being there to tag along and put up with my extravagant and demanding ways: your faith in my choices and reservations are what made *Everybody Eats There.*

—M.G.

351

Index

355

356

357

George's, 79
Georges, Jean, 324
George V Hotel, 99, 102, 117
Gere, Richard, 233, 236, 271
Gerhartz, Gustave, 137
Gerhartz, Hilda, 137
Gerhartz, Vreni, 136–38
Gero, 248–49, 250
Getty, Gordon, 281
Getty, J. Paul, 60, 62, 103, 124, 127
Giamatti, Paul, 283
Giambi, Jason, 40
Gibson, Mel, 238
Gielgud, John, 56
Gilbert and Sullivan, 63
Gill, A. A., 61
Gino, 21–24
Giorgio, 327, 328, 330–32, 334
Giuliani, Rudolph, 26, 40
Givenchy, Hubert de, 128
Global Dining, 223
Godard, Jean-Luc, 184
Godiva, 215
Goethe, Johann Wolfgang von, 152
Goin, Suzanne, 274
Goldin, Nan, 105
Goldman, Ron, 298
Goldsmith, James, 79, 80, 93
Goldwyn, Samuel, 109, 124, 340
Gollancz, Victor, 62
Gong Li, 206, 207, 340
González, Antonio, 172–73
González, Antonio, III, 173–74
González, Antonio, Jr., 173
Gorbachev, Mikhail, 218
Gordon, Michael, 295–96, 328
Gore, Al, 303
Gore, Lesley, 41
Gotti, John, 18
Goulandris, Basil, 62
Goya, Francisco, 172
Grace, Princess, 62; see also Kelly, Grace
Grade, Lew, 66
Graham, Rodney, 49
Grammer, Kelsey, 317
Grant, Cary, 48–49, 130, 164, 173, 189, 191, 252, 292, 339
Grant, Hugh, 79, 128, 190, 191, 331
Gray, Rose, 57, 82
Grazer, Brian, 319

Great American Disaster, 310
Greene, Gael, 11, 101
Grendene, Leticia, 267
Grendene, Miky, 267
Grey, Brad, 294, 319, 341
Grill, 319, 336
Gritti Palace, 140, 144
Groom, Winston, 35
Grotta Azzurra, 16, 67
Grubman, Alan, 319
Guérard, Michael, 101
Guinea Grill, 311
Guinness, Alec, 66, 67
Guinle, Jorginho, 252
Guinle, Otávio, 252
Gulbenkian, Nubar, 62, 85, 103, 127
Gundel, 46
Gwathmey, Charles, 40
Gyllenhaal, Jake, 280

Hakkasan, 91–92
Halberstam, David, 35, 38
Haldeman, H. R., 44
Hall, Jerry, 188
Hal's, 337
Halston, 7
Hamasaku, 339
Hambro family, 93
Hamburger Hamlet, 310, 328, 339
Hamill, Pete, 35, 38
Hamilton, George, 260
Hanks, Tom, 106, 116, 210, 330
Hanover family, 89, 295
Hansen family, 93
Hapsburg family, 3
Hard Rock Cafe, 309, 312
Hard Rock Hotel, 323
Harriman, Pamela, 115
Harrison, George, 236, 267, 304
Harrods, 90, 215
Harry's (Paris), 259
Harry's Bar, 55, 74, 75, 79–81, 129, 139–46, 179, 255, 259, 324
Harry's Café de Wheels, 241
Hartnett, Angela, 71
Harvey, Laurence, 67, 311
Hasegawa, Kozo, 196, 223
Hawks, Howard, 340
Hawn, Goldie, 318, 322

361

Prudhomme, Paul ("K-Paul"), 16, 17
Puck, Barbara, 303
Puck, Wolfgang, 17, 113, 196, 205, 213,
220, 233, 237, 240, 257, 273, 278,
295, 299, 300, 302–3, 305, 306, 309,
311, 319, 320, 326, 327, 339
Pulitzer, Lilly, 31
Putin, Vladimir, 172, 200
Puzo, Mario, 35
Pyramide, 177

Qaddafi, Muammar, 154
Quaglino, 88
Quant, Mary, 67, 90
Quasimodo, 96
Queensberry, Marquess of, 70
Quilted Giraffe, 17
Quo Vadis, 16, 30, 66, 70

Rabelais, 152, 153
Racquet Club, 29
Radcliffe, Daniel, 236
Radziwill, Lee, 108
Raft, George, 20, 23
Rainbow Room, 232–33
Rainia, Queen of Jordan, 160
Rainier, Prince, 62, 124
Rampling, Charlotte, 105
Ramsay, Gordon, 61–62, 63, 64, 68, 70,
71–73, 93, 151
Rao, Anna, 20
Rao, Charles, 20
Rao, Louis, 20
Rao, Vincent, 20
Rao's, 18–21, 23, 24
Rather, Dan, 43
Rattlesnake Club, 48
Rauschenberg, Robert, 10, 43, 104
Reagan, Ronald, 280, 303, 339
Rebozo, Bebe, 269
Redgrave, Michael, 56, 62
Red Lobster, 219
Redstone, Sumner, 129, 332, 341
Reed, Carol, 62
Reeves, Keanu, 54, 104
Regency Hotel, 49
Regine, 34, 270
Reichl, Ruth, 177, 278

Reiner, Rob, 296, 319
Rembrandt, 212, 214
Reno, Jean, 185
Restaurant de La Tour d'Argent. *See* La Tour
d'Argent
Reuben's, 51
Rice-Davies, Mandy, 67
Rich, Frank, 19
Richard, Cliff, 87
Richards, Keith, 66, 79, 104, 178, 319
Richards, Lucie, 79
Richards, Trish, 239
Richie, Lionel, 322
Richie, Nicole, 7, 322
Riley, Pat, 263
Rio de Janeiro, 251–54
Ripert, Eric, 26
Ritchie, Guy, 72, 331
Ritz, 117, 246
Ritz, Caesar, 63
River Cafe, 57, 82–84
Rivers, Joan, 35
Robuchon, Joel, 129, 224–26, 227, 229
Rockefeller family, 3, 252
Rockpool, 237–40
Rockwell, David, 313
Rodgers, Judy, 274, 277, 278
Rogers, Ginger, 93, 252, 291
Rogers, Richard, 82–83
Rogers, Ruth, 82, 84
Rogers, Will, 262
Rohatyn, Felix, 43, 46
Rohmer, Sax, 207
Romagnoli, Elisabetta, 151
Romagnoli, Franco, 147–48, 149, 150, 151,
156
Romagnoli, Mario, 149
Romanoff, Mike, 62, 292, 299
Rome, 146–59
Ronaldo, Cristiano, 180
Roosevelt, Eleanor, 62
Roosevelt, Franklin, 98, 117
Roosevelt, Theodore, 98
Roosevelt family, 29
Root, Waverly, 107, 139
Rosati, 166
Ross, Harold, 291
Rosti, 296
Roth, Philip, 34
Rothko, Mark, 43

369